Rebuilding Poland

Rebuilding Poland

Workers and Communists, 1945–1950

PADRAIC KENNEY

Cornell University Press

Ithaca and London

HX
315.7
.A6
K46
1997

Padraic Kenney received the Eugene M. Kayden University of Colorado
Annual Faculty Manuscript Award for this manuscript. Cornell University
Press gratefully acknowledges a subvention from the Kayden Advisory
Committee of the University of Colorado at Boulder, which aided in bringing
this book to publication. Research for this book was supported in part by a
grant from the International Research & Exchanges Board (IREX), with funds
provided by the National Endowment for the Humanities, the United States
Information Agency, and the U.S. Department of State, which administers the
Russian, Eurasian, and East European Research Program (Title VIII).

Copyright © 1997 by Cornell University

First published 1997 by Cornell University Press.

Library of Congress Cataloging-in-Publication Data
Kenney, Padraic, b. 1963
    Rebuilding Poland : workers and Communists, 1945–1950 / Padraic
Kenney.
        p.   cm.
    Includes bibliographical references (p.   ) and index.
    ISBN 0-8014-3287-1 (cloth : alk. paper)
    1. Communism—Poland—History.   2. Working class—Poland—History.
3. Poland—Economic conditions—1945–1980.   4. Poland—Social
conditions—1945–   I. Title.
HX315.7.A6K46   1996
338.9438—dc20   96-21388

Printed in the United States of America

This book is printed on Lyons Falls Turin Book,
a paper that is totally chlorine-free and acid-free.

FEB 7 1997

7302

For Izabela, Maia, and Karolina,
for Moira and Shelagh,
and for my parents, Michael and Sara

Contents

Illustrations

Figures and Maps

Figures

Maps

Acknowledgments

This book has its origins in a semester spent in Moscow more than twelve years ago. I was intrigued, there and upon my return to the United States (and later in Toronto, where I studied Russian history with Robert Johnson and John Keep), by the complex and multiple meanings of the Russian revolution which ordinary people employed, and by the challenge of confronting the social and political histories of revolutionary change. As I have moved some distance away from those earlier interests, the work of the pioneers in Russian social history (including many teachers and friends) still inspires me.

From these influences came a desire to write for the beginnings of Poland's communist state what so many have been doing for the Soviet analogue.

I have been continually challenged to make a problem that fascinates me—the reception and reinterpretation of communism by Polish workers—accessible to a wide audience. At the University of Michigan, Roman Szporluk and William Rosenberg were demanding critics who forced me to pay careful attention to the historiographical implications of my work. I am grateful for theoretically rigorous readings by Michael Kennedy and Howard Kimeldorf. Barbara Engel, Jeffrey Kopstein, Norman Naimark, Andrzej Korbonski, Fred Anderson, Robert Pois, Henryk Szpigiel, and especially John Connelly and Antony Polonsky, the readers of the book manuscript for Cornell University Press, have offered invaluable comments. Finally, I have had two conscientious editors through many drafts: my father, Michael Kenney, and Roger Haydon of Cornell University Press.

During my research trips, Polish friends were exceedingly generous with their time and hospitality. Indeed, my research would not have been possible without the generosity of Marek Czapliński and his family and Krystyna and Marian Ziółkowski, my parents-in-law. Many colleagues—too many to mention them all here—have shared their knowledge and unpublished work with me—in particular, Jędrzej Chumiński, Darek Jarosz, Ewa Karpińska, Kazimierz Kloc, and Grzegorz Sołtysiak. Their scholarship and their friendship have, I hope, left their mark on this work. I have also been fortunate to have the guidance of pioneers in the study of modern Poland: Krystyna Kersten, Andrzej Paczkowski, Hanna Świda-Ziemba, Tomasz Szarota, and Irena Turnau. This work is the first in any language to interpret most of the archival materials I consulted; it was made possible by the assistance of many archivists and librarians. I also thank the workers I interviewed in Łódź (with the expert assistance of Ewa Karpińska) and Wrocław. I hope that I have been in some way faithful to their understanding of their lives.

Parts of Chapters 5 and 6 appeared in "Remaking the Polish Working Class: Early Stalinist Models of Labor and Leisure," *Slavic Review* 53 (Spring 1994): 1–25. A version of Chapter 2 was published as "Working-Class Community and Resistance in Pre-Stalinist Poland: The Poznański Textile Strike, Łódź, September 1947," *Social History* 18 (January 1993): 31–51. I thank the American Association for the Advancement of Slavic Studies, publisher of *Slavic Review*, and Routledge, publisher of *Social History*, for permission to incorporate that material here.

The research for this book was supported by three grants from the International Research and Exchanges Board, with funds provided by the National Endowment for the Humanities and the United States Information Agency. Further research was funded by grants from the University of Colorado's Council on Research and Creative Work. Writing was supported first by a dissertation fellowship from the American Council of Learned Societies and the Joint Committee on Eastern Europe and then by a semester's leave from the Department of History at the University of Colorado. My sister, Moira Kenney, and William Semann prepared the maps; Christopher Gerlach, Bartosz Marczuk, and Maciej Kamiński helped process the data.

I am grateful to my wife, Izabela Ziółkowska-Kenney, for her companionship and support.

Finally, two good friends could not see this book's completion. I wish to remember Tadeusz Bojanowski and Kalina Kloc and dedicate this book to their memory.

PADRAIC KENNEY

Boulder, Colorado

Abbreviations in Text

(For abbreviations used in footnotes, see Sources.)

CRZZ (Centralna Rada Związkow Zawodowych): Central Trade Union Council

KCZZ (Komisja Centralna Związkow Zawodowych): Central Trade Union Commission

MWP (Młodzieżowy Wyścig Pracy): Youth Labor Competition

PKWN (Polski Komitet Wyzwolenia Narodowego): Polish Committee of National Liberation

PPR (Polska Partia Robotnicza): Polish Workers' Party

PPS (Polska Partia Socjalistyczna): Polish Socialist Party

PSL (Polskie Stronnictwo Ludowe): Polish Peasant [Popular] Party

PZPBW (Państwowy Zakład Przemysłu Bawełnianego/Wełnianego): State Cotton/Wool Industry Plant

UB (Urząd Bezpieczeństwa): Security Apparatus

WRN (Wolność, Równość, Niepodległość): Freedom, Equality, Independence

zł: złoty

ZMP (Związek Młodzieży Polskiej): Union of Polish Youth

ZWM (Związek Walki Młodych): Union of the Youth Struggle

Rebuilding Poland

Continuities in Twentieth-Century Polish Society

Since the fall of communism, politicians in Poland have tried to reach back past the entire communist era and portray the post-1989 state as the "Third Republic," the direct successor of the interwar Second Republic. In the public imagination, fifty years of Polish history thus become an anomaly, a nightmare from which one awakens burdened with the aftereffects of stalinization. But now that the communist era is over, the task of situating that period in modern Polish history is increasingly important; the end of state communism in Europe is an occasion not to file away an era as mercifully resolved but to pick it apart and to understand how it operated. Our understanding of Polish communism must begin with its origins. To that end, this book employs the tools of social history to search for continuities and indigenous contexts for the ostensibly working-class-based revolution that gave birth to the Polish People's Republic (PRL). Although the communist state was hardly the product of native social aspirations, Polish society did affect the nature of the transformations of 1945–50, forcing the regime to evolve in response to social demands. Ultimately, the fall of communism itself was the result of the breakdown of state-society relations.

Since its beginning, the communist period has been approached from one general viewpoint in the West and in Polish independent historiography. The earliest work concentrated on the illegitimacy of the Polish communists and the foreign origins of their support, emphasizing the communists' political machinations to gain and maintain power and to exclude their opponents.[1] In *The Soviet Bloc: Unity and Conflict*, perhaps the most important work of the totalitarian school of historical study, Zbigniew Brzezinski expanded on these themes, looking beyond party and international politics to the role of economic and social policy in the communist drive for total control. *The Soviet Bloc* also draws attention to the implications for the communists' success of the shift of Poland's borders, the destruction of Poland's intellectual and economic elites by the Nazis during the war, and the appeal of early communist policies such as radical land reform and nationalization of industry. Brzezinski highlighted diversity within the Soviet Bloc—in particular, the extent to which Polish communists differed from their counterparts elsewhere in Eastern Europe in the lesser degree of repression they exerted and their greater accommodation of national identity.[2]

While subsequent studies have added nuance to Brzezinski's work, retreating from a more rigid totalitarian model, they have changed our view of the communist takeover very little. Recent histories by both Polish and Anglo-American historians have continued to emphasize the means by which the communists secured power, tempering their political narratives with acknowledgment of the varied ways in which society responded to communist power. The story remains essentially the same: although after their 1944 assumption of power the communists offered cultural concessions and socioeconomic progress in order to achieve total political dominance by 1947-48, the people of Poland played no role in the determination of their future.[3]

The political drama these histories relate is compelling, straightfor-

---

[1] M. K. Dziewanowski, *The Communist Party of Poland* (Cambridge, Mass., 1959); Stanisław Mikołajczyk, *The Pattern of Soviet Domination* (London, 1948); Arthur Bliss Lane, *I Saw Poland Betrayed* (London, 1949).

[2] Zbigniew K. Brzezinski, *The Soviet Bloc: Unity and Conflict*, 2d ed. (Cambridge, Mass., 1967). Other comparative works include Hugh Seton-Watson, *The East European Revolution* (New York, 1951); Jerzy Tomaszewski, *The Socialist Regimes of East Central Europe: Their Establishment and Consolidation, 1944-1967* (London, 1989); Wlodzimierz Brus, "Stalinism and the 'People's Democracies,' " in *Stalinism: Essays in Historical Interpretation*, ed. Robert Tucker (New York, 1977), 239-56.

[3] Norman Davies, *God's Playground: A History of Poland*, vol. 2: *1795 to the Present* (New York, 1982); Jaime Reynolds and John Coutouvidis, *Poland, 1939-1947* (Leicester, U.K., 1986); R. F. Leslie, ed., *The History of Poland since 1863* (Cambridge, 1980); Andrzej Paczkowski, *Pół wieku dziejów Polski, 1939-1989* (Warsaw, 1995); Krystyna Kersten, *Narodziny systemu władzy: Polska, 1943-48* (Warsaw, 1984) (in English as: *The Establishment of Communist Rule in Poland, 1943-1948*, trans. John Micgiel and Michael H. Bernhard [Berkeley, Calif., 1991]).

ward, and correct but seriously incomplete. As much as they have told us about Polish–Soviet relations and about the development of the planned economy and a repressive regime, they have been unable to tell us what the communist experience was actually like. What did people think about communism? What did they dislike or like about it? How did they survive? How did the regime exercise its power, and did anything hold it back? What were the communists' goals as regarded society, and did they achieve them? If not, why not? These questions have until now been unanswered, leaving us with insufficient clues to communism's downfall, not to mention its revived popularity since 1989. The relationship between society and state at the beginning of the era can tell us much about why the regime lasted as long as it did, and why and how it fell.

This book is not a quixotic attempt to show that the communist takeover was a popular revolution or that the communist state initially possessed much legitimacy beyond the goods it dispensed. Indeed, any historian who would write a social history of this period in Eastern Europe must acknowledge one fundamental fact: without the Soviet Army's occupying Poland, the communists could not have taken or held power. Rather, this book shows how social continuities and logics help us place this period in Polish history and help us grasp the dynamics of the communist system. The imposition of stalinism[4] does not relieve us of the need to understand what happened and how and to recognize all the forces, internal as well as external, social as well as political, that shaped postwar Poland. Social history is not merely a complement to the political narrative but a transformation of it. It does not simply show us what else was going on backstage but recasts and rewrites the entire play.

The social bases of the political transformation of Eastern Europe have been explored with some success in other countries of the region.[5] Of all Eastern European societies, the Polish case is particularly intriguing, for Poles were apparently the least accepting of communism. Although

[4]I have used the term *stalinism* in lowercase throughout this book in an effort to separate the system from its founder.

[5]Norman Naimark, *The Russians in Germany: A History of the Soviet Zone of Occupation, 1945–1949* (Cambridge, Mass., 1995); Martin Myant, *Socialism and Democracy in Czechoslovakia, 1945–48* (Cambridge, U.K., 1981); Jon Bloomfield, *Passive Revolution: Politics and the Czechoslovak Working Class, 1945–48* (New York, 1979); Bogdan Denitch, *Legitimation of a Revolution: The Yugoslav Case* (New Haven, Conn., 1976); Charles Gati, *Hungary and the Soviet Bloc* (Durham, N.C., 1986).

crudely framed, the juxtaposition of the resistance of 1939–44 (not to mention of the previous 150 years) in the name of democratic ideas with the relative peace of the establishment of communist power, is provocative especially given the traditional antipathy between Poles and Russians. The second attraction of Poland as a subject is its importance to the bloc. As the largest and most populous country in Eastern Europe and a leader both industrially and agriculturally, Poland was, as Brzezinski put it, "the primary objective of Soviet policy in East Central Europe," the key to domination of the region—and since 1980, the key to the bloc's disintegration.[6] It is the logical point at which to begin an understanding of communism in Eastern Europe.

Yet Polish history remains trapped by the twin dramas of 1944–45 and 1980–81. In order to understand the communist era, we must recognize that 1945 was a period of revolution and chart the continuities linking that era to the prerevolutionary world. Because *revolution* commonly denotes a dramatic and systemic change that addresses popular needs and desires, scholars have shunned this term for the events of 1945. Alone among Polish scholars, Tadeusz Łepkowski has argued for an understanding of the birth of the communist state as a "clash of two revolutions."[7] But communist Poland was really the product of two revolutionary transformations. The first, roughly 1945–47, was an economic and social revolution: the economy was transferred from private or Nazi hands into the hands of the state, while workers and peasants were anointed the new ruling class. The second revolution, of 1948–50, was both political and social. On the one hand, the communist party gained ascendance over the Polish state and Polish society; on the other, this was the beginning of mass advance by workers and peasants into education, industry, and the bureaucracy. The opposition movements, which culminated in the Solidarity movement of 1980–81 and paved the way for the fall of communism, were in large part the products of conflicts between the popular desires and the imposed parameters of those two revolutions.

Solidarity's power lay in its nature as a community, or even a "cultural-political class."[8] Thus, our interpretation cannot be limited to the

---

[6]Brzezinski, *Soviet Bloc*, 9.
[7]Tadeusz Łepkowski, "Myśli o historii Polski i Polaków," *Zeszyty Historyczne* 68 (1984): 120–29.
[8]Jan Kubik, *The Power of Symbols against the Symbols of Power: The Rise of Solidarity and the Fall of State Socialism in Poland* (University Park, Pa., 1994), 235–38.

immediate context of 1980–81; we must explore the roots of that culture and that politics. Several recent studies have moved back from 1980, searching for the origins of Solidarity. It is impossible, however, to find them unless workers are subjects not only when they are engaged in organized oppositional activity and unless it is recognized that communist repression was not the only influence on workers' experience.[9]

A more complete history is possible only with access to new kinds of sources. This book draws on state, party, secret police, trade union, and factory archives—most of them never before used—as well as oral interviews and published propaganda in order to tell a new story. To tell that story requires careful attention to the hidden meanings of the most unlikely materials and to read in documents and reported actions not simply a record of what transpired but what the authors and their subjects believed should or would happen and what it meant. As we shall see, this task becomes more difficult as ever more formulaic official language reveals less and less about society and more and more about the intentions of its users.

One purpose of such an approach is to allow for a comparative understanding of communist societies. The social history of such regimes, whether they are called totalitarian, authoritarian, leninist, stalinist, socialist, state-socialist, state-capitalist, or communist, has been most successfully written about the Soviet Union and its twin transformations of 1917–21 and 1928–32. Scholars have documented the aspirations and beliefs of workers, peasants, soldiers, bourgeoisie, and intellectuals and shown the extent to which the Soviet regime was the product of societal resistance or accommodation as well as indirect negotiation with certain social groups.[10] A comparison of the Soviet Union with other examples from the Soviet Bloc could shed much light on the question of whether the Soviet experience was unique. For example, is a state-socialist revolution possible because of a particular mix of a small, politically conscious proletariat and masses of easily mobilized peasant-workers? What is the relationship between such a revolution, which echoes popular de-

[9]Lawrence Goodwyn, *Breaking the Barrier: The Rise of Solidarity in Poland* (New York, 1991); Roman Laba, *The Roots of Solidarity: A Political Sociology of Poland's Working-Class Democratization* (Princeton, 1991). In contrast, see Robert Blobaum, " 'Solidarność' a tradycje polskiego ruchu robotniczego: Kilka uwag historyka," *Aneks* 39 (1985): 148–61. There is a large literature in Polish on the upheavals of 1956 and 1970–71.

[10]See Ronald Grigor Suny, "Toward a Social History of the October Revolution," *American Historical Review* 88, no. 1 (1983): 31–52, and the debate initiated by Sheila Fitzpatrick in *Russian Review* 45, no. 4 (1986).

mands for land, bread, and workers' control, and a stalinist type of revolution from above? Most important, is there such a thing as *stalinism,* or does the disparity between the Soviet Union and Eastern Europe make such a term meaningless? This book should make possible a comparative examination of societies under communist or authoritarian rule.

The necessary starting point is to study the role of the industrial working class—the titular vanguard of the revolution—which has been so well studied for the Soviet Union.[11] Such an analysis of Poland addresses important issues in the literature on the working class and social transformation. One of the key issues in the field today is the problem of resistance in authoritarian regimes. How can workers resist, and do what James Scott termed "everyday forms of resistance" accomplish anything?[12] Poland's working-class communities, founded on shared work experience, cultural rituals, and urban structures, drew on their traditions and ideas about shared identity to articulate beliefs about themselves, their work, and their place in society. This made the working class in Poland more powerful than the communists expected; it gave workers the tools to influence and survive the system in which they lived and to reemerge as a social actor in 1956 and after.

All this adds up to a *moral economy* of the Polish worker. The concept of moral economy, as articulated by E. P. Thompson and others, refers to a set of values—generally embracing ideas of egalitarianism, social justice, and basic collective rights—embedded in the culture of a community (a moral community) that enable collective, usually spontaneous action against those whom the community holds responsible for disrupting its ability to maintain a standard of living.[13] When workers demanded that their employers answer for high prices on the free market, when they struck in quixotic solidarity with the workers of another factory, and when they resisted higher norms or threatened workers who beat norms, they expressed a moral economy that outstripped the power of any formal organization to oppose the commu-

[11] Particularly important are William Chase, *Workers, Society, and the Soviet State: Labor and Life in Moscow, 1918–1929* (Urbana, Ill., 1987); Hiroaki Kuromiya, *Stalin's Industrial Revolution: Politics and Workers, 1929–1932* (Cambridge, U.K., 1988); William G. Rosenberg and Lewis H. Siegelbaum, eds., *Social Dimensions of Soviet Industrialization* (Bloomington, Ind., 1993); others are cited in later chapters.

[12] James Scott, "Everyday Forms of Resistance," in *Everyday Forms of Peasant Resistance,* ed. Forrest Colburn (Armonk, N.Y., 1989), 3–33.

[13] See E. P. Thompson, *Customs in Common* (New York, 1991), chaps. 5 and 6.

nist state. The nature and results of this conflict are the subjects of this book.

It is difficult to talk about "the workers" or "the working class" as a whole, for Polish working-class communities were overlaid with various, sometimes competing, identities, including class, nation, gender, and generation. These social identities provided the basis for collective resistance to economic, social, or political repression. Class identity, both within the factory and outside, is naturally the most important to my analysis. When workers saw themselves as a community based in labor, when they opposed employers or the state as employers or the communists as oppressors of workers, they were expressing class identity. In order to understand class, we need to discover, first, how the economic and political contexts and community and factory experience shape or inhibit collective identity and, second, how that identity is related to collective action. Class identity, even under stalinism, was an essential prerequisite to collective resistance.[14]

Understood as an identity, class is thus subjective; it never includes all workers because many who are objectively workers do not consider themselves so. (Because of the way in which the communists thought of workers, *worker* in this book will usually mean "blue-collar" or "industrial worker.") In communist Poland, of course, class also had an objective political meaning, defined by party or state leaders. The interpretation of class identity therefore offers the opportunity to analyze state intentions and their efficacy by stripping away the propaganda of class to discover how the ostensible subjects of the revolution really behaved and how subjective class compared with the official version. As Stanisław Ossowski has observed, class consciousness is particularly likely during times when a middle class is subdued or weak, as was the case in postwar Poland.[15]

Like class, nation is important not so much as an objective phenomenon but as a constructed one, both produced from above and imagined in different ways by different social groups.[16] Workers often saw them-

[14]See Ira Katznelson, "Working-Class Formation: Constructing Cases and Comparisons," in *Working-Class Formation: Nineteenth-Century Patterns in Western Europe and the United States,* ed. Ira Katznelson and Aristide R. Zolberg (Princeton, 1986), 3–41.

[15]Stanisław Ossowski, *Class Structure in the Social Consciousness,* trans. Sheila Patterson (New York, 1963), 95–96.

[16]For competing yet complementary views on this process, see Benedict Anderson, *Imagined Communities: Reflections on the Origins and Spread of Nationalism,* rev. ed. (London, 1991), and Ernest Gellner, *Nations and Nationalism* (Ithaca, N.Y., 1983).

selves as Poles (or Catholics) in contrast to authorities whom they perceived as non-Polish or less Polish. In 1945–49, national identity paradoxically sharpened as Polish society approached homoethnicity; without the Germans and the Jews, two traditional foci of Polish separateness, and against the threat of two foreign aggressor/occupiers— the recently-departed Germans and the Soviets—Poles re-created antagonistic relations. One of the purposes of decoding national identity is to determine whether workers saw the communists as authentically Polish or not, and thus suggest answers to what must be one of the central questions in the social history of communist Poland: did Poles consider the regime to be foreign?

Class and nation could perhaps unite all workers; other identities divided them. The working class in 1945 was in the midst of a dramatic transition within a set of interrelated identities of experience: urban/rural, male/female, skilled/unskilled, old/young. Sometimes the division between the "old" workers of pre-war urban roots and factory experience and the "young" arrivals in the city and factory was clear and keenly felt. Other times the categories did not match so neatly: older workers might be recent arrivals from the countryside; many younger workers were as much a part of the old urban culture as were their parents. Depictions of age or skill cannot be taken unexamined; as with class or nation, attention must be paid to the objectives of those assigning such identities. Generational distinctions were often the product of observers' ideas of the working class. For example, old communists might use the phrase *young workers* to mean undisciplined newcomers; the term *old workers* might imply party activists' impatience with strikers' intransigence. Finally, gender shaped patterns of conflict and accommodation, often in unpredictable ways.

As we will see, political and economic forces also tore Polish labor communities apart; even then, however, workers were able to contest and alter the state's efforts. The terrain of the shop floor was a key area of worker-state conflict in the founding years of the postwar order. Employers and the party used speedups, discipline, enthusiasm campaigns, and incentives to raise productivity and achieve domination over the urban work force. In response, workers defended their control of the labor process. "Workers' control" usually implies worker participation in supervision or management (a kind of control also evident in 1944–45). The broader definition of *control* used here signifies the incorporation of the factory, the work station, and the work day into the rhythms and patterns of a community; in defending that relationship, workers simply asserted the values of that shared identity. Workers' communities themselves, in other words, became a terrain of struggle; workers sought to maintain control over their lives and the relationship between their home and their work. Such an idea of control is appropriate given the expansive nature of the state and its ideologically driven interference in workers' lives; workers could seek control not only when they had powerful resources at their disposal (as in the Russian Revolution). Employing a broader definition allows us to recognize this desire for control even when workers are unable, due to structural limitations of state, community, or family, to seek total control of the factory. Their action need not be interpreted as a weaker version of traditional control but as a way to achieve similar goals with more limited resources.[17]

Another way in which workers defended their community was through mobility. There were three kinds of mobility important in the early postwar years. Two are quite familiar: promotion into administrative, technical, and party positions; and migration into the cities. While these processes contributed to communist mastery of society and the working class, the communists could not control who benefited and how those who advanced saw themselves.[18] New workers or administrators gained experiences and skills over which the communists had little influence; thus, migration and promotion became unexpected weapons in the hands of their beneficiaries. Lateral mobility—movement between jobs or cities—was also a powerful weapon in workers' hands. By switching factories at will, workers asserted their right to decide how and where they would work and denied the state the right to establish labor communities according to its own rules.

Of course, against all these tools in the hands of the workers were those in the hands of the state, which are equally important to understanding the social nature of stalinism. State strategies of manipulation, persuasion, and repression cannot easily be separated from the actions of society. One great obstacle to examining the state's role, however, is determining just what the state is. In a communist state, the party that establishes the ideological parameters for governing becomes so closely identified with state power—the formal establishment of rules for gov-

---

[17]On the labor process and class conflict in communist states, see Michael Burawoy, *The Politics of Production: Factory Regimes under Capitalism and Socialism* (London, 1985), chap. 4.
[18]George Kolankiewicz, "The Working Class," in *Social Groups in Polish Society*, ed. David Lane and George Kolankiewicz (London, 1973), 91–95.

erning society—that it becomes difficult to separate the two. The difference between them, in fact, was also difficult for the subjects of this book to perceive. Poles often used (and still use) the term *władza*—"authorities" (or even "the powers")—to describe government, embracing both actual state officials and anyone else who wields power. The term included, for example, factory directors who reported to the Ministry of Industry. Workers generally reacted to and categorized their employers as they would capitalist owners, yet they clearly recognized that these employers were different in their access to state resources—as is evident in many of the strikes described later in the book. Directors were likely to be not only party members (a fact in itself not necessarily indicative of political power) but party advocates as well; if not, they were likely to have a close assistant who did represent the party's interests in management. On the other hand, management often sacrificed the interests of the state to please workers, while local party or union representatives often acted on their own, supporting worker interests over state interests. It is tempting to follow the workers' lead and, in exasperation, lump them all together as "the authorities." Very often, I use this term to reflect the workers' perspective; however, it is often necessary to be attentive to differences among various authorities—to recognize that politics in early communist Poland was not nearly as uniform or effective as communist leaders might have wished.

To examine these issues, this book compares worker experiences of 1945–50 in two cities, Łódź and Wrocław. The choice of cities was somewhat serendipitous. I was drawn to Wrocław, the city where I began my acquaintance with Poland in the mid-1980s, because of its unusual rebirth on the ruins of a nearly empty German city in 1945. Remade as Polish, with an invented national identity, it enjoyed an early reputation as the capital of Poland's "Wild West" [*dziki zachód*] a free-spirited city of brigandry and rugged pioneers.[19] The focus of dozens of studies in Polish over the past forty years, it remains almost unknown in English-language scholarship. Łódź, meanwhile, is an equally attractive subject because of its mystique as an old proletarian city, the scene of great strikes in the Russian Empire and the interwar years and of nearly forgotten strikes in 1945–48. Comparison of these two cities adds up to more than the sum of their parts; this is not merely a study of two

---

[19]Another name for the region was "Mexico" (*Meksyk*). Jędrzej Chumiński, "Czynniki destabilizujące proces osadnictwa we Wrocławiu (1945–1949)," *Acta Universitatis Wratislaviensis* 1512: *Socjologia* 10 (1993): 64.

cities, no matter how important they are individually. It is a study of Poland as a whole in which Wrocław and Łódź are examples of the range of experience in communist Poland. Differences between these two cities yield insights into the ways in which the state used social forces to its benefit. Łódź was representative of Poland's past, Wrocław of its future. Labor community and working-class tradition provide both the foundation for working-class resistance in Łódź and, in their absence, some of the reasons why workers in Wrocław failed to resist in the same way.

Observers of Eastern Europe (beginning with Stalin himself, who quipped that applying socialism [as he understood it] in Poland was like putting a saddle on a cow) have always highlighted the fundamental incompatibility between the communist state system perfected in the Soviet Union and countries of democratic, relatively urbanized traditions. What has not been explored is how social traditions and established communities actually interacted with communist power. Political traditions were only weak opponents of the new regime; the war displaced prewar Poland's political leadership to London, leaving the communists unassailable at home. But as a society—in some ways greatly changed, in others quite intact—prewar Poland did interact with the postwar regime, its identities conflicting with the forms projected in the communist social vision.

This case was particularly true for the industrial workers. While many scholars have assumed that the Polish working class was born anew in 1945, this assumption is as clearly mistaken as it would be, for example, to ignore the mental baggage that immigrants brought with them to America.[20] To note the importance of pre-1939 traditions to the 1945 revolution is not to say that the one created the other but only to recognize the influence of memory on the participants of the later drama.[21] My introduction cannot do justice to the complexity of experiences in interwar and wartime Poland, but it can offer an outline of working-class experience and communities before 1945, with particular attention paid to Łódź.

[20]Jolanta Pietrasik observes this misinterpretation among Polish sociologists in "Struktura społeczna w Polsce w latach 1944–1949 (przegląd literatury)," in *Elity władzy w Polsce a struktura społeczna w latach 1944–1956*, ed. Przemysław Wójcik (Warsaw, 1992), 95.

[21]See Norman Naimark, "Revolution and Counterrevolution in Eastern Europe," in *The Crisis of Socialism in Europe*, ed. Christiane Lemke and Gary Marks (Durham, N.C., 1992), 65–67.

Before 1918, Poland was divided among three empires, with most of the center and east belonging to Russia, Galicia in the southeast to Austro-Hungary, and Silesia and the west to Germany. This division, and the relation of the several parts to their respective empires, greatly affected the economic and social course of independent Poland. Russian Poland, which included Łódź, was by the late nineteenth century the most industrialized part of the Russian Empire and a crucial link to the West. Although its residents were subject to cultural persecution, German industrialization and political integration made Prussian Poland the most economically advanced region in both interwar Poland and the post-1945 state. The same was true for a fourth area, the lands awarded to Poland in 1945 (including Lower Silesia, where Wrocław is located), which had not been part of any real or imagined Polish state for centuries.

One could not speak of a single Polish working class in 1918 because regional identity was more powerful than national identity (and remained so even after World War II). Independent Poland had both to unite these three societies and build a state that might survive between Germany and the Soviet Union. While neither task was accomplished, industrialization between the wars, particularly in state-sponsored developments such as the port of Gdynia, drew workers from all over Poland; Warsaw, too, was a magnet for job seekers from the entire country. Poland slowly became a more urban and industrial country.[22]

Interwar Poland was hardly a modern country by Western standards. Yet there were a number of Polish cities with an industrial tradition in metals, textiles, and mining that reached back to the mid-nineteenth century. The 5 million blue-collar workers (with their families, nearly 11 million or almost one-third of the population) were a powerful voice in Polish society;[23] more than one government fell or was weakened by labor unrest. In 1921–23, hyperinflation provoked a national wave of strikes, including a national general strike on 3 November 1923 and a worker uprising that took over Kraków two days later. During the world depression of the early 1930s, nearly every working-class family expe-

---

[22]Zbigniew Landau and Jerzy Tomaszewski, *The Polish Economy in the Twentieth Century* (London, 1985); Ferdynand Zweig, *Poland between Two Wars: A Critical Study of Social and Economic Changes* (London, 1944).

[23]Zbigniew Landau and Jerzy Tomaszewski, *Robotnicy przemysłowi w Polsce, 1918–1939: Materialne warunki bytu* (Warsaw, 1971), 29. Landau and Tomaszewski's figures are somewhat higher than those one might estimate from statistical yearbooks because they include transport workers, agricultural laborers, and unemployed workers.

rienced unemployment, part-time work, or dislocation. In a wave of nationwide labor conflict lasting roughly from 1930 to 1937 and directed against an increasingly right-wing regime, Polish workers invented the sit-down or occupation strike.[24]

A wide variety of political parties and trade unions represented workers in the interwar years. Communists never enjoyed majority support among workers but were a constant, if often illegal, force on the political scene.[25] Most major urban parties also controlled their own trade unions so that while perhaps only 1 or 2 percent of the workers were active in a political party, nearly 20 percent of the workers expressed some political involvement through membership in a trade union in the late 1920s and 1930s. Before 1926, the total was close to 35 percent. From left to right, these included unions of the Communist Party of Poland (KPP) and the Polish Socialist Party (PPS) (together usually referred to in the historiography, along with socialist Jewish and German unions, as the "class unions"); the centrist National Workers' Party; the Christian-Democratic unions; government-run unions; and, farthest right, the union of the National Democratic Party.[26]

Postwar workers could draw several salient memories from these experiences. The first was that of organized labor conflict. As logical as it might seem to the postwar communists that the new employers (that is, themselves) were different, this change seemed to workers a semantic shift at best; moreover, the fact that prewar strikes were often led by communists and socialists activists stymied party leadership after 1945. With communists speaking like managers, and managers representing the party, workers could be forgiven for deciding that nothing had

---

[24]Laura Crago, "Nationalism, Religion, Citizenship, and Work in the Development of the Polish Working Class and the Polish Trade Union Movement, 1815–1929: A Comparative Study of Russian Poland's Textile Workers and Upper Silesian Miners and Metalworkers" (diss., Yale University, 1993), chaps. 6–8; Łepkowski, "Myśli o historii Polski i Polaków," 95–101; Janusz Żarnowski, *Społeczeństwo Drugiej Rzeczypospolitej, 1918–1939* (Warsaw, 1973); Feliks Gross, *The Polish Worker: A Study of a Social Stratum* (New York, 1945), 130–42.

[25]On communist constituencies in the interwar period, see R. V. Burks, *The Dynamics of Communism in Eastern Europe* (Princeton, 1961).

[26]Ludwik Hass, "Aktywność polityczna i organizacyjna klasy robotniczej Drugiej Rzeczypospolitej," *Dzieje Najnowsze* nos. 1–2 (1983), 19–44; Ludwik Hass, "Opcje i preferencje polityczno-społeczne robotników Polski międzywojennej," in *Wokół tradycji kultury robotniczej w Polsce*, ed. Anna Żarnowska (Warsaw, 1986). On interwar politics see Jerzy Holzer, *Mozaika polityczna Drugiej Rzeczypospolitej* (Warsaw, 1974), and Joseph Rothschild, *East Central Europe between the Two World Wars* (Seattle, 1974), chap. 2.

changed from the capitalist era. On the other hand, the corollary to prewar conflict, as the communists argued, was the memory of extreme poverty and despair, which contrasted with the hope of 1945. But again, impressions differed; workers interpreted these memories very differently from the way the communists portrayed them.

Second, the interwar period saw a rapid decline in the efficacy of working-class politics. As national politics moved steadily rightward, labor parties or unions—at first the communists, then the socialists, but by the late 1930s even the Christian labor activists—found themselves isolated and powerless at the national level. Workers could conclude that nothing would be gained by participation in formal politics. Workers' lack of interest in, as opposed to antipathy toward, communist politics in postwar Poland echoed this experience.

Finally, the interwar and war periods prepared workers to accept the communists' key industrial program: nationalization of the factories. The trend in the interwar period was toward increased government involvement in industry; in 1919, the government even attempted to expropriate some factories from their owners. The severe unemployment of the 1930s etched on the Polish mind the image of heartless capitalists—often perceived as foreign (German) or non-Polish (Jewish)— who were throwing workers on the street. The war then annihilated the country's economic elite of all nationalities; many of those who were not murdered by the Nazis had either spent the war abroad (a damning fact in a country where patriotic heroism and suffering were highly valued) or had shown their wealth a little too conspicuously during the occupation. Others had no factory to return to because their property was destroyed by the Germans or removed by the Soviets. The logic of reconstruction, in light of all these factors, required state direction in the reconstruction of the economy.[27]

As my brief outline shows, migration to the cities, violent class conflict, unemployment and poverty, and pluralist labor organization were all familiar experiences to the prewar Polish worker and were thus part of the collective memory of postwar labor communities. In cities where

[27]Zweig, *Poland between Two Wars*; Crago, "Nationalism, Religion, Citizenship, and Work," 280. In interwar Poland, moreover, workers in state-run industry, with better benefits and job security than those in the private sector, considered themselves a labor elite. See many of the memoirs in *Pamiętniki bezrobotnych* (Warsaw, 1933; 2d ed., Warsaw, 1967). On capitalists during the war, see Tomasz Szarota, *Okupowanej Warszawy dzień powszedni* (Warsaw, 1973), 170–81.

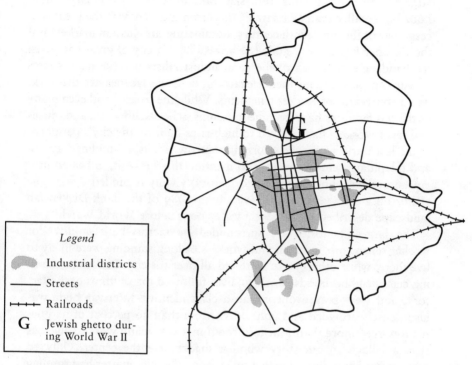

Legend

Industrial districts
Streets
Railroads
G Jewish ghetto dur-
ing World War II

Map 1. Łódź, 1946

industry had been developed for half a century or more, several generations of worker families had established deep roots, reflected in the
strength of their conflicts with employers and the state. Łódź has been
Poland's preeminent worker city in the twentieth century, from the revolution of 1905–7 to the huge strikes of the 1930s, to today when the
city's hard times seem to epitomize Poland's difficulties in adapting to
Western markets and the decline of the socialist welfare state.

Almost completely lacking in natural defining features such as rivers
or hills, Łódź is a sprawling city that reminds Poles from other cities of
a great village. Any structure it has is imparted by its factories. From a

---

[28]Julian K. Janczak, "Ludność," in *Łódź: Dzieje miasta*. Vol. 1: *do 1918r.*, ed. Bohdan
Baranowski and Jan Fijałek (Warsaw, 1980), 210.

tiny village in 1820, it grew to a city of 314,000 by 1900, the second
largest in the Polish lands. (Prussian Breslau/Wrocław was larger than
Łódź but smaller than Warsaw.)[28] Its cotton industry was the great success story of the nineteenth century, dominating the Russian market until
the October Revolution. Łódź has always been a city of great contrasts:
the handsome mansions of the great industrialists line the main streets
downtown; just behind their elegant fin-de-siècle facades are the dark,
damp courtyards of worker tenements. While the palaces and even many
of the old factories have become museums, schools, libraries, and offices
and most workers have moved to high-rises built on the city's periphery
in the last thirty years, the poorly lit, narrow streets, crumbling facades,
and dilapidated entryways (not to mention the dimly lit, unheated provincial archives, housed in an old factory) vividly reminded a first-time
visitor on a snowy November evening in 1989 of the dank Dickensian
landscape described by Władysław Reymont before World War I.[29]

The largest factories are surrounded by factory-built *famułki,* or
worker tenements; foremen and workers of long standing were likely to
live there, while others were scattered all over the city. In various working-class neighborhoods, workers' lives followed the rhythms of the factory, and were played out within a class identity. Interwar Łódź was
also densely crowded and unhealthy. More than 30 percent of its population lived more than four to a room in 1931; many workers lived as
if in a village, in one-story wooden shacks near the center. Only 10
percent lived in buildings with a toilet, and only one-quarter had running
water; 15 percent had no electricity. In each respect, Łódź lagged far
behind other large cities in Poland.[30]

In contrast, Wrocław (Breslau until May 1945) had been the administrative and trade capital of German Lower Silesia. It was the largest
city in the lands that Poland acquired in 1945. Unlike Łódź, whose ar-
chitecture, landscapes, and social relations evoked certain traditions and
cultures for much of its population, Wrocław had not been commonly
associated with the idea of Poland for many centuries. The ancient
traditions of Polish presence in Wrocław and the intellectual life of the

---

[29]Władysław Reymont, *Ziemia obiecana* (1899), in English as *The Promised Land* (New
York, 1927).
[30]Wacław Piotrowski, *Społeczno-przestrzenna struktura miasta Łodzi. Studium ekologiczne* (Wrocław, 1966). See Krystyna Piątkowska, "Research in the Chair of Ethnography
of the Łódź University,"*Ethnologia Polona* 12 (1986), 225–33; much work has been done
as undergraduate theses at the Katedra Etnografii, Uniwersytet Łódzki. Adam Ginsbert,
Łódź: Studium monograficzne (Łódź, 1962), 140–41.

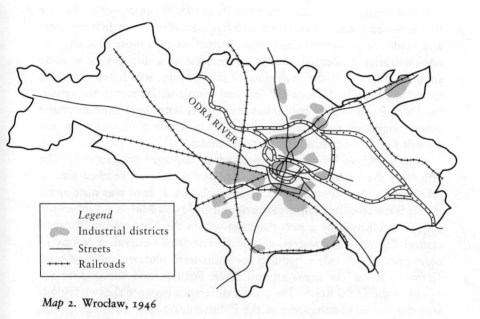

Map 2. Wrocław, 1946

tiny Polish community in Lower Silesia in the eighteenth and nineteenth centuries and its suppression in the interwar period had not made the city seem Polish. To those who now came to the city, the geography of Wrocław was unfamiliar, its history alien.

Of almost one million Germans at the start of the Red Army's siege of "Fortress Breslau" in January 1945, only 150,000 still remained among the ruins upon liberation on 8 May. The siege severely damaged the city's center and leveled two huge swaths of residential neighborhoods to the west and south of downtown, on the front lines of the battle.[31] Huge mountains of rubble blocked the streets, and the empty shells of buildings loomed above. Even in ruins, Wrocław was impressive; it is still unlike other Polish cities of its size. A belt of administrative buildings and spacious parks surrounds an old-town core. The center of the city survived the Red Army's siege, preserving a dense network of small factories, workshops, workers' apartment houses, and baroque churches stamped by several centuries of Prussian order. What still

---

[31]On the war, siege, and liberation, see Marek Ordyłowski, *Życie codzienne we Wrocławiu 1945–1948* (Wrocław, 1991), 7–22.

strikes a visitor to Wrocław today is its insularity, an aspect of the city that imposed a kind of isolation and fragmentation on its first residents and made the process of community formation even more difficult. The administrative-residential core is surrounded at a distance by satellite suburbs annexed at the beginning of the century, which are separated from the center by factory districts and farmland. Nearer to the center, the Odra River and its tributaries and moats both divide and surround other neighborhoods, creating a sense of space unlike that in the crowded cities of central and eastern Poland.[32]

As in Wrocław, World War II profoundly damaged Polish society. The effects of the Nazi occupation on those who survived reached also to relations between workers and between classes. Poland was once again divided; the so-called Fourth Partition of the 1939 Molotov-Ribbentrop pact was followed by a new partition within the Nazi empire. Most of central Poland was assigned to the Government-General, a colony of sorts under Nazi rule scheduled for short-term plunder and long-term Germanization. The areas around Łódź, Poznań, and Silesia were annexed to the Third Reich. The crucial difference between the two regions was the degree of toleration of the Polish nation. The Polish language, and indeed Polish identity in general, was permitted in the Government-General and forbidden in administration and schools in the Third Reich. Thousands of Germans migrated to the newly annexed lands, making contact with Germans other than soldiers and police unavoidable, which was not the case in the Government-General.[33]

Workers in the annexed lands faced a significantly tougher factory regime, with lower pay and rations and greater discipline, than did their colleagues to the east. The virtual lack of any underground organization in the annexed lands meant that the Polish worker was completely deserted, left to cope with the Germans alone. The harshest conditions were endured by the nearly 2 million workers on forced labor (including agricultural labor) in Germany; workers in the annexed lands were particularly vulnerable candidates. While many regarded forced labor as preferable to the dangers at home, they found themselves working vir-

[32]K. Małeczyński, M. Morelowski, and A. Ptaszycka, *Wrocław: Rozwój urbanistyczny* (Warsaw, 1956).

[33]Jan Gross, *Polish Society under German Occupation: The Generalgouvernement, 1939–1944* (Princeton, 1979); Czesław Łuczak,*"Kraj Warty" 1939–1945: Studium historyczno-gospodarcze okupacji hitlerowskiej* (Poznań, 1972); Mirosław Cygański, *Z dziejów okupacji hitlerowskiej w Łodzi* (Łódź, 1965).

tually for nothing, completely deprived of even the rights enjoyed by workers in Łódź. They did, however, usually live in camps with other Poles and occasionally were allowed vacations home. Many were in factories for the first time and brought back new skills and training when they returned to Poland.[34] The war also caused other notable population movements, especially migration into the cities. Particularly in the annexed lands, where workers were needed to take the place of those taken to Germany, thousands of peasants came to work in factories for the first time, especially in the last year of the war. The numbers of women in factory work also rose dramatically. These movements were only the start of rapid social advance that exploded after Poland's liberation.[35]

At the very least, the war experience transformed Polish workers' political engagement. The war generally moved society to the left, away from the discredited right-wing parties. As Franciszek Ryszka explained, even as the war experience "forced one to think 'politically' "—that is, to be aware of the force of political ideas and their role in transforming Poland—it left people hesitant to take a position; they were "far from support, but not disposed toward a fight against the new authorities."[36] This paradox can be resolved, however, by recalling the lack of interest in politics mentioned earlier. Opposition politics seemed no more promising after the war than official politics, because the war made political consensus a virtue by removing and discrediting political options. The later years of the war saw the convergence of communist and noncommunist public positions on social and economic issues. The possible reconstructions of Polish industry, as articulated by political forces in the

[34]Feliks Gross, *Polish Worker*, 163–242; Szarota, *Okupowanej Warszawy dzień powszedni*, 134–61; Władysław Rusiński, *Położenie robotników polskich w czasie wojny, 1939–1945, na terenie Rzeszy i "obszarów wcielonych,"* 2 vols. (Poznań, 1949, 1955), 2: 162–72; Czesław Łuczak, *Polscy robotnicy przemysłowi w Trzeciej Rzeszy podczas II wojny światowej* (Poznań, 1974); Herbert Szurgacz, *Przymusowe zatrudnienie Polaków przez hitlerowskiego okupanta w latach 1939–1945: Studium prawno-polityczne* (Wrocław, 1971).

[35]Kazimierz Wyka, *Życie na niby* (Kraków, 1984), 145–50; Jan Gross, "Social Consequences of War: Preliminaries to the Study of Imposition of Communist Regimes in East Central Europe, *East European Politics and Societies* 3 (Spring 1989), 203; Czesław Madajczyk, *Polityka III Rzeszy w okupowanej Polsce*, 2 vols. (Warsaw, 1970), 1:247, note 32; Czesław Łuczak, "Polska klasa robotnicza w latach wojny i okupacji," *Z Pola Walki*, nos. 1–2 (1982): 54; Kazimierz Piesiewicz, "Social and Demographic Consequences of World War II and the German Occupation in Poland," *Oeconomica Polona* 1983:1, 79–82.

[36]Franciszek Ryszka, "Ideowo-polityczne podstawy przemian," in *Polska Ludowa, 1944–1950: Przemiany społeczne*, ed. Franciszek Ryszka (Wrocław, 1974), 25, 51. See Łepkowski, "Myśli o historii Polski i Polaków," 112.

country in 1944, included neither capitalism nor Soviet-style statization. The nationalization of Polish industry, one of the key aspects of reconstruction, was a development expected and desired by most segments of society and most of the surviving political spectrum. The communist position—expressed for public consumption in the December 1943 manifesto "What are we fighting for?"—was remarkably similar to that of the underground arm of the government-in-exile (itself the product of compromise among widely divergent political parties) in a document issued the following spring. Both were revolutionary programs that proposed a bold restructuring of Polish society, including the socialization and planning of much of the economy and limits to the right to private property.[37]

The war's effect on social relations was similarly contradictory. On the one hand, as Jan Gross has written, the workers' complete alienation from their German employers meant that "Work . . . suddenly lost its capacity for binding the social fabric together."[38] Yet the war also reaffirmed national and class solidarities—rather, given Gross's observation, it allowed for the reformation of new solidarities adapted to the postwar world. Repression as a nation was an experience shared by all Poles regardless of class; few Poles remained in any position of authority, and many from the *inteligencja* found work in factories. When Poles after the war sought eagerly to recapture familiar prewar relationships, the easiest one to revive was national identity. That reawakening is not a pleasant topic, for it brings us to Polish experience of the Holocaust. Polish ambivalence toward the Jews, their perception of being simultaneously martyrs themselves and witness to others' martyrdom, has shaped their understanding of their own suffering. The meaning of the prewar Jewish community and the Holocaust for

[37]"O co walczymy," in *Kształtowanie się podstaw programowych Polskiej Partii Robotniczej w latach 1942–1945 (wybór materiałów i dokumentów)* (Warsaw, 1958), 140–69. See Antony Polonsky, "The Beginnings of Communist Rule in Poland," in *The Beginnings of Communist Rule in Poland*, ed. Antony Polonsky and Bolesław Drukier (London, 1980), 9–10; and Marek Nadolski, "Programy przeobrażeń ustrojowych w Polsce komunistów i ugrupowań prokomunistycznych w latach 1941–1948, in *Elity władzy*, 151–74; "O co walczy Polski lud," in *Armia Krajowa w dokumentach 1939–1945* (London, 1976), 3:361–69; see Kazimierz Przybysz, "Program przeobrażeń ustrojowych w Polsce w myśli politycznej Rady Jedności Narodowej oraz opozycji demokratycznej lat 1945–1947," in *Elity władzy*, 122–28. On the economic underpinnings of nationalization, see Gross, "Social Consequences of War," 201–2.

[38]Gross, "Social Consequences of War," 202.

Polish workers is difficult to define. Listening to workers express national antagonisms, one has the impression of people who are searching to re-create prewar national relations as if they are sensing an amputated limb. At the same time, they try to erase the Holocaust from their memory, just as they removed the physical evidence: in the summer of 1945, worker families took apart the empty houses of the Łódź ghetto in Bałuty for fuel.[39]

The war truncated social relationships, removing long-time political and economic elites and leaving a nation consisting largely of workers and peasants. "German" and "Jew" had been shorthand for the bosses of industry, the causes of the Polish workers' misery. After the war, there were neither Germans nor Jews in any appreciable number; their disappearance left national and class conflicts uncertain and surprisingly volatile, especially in established cities such as Łódź. Thus, in the communist era, "national" conflicts often concealed class antagonisms and vice versa.[40]

The working class irrevocably became "Polish," and working-class identity was strengthened by the war. As onerous as it was, wartime factory work could also be a refuge less stressful than home or the streets. "Work," wrote one worker after the war, "gave one protection. . . . A working Pole became a more invisible, gray, colorless, nameless robot—and thus found some security from persecution."[41] Workers as a group suffered less social displacement than did many other groups—that is, most stayed in their jobs. They were likely to discover that they were more suited to the factory than to trying their hand, for example, on the black market. Kazimierz Wyka observed during the occupation that, while most workers traded what they could, they did so only to feed their families; intellectuals or peasants made a living at it.[42] Even more than before the war, the factory became the locus of class identity. Within the factory no Polish workers were privileged; therefore, a certain shop-floor solidarity emerged that even allowed workers to win certain small concessions from their German employers. Looking at the survival of Poland's urban com-

[39]AAN KC PPR 295/V/5, kk. 33–35. On the Holocaust in Łódź, see Icchak (Henryk) Rubin, *Żydzi w Łodzi pod niemiecką okupacją, 1939–1945* (London, 1988).
[40]See Naimark, "Revolution and Counterrevolution," 68.
[41]Quoted in Rusiński, *Położenie robotników,* 2:85.
[42]Wyka, *Życie na niby,* 148–49; Kazimierz Szymczak, memoir in *Pamiętniki robotników z czasów okupacji* (Warsaw, 1949), 1:9, 28–35.

munities, a 1944 American analysis predicted that communism would find fertile ground in its traditional industrial base.[43]

If these trends might in some way be advantageous to the communists (although we shall see that they usually were not), the war also encouraged behavior that fostered postwar conflict. First, the Nazi occupation was an excellent school of resistance. Unable to strike to improve their lot, workers learned to steal and commit sabotage, particularly in the annexed lands, where few workers belonged to resistance organizations. For some, sabotage may have been aimed at hurting the Nazi war effort; certainly, many histories have glorified it in this way.[44] For most, theft was simply a matter of survival; both theft and sabotage, whatever their purpose, were individual efforts radically different from prewar collective resistance. Postwar observers claimed that these techniques bred a disrespectful attitude on the part of the workers toward the workplace and the employer and demoralized workers.[45] In general, workers had learned to make do without state and economic structures during the war, which, as we will see, encouraged a syndicalist idea of factories in the hands of the workers or the nation. Certainly, resistance after the war was unlike anything the communists were used to: supportive of consensus yet suspicious of mass organizations; collective but without ringleaders or formal rules authorities could understand; individual but with collective aims; frequently anarchic but with demands often directed to the wrong authorities.

The first half of this book deals with the revolutionary transformation of 1945–47. Chapter 1 introduces the key institutional players in Polish politics and the economy in 1944–47, and situates in a social context the key political events of the first three postwar years. Chapters 2 and 3 examine the working-class communities in Łódź and Wrocław. In Łódź, the working class reemerged and reasserted itself after the war as a moral community of Polish workers who were waging a struggle

[43]Rusiński, *Położenie robotników*, 2:75; OSS Research and Analysis, "Postwar Poland," 21–22, U.S. State Department Records, Poland, 1944–49, reel 1.

[44]Łuczak, *"Kraj Warty"*; Marian Malinowski et al., *Polski ruch robotniczy w okresie wojny i okupacji hitlerowskiej, wrzesień 1939–styczeń 1945: Zarys historii* (Warsaw, 1964); Piotr Matuszak, *Ruch oporu w przemyśle wojennym okupanta hitlerowskiego na ziemiach polskich w latach 1939–1945* (Warsaw, 1983).

[45]Madajczyk, *Polityka III Rzeszy*, 2:42; W. Sokorski, introduction to *Pamiętniki robotników z czasów okupacji*, 10. Wyka takes a more optimistic view in *Życie na niby*, 149–50.

for control over factory and community; the absence of such community in Wrocław had significant consequences.

The second half of the book treats the stalinist revolution of 1948–50. Chapter 4 returns to the social context of politics, exploring how the communists attempted to establish control over society by using societal desires as an excuse to impose authoritarian rule. Chapter 5 discusses the rise of labor competition as a way of mobilizing workers to produce and participate in the new society with promises of material reward, fame, and advancement. Chapter 6, by looking at the manipulation of models of work and the worker from above and below, shows how workers found ways to resist the deconstruction of working-class identity. In the conclusion, I weigh these two efforts—the workers' to defend and retain control over their moral community, the authorities' to control factory and society—against each other. A reconsideration of the nature of state and society in stalinism leads to a question critical to the history of communist Poland: what produced the system of the early 1950s? To put it another way, was there a revolution (or two) in Poland after World War II? If so, whose was it?

Part I

Revolution in the Factories, 1945–1947

1 The Struggle for the Factory

The agreement of the Allied powers at Yalta in February 1945 promised "free and unfettered" elections throughout Eastern Europe. Within a few months events in nearly every country discouraged such hopes; the Poles, whose democratic traditions were among the strongest in the region, were in this regard the most bitterly disappointed. But for almost three years political battles in Poland were fought with the language and forms of democratic politics. Whether this was because of an elaborate communist ruse, Western pressure, or a half-hearted attempt to make the "national road" to communism work in such a framework, the period, as experienced by the ordinary Polish worker, was in many ways fundamentally different from the succeeding forty years.

This discourse of democracy dominated Polish life far beyond formal politics because it allowed for many different interpretations of the concept. Many workers felt empowered to lay claim to their factories in the name of democratic change, and labor institutions harbored activists of widely divergent views. Indeed, much of society hoped that the war, having wreaked social, economic, political, and cultural destruction on the old republic, might afford the opportunity for a new Poland, in which those groups underprivileged before the war would find more equity and power. Czesław Bobrowski, an architect of the planned economy, recalled that "despite the sharp antagonism between government and society, at that time both sides of the conflict rode in one wagon." Worn out by war and not ready to concede defeat, people were willing to believe in and support the regime's efforts to rebuild the country, craft new social programs, and spread a mass Polish culture.[1]

At the same time, however, the Polish state and its institutions, most particularly the quasi-state Polish Workers' Party (Polska Partia Robotnicza, PPR), engaged in a struggle for ideological and political supremacy. Thus, the first years of communist power have come to be characterized in the historiography as a civil war. According to this interpretation, this war was both military (between underground anticommunist groups and the Polish communist and Soviet forces) and political (between government and opposition parties). While workers rarely participated in the conflict, which took place mostly outside urban areas, its battles did influence state-worker relations. Yet "civil war" fails to describe the revolution of 1945–47, because it conflates complex social conflict with struggle for control of the state.[2]

With the firm backing of Stalin and the Soviet Army, a group of Polish communists created the PPR in 1942 and then set up a provisional government, the Polish Committee of National Liberation (Polski Komitet Wyzwolenia Narodowego, PKWN), on 22 July 1944, on the heels of the advancing eastern front. The committee began to act as a government despite the continued existence of an internationally recognized government-in-exile in London. Without the Soviets, the two strongest political forces would most likely have been the Polish Socialist Party (Polska Partia Socjalistyczna, PPS)—a party respected before the war and prominent in the underground resistance—and the Polish Peasant Party (Polskie Stronnictwo Ludowe, PSL), left agrarians whose leader, Stanisław Mikołajczyk, was the only politician of stature to return from London. Stalin's backing meant, however, that the PPR was the clear senior partner in an alliance formed with the PPS (and several minor parties). The Government of National Unity, a coalition hammered out in Moscow and formed on 28 June 1945 with Western recognition, included members of all these parties. It implemented the two major expressions of democratic politics: a referendum on government policies in June 1946 and a parliamentary election in January 1947. Both events

---

[1]Quoted in Hanna Świda-Ziemba, "Stalinizm i społeczeństwo polskie," in *Stalinizm*, ed. Jacek Kurczewski (Warsaw, 1989), 39.

[2]See, for example, John Micgiel, "Coercion and the Establishment of Communist Power in Poland, 1944–1947" (diss., Columbia University, 1992), and Krystyna Kersten, *Narodziny systemu władzy: Polska, 1943–48* (Warsaw, 1984). For a review of this concept, see Andrzej Werblan, *Stalinizm w Polsce* (Warsaw, 1992), 16–17.

were marked by bitter and sometimes bloody rivalry between the communist-allied bloc and the legal opposition. In both cases, results were fixed through intimidation and fraud, but the West chose not to make this cause for confrontation with Moscow, allowing the communists to consolidate power and bring "democracy" to an end.

The State and the Party in the Factory

It is difficult to identify the "authorities" in early communist Poland. Communist regimes tend to promote an ambiguous role for the party—does it actually rule, or merely 'guide', as party leaders like to claim?—and this ambiguity was real in Poland in 1945–47. There were in fact two major parties in power: the PPR ruled alongside the PPS, and the first two prime ministers (Edward Osóbka-Morawski and Józef Cyrankiewicz) were socialists. As closely allied as these parties were, they engaged in fierce doctrinal debates on key economic and social issues until their merger in December 1948. Other parties—even the anticommunist PSL—were represented in government.

PPR members, however, directed most of the key ministries, including the Ministries of Public Security and Industry and Commerce. The latter was directed from 1944 to 1949 by Hilary Minc, certainly one of the three or four most powerful men in Poland and a key figure in the PPR. To say the least, there was a close relationship among the various ministries, the PPR and PPS, and the trade unions. It is too simple to state merely that the PPR manipulated or controlled its partners; nonetheless, they were hardly competing interests. It is helpful to think of the pre-stalinist Polish state as a corporatism of unequal partners: the ministries, parties, and unions—institutions whose personnel, programs, and powers overlapped significantly—cooperated with one another in the control of the society and the economy. Although most of these institutions eventually became part of the communist *nomenklatura*, compliance in the pre-stalinist years was not automatic, and control was incomplete. Rather than attempt to delineate precisely the power of each of these institutions, in this chapter I will examine the struggle among them (and with the opposition) for control of the factory.

A decree of January 1946 nationalized all factories of fifty or more workers, as well as smaller factories of particular importance.[3] Most had

---

[3] *Upaństwowienie i odbudowa przemysłu w Polsce (1944–1948): Materiały źródłowe,*

Hanging of a banner announcing that the I. K. Poznański mill is a state enterprise (probably January 1946). Photographer unknown. Archiwum Akt Nowych, Warsaw.

long ago been de facto nationalized when the prewar and wartime owners disappeared. For most workers, then, management meant the state. Workers at a Łódź slaughterhouse realized the implications this situation had for labor relations after their cooperative was taken over by a state firm. "We don't have the slightest influence on work and pay conditions," they complained to union officials in September 1945, "because [the director] constantly reminds us this is a state firm and thus shuts our mouths, because after all we cannot and do not want to fight with the state."[4] The director of a state firm represented the Ministry of Industry and the central planners and thus could always avoid addressing

---

2 vols., ed. Hanna Jędruszczak (Warsaw 1967–69), 1:339–344; Stanisław Jankowski, *Od-budowa i rozwój przemysłu polskiego w latach 1944–1949* (Warsaw, 1989); Tadeusz Kowalik, *Spór o ustrój społeczno-gospodarczy Polski, 1944–1948* (Warsaw, 1980). For a comparative view, see Wlodzimierz Brus, "Postwar Reconstruction and Socioeconomic Transformation," in *The Economic History of Eastern Europe, 1919–1975*, vol. 2: *Inter-war Policy, the War, and Reconstruction*, ed. M. C. Kaser and E. A. Radice (Oxford, 1986), 596–608.

[4]ARZ KCZZ WO 141, k. 265.

workers' complaints by pleading lack of authority—or, as happened with similar frequency, give in to workers' demands and confound the plans of the Warsaw bureaucracy.[5] In the same way, though workers at first tried to attack management without confronting the state, they eventually learned to oppose the state as well, or they used the rhetoric of nationalization to their advantage. Workers called to an April 1946 meeting in the Elektrobudowa/M3 factory in Łódź "maintained categorically that meetings should take place during work and not after, since we are 'state workers' and work for the state."[6] Thus, from the perspective of both directors and workers, nationalization inherently politicized labor conflict.

Although the postwar order was supposed to be different, factory administration appeared to the worker to be just like it was before the war: management set work regulations and pay, and distributed services. Indeed, the earliest managers came from prewar factory technical administration because qualified people of any affiliation, let alone those who were ideologically reliable, were in short supply; even the PPR Central Committee warned against anti-intellectual tendencies in industry. In 1945, 76 percent of a sample of factory directors had higher technical education; only 24 percent belonged to the PPR and 52 percent were unaffiliated. Management's transformation from prewar *inteligencja* to promoted proletariat began only in 1948–49: the percentage of directors with higher technical education was still 63 percent in 1947 but had dropped to 30 percent two years later; party membership climbed from 65 percent to 83 percent in the same period.[7]

The ideological struggle in management was sharpened by the growth of economic planning. At the end of 1946, a three-year economic recovery plan was unveiled, coinciding with the parliamentary election and the beginnings of an improvement in living conditions.[8]

[5]See subsequent chapter, and also AAN MPiOS 750, k. 30.

[6]AAN MPiH 144, k. 175.

[7]Sample size in 1945 was twenty-five and averaged thirty-eight over six years. Halina Najduchowska, "Dyrektorzy przedsiębiorstw przemysłowych," in *Przemysł i społeczeństwo w Polsce Ludowej*, ed. Jan Szczepański (Wrocław, 1969), 82–84. AAN KC PPR WO 295/IX/382, kk. 57–58. On industrial administration, see Hanna Jędruszczak, "Miasto i przemysł w okresie odbudowy," in *Polska Ludowa, 1944–1950: Przemiany społeczne*, ed. Franciszek Ryszka (Wrocław, 1974), 312–14; Jankowski, *Odbudowa i rozwój*, 168–76.

[8]Janusz Kaliński, *Plan odbudowy gospodarczej* (Warsaw, 1977); Janusz Kaliński, "Planowanie gospodarcze," in *Gospodarka Polski Ludowej, 1944–1955*, ed. Janusz Kaliński and Zbigniew Landau, 150–53.

With every year of the plan (1947–49), production targets, and thus management reliability, became more politically necessary. "Industry has become fertile ground for PPR politics," complained the PPS circle at a Łódź garment factory to Prime Minister Józef Cyrankiewicz in 1947. "The positions of directors, personnel directors, and other key positions in industry are being filled mostly with people who are semi-literate or lack appropriate qualifications; the level of Party values is considered a qualifying criterion."[9] *Party* and *management* were beginning to mean the same thing.

The key agent of PPR influence in the factory was the personnel director (*personalny*), who reported to the Ministry of Industry. By 1948, at least, the personalny was almost certainly a PPR member—indeed one of the best the party had to offer.[10] Owing allegiance neither to management nor workers, the personnel director filled the vacuum left by the stymied factory council (discussed later in this chapter), and to some extent supplanted the trade union as well. Nevertheless, although the position later became legendary as a conduit to the Security Apparatus (Urząd Bezpieczeństwa, UB), it cannot be said that the personalny was an effective tool of the party before 1947. A Ministry of Industry instruction of February 1946 made only brief mention of the personalny's duty to "observe and evaluate relations between the enterprise and the local governmental and socio-political organizations."[11] Later that year, the PPR Central Committee was actually trying to rein in the tendencies of some personnel directors to side with workers in norm and wage disputes.[12] Six months later, as the PPR's Political Bureau affirmed the personalny's role in attracting workers to the party, it maintained that "personnel directors who are party members ought to influence the group of people among whom they work, in order to educate them, to bring them near, and eventually draw them into the Party, but the form of that influence should be conversations and comradely discussions, not administrative pressure."

Even in this internal directive, party leaders were at pains to stress administration over ideological work: "The *personalista* [sic], while a

---

[9] AAN CKW PPS 235/XV/59, kk. 40–42.
[10] Of twenty-four personnel directors in factories surveyed by the Wrocław PPS in April 1948, eighteen were PPR members, one belonged to the PPS, three had no affiliation, and two were unknown. WAP WK PPS 36/XIV/19, kk. 176–77.
[11] AAN MPiH 112, kk. 9–12; see "I Zjazd PPR," *ARR* 11:257.
[12] 2 November 1946, AAN KC PPR 295/IX/382, n.p.

member of the Party, . . . may not however act in the name of nor represent the Party in the factory. The *personalista* is not a Party functionary, but a Party member/state employee. Blurring of the borders between the state and Party apparata is impermissible. The *personalista* may not accept Party orders which do not agree with Ministry of Industry instructions."[13] This was theory; in practice, the personnel director could exert considerable pressure on workers in the name of his party and the state—could become indeed the unofficial ruler of the factory. As a member of management, the personalny took part in production decisions, exercised control over administrative appointments, and monitored the work of the factory council. He or she was an embodiment of the PPR's image and was a main conduit of party propaganda into the work force. A worker at a Wrocław sugar refinery was not far wrong when he lamented in June 1948 that "the *personalny* is the lord of life and death."[14]

One of the reasons that the PPR was so successful in developing the personnel director as a tool was that its understanding and execution of the task of winning over the workers was quite different from that of the PPS. The PPR was concerned above all with numbers and the control of key positions—personnel director, top management, and factory council chair—while the PPS often neglected these positions in favor of persuasive arguments, hoping to win workers to the cause of socialism rather than just to the PPS. The PPR appeared to make the transition to postwar politics more easily than did the PPS.[15] As a result, the PPR eventually became the central labor institution in the workplace. First, however, the party battled with the PPS, other political organizations, management, and the workers for control of factory politics and the labor community.

Because it focused on management, the PPR was slow to gain formal control of the shop floor. Faced with the enormous tasks of rebuilding and obsessed with their numerous enemies, party leaders hoped they could trust the workers while they concentrated on winning over other classes in society. They apparently believed in their ability to mobilize

[13]The document concluded: "Party authorities direct and give political direction to the work of personnel directors, just as they give direction to all comrades working in the state apparatus." AAN KC PPR 295/V/6, kk. 69–76.

[14]WAP III KD PPR 33/VI/6, k. 51. See also ARZ KCZZ WE 85, n.p. (24 February 1947).

[15]AAN CKW PPS 235/VI/4, k. 21; AAN MIiP 82, k. 10.

and win the masses and in the basic approbation of regime policies by the Polish working class. In December 1946, there were barely four thousand PPR circles in factories, while there were more than ten thousand state firms in addition to thousands more cooperatives and private firms.[16] The Central Committee created a labor department only in June 1945 as the result of a resolution of the PPR Secretariat, which cautioned that unions were growing too close to the government and distant from workers. The same resolution also called for every party member to belong to and participate in a trade union.[17] By 1946, debates within the Central Committee revealed a stronger concern that unions might meddle too much in management affairs instead of ensuring that production goals were met. Still, defense of "workers' rights" (that is, social welfare) remained one of the tasks that party leaders assigned to the unions rather than taking on themselves.[18]

At the same time, the PPR leadership, like revolutionary parties everywhere, continued to worry about popularity and faulted the party's local organizations. At a Central Committee plenum in September 1946, PPR General Secretary Władysław Gomułka warned of weakness in the PPR, which "generally stands on a low level of political consciousness. . . . It seems, comrades, that not enough attention has been paid to education, and to the politicization of the Party masses." Gomułka blamed factory party circles, which met rarely and were unattractive to new or prospective members. "I talked with some comrades," he continued, "who put it this way: 'Even if we organize a Party circle, it is so boring that people yawn, and sleep, and don't listen.' " Such indifference was especially the case in the large factories, Gomułka complained, demanding: "Who organizes mass work there if our Party is weak?"[19] As party membership expanded, party circles lost their ideological effectiveness. At first, a circle might act as a leveler, bringing together workers and directors in one organization. Eventually, however, many larger factories had separate circles for management and workers.

While the PPR in late 1946 and early 1947 was in the ascendance, it was ill-prepared to control the factory. PPR Central Committee inspec-

---

[16]Two years later, there were more than 10,000 PPR factory circles. *Partia w cyfrach, 1944–1948* (Warsaw, 1948), part 2, table 2A; *RS 1947*, 65.
[17]"Dokumenty PPR i PPS dotyczące działalności związków zawodowych," *KHRZ*, nos. 2–3 (1964): 191–92.
[18]AAN KC PPR 295/IX/382, k. 97.
[19]*ARR*, 10:337–38, 341.

tor Julian Kole visited Łódź in October 1946 (presumably in response to concerns raised by Gomułka) and found a disturbing alienation between the party and the workers of Poland's most industrial city:

> Neither the [PPR circle] secretary nor the district instructor knows what factory issues will be discussed [at a circle meeting]. Everything is improvisation. People have their say and that's it. There are no prepared resolutions on what the circle is to do in its jurisdiction for any of the points on the program. At all the circle meetings [that I attended], there was a report on the last Central Committee plenum. It is characteristic that there was no discussion of that report at any circle. How can this fact be explained? Comrades [in the circles] maintain that one reason is the rally nature and style of these reports. Things liven up only with discussion of economic or factory issues. . . . Most comrades leave the meeting in a pessimistic mood; only the words of the "Internationale" pick up the mood.[20]

Kole also visited the Barlicki mill, site of a recent strike. The PPR had reacted to the conflict by calling off a scheduled meeting. "It is practically a rule of thumb," Kole remarked, "that during important political actions or strikes, circle meetings do not take place. . . . The circle is not there while the conflict is settled. This has no [positive] effect on the cementing of the circle's relationship [with] the masses."[21] Recruitment of new members was haphazard at best. Kole described a PPR recruitment effort at the Scheibler and Grohman mill, Łódź's largest factory: "The turnout was not bad, mostly women. . . . After the speech, a [PPR youth organization] member spoke; he said a few words about the Nuremberg verdict, read a resolution, and the meeting ended with the singing of the 'Rota.' Some of the workers were dissatisfied. The same signals were found at other factories visited. [Our] comrades are afraid to do battle with oppositionists and malcontents, [and this fear] has a negative effect on workers."[22]

The PPR, in short, was unable to put on an attractive front for potential recruits in the factory. Kole listed several reasons. First, the PPR was forced into the role of factory police, punishing theft: "In most cases, our Party members have changed into UB agents or actual 'thief-

---

[20] AAN KC PPR 295/XI/10, kk. 28–29.

[21] Ibid., 31–32.

[22] Ibid., 35. The "Rota," a patriotic song composed by turn-of-the-century poet Maria Konopnicka, is a call to resist foreign oppression. It begins: "We will not forsake the land of our fathers; / we shall not let our tongue be buried. / We are a Polish nation, a Polish people."

catchers.' Instead of agitation and propaganda, they conduct police actions." Management or local PPR leaders often used party members for unpopular tasks such as searching workers at the end of the day or breaking strikes. Some PPR activists saw themselves as management's right hand and willingly supported the director not only in condemning or punishing theft and sabotage but even in pay and work issues. They were slow to condemn the excesses of directors and bureaucrats—who were more likely, after all, to be party members than were ordinary workers.[23] It was also to the advantage of the factory councils and trade unions to present the PPR in this role. A popular view held that the factory council was for shop issues while the PPR was for "higher" issues, such as supervising the factory council and management and monitoring production.[24] This image, which was not far from the Party's eventual role, was not likely to foster worker support.

For both labor parties, factory circles were a new form of work; there had been no such party cells before the war. Moreover, the PPR at liberation was mostly a small core of activists. While the party grew very quickly, reaching a temporary peak of just over 300,000 nationwide in April 1945 before declining to about 235,000 in December, it was still a relatively small organization; the number of "mobilized" or "conscious" members was vastly smaller. Most belonged in name only, taking little part in party affairs. Organizing a circle in the factory did not mean real PPR influence. If party activists hoped that workers would mobilize themselves, translating support for regime initiatives such as nationalization into political enthusiasm, the 1946 referendum and the 1946–47 strikes showed otherwise.[25]

The PPR's problem was that it attempted to expand in a society where people already had organizational allegiances or else felt an antipathy toward politics of any kind. This was particularly the case in established communities such as Łódź. Even in early 1946, a survey of PPR circles in one district found real isolation, precisely because of what might be termed the PPR's organizational superfluity. There were only a handful of members in several factories, with little or no effort made to reach out to nonmember workers. Activists at the Wicke factory tried hard to

[23]Ibid., 35–36. Also AAN MPiH 144, kk. 1–3; AAN MPiH 215, n.p. (Wagner factory). See chap. 2.

[24]ŁAP KW PPR 1/XI/2, n.p. (May 1946).

[25]On national party membership, see Jaime Reynolds and John Coutouvidis, *Poland, 1939–1947* (Leicester, U.K., 1986), 175–97, esp. 181.

find excuses: there were only five PPR members because "the mood among workers shows *sanacja* tendencies [a reference to the 1930s dictatorship], and this causes a misunderstanding among the workers." At the large Eitingon mill, where there were thirty-three members, activists felt that since most workers were "older, [and] don't understand what the Party is," it was sufficient simply to hand out "declarations of intent to join the Party" and hope for a response.[26]

In addition, the PPR's commitment to economic efficiency and political power frequently drove it to oppose worker actions at the cost of popularity. After a September 1945 strike wave in Łódź, a Ministry of Industry inspector lamented that "the political parties have utterly no control over the situation. They limit themselves to arranging the return to work of Party elements, despite the hostile attitude of the workers. . . . The low activity of the political parties has a deleterious effect on the organization of life; they cannot accomplish the tasks which they are assigned. Certain actions of the parties (like, in my opinion, strike breaking . . .) bring them worker antipathy."[27] Thus, the communists were on the defensive; not only did many party members join strikes, but those that did not found themselves threatened or attacked by other workers.[28]

Even at the top, the PPR's attitude toward strikes was in 1945 surprisingly ambiguous, allowing that strikes were theoretically possible. In March, trade union chief Kazimierz Witaszewski asked textile workers only to "renounce strikes for the duration of the war." Hilary Minc complained in September 1945 of workers' "indulgent attitude toward strikes, which cost little and carry no risk. There is a peculiar feeling that everything is allowed in democratic Poland. . . . No one has managed to tell the workers that not everything is possible in Poland right away, that some things are still impossible." Minc used the demands of reconstruction, not of socialist order, to explain the need for greater discipline. Perhaps, he implied, workers would regain that right when this battle had been won. Łódź trade union leader Aleksander Burski finally asked workers to reserve that "sacred weapon" for the battle with reactionary forces.[29]

---

[26]ŁAP KD PPR Górna-Prawa 1/VI/65, kk. 21–22.

[27]AAN MIiP 82, kk. 9–10.

[28]Gomułka acknowledged at a PPR Central Committee plenum in October 1945 that PPR members often supported strikes. Janusz Gołębiowski, *Walka PPR o nacjonalizację przemysłu* (Warsaw, 1961), 268–69.

[29]ARZ KCZZ WO 125, k. 20; Minc speech reprinted in *Życie Warszawy*, 22 November

Party leaders thus treated the strike with respect and fear as they sought to define their role in labor relations. Even in 1945, however, the PPR tried out language reminiscent of that of its capitalist predecessors. "The workers . . . do not really understand the enormous work of the Government and the political parties," explained one report, "and are more interested in their own needs and their individual standard of living." By 1947, Central Committee member Stefan Jędrychowski could state categorically that a strike "was a weapon which is excluded from the working class arsenal. . . . [It is] directed at the class itself, since . . . there is no factory-owner's profit which could be taken away." Instead, Jędrychowski advocated the struggle for higher production and less time lost. Nevertheless, strikes were not specifically outlawed.[30]

The Polish Workers' Party was not just another social institution searching for more members and greater influence. It pretended to have responsibility for a wide range of social issues—such as housing, fuel, and food supply. It also assumed supervision, welcome or not, over the activity of factory councils and trade unions (and also factory management). The failures of these organizations thus compromised the PPR as well, even if the workers did not necessarily equate them with the party. PPR strategy required that local party leaders act as representative of the new order by reaching beyond the safe confines of the party to contact the nonparty masses; yet Kole noted a "fear of the masses among the Party rank-and-file. The factory councils do not hold worker meetings in the factories. The trade unions do not organize meetings of factory council chairmen, the Party does not energize the factory councils, and thus the masses are left to fall prey to whispered propaganda."[31]

The drive for a tighter party organization in the factories came in the wake of widespread worker unrest in 1946–47. Drawing conclusions from the great strike of September 1947 in Łódź, PPR ideologist Roman Zambrowski argued that mass membership, not the dedication of a few, was the key to control: if the thirty-odd "old mobilized cadres" at the Poznański mill (the center of conflict) tried to stop the strikers, "the women would have broken their bones and we would have achieved

---

1984; "I Zjazd PPR," ARR, 11:257. A PPR delegate to a Łódź postal strike used military imagery to make a similar point: "a state worker, like a soldier, may not leave his post." ŁAP WRZZ 253, n.p.

[30] ŁAP KD PPR 1/VI/66, kk. 17, 24–25; AAN KC PPR 295/XI/2, k. 14; Walery Masewicz, *Strajk: Studium prawno-socjologiczne* (Warsaw, 1986), 205–11.

[31] AAN KC PPR 295/XI/10, kk. 25–26.

nothing, but 600 PPR members broke the strike."[32] Thus, in November the Party's Central Committee took the step of placing the 110 largest factories (with a total of more than 280,000 workers) under its direct control; the leadership could now keep its finger on the pulse of the most important centers of industry rather than rely on provincial officials' reports.[33]

The PPR's chief ally in its attempts to control the factory was the Security Apparatus (UB), the police organ, which, like its counterparts throughout the region, was essential to the acquisition and holding of political power. From the beginning, of course, the UB was an unpopular institution that Poles were quick to compare to the recently departed Gestapo. Nevertheless, while the UB was ruthless in its repression of certain opposition groups, its presence in the factory was even weaker than that of the PPR. The UB had difficulty recruiting functionaries who were reliable, competent, and intelligent. As late as August 1947, the various provincial offices of the UB controlled only 228 resident agents (that is, full-time employees of the ministry), 568 agents, and 8,194 informers in all of Polish industry. The entire Lower Silesian province had just two residents in industry plus 88 agents and 618 informers. While the numbers in the city of Łódź were higher (43, 34, and 555, respectively), they were weakest where they were needed most—in the textile industry. Some of the largest factories had no agents at all. Moreover, some 10 percent of the residents and agents, and about one-quarter of the informers were classified as "not working"—in other words, paper agents. (An informer meant a contact only; UB reports frequently noted that many informers and even agents did not necessarily exist but only served to inflate figures.)[34] Vice-Director Zdzisław Szymczak critiqued the apparatus's work in industry at an April 1947 meeting of provincial UB chiefs. He complained that the ministry's provincial offices were not taking reports of sabotage seriously, only registering their occurrence. The UB's efforts to combat strikes were in an even worse state, because

[32] AAN KC PPR 295/IV/1, k. 22.
[33] AAN KC PPR 295/IX/5, kk. 15–17.
[34] MSW MBP 17/IX/38, t. 1, kk. 6, 9; t. 2, n.p.; AAN MIiP 82, k. 10. Recruiting problems were a frequent subject of discussion in the ministry. See documents in *Aparat bezpieczeństwa w latach 1944–1956: Taktyka, strategia, metody, część I: Lata 1945–1947*, ed. Andrzej Paczkowski, *Dokumenty do dziejów PRL, zeszyt 5* (Warsaw, 1994). On repression by the UB and other security organs, see Andrzej Paczkowski, *Pół wieku dziejów Polski, 1939–1989* (Warsaw, 1995), 164–70, 238–45, and Micgiel, "Coercion and the Establishment of Communist Power," 41–59.

more resources had been devoted to the sabotage issue. Only where UB operatives had focused on recruiting foremen had they gained any solid information about workers' activities and moods.[35] Indeed, these shortcomings would be amply evident after the Łódź strikes of the fall of 1947. To speak of an all-powerful security apparatus at this point would be misleading at best. The constraints of ideology and cadres continued to hold back the regime in the factory into the stalinist years.[36]

The Failure of a Labor Opposition Politics

For a labor historian, the study of political opposition in communist Poland is a frustrating challenge for the simple reason that no opposition group (with the partial exception of the PPS, including its outlawed right wing) paid serious attention to workers until 1976. In most cases, the lack of attention to any social groups is striking. With such a rich tradition of pluralist labor politics before the war, why did a similar political opposition not emerge after 1945? The obvious answer is that it was repressed by the communists. Indeed, although during the "democratic" period, PPR leaders tolerated legal opposition among intellectuals and peasants, they looked especially harshly on any encroachment onto their turf. To complete this picture, however, we must also recognize other obstacles to such an opposition (whether led by the PPS, the PSL, the Catholic church, or the underground opposition), including the limitations these groups had as organizers among labor. The various opposition groups showed in their propaganda a marked preference for *high*, or formal, politics, agitating almost exclusively around larger political abstractions such as anticommunism and sovereignty, and restricting themselves to polemic description of social problems. In part, this

---

[35] *Aparat bezpieczeństwa w latach 1944–1956*, 84–89. The reality of sabotage (see Chapter 4) probably bore little resemblance to Szymczak's fulminations; he admitted that his evidence was mostly anecdotal.

[36] The role of the military in the factory at this time, meanwhile, is still murky. The railroads were militarized throughout the late 1940s. In December 1945, Aleksander Burski spoke warmly of the effect that the military's cultural/educational patronage in factories had on worker unrest. "I Zjazd PPR," *ARR* 11:258; see Ignacy Blum, *Z dziejów Wojska Polskiego w latach 1945–1948* (Warsaw, 1960). With the prominent exceptions of the Recovered Territories and Upper Silesia, Soviet Army presence in most Polish factories declined rapidly after war's end in May 1945. See Ryszard Nazarewicz, "Raporty generałów," *Polityka* 13 February 1988; AAN KC PPR 295/V/5 kk. 40–44. The opening of new archives may well reveal a greater military presence in Polish industry.

approach can be explained by a belief that the struggle to regain Polish sovereignty and democracy took precedence over issues of concern to particular constituencies.[37] An understanding of opposition's failure to organize labor can shed some light on the forms that worker resistance took in this period.

Workers in 1945–48 (indeed, until 1956) were disinclined to engage in debate over national issues or to participate in political organizations; their lack of interest in formal partisan politics was a valuable asset for the ruling parties. The simple fact of repression is not sufficient to explain this disinclination, for (as we will see in subsequent chapters) the regime had relatively little control over workers in other ways. In part, exhaustion after the war accounted for this mood. While many Poles had an idea of what kind of Poland they hoped to have after the war, they felt that simply regaining independence was more important. It was difficult, even if one was suspicious of the government's intentions, to summon the energy to continue fighting. Thousands took part in the so-called civil war, but millions did not. For the latter, the sheer challenge of the reconstruction of everyday life was absorbing enough. A report by the underground organization Freedom and Independence (WiN) in June 1945 conceded that "the absorbing power of everydayness has begun to break apart the antipathy [*negacja*] toward the Lublin government [PKWN]. . . . Centers of conspiratorial work have lost contact with society as a whole, and have partly lost their popularity. . . . Society's solidarity with the pro-London orientation is beginning to break."[38]

That the PPR itself misunderstood society can be seen in its pronouncements about opposition. People "on the sidelines" (in PPR terminology) were often classified as the opposition (increasingly so as the referendum and election campaigns heated up) yet never with any evidence about the nature of their political beliefs. Their indifference or cautious neutrality seemed like hostility to frustrated politicians and was treated as such. There were indeed dozens, perhaps hundreds, of underground opposition groups in Poland in the first postwar years. Many may have been no more than a name and have left behind no documentation; there were few, if any, in factories or focusing on workers.[39]

---

[37]On the postwar opposition, see Marek Latyński, *Nie paść na kolana. Szkice o opozycji lat czterdziestych* (Warsaw, n.d.), and Andrzej Friszke, *Opozycja polityczna w PRL, 1944–1980* (London, 1994), 7–66.

[38]Quoted in Gołębiowski, *Walka*, 295.

[39]One group that did appeal to workers (with unknown success) was the Nationwide

Much of our information about contacts between the underground and the workers comes from PPR and UB leaders who feared such contacts. The PPR Political Bureau declared, after a September 1945 wave of strikes in the Łódź area, that it detected "dangerous signs of a rise in the activity of the NSZ [National Armed Forces, a radical-right armed organization] among the Łódź working class, and the ominous phenomenon of PPR passivity in regards to NSZ infiltration of the factories." It resolved to send no one less than Gomułka and Minc to Łódź to address the problem.[40] But there is no evidence of such infiltration. The PPR and UB simply interpreted any dissatisfaction in terms of organizations and political struggle, just as they would suspect sabotage in any fire or work accident.

Although allied with the communists, the socialists were the most likely source of opposition. Because of its long national traditions and the presence of many independent-minded politicians in its ranks until unification with the PPR, the PPS was a magnet for workers who valued political independence and plurality and for the labor-oriented underground. Many in the underground placed their faith for a free Poland in the PPS, hoping that it might provide a nucleus for a challenge to PPR dominance.[41] WiN issued a lengthy appeal entitled "To Polish Socialists," calling upon the PPS to defend the interests of its traditional supporters: "Don't allow yourselves to be pushed out of the trade unions and factory councils, but instead dominate them and use them in the struggle for the rights of workers and of your Party. . . . Hurry to the aid of your worker members who are arrested or thrown out of work. Don't allow yourselves to be separated from the working masses; don't lose your influence on them; teach them, advise them in their little everyday problems, and constantly shape them in your genuine Polish socialist

---

Polish Organization of Working People (with the awkward acronym ONPOLP), perhaps affiliated with WiN. Its appeals lamented the betrayal of Poland and the socialist cause (including the failure of workers' control) because workers were misled by faith in the PPS. As one leaflet exclaimed: "It is a shame and dishonor for every worker if, by remaining in the ranks of the PPS, he contributes to the treasonous behavior of today's PPS." "W sprawie PPS," MSW MBP 41/231, k. 191; other documents in this folder, and MSW MBP, 41/230, n.p. A similar WiN document appears in MSW MBP, 41/229, n.p. An incomplete list of underground organizations is in an internal Ministry of Internal Affairs publication, *Informator o nielegalnych antypaństwowych organizacjach i bandach zbrojnych działających w Polsce Ludowej w latach 1944–1956* (Warsaw, 1964).

[40] AAN KC PPR 295/V/2, k. 19.

[41] MSW MBP 17/IX/77, t. 2.

direction."[42] This, too, was the rhetoric of the PPS's outlawed right wing, WRN (Freedom, Equality, Independence). Very little can be said with certainty about the WRN because the PPR was in the habit of ascribing every sign of trade union independence to the *"wuerenowcy"* (WRN members). UB Colonel Julia Brystygierowa reported to a briefing of provincial UB chiefs in April 1947 that nine unions (of which only the railroad workers' union was made up primarily of workers engaged in manual labor) contained "WRN groups." But even Mieczysław Moczar (Łódź UB chief, later Minister of Internal Affairs) was forced to admit at the same meeting that "so far we have not been able to find the WRN in [the ranks of] the PPS."[43]

Thus, for all their talk about reactionary forces, PPR leaders continued to see the PPS as the greatest threat in the factory. The Łódź PPS, led by Henryk Wachowicz, was notoriously independent; in mid-1945, the PPR claimed that the PPS controlled nearly all smaller trade unions in the city.[44] In the 1946 May Day celebrations, the PPR sought to enforce a parade under jointly carried banners. Some of the workers at the Herszenberg and Halberstadt factory in Łódź objected to the caricatures (presumably of Mikołajczyk, Churchill, and so on) to be carried by the PPR. A schism ensued, with most workers marching apart from the PPR, unofficially with the PPS. That same year, the two parties marched separately in Wrocław, in what a PPR observer described as a "subdued" procession, without songs or slogans.[45] At the September 1946 PPR plenum, Gomułka warned of the danger from a "hegemonistic" PPS. He turned special attention to PPR–PPS relations in Łódź, where he accused the PPS of completely rejecting the idea of a united front, but he noted that the same problem was evident elsewhere. To the PPR, even such separatism seemed threatening.[46]

---

[42]No date, but probably 1947. MSW MBP 41/233, kk. 87–94. See Zygmunt Woźniczka, *Zrzeszenie Wolność i Niezawisłość, 1945–1952* (Warsaw, 1992), 184.

[43]MSW MBP 17/IX/77, t. 2, n.p.; see also comments by Brystygierowa at 22 December 1948 briefing, t. 3, k. 201. On the WRN in general, see Micgiel, "Coercion and the Establishment of Communist Rule," 164–69.

[44]AAN KC PPR 295/IX/436; ŁAP KW PPR 1/XI/1, n.p.

[45]ŁAP WK PPS 22/XII/7. In 1945, PPS activists at the Hirszberg factory in Łódź refused to show up for the parade at all, returning instead (as the PPR alleged) to the factory to drink vodka. AAN KC PPR 295/IX/32, k. 1. In Wrocław, see 295/IX/49, k. 138; WAP KW PPR 31, k. 59.

[46]*ARR*, 10:334. Ignacy Loga-Sowiński, the PPR leader in Łódź, blamed overworked PPR activists and the unwillingness of PPR-member directors to take part in party meetings (360–61).

In uneasy cooperation, the two parties began the national referendum campaign in early 1946. A bloc of government parties asked voters to approve the abolition of the Senate, the nationalization of factories, the redistribution of land, and the new borders with Germany. The campaign was important because it marked the first use of the new political language in public. Now communist politics, although they still had little importance in the daily lives of most Poles, became less easy to ignore or avoid, and the distance between the government parties and the political opposition widened. With geopolitical issues at least partially resolved, the regime turned to society and imposed its own political interpretation on social issues. This first attempt to enforce some political unity on workers failed.

The campaign reflected the problems with party organization already noted: activists still unprepared for mass politics were unable to make effective contact with the electorate. The Łódź Information and Propaganda Bureau reported that lack of interest in political meetings was matched by the indifference of the PPR and PPS, which "display rather lively, but limited activity—that is, locally, among their own members. One cannot find a propaganda program . . . to attract nonparty people on the sidelines into political life."[47] Successful programs would have to downplay politics; one example was a series of concerts that the Central Workers' House of Culture of the Workers' University Society organized in sixty-one factories in the last two weeks of the campaign, in the belief that a clever linking of the topic with art "is the only way to reach the minds and hearts of the workers." Such a concert usually opened with a speech by a union representative. Up to 1,500 workers attended, and the response was enthusiastic. One factory council representative exclaimed:

If only you citizens would come with such concerts, there would be no speech which workers would not want to hear, for even if the speech . . . itself were very interesting and dealt with the most burning issues, . . . it is tiring, and the workers don't listen, and even leave. But today I did not see even one person leave. You heard yourselves how workers yelled "Give us more!" and at the conclusion, when the artist said "Remember June 30—everyone with their 'Three Times Yes' card to the voting urn!"—how the whole hall began to applaud and shout.

[47]ŁAP WUIiP 31. See also MSW MBP 17/X/10 t. 1, k. 9.

Enthused another: "Wonderful concert! The mood of our railwaymen has changed 180 degrees. . . . I am certain that . . . there won't be a single railwayman here who would vote 'no.' "[48]

Such strategies were usually beyond the abilities of local organizations. At the M3 metal factory in Łódź, the personnel director did not exaggerate the problem by much:

> In the factory, there is very little interest on the part of the political parties and the trade union in the matter of the Popular Referendum. . . . The factory council by itself is not involved, for it is so convenient for them to quit work and go home, not to a meeting; . . . if a worker comes to the factory council with a question, he is sent to the trade union, or [the council] immediately telephones [the union] to find out what to answer to this or that question. The political parties . . . do not try to hold meetings enlightening [the workers] as to what the Popular Referendum is, for the whispered propaganda campaign is quite lively in our factory, and I don't want to exaggerate, but I don't know if 20 percent will vote three times "Yes," and the rest will be for giving the factory back to Mr. Jaroszyński [that is, voting no on question two, about nationalization].[49]

Officially, 68 percent, 77 percent, and 91 percent of voters nationwide approved the three questions, respectively.[50] The real results (kept secret but carefully analyzed by political leaders) were more sobering. The government parties lost the first two questions, gaining just 31 percent on the first (which the opposition PSL had made a test of its support) and 45 percent on the second; a smaller majority of 68 percent approved the new borders.[51] One PPS leader explained workers' apparent rejection of even nationalization as due to a lack of understanding: "The worker saw the economic policy of management, which often did not see indi-

[48]ŁAP WRZZ 114, n.p.

[49]AAN MPiH 144, k. 176. The PSL joined the PPR and PPS in calling on its supporters to approve question 2. Some underground groups called for a no on this question, apparently because they associated the land reform part of the question with the institution of Soviet-style collective farms, not because of any support for private industry. Nationalization was rarely if ever challenged in underground pamphlets. See for example documents in MSW MBP 41/230, zeszyt 5.

[50]Tadeusz Marczak, *Propaganda polityczna stronnictw przed referendum z 30.VI.46r.* (Wrocław, 1986), 198. On the referendum, see also Kersten, *Narodziny systemu władzy*, chap. 6.

[51]AAN Referendum, II/29 (122), k. 1.

vidual [workers], only numbers, or its own egotistical interests. We could not fight as needed, and mobilize forces."[52]

Drawing lessons from the referendum results, the PPS and PPR prepared to go on the offensive—but not necessarily together. The PPR raised the stakes of the battle at its September 1946 plenum, proposing that the two parties merge. Through 1947 it was not certain which party would have more support, and could thus dominate a unified party. Both parties believed that they had emerged from the referendum stronger, wiser about their ally, and ready for the tasks ahead. The referendum had helped to polarize society; one provincial PPR committee noted that people now tended to join either the PPR or the most anticommunist of the underground organizations.[53] The director of a Łódź electronics factory was challenged to choose sides, "to go either to the left or right, [for] the straight road leads right to the cemetery." A worker at the same factory, arrested for membership in an underground partisan group, drew the same conclusion and asked to join the PPR.[54] PPR membership increased from just under 350,000 on the eve of the referendum to more than 550,000 before the parliamentary election seven months later. The PPS also grew dramatically in this period, from just under 200,000 at the end of 1945 to almost 440,000 a year later. PPS leaders felt that a potential alliance would be between at least equal partners, with the PPS as the driving force of the nation.[55] The struggle between the two parties would be waged at a number of levels in the government, in local administration, and in the party press, as well as over control of the factory councils and unions.

In a period of mass growth and swift propaganda campaigns the PPS was hindered by its emphasis on the quality of its cadres. In contrast to the PPR, which was concerned about political battles, PPS leaders issued a circular on factory councils that called for "the best comrades, as far as intellectual and moral level is concerned, to enter the factory councils." Such comrades would be those "who enjoy an appropriate level of respect and popularity among the work force. . . . The Party . . . may not allow incompetent or simply compromising actions on the part of

[52]Tadeusz Ćwik, quoted in Jerzy Jagiełło, *O Polską drogę do socjalizmu* (Warsaw, 1983), 93–94.
[53]Marczak, *Propaganda polityczna*, 212.
[54]AAN MPiH 144, kk. 39–40.
[55]Bronisław Syzdek, *Polska Partia Socjalistyczna w latach 1944–1948* (Warsaw, 1974), 348–49. Reynolds and Coutouvidis, *Poland, 1939–1947*, 236, 278–87.

Election poster, 1946. "Who Is to Rule in Poland—Them or Us? Vote for the Democratic Bloc." Archiwum Akt Nowych, Warsaw.

comrade factory councilors to lower its authority or trust of the masses."[56] At Wrocław's Pafawag, this was more and more difficult to achieve as the factory grew:

> The percent of thoroughbred, disciplined, skilled employees is declining sharply. The element which now arrives is drawn from people with very little factory familiarity, if any—residents of villages and small towns, and people from "beyond the Bug [River] [that is, Poland's former eastern territories—the kresy]." . . .
>
> Workers who are skilled and unselfishly devoted don't have time to concern themselves with social matters, and take a minimal role in propaganda campaigns. PPS members, even old Party comrades, don't reveal [their party affiliation], placing work in rebuilding such an important workplace first, above some participation in Party life.
>
> Comrades from the fraternal PPR, however, are less devoted to skilled work, and are more active in recruiting the incoming element to the Party, and as a result they achieved an overwhelming majority in the first constituted factory council.
>
> This affects production to some degree. The . . . PPR cell is quite active, organizing constant meetings and sessions during work hours, and gathering an ever larger group of workers.[57]

A key battleground was the factory council. At the PPR Central Committee's July 1945 plenum, Roman Zambrowski warned that the party was losing influence in some factories; the Secretariat issued a circular in September that characterized upcoming factory council elections as "a serious political battle" and outlined tactics for breaking PPS insistence on separate candidate lists.[58] In subsequent elections, party circles usually either nominated candidates or drafted them onto both party and nonparty slates, seeking to control the process of workplace democracy as closely as possible. A PPR report of the campaign at the Steinert cotton mill in Łódź offers a glimpse into the election procedure:

---

[56]"Dokumenty PPR i PPS dotyczące działalności związków zawodowych," 207-8, also 204-6; October 1946 membership drive: AAN CKW PPS 235/VII/12, kk. 42-45.

[57]September 1946, WAP WK PPS 36/XIV/20, kk. 69-70. See also WAP WK PPS 36/XIV/20, kk. 124-25.

[58]ARR, 7:162; "Dokumenty PPR i PPS dotyczące działalności związków zawodowych," 193-95. The circular explained that the system of joint lists (in which workers could choose particular candidates from the agreed-upon joint list) "makes it fully possible to uncover the influence of particular parties . . . without a battle between them." See also "I Zjazd PPR," ARR, 11:259.

PPS and nonparty workers were present at a meeting of our cell, and together we planned a slate of candidates to the factory council. At a general meeting . . . we announced the slate to the workers, who received it rather unfavorably, demanding more nonparty [candidates] and the removal of Klimczak, a PPS member; they wanted to choose another in his place, but the district PPS guaranteed that Klimczak would fulfill his duties. The [election campaign] meetings were quite stormy, and the workers felt a personal dislike for certain PPR members.

[Question:] Do the non-Party [workers] who are candidates to the factory council have the trust of the masses, and are they honest people?

[Answer:] Yes, they are honest workers.[59]

At the Geyer mill, the PPR countered the same demands for more nonparty representation with the response that, after all, they had been working hardest to rebuild the country. Party leaders agreed upon a balance of nine members each from PPR, PPS, and nonparty slates, plus three youth candidates (split the same way). In the actual voting, however, PPS members allegedly refused to vote for PPR candidates; and the council ended up with four PPR members, twelve each PPS and nonparty members, and two youth representatives; one particularly unpopular PPR candidate was not elected.[60] Overall, the elections in Łódź ensured party-dominated representation of nonparty workers: while PPR membership was rarely above 4 or 5 percent in the larger factories, PPR members usually accounted for one- to two-thirds of a given council.

Not that the PPS was defenseless. Through 1947, PPS and nonparty activists dominated the lower levels of many unions. The PPR at a factory in Łódź accused the PPS in March 1947 of indiscriminately "accepting members whom the PPR would never take. That's why their membership is 100 members, while the PPR has only 59." Like their leaders, PPR members connected numbers to power.[61] The battle for the factories sometimes took on a desperate, even violent edge, as in PZPW No. 4 in Łódź during a February 1947 union election. A PPR representative found the agitation of his PPS comrades incomprehensible: "One name, of PPR comrade Płoszyński, was mentioned, and the gathering responded with enthusiasm (chanting his name); when a second name, also of a PPR comrade, was mentioned, he was also favorably received by all. Just then a storm erupted; as if pulled by a string, all the PPS

[59] ŁAP KŁ PPR 1/VI/141. k. 1–4.
[60] Ibid., kk. 3–4.
[61] AAN MPiH 144, k. 89.

members began to create a tumult, jumping . . . about the stage waving
their hands, shouting names of PPS [candidates] into the ear of the union
representative. . . . They acted like madmen on stage, dancing something
like the 'Swing' . . . and in a possessed manner shouted that this was
unjust. *But what was unjust?*" Three women (apparently from the PPS)
attacked a PPR factory leader; one yelled: "We should finish with you
once and for all, you son-of-a-bitch, I'll show you; you are always trying
to clobber us over the head."[62]

Tensions were highest on the railways, where union activists fiercely
defended their independence and the PPS enjoyed substantial support—
controlling nearly half the seats on regional union boards. A May 1947
PPR report accused the PPS of "opposition demagoguery": "Whispered
agitation is being conducted to the effect that the PPS is fighting for a
pay raise for railwaymen, but is unfortunately helpless at the moment
because the PPR is playing first fiddle against that raise." The socialists,
the report continued, supported demilitarization of the rails and were
trying to break the railway union into two separate party unions.[63]

In fact, all political players in 1945 attached great importance to the
unions as a means to political power and hoped to influence them. One
other organization with echoes of prewar labor traditions was the Labor
Party (SP), a Christian Democratic party legal until 1950. Some prewar
activists briefly flirted with the idea of reviving the prewar Catholic trade
unions but quickly gave up; the party remained small and confined itself
to parliamentary activity.[64] In Łódź, the UB reported in May 1946 that
the SP showed "rather large initiative in factories and municipal offices
in Łódź"; in some factories there and elsewhere, 30 percent of the politically active workers were SP members.[65] But the odds against such

---

[62] ŁAP KŁ PPR 1/XI/18, kk. 54–55.

[63] ARZ KCZZ WO 309, kk. 29, 31; see Janusz Jarosiński, "Problemy pragmatyki
służbowej kolejarzy w działalności Związku Zawodowego Pracowników Kolejowych w
latach 1944–50," *KHRZ*, nos. 1–2 (1983): 1–2, 25–42. On PPS influence in the trade
unions, see Syzdek, *Polska Partia Socjalistyczna*, 301–16, and Grzegorz Sołtysiak,
"Działalność socjalna związków zawodowych w Polsce w latach 1944–1945," *Kwartalnik
historii i teorii ruchu zawodowego*, no. 2 (1989): 18–20.

[64] A former Christian labor activist recalled that a group in Łódź considered forming a
"purely national" anti-Bolshevik union in January 1945; the idea was dropped because so
many former unionists had already gone over to the official unions. Stanisław Małolepszy,
CRZZ Library memoir 469, 1–4. On the SP, see Waldemar Bujak, *Historia Stronnictwa
Pracy, 1937–1946–1950* (Warsaw, 1988).

[65] MSW MBP 17/IX/10, t. 1, k. 10. See also talk by Julia Brystygierowa at briefing for
provincial UB chiefs, 28 April 1947, MSW MBP 17/IX/77, t. 2., and Andrzej Andrusiewicz,

organization were enormous; a Catholic trade union would have directly threatened the state's monopoly on labor organization.

In general, the two major centers of legal opposition at the time—the peasant party and the Catholic church—stayed clear of social organizing. The left-agrarian PSL, the lone legal voice for negotiation, democracy, and the rule of law, became the focal point of national political opposition. At the height of its power in the summer and fall of 1946, it claimed some 800,000 members, more than either the PPR or PPS, and seemed about to break up the government coalition by forming an alliance with those in the PPS who sought to resist PPR hegemony. The evident foolhardiness of treading on the PPR's turf and the need to focus meager resources on its rural base kept the PSL away from labor agitation.[66] Its platform was generally pro-labor: the PSL supported economic restructuring in the worker's favor but opposed state control of the economy. The party "does not defend capital," explained a PSL activist, "but cannot allow the state to become a capitalist; the worker, too, would be dissatisfied with this, since if the state became a capitalist it too could exploit the worker." Party leader Vice Premier Stanisław Mikołajczyk echoed this point in a speech to workers in Katowice in April 1946.[67] Although the PSL devoted little time to analysis of industrial and labor issues, it nevertheless won some worker support because of its independence; a UB report from mid-1946 noted that the city of Łódź was the only place in that province to experience a rise in PSL membership despite the lack of organizational effort among workers. The PSL boasted some worker circles, particularly among public utilities workers, and was strong among workers in the handicrafts. Romuald Turkowski that estimates that some 7,350 workers in four cities were members in 1946.[68]

"Stronnictwo Pracy (1945–1950)," *Z Pola Walki*, no. 1 (1986): 136. For echoes in Wrocław, see AAN KC PPR 295/VII/210, k. 62.

[66]The PSL's greatest nonpeasant constituency was among white-collar workers. It controlled the Teachers' Union and was powerful in several others. Romuald Turkowski suggests that the UB worked especially hard to counteract or eliminate PSL influence among workers. *Polskie Stronnictwo Ludowe w obronie demokracji, 1945–1949* (Warsaw, 1992), 72–101, esp. 96–99.

[67]K. Bagiński, quoted in Turkowski, *Polskie Stronnictwo Ludowe*, 97; Reynolds and Coutouvidis, *Poland, 1939–1947*, 246. See also Przybysz, "Program przeobrażeń ustrojowych," 140, and Gołębiowski, *Walka*, 297–306, citing articles from the PSL daily *Gazeta Ludowa*.

[68]MSW MBP 17/IX/10, t. 1, k. 14, also k. 10; Turkowski, *Polskie Stronnictwo Ludowe*, 97. On PSL worker circles, see Henryk Komarnicki, *Rola i miejsce PSL w systemie*

For its members and sympathizers, support of the PSL had clear political meaning. Allegiance to this symbol of opposition meant commitment to a political struggle against the communists. But the PSL was a
party more like the PPS than the PPR, stressing high politics and ideas
above mass mobilization. Unlike the PPR, whose every member was
mobilized by the leadership for political campaigns, the PSL was not a
party whose members carried out directives from above or did battle for
an ideology; rather, membership functioned as a support for the activities of the elite. The PSL was faithful to a tradition of parliamentary
negotiation and saw the future of Poland in this way. Thus, the PSL
member was not as politicized as his or her PPR counterpart (no matter
how apathetic the latter might be). Indeed, because it opposed the hy-
perpoliticization of life under PPR leadership, membership in the PSL
could also be a way to protest politics in general. But with its fate so
closely tied to the survival of parliamentary politics, the PSL was devastated by the official referendum results and the similarly rigged parliamentary election of January 1947.

Determining the role of the Roman Catholic church in labor communities is similarly difficult. On the one hand, the church was a constant presence in the Polish worker's world and furnished a social
identity as well as an intrinsically anticommunist world view that was
constantly evident in workers' lives. On the other hand, the church never
addressed workers *as* workers—that is, as a constituency with particular
needs. The time when the Polish church would embrace human rights
as a cause was still thirty years away. There is no evidence of a ministry
of any kind among the workers. Therefore, inasmuch as the church addressed the worker as a Pole or a Catholic, it defused rather than enhanced labor conflict until workers found a way in the 1980s to link the
two languages. Nevertheless, the history of the Catholic church's local
activity during these years has yet to be written; many individual examples of contact will surely be found.[69]

---

społeczno-politycznym Polski Ludowej 1945–47, (Warsaw 1987), 172–74. On PSL–PPS
relations, and for PSL numbers, see Reynolds and Coutouvidis, *Poland, 1939–1947*, 260–
67.

   [69]Studies of the church in communist Poland rarely devote more than a few pages to
the years 1945–48 and none at all to relations with society. See Jerzy Kłoczowski, Lidia
Müllerowa, and Jan Skarbek, *Zarys dziejów kościoła katolickiego w Polsce* (Kraków,
1986), 379–82, and Kersten, *Narodziny systemu władzy*, 166–68, 254–65, 283–84, 355.
On the lack of social activism in the church, see also Tadeusz Łepkowski, "Myśli o historii
Polski i Polaków," *Zeszyty Historyczne* 68 (1984): 113–14.

Party and UB leaders maintained their suspicions of the church. The fact that most workers retained their ties to the church—contributing, for example, to church rebuilding funds—was a threat to the Party's claim to embody working-class politics. Delivering a UB briefing on the clergy and workers in October 1947, Julia Brystygierowa urged her colleagues "firmly and ruthlessly to prevent the clergy and Catholic organizations from encroaching upon worker ground; to pass on information about every sign [of such activity]." Although the party sounded the alarm, evidence was hard to come by; the UB report uncovered, for example, only one report of a member of the clergy's speaking out against labor competition—at a funeral for two workers killed in a work accident.[70] The PPR nevertheless had reason to be worried, for workers surely drew their own conclusions from what they heard in church, no matter what the intended message.

What was the significance of all this political conflict, real and imagined? Outside the forests, where the new regime waged armed battle with the partisan underground, was Poland in a civil war? At least within the cities, it would be more appropriate to speak of a war of nerves and expectations, one that did not necessarily engage the concerns of rank-and-file Polish workers. As will be seen, labor conflict during this entire period centered not on opposition to or support of a political line but on workplace and community issues. "Civil war" suggests a battle between two camps, yet people did not share common goals in 1945–47, except for those (such as peace and reconstruction) that the communists shared, too. Moreover, after the events of 1939–45, it was easy to lose faith in one's ability to affect the course of national events by engaging in politics, no matter how obvious the consequences of communist triumph might be. Even shortly before the election, an informant in Wrocław reported that "interest of society as a whole in the election is, except within the political parties, minimal."[71]

In place of political engagement, popular apprehensions found an outlet in a nationwide rumor mill from spring 1946 through the elec-

---

[70]MSW MBP 17/IX/38, t.1, kk. 8, 27; MSW MBP 17/IX/77, t. 2 (reprinted in *Polityka*, 6 October 1990); Nevertheless, although the Łódź PPR watched churches carefully the Sunday after the Poznański strike, it was unable to come up with any evidence of church involvement. AAN KC PPR 295/IX/228, kk. 12–14. On the apolitical stance of the church in Wrocław, see WAP Urząd Wojewódzki VI/40, k. 103.

[71]AAN MLiP 552, k. 129. See also ibid. 553, k. 105. For an independent perspective along these lines, see Aleksander Janta, *Wracam z Polski 1948* (Paris, 1949), 31–36.

tion. The indignant (or enthusiastic, depending on the aggressor) coverage of the first blows of the cold war in the official press stimulated rumors that World War III was imminent or that Soviet troops were on the move to annex Poland. After six years of war, and in a country where news was controlled, almost anything was believable. The Soviet Army, reinforced by three million troops, was expected to enforce a PPR-bloc victory; specially-sent Soviet troops would be allowed to vote in the election, and Soviet troops were heard to say that "if we win the election, we will leave." There were two schools of thought on the election results. One warned that Poland would become the seventeenth republic of the Soviet Union, that *kolkhozy* would be introduced, and that PSL members would be shipped to Siberia. The other perspective hoped for a reversal—that Mikołajczyk would reveal his program and "dazzle the Poles" right before the election, or that the underground forces would rise up to ensure fair voting and the PSL would win. By election day, 17 January 1947, the more pessimistic version dominated; most of Poland expected a dramatic international conflict. British and American troops, some said, would come to monitor the voting; a rumor in Wrocław said that British paratroopers had landed in Warsaw and fought street battles with Polish police. In Pabianice near Łódź, residents predicted the imminent transit of five million Soviet troops headed west to fight; Soviet tanks painted with the slogan "To London" were reported on the highway near Wrocław.[72]

Given the tense atmosphere, the fact that the election actually passed in relative quiet was a significant victory for the government bloc, even more important than the announced vote totals. The methods by which the bloc of parties led by the PPR assured victory have been studied extensively elsewhere; opposition activists were harassed, jailed, or even killed, and PSL lists were declared invalid in many of its strongholds.[73] The regime engineered its victory especially carefully in the factories: trade union and party leaders worked out down-to-the-minute voting schedules; workers met at assigned places and then marched together to the voting booth, sometimes with pieces of paper marked with a '3' (the number of the Democratic Bloc's list) pinned to their coats. While there were many factories where the plan fell apart and workers did not vote, the PPR bloc succeeded for the first time in forcing political participation

[72]AAN MIiP 84, kk. 1–23.
[73]See Kersten, *Narodziny systemu władzy,* chap. 7.

Election march, 17 January 1947. Workers of a Warsaw(?) factory march to vote. Banner reads: "State Wine and Juice Factory. We Vote for Improvement of the Lives of Workers, Peasants, and the Working *Inteligent*." "3" refers to the place of the government bloc on the ballot. Muzeum Niepodległości, Warsaw.

on much of Polish society.[74] But although the falsification of results was probably evident to all, the expected confrontation—not to mention World War III—did not happen. This fact both deflated popular political interest and emboldened the PPR; over the next year, it virtually eliminated the illegal underground and neutralized the legal opposition. The PSL's Stanisław Mikołajczyk fled the country and near-certain arrest in October. Popular faith in the opposition's potential evaporated; politics, in the sense of democratic contest, was over. The PPR and PPS experienced a great upsurge in membership, because many now realized that

[74]AAN KC PPR 295/XIII/18, kk. 75–77; ŁAP WRZZ 402, n.p.; WAP KW PPR 1/V/36, kk. 96–97.

a party card might be a ticket to promotion or a means of survival. The PPR grew by more than 52 percent from December 1946 to June 1947, to almost 850,000 members, while the PPS more than doubled, to about 660,000.[75]

The aftermath of the election marked the end of the hopeful period of state-society relations, yet the Polish communists still had a long way to go toward total control of society. What they had achieved was something else: the preeminence of the PPR both as a political voice and a social and economic organizer. The ability of the PPR to repress the political opposition and secure electoral victory, and subsequent Soviet pressure to reorient the revolution toward stalinist uniformity, confirmed the party's dominance of the Polish state and its belief in its ability to organize society in the way that it wished. The PPR drive to unify the two main parties accelerated in early 1947, and its rivalry with the PPS in the factories intensified. It was time for many workers to choose between parties or between membership and nonparty status. Despite the likelihood that the PPR would swallow up the PPS, many now turned to the latter. The Wrocław PPS reported that

> The attitude of the population to the PPS is clearly positive, manifested of late in concern about the meaning and future of our Party. Proof of this can be found in the continuing enlistment in the ranks of the PPS despite harassment and purges in the workplaces.
>
> The PPR, as a result of recent unpopular moves, has lost much good will among the people of this province. . . . The MO [Civil Militia] and Security [UB], because of their nearly total domination by the PPR, . . . are officially regarded by the population as executive organs of the PPR.[76]

The battle within the factory between the PPR and PPS was real; both on paper and in the minds of many workers and factory activists, the PPS was the equal of the PPR. But the battle was merely a reflection of the intense struggle for economic control of the factory and the shop floor, which contributed greatly to the labor conflict of 1945–49. The

[75] *PPR: rezolucje, odezwy, instrukcje i okólniki Komitetu Centralnego I.47–XII.48* (Warsaw, 1973), 287; Jaime Reynolds, "Communists, Socialists, and Workers: Poland, 1944–1948," *Soviet Studies*, 30, no. 4 (1978): 539. On the other hand, it is difficult to treat party numbers too seriously after reading the 1948 report of the PPR party circle at a Wrocław tram depot. There had been no PPS circle there, but "with a cooperative effort [i.e., with the PPR's help], a PPS circle was organized at depot I and now has 20 members." WAP 2d KD PPR 32/VI/2, kk. 47–49.

[76] WAP WK PPS 36/VI/3, kk. 35–36.

struggle began over control of the basic labor institutions: the factory councils and the trade unions. Just as workers found little value in the political conflict around them, so too they soon discovered that they were without any labor organization either.

The Subordination of Organized Labor

Nationalization of industry was a popular idea; however, it raised a further difficult question: if factories were no longer the property of private capital, to whom did they belong? Was industry the property of society, or the workers in particular, or was it to fall under state control?[77] The manifesto of the PKWN was remarkably inclusive and democratic, suggesting even that much private property would eventually be returned.[78] The form that factory administration ultimately took—of Soviet-style state control—had not been decided upon by the end of the war, even within the PPR. At a February 1945 party plenum, Minister of Industry Hilary Minc, later the chief architect of the stalinist economy, promoted a mixed economy, in which the state would control only the "commanding heights," leaving certain private industries and cooperatives in place to "contribute to economic reconstruction;" Minc even hinted at "further democratization of the economy."[79]

Amid the relative political confusion at the end of the war, workers in dozens of factories in liberated Poland took social and economic transformation into their own hands. Small groups of workers began to defend, liberate, rebuild, and activate their factories in late 1944 as the German Army retreated from eastern and central Poland. Worker activists took advantage of the absence of local political forces in the liberation period and of the pressing need for immediate economic reconstruction; with the tacit approval of the nascent government, they ran their factories or chose new administrations. What began as a continuation of wartime worker resistance briefly promised to sprout into

[77]On the debate over nationalization, see Kazimierz Kloc, *Historia samorządu robotniczego w PRL, 1944–1989,* SGPiS: Monografie i opracowanie, 351 (Warsaw, 1992), 13; Henryk Słabek, "Ogólne aspekty polityki PPR i PPS w kształtowaniu nowych stosunków przemysłowych," *Z Pola Walki,* no. 1 (1978): 35–69.

[78]*Kształtowanie się podstaw programowych Polskiej Partii Robotniczej w latach 1942–1945 (wybór materiałów i dokumentów)* (Warsaw, 1958), 502–10.

[79]*The Beginnings of Communist Rule in Poland,* ed. Antony Polonsky and Boleslaw Drukier (London, 1980), 406–8.

a foundation of workers' democracy but ended as a barely remembered forerunner of the workers' councils of 1956–57 and 1980–81. The significance of this movement is the subject of some debate. Were councils "spontaneous," "purely workerist," and "part of the democratic independence movement,"[80] or simply a camouflage for union activists and technical intelligentsia with an agenda not necessarily identical to that of the workers?[81] In 1944–45, at least, the councils were more likely the former.

The council movement challenged official ideas of factory nationalization; after defending and rebuilding their factories, workers were not likely to hand them over to the Soviets, the government, or a private employer. How workers imagined control would work on a larger scale, in contacts between firms and with the government, is not clear; their immediate purpose was to take control of their own factory. Although the leaders or organizers of a factory committee were often PPR members, the movement was not directed by any party. Nevertheless, the factory councils had a special role to play in the communist vision. They were to be the cornerstone of a popular government linking the working class to its ostensible representatives in government. The communists in occupied Warsaw, for example, called in February 1944 for the creation of factory committees that would contain representatives of "all political options which are in the workplace, and to whom the good of Poland is close to heart."[82] The PPR, or at least its more practical-minded membership, ultimately preferred one-person management; this lesson, at least, was drawn from Soviet experience. But factory councils also had practical value in the period of liberation.

A statute regulating the activity and rights of factory councils was finally approved on 6 February 1945.[83] Ignoring already existing councils, it called for the formation of employee representation (*przedstawi-*

---

[80]Kloc, *Historia samorządu robotniczego*, 19.

[81]Robert Biezenski, "Workers' Self-Management and the Technical Intelligentsia in People's Poland," *Politics and Society* 22, no. 1 (March 1994): 60–61. Others, such as Tomasz Żukowski (*Związki zawodowe i samorząd pracowniczy w polskich zakładach przemysłowych w latach 1944–1987* [Warsaw, 1987], 18–19, 26–28), have seen factory councils as merely the product of manipulation from above.

[82]Gołębiowski, *Walka*, 55. Citing Home Army documents, Gołębiowski mentions similar PPR-led factory committees during the war (54 n. 132).

[83]"Pierwsze dokumenty normujące podstawy prawne tworzenia i działalności związków zawodowych w początkach Polski Ludowej," ed. Andrzej Nieuważny, *KHRZ*, no. 4 (1986): 55–60. See Kloc, *Historia samorządu robotniczego*, 25–26.

cielstwo pracownicze) by secret ballot in all public or private factories of twenty workers or more, in a ratio as low as one representative per ten workers. Councils were to be the "representation [*zastępstwo*] of the labor interests of the employees of a workplace before the employer, and [embody] vigilance over the strengthening and improvement of production in the workplace, in accordance with the general guidelines of the state's economic policy." As such, factory councils were an arm of the would-be workers' state. They were instructed to "cooperate with state organs or with [local government] in social control of the factory's economic activity." The workers' representatives, councils were to monitor working conditions, collective agreements, and factory social and cultural organizations; participate in the establishment of work rules and employment procedures; take part in the distribution of goods to workers; and mediate worker-employer disputes. Management was to call regular meetings with the factory council to discuss workplace issues such as productivity, labor discipline, safety and work hygiene, and new technical information. In other words, the factory council was only an intermediary between workers and management. At the same time, the state stepped between workers and management: council resolutions on production or technical issues, for example, had first to be submitted to the appropriate industrial association in the Ministry of Industry for approval before being brought to management. The very name "council" (*rada*) implied an advisory role; the first spontaneous organizations had been called committees, suggesting administration.

Despite these restrictions, factory councils could still consider themselves independent bodies because the decree left the relationship between factory council and trade union undefined. Still more important, the decree did not specifically remove the factory councils' right to choose a factory director or assign this task to another body. Many councils had in the previous months elected directors and management, and performed other quasi-managerial actions. Even as his ministry was issuing this rather restrictive decree, Hilary Minc declared in a February 1945 speech that "the workers' representatives should be elected first, and they should then decide on who are to be managers in their factory. They must be given the power to say 'No, that man is bad, but this man is good.' "[84] The trade union biweekly *Trybuna Związkowca*, in an article entitled "The 'Great Charter' of Workers' Rights," remarked that

[84] *The Beginnings of Communist Rule in Poland*, 409.

"the worker thus becomes one of the essential regulators of the organization of an enterprise, and becomes completely equal with the employer in the workplace." The paper used the words "co-responsible" and even "co-owner" [*współgospodarz*] to describe the workers' role.[85]

Factory councils continued their essentially syndicalist practices—what the PPR termed *sekciarstwo* (sectionalism)—through 1945. Councils self-appointed or chosen by workers in the first weeks after liberation saw their factories as their own, defended them against outside intervention, and attempted to restructure them themselves. They attempted, for example, to nationalize small factories not yet targeted by the state and to choose their own director from among themselves or from among respected prewar technicians. Or, taking official pronouncements about the working class literally, they regarded the factory as belonging to the workers. One of the most contentious issues was that of specialists sent from "outside"; councils resented the idea that an outsider might know better how to run their factory. Industry spokespeople depicted strong councils as dictatorships that ignored management. "Factory councils believe their powers entitle them to much more than is actually the case," complained the Garment Industry Association in April 1945. "They take away management's right to speak in the factory, and do not admit the people we send [to the factory], often creating a sort of monopoly, a closed fortress."[86]

Political representation in the factory did not, party leaders discovered, mean reliable control over a council. In 1945, both party circle and factory council tended to champion local interests. The PPR was as yet far from centralized, and the PPS much less so. Local party activists saw themselves as bulwarks of the revolution in their factory and city; their local patriotism or unguided enthusiasm made Warsaw's attempts to plan the economy more difficult. Respected noncommunists of various stripes often occupied seats on factory councils. In the Kindler mill in Pabianice, for example, a strike in late October 1945 (discussed in Chapter 2) postponed council elections. Strikers chose many of the same workers advanced as council candidates to be delegates to strike negotiations with the PPR and management. The previous (appointed) council, reported an investigative commission, had lost its popularity because of various shady deals; it looked as though the new members would not only represent the workers' choice but bring experience with strike lead-

[85] *Trybuna Związkowca* 2, 1 May 1945.
[86] ŁAP WRZZ 46, k. 22.

ership into their new positions. At least officially, the possibility that a worker-run factory's coming to a halt would both harm the economy—especially before the war was over—and tarnish the image of a successful worker-run Poland was a key reason for the state's ambivalence toward the council movement. State economic administration could not tolerate political unreliability any more than it could afford economic instability.[87]

If the factory councils were to be the realization of worker democracy in the factory, the trade unions, in the vision of the creators of the new Poland, would be the organizational voice of a united working class. This conception of the role of the unions had roots in the Soviet-style state union; indeed, the unions' fate in Poland after the war paralleled that of the unions and union activists after the Bolshevik Revolution, when a very early period of union pluralism gave way to increasing centralization and state control. In early 1947, while he warned the Central Committee of the dangers of syndicalism, Hilary Minc praised the way in which Lenin had managed the unions.[88]

The trade unions were creations of activists allied with the new regime; most had been activists in the prewar class unions as well. The Central Trade Union Commission (Komisja Centralna Związków Zawodowych, KCZZ, the name of the communist unions in the interwar period) united thirty-four unions set up along industrial rather than regional lines and encompassing both blue- and white-collar workers.[89] The First Congress of Trade Union Delegates in Lublin in November 1944 expressed ideals similar to those in the PKWN's manifesto: unions were to be free, independent, and nonparty—yet not apolitical. The new KCZZ, the congress declared, "stands on the same positions as the old KCZZ, but bases its activity in new democratic forms."[90]

As did the factory councils, the KCZZ faced irresolvable contradictions. Even at its First Congress, it presumed to speak as a mass organization representing all workers, including white-collar workers. This approach made class struggle a rather cumbersome project; a union that

---

[87]ŁAP DPB 20, n.p.; Gołębiowski, *Walka,* 107–9.

[88]*ARR,* 7:283–86.

[89]The legal foundation for the new unions remained the 1919 law on trade unions, which was in force until 1949. On KCZZ structure, see Kazimierz Kołakowski, "Struktura organizacyjna ruchu zawodowego w Polsce Ludowej i jej przemiany w latach 1944–1975," *KHRZ,* no. 2 (1976): 58–80.

[90]Jakubowska, "Kształtowanie się," 4. See also Jerzy Musiał, "Kronika 40-lecia ruchu zawodowego w Polsce Ludowej, XII.44–XI.45," *KHRZ,* nos. 1–2 (1985): 95–122.

embraced all employees could hardly have the same positions as a blue-collar union. What exactly could such a union do, and how was it different from the labor parties that were also welcoming managers into their midst? More than mere "forms" would have to be changed to work with a state that was also the main employer in industry. Like their counterparts in the councils, early trade union activists leaned toward syndicalism. Even the Executive Department of the KCZZ itself in April 1945 argued that "the activation of state industry, and the normal functioning of the factories, is as impossible without the participation of representatives of the working class [that is, the unions] in management as without the participation of specialists." It charged that some directors "work with the help of old methods, not taking into account the new attitude of the working class to the economic problems of the state; they circumvent representatives of the working class in deciding fundamental issues." To strengthen the role of the working class in management, the KCZZ called for trade unions to work with the government to develop economic plans; to monitor the fulfillment of those plans in the factories; and to nominate directors of factories, industrial associations, and so on. This last task did not imply workers' control through the factory councils; the KCZZ recognized the principle of one-person rule (jedynowładztwo) in the factory. But the trade unions were to be, as a combination of workers representation and politicians, the foundation for the new economic order.[91]

The tension between mass organization and bureaucratic necessity reached a climax at the First Congress of the KCZZ in November 1945, which attempted to resolve the ambiguities of union work. In the weeks leading up to the Congress, workers, factory councils, and union locals from across the country sent hundreds of petitions, resolutions, and letters, either as instructions to elected congress delegates or as independent appeals. While some followed formulas supplied by the KCZZ itself (for example, rote denunciations of the alleged murder of workers by anti-communist partisans), many others raised complaints and issues that reflected poorly on the unions or revealed syndicalist pressures from below.[92]

[91] Trybuna Związkowca 2, 1 May 1945.
[92] Petitions can be found in ARZ KCZZ WO, 14, 18, 19, 40, 41. See a Ministry of Information and Propaganda circular from June 1945 in Andrzej Krawczyk, Pierwsza próba indoktrynzacji: Działalność Ministerstwa Informacji i Propagandy w latach 1944–1947. Dokumenty do dziejów PRL, zeszyt 7 (Warsaw, 1994), 74–75.

The Congress responded rhetorically to some of workers' most urgent demands, calling for pay reform; fair distribution of food, clothing, fuel, and apartments; and punishment of speculators. But the tasks of the labor movement, outlined in the resolutions of the Congress, were very different. They included support of national reconstruction, improvement of productivity and labor discipline, support of the workers' cooperative movement, promotion of talented workers into managerial positions, supervision of the factory councils, avoidance of conflict in the factories, raising workers' political culture, and the creation of a mass trade union.[93] With this list of tasks, most alien to the traditional union, the trade union apparatus distinguished itself from prewar unions but did not resolve its ambiguous position.

This ambiguity was evident in the fate of the factory councils. Like the state and the PPR, the unions opposed councils' independence. Yet the authorities could not abolish the councils, for they were essential to securing workers' cooperation or participation in economic restructuring. Even more, they echoed worker traditions, which the union saw symbolic political value in preserving. The fact that the factory councils retained a central role in pay and *aprowizacja* (food supply and distribution) issues indicates the importance that these bodies had for the state. Although the challenge of meeting such demands in 1945–46 was nearly impossible to accomplish, councils enjoyed some autonomy and could take credit when food or money was forthcoming from above.[94]

Yet even as the February decree became law on 20 May, the period of greatest freedom for factory councils was coming to an end. With the war now over, the state's need for "spontaneous" assistance declined; factory councils that tried to elect directors or regulate production could only be a nuisance. A new Ministry of Industry decree aimed to curtail syndicalism by delimiting the role of factory councils more clearly.[95] Issued just ten days after the first decree took effect, it rejected any idea of factory council comanagement, affirming the director's "full responsibility for the fate of the company entrusted to him." Councils were to cooperate with management—particularly on issues related to work practice and social welfare—and to give advice in technical or admin-

[93] Musiał, "Kronika," 120–21.
[94] Kloc, "Historia samorządu robotniczego w PRL, 1944–1980" (habilitacja, SGPiS, Warsaw, 1985), 33–35.
[95] Reprinted in *Trybuna Związkowca* 5, 15 June 1945. See also Kloc, "Historia samorządu robotniczego," 38.

istrative matters. Direction in these areas and the awarding of bonuses were "exclusively reserved for the director." In this way, factory councils were reduced to a sort of office for worker affairs within the factory bureaucracy. Production issues—including bonuses through which management would encourage greater productivity—lay explicitly beyond the councils' domain. Although the decree left no doubt that power to appoint management lay exclusively with the administration of the particular industry, doubt still remained: What exactly did it mean, for example, that the factory council had "supervisory" powers in certain areas?[96] Nevertheless, the decree marked the beginning of the end of the factory council era. Within this straitjacket, it would be difficult to achieve anything.

Authorities hoped to shore up councils' authority among the workers with elections to new councils, under the rules set by the decrees, in the fall of 1945. In fact, the opposite effect occurred. Union officials in the Łódź region immediately set about dissolving councils that been formed in the first days of liberation, replacing them with temporary councils until elections could be held. This action fostered an impression in workers' minds that councils were powerless and could be dissolved at any time.[97] Only the PPR showed much enthusiasm for the elections. Łódź Province UB chief Mieczysław Moczar reported that 30 to 40 percent of workers did not participate in the voting; he attributed this "not to a political boycott, but apathy."[98] With these elections the factory council became a part of the labor bureaucracy, yet it remained an echo of a certain vision of labor organization incompatible with the demands of the state-run economy. In their search for authority, the councils could either embrace the workers (as syndicalists) or management (as another bureaucracy). Some joined the workers against management, or turned a blind eye to lack of discipline, theft,

[96]See ARZ KCZZ WO 148A, n.p.

[97]The Łódź Labor Inspector noted that such illegal actions also helped to lower workers' respect for the law, "which is not very high as it is, due to the war." AAN MPiH 961, k. 5.

[98]MSW MBP 17/IX/77, t. 1, k. 2. These numbers also reflect the high absentee rates in the factory, then ranging from 10 to 30 percent. Sample election results in ŁAP KW PPR 1/XI/11. For PPR–PPS tactics in the election, see Władysław Stefaniuk, *Łódzka organizacja PPS, 1945–1948* (Łódź, 1980), 82–89. In Łódź, the elections took place from October to December; the timetable was probably similar in other established cities. In Wrocław, where most factories were not yet operating in 1945, elections took place later and over a longer time.

and strikes; those who sought their place in the hierarchy made a fatal mistake. Failing to resolve issues, the councils only expanded bureaucracy. As a council member in Wrocław admitted, "Our factory, instead of producing lathes, is beginning intensively [to produce] protocols of conferences."[99]

No longer the organs of worker power they had hoped to be in early 1945, councils were more a hindrance to economic planning than they were co-managers and could meet neither worker expectations of economic control nor address their basic daily needs. Workers suspected that complaints brought to council members would be leaked to management. They ignored general meetings called by councils and turned to the PPR or directly to management with their concerns. As management marginalized the councils from above, so workers repudiated them from below. For example, councils were an issue in strikes in Łódź throughout 1946. Workers expected their representatives to be workers and to continue to work. As the personnel director at the Barciński mill reported after a strike there in March 1946, "The factory council . . . does not at this moment represent the workers' interests, since the majority of the council members chosen in the fall of 1945 were workers, and are now in supervisory positions in the company." Strikers at the Ramisch mill in October 1946 were outraged that the council had but one worker member who "as chair of the factory council does not work and [so] has broken away from the workers"; in response, authorities added two workers to the council.[100]

Factory councils were thus suspended between insubordination and deference. One industry executive linked council attitudes to party politics. He reported that, where the majority of council members were PPS members, the council "regarded itself as the only power in the factory"; where PPR members dominated, councils tended to be "little interested in factory affairs." Many of the latter actually surrendered their powers

[99] WAP KW PPR 1/XII/45, kk. 38–39, 51–52; Szymon Goldman, "Z kroniki dolno-śląskich związków zawodowych z lat 1945–1948," *Biuletyn Biura Historycznego CRZZ*, nos. 2–3 (1964): 2–3, 85–87. A Wrocław PPR leader admitted that "in some places, factory councils are hated by the workers, [because] people are freed from work, and do nothing all day." AAN KC PPR 295/XIII/2, kk. 21–23.

[100] AAN MPiH 214, kk. 10–11; AAN KC PPR 295/XI/10. For other examples of disputes between workers and councils, 1945–47, see Kloc, "Historia samorządu robotniczego," 52–55, 96; AAN KC PPR 295/IX/32, k. 8; AAN MPiOS 803, k. 151; ŁAP WUliP 32, k. 13; ŁAP WRZZ 66, n.p.; WAP KW PPR 1/XII/33, kk. 170–71; AAN KC PPR 295/XIII/18; AAN KC PPR 295/IX/47, kk. 4–5.

to the factory personnel director, who was usually a PPR member.[101] Many workers had begun to recognize that factory councils could also be a means to control, discipline, and mobilize them. Some officials stated this aim explicitly—for example, this speaker at a Metalworkers Trade Union conference in March 1945: "The factory council must explain the situation to the workers, condemn harmful individuals, register them, announce [their names], castigate them at every step and demand public explanations at open meetings, and if that doesn't help—throw them out. Then the worker will take care of his reputation, and will begin to work honestly. If the factory council carries out its task well, the quality and quantity of production will be better."[102] In this role, the factory councils failed. Councils that embraced their production-mobilization duties found that workers wanted something else entirely: note the bewilderment of one council chairman (at a Łódź textile mill) in October 1947: "Workers come unwillingly to a meeting after work, and when they do, they talk about butter, about pay, and the meeting becomes chaotic."[103]

The councils' failure as intermediary bodies also helped to further the breakdown in communications that made conflict more likely. The decrees of 1945 had divided the factory and labor policy into two separate areas: economic/production policy and social policy. The factory council—and, by extension, the working class—was now expected to confine itself to action in the latter sphere only. However low production may have fallen in 1946–47, successes (measured in rebuilt factories and accelerating production) were notable. Social welfare, meanwhile, was stretched thin by the war, returning refugees, severe food shortages, and the rhetoric of entitlement proffered by the state. The factory councils were trapped by exigency and politics; they were administrators with nothing to offer, advocates with no one listening, worker representatives without worker support. While factory councils or individual members could and did, despite their relative lack of credibility, support worker demands and play a role in labor conflict, indecisive or compromised councils more often helped fan the flames of conflict. After their sub-

---

[101] AAN MPiH 167, k. 217.

[102] ARZ KCZZ WO 84, kk. 42–43. About the same time, some people in the Ministry of Industry expressed the idea that councils served an educational function, alerting the worker to his or her true interests and those of the state. See Żukowski, *Związki zawodowe*, 18.

[103] ŁAP DK PPS Łódź-Zielona, 33/X/1, k. 82.

ordination to formal union control in January 1947, factory councils would not reappear as an autonomous voice in the factory until 1956.

The decline of the councils did not mean victory for the unions, however. The state had made its views on independent unions clear from the beginning. An April 1945 memo from the Ministry of Labor and Social Welfare deplored cases of unauthorized local union organizing, even when condoned by the Ministry's Labor Inspectorate. It reminded inspectors that "the working strata take an active part in the formation of the new reality . . . effectively and concretely only through their united and strong organizations" and advised them to register only unions that belonged to official structures.[104]

The state preferred that the unions become liaisons with the social welfare bureaucracy. Like the factory council activists, some unionists welcomed this role. They believed they could be most effective participating in the state bureaucracy as worker representatives. Major tasks of the union noted by the KCZZ biweekly *Trybuna Związkowca* (Unionist's Tribune) in 1945 included the quality of rationed bread, the quality of cafeteria meals, coal shortages, and worker housing. Union activists' memoirs portray their efforts to establish their union as a goal in itself, not as a means to help workers or win concrete demands from employers. Battles to win more food for workers or the like were, according to these accounts, won bureaucratically, through paperwork and lobbying. Even when unions at the local level came into conflict with factory management, they preferred to avoid conflict, passing concerns on to others. The problems in a 650-worker textile factory in Łódź seemed to invite traditional union-employer antagonism: "There are very strange dealings. Union representatives are virtually banned from entering the factory. Workers are not registered with Social Insurance, though the appropriate sums are deducted from their wages. There are two cafeterias—one for the office employees, one for the workers. This is undemocratic and not in practice anywhere [else]. Pay is irregular, and is several weeks behind." The author of this report, from the Textile Workers' Trade Union headquarters, believed, however, that it was not the union's job to protest or alter this situation itself: "Perhaps the proper authorities will reform these practices?" he concluded wistfully.[105]

---

[104] AAN MPiOS 12, k. 116.

[105] *Trybuna Związkowca* 8, 1–15 August 1945. The article also gave examples of factory directors removed and even jailed upon the recommendation of the union, which discovered evidence of embezzlement. For other examples of union bureaucratism, see *Wspom-*

Workers became almost incidental to unions' bureaucratic work. The drafting of industry-wide collective labor agreements in the second half of 1945, for example, took place mostly without workers' input or knowledge. All agreements followed models drawn up by the Ministry of Labor and Social Welfare and the Ministry of Industry. While there was some variation among the agreements on certain points, they were remarkably similar. Admitted a Metalworkers Trade Union official in September 1945: "The collective agreement should be agreed upon with the masses before it is signed, regardless of all the difficulties this entails. With the present agreement, some sections knew nothing about it even after it was signed."[106] Factory management, meanwhile, knew how to manipulate the unions. KCZZ leader Kazimierz Witaszewski complained to a 1947 PPR Central Committee plenum that directors were telling workers who made demands: "Go to the union. If they agree, I'll give it to you."[107] In other words, all sides knew there was little that could be done to satisfy workers. As they passed responsibility from one to another, they swiftly made it clear that workers had no advocate.

It was impossible for union leaders to avoid their ambiguous, awkward position. Although representatives of the workers' state, they could not always deliver on their promises. In July 1945, the Textile Workers' Union issued a desperate appeal, noting that collective agreements and wage scales had become fiction, because the workers received neither food nor pay: "In this state of affairs, the union loses the authority and trust which it enjoyed until now. . . . [W]orkers in the factories hiss at union representatives, saying that [they ought to] leave politics aside and explain rather when [workers] will finally get enough food so that their children will not waste away from hunger."[108] Unionists in Łódź understood why they bore the brunt of workers' anger: "Trade unions, bringing their case to the workers, often rely on the promises of those so-called bureaucratic agents. That's how it was with fuel, and with aprowizacja, and many other things. All this ended in fiasco. It is time finally to put an end to these methods, because they compromise us in

nienia działaczy związkowych, 2 vols.: *1909–1949* and *1944–1972* (Warsaw 1971, 1974). Salomea Kowalewska, "Wzór osobowy i pożądane postawy pracowników w przemyśle," in *Przemysł i społeczeństwo*, 217-18.

[106] ARZ KCZZ WO 84, k. 309; Sołtysiak, "Działalność socjalna," 31-32.
[107] AAN KC PPR 295/II/5, kk. 66-67.
[108] ARZ KCZZ WO 125, k. 66. For other examples of confrontation in 1946, see ARZ KCZZ WE 138, n.p.; ARZ KCZZ WE 139, n.p.

the eyes of the workers. We get certain information, we release it to the masses, and when it is time to deliver, nothing happens. All the dissatisfaction and hatred falls on us. It will come to the point that no unionist will be able to appear in a factory."[109] Activists from the food industry trade union blamed the press, which "announces to the worker [that] there will be such and such a raise. Everyone is happy, but we know from the start that there is nothing special to give them."[110]

Unions were virtually invisible in factory conflict and in workers' memories; their bureaucratic efforts on behalf of workers were behind the scenes and were unremarked by their constituents. Facing conflict, embattled unionists simply retreated from the workplace. During a November 1945 strike at the John metal factory in Łódź, for example, the union took no position at all. Union leaders preferred to remain quiet during a strike rather than antagonize the workers or run afoul of the state. The following summer a PPR investigator found unionists at Poland's largest textile mill virtually in hiding from the workers, unwilling and unable to help workers or to prevent them from striking.[111]

It is imprecise, however, to label the unions in these first years as "pro-government" or "antiworker". Union activists were testing a new role in the communist state—as a fighter for democracy against the remnants of reactionary capitalist Poland. An editorial in *Trybuna Związkowca* in June 1945 articulated this concept of class struggle without real classes:

> The class struggle continues, and will continue until total victory. And it must be waged everywhere, most energetically and with every means which might assure its effectiveness. . . . With whom should the laboring class struggle for improvement of its lot in Democratic Poland, if the government is supported by [the working class] which itself is co-manager of the country? Well, the struggle . . . should be waged with every bureaucratic deviation from published rulings; every occurrence of conscious sabotage; every occurrence of passivity and indolence . . . ; as well as *every occurrence of lack of work discipline, inappropriate attitude to national property, or low labor productivity.*[112]

[109] ARZ KCZZ WO 141, k. 188.
[110] ARZ KCZZ WO 284, n.p.
[111] ŁAP WK PPS 22/XII/2, n.p.; AAN KC PPR 295/IX/32, k. 21.
[112] "Walka klasowa w Polsce demokratycznej," *Trybuna Związkowca* 4, 1 June 1945. Emphasis in original.

Such struggles were hardly the stuff to rouse workers' enthusiasm. Moreover, without these tasks (and the material problems eventually declined in urgency while traditional class enemies became harder to find) the unions' only task was to enforce labor discipline and productivity. The defense of industrial production goals soon brought the unions into direct conflict with the workers, and the strike waves of 1945–47 grew more antagonistic toward organized labor.

Until late 1947, however, the trade unions were not full-fledged members of the state–party mobilization apparatus. Until that time, the union remained primarily a social welfare office and an arbiter of labor peace. The former role, including the monitoring of aprowizacja, employment, pay, housing, vacations, child care, and other social issues, could win fragile worker support; however, as with the factory councils, it could also expose the unions to harsh criticism when they could not deliver. The KCZZ's failure to win acceptable pay increases in the fall of 1945, for example, only exacerbated strike moods throughout the country and made the unions appear harmless to the government and useless to the workers.[113] The propaganda campaign to secure housing for the workers (with the slogan "Let's move workers from attics and basements to sunny apartments") was also unsuccessful; little new building was done in the first few years. Local campaigns such as the Workers' Housing Action in Łódź produced at best symbolic results: only a few workers in the direst straits acquired apartments in abandoned palaces, while the rest received nothing.[114]

The creation of mass organizations is, in one sense, a natural goal of trade union activity, and unionists in Poland after 1945 were in a position to achieve this goal. Thus, they supported universal (as opposed to voluntary) membership, with union dues automatically deducted from workers' paychecks, and the existence of only one union organization. Yet this image depended on the KCZZ's ability to achieve progress; the contrast between potential and actual achievements was all the greater, and the resentment of the unions all the deeper, as a result of union rhetoric. Administering social welfare problems, the unions worked within the bureaucracy, and workers came to see bureaucracy and its rules as unjust.

[113]Sołtysiak, "Działalność socjalna," 25–26.
[114]Helena Gnatowska, *Rola Polskiej Partii Robotniczej w kształtowaniu i realizacji polityki socjalnej Polski Ludowej, 1942–1948* (Białystok, 1986), 143–46; Kazimierz Przybył-Stalski, "Robotnicza Akcja Mieszkaniowa," in *Takie były początki,* ed. Władysław Góra et al. (Warsaw, 1965), 474–81.

Union leaders did not intend or welcome their role as enforcers of labor peace; they seemed genuinely to believe that workers could win improvements in their lives without strikes, thanks to an efficient and popular social services bureaucracy. Like Lenin's nemeses of forty-five years before, unionists preferred an "economist" position, forsaking the terrain of labor relations to the party. The KCZZ had claimed publicly in late 1945 that "trade unions have the complete ability to achieve all just demands advanced by the world of labor without strikes and harsh conflicts."[115] Yet strikes occurred frequently on both these issues and those that the KCZZ deemed already obsolete, and the unions were forced to deal with them. One can easily imagine the frustration of a union leader in 1947 who, "screaming and stamping his feet," tried to head off a strike at the Barlicki mill in Łódź but instead provoked the strike.[116]

Both factory councils and trade unions had backed themselves into a bureaucratic corner by accepting their state-imposed mandate and focusing on problems—aprowizacja and other social issues—that could not be resolved to anyone's satisfaction. The logical next step, taken in a January 1947 ministry decree on factory councils that amended the decree of February 1945, was to incorporate the factory councils into union bureaucracy. The most fundamental change in the law was contained in the first article, which now stated that factory councils were "an organ of employees' trade unions," not "a new organ of labor organization." Supervision of council elections was transferred from the labor inspector (or the council itself, if already existing) to the unions, which also received power to dissolve factory councils if deemed necessary. Nevertheless, some aspects of the decree suggest that it was not the authors' intent to silence the factory councils but rather to protect councils from the influence of management. Indeed, the decree actually appeared to double workplace democracy by creating an entire parallel elected structure: factories of more than one hundred workers were to elect one shop steward (*mąż zaufania*) for every twenty-five workers to act as a "liaison between the workers . . . and the factory council."[117] The duties of this new parallel link between workers and the union were not further defined; indeed, the shop stewards did not play a significant

[115]Sołtysiak, "Działalność socjalna," 33. See also "Łódź pracująca o strajkach—rezolucje ORZZ," *Trybuna Związkowca* 12, 1–15 October 1945.
[116]ŁAP KŁ PPR 1/VI/141, k. 62.
[117]"Pierwsze dokumenty normujące podstawy prawne," 60–63.

role in labor relations. According to one memoirist, they were actually agents of mobilization: their chief tasks were "work place organization, and [promotion of] personal culture and a social attitude toward the tools of work." Factory councils, for their part, perceived shop stewards as a threat to their powers, especially when the council had already been weakened by the union or management.[118]

Trade unionists may have imagined that allegiance to the national union structure could give the councils greater influence than before. The effect of the decree was the opposite, for several reasons. First (as perhaps the ministers who signed the decree anticipated) the trade union apparatus was no match for the "economic nomenklatura"[119] of Hilary Minc's Ministry of Industry. Second, the unions quickly emerged as organs of council repression. They frequently dissolved intractable factory councils, appointing temporary, more docile councils in their place until the next election. A factory council member who filed a complaint might be removed by the union from the council and even transferred to another factory.[120] Meanwhile, management continued to suppress council members; those who did not want to risk being fired or losing access to the factory "went on bended knee" before management.[121]

As we will see in subsequent chapters, the success of unions and factory councils in the early years depended in part on the nature of the local community. But as is often the case for unions, the strength of state and management was even more important. This, and the unions' increasing irrelevance to the political battles of 1947 and later, accounted for the remarkable isolation of organized labor in communist Poland. In 1947–48, unions formally became organs of worker mobilization; the various campaigns of those years, described in Chapters 4 and 5, marked the culmination of the unions' retreat from worker advocacy.

By 1947, the councils and unions were clearly under state–party control; as a result, labor conflict moved farther and farther from the realm of formal organization. Both political opposition and labor institutions had difficulty articulating the demands of the workers, and by 1947 workers did not expect them to do so. Without such representation,

[118]Eliasz Leppert (hydrometer factory, Wrocław), CRZZ Library memoir 650. WAP KW PPR 1/XII/24, k. 80. See August 1947 KC PPR instruction on the training of shop stewards in "Dokumenty PPR i PPS dotyczące działalności związków zawodowych," 200–201.

[119]Kloc, "Historia samorządu robotniczego," 47.

[120]See 1947 Lower Silesian labor inspector's report, AAN MPiOS 750, n.p. For an example, see AAN MPiH 173, kk. 100–101.

[121]AAN KC PPR 295/XIII/7, kk. 96–97.

which was endangered already in 1945 and had virtually disappeared by the 1947 election, workers instead represented themselves. The unrest of 1945–48 was the independent and unorganized product of their moral communities, with union or party participation the exception that proved the rule. Both conflict and contact between society and state took place without formal politics; the state and the PPR found it difficult to monitor, let alone control, labor conflict and were thus forced to adapt to it in subtle ways. The following chapters will examine workers' aspirations in the cities of Łódź and Wrocław in the years 1945–47 until the state and the PPR discovered ways of controlling the Polish working class and shaping it to meet the needs of the People's Republic.

2   On Strike in Łódź

As they marched across Poland with the victorious Soviet Army, the PPR elite searched for signs of the future they planned to build. Entering Łódź on 20 January 1945, Ignacy Loga-Sowiński waxed enthusiastic about the city where he would soon be party leader:

> I arrived in Łódź Saturday evening. I was in Lublin when the Red Army entered the city and when the Polish Army arrived. I was also in Praga [Warsaw's right bank, liberated August 1944]. There can be no comparison. Only Łódź, the capital of the Polish proletariat, could burst forth with such universal, spontaneous enthusiasm. Everyone hung out flags, red and white-and-red. Red Army officers told me how people carried them [on their shoulders] and kissed them.... [1]

For just over five years, Polish identity in Łódź had been severely repressed on a scale much greater than in many other Polish cities. Łódź had served as a reservoir of human material to be exploited and an industrial plant to be exhausted. Its textile workers, easily exchangeable and expendable, lacked the bargaining strength of those who were more essential to the German war effort (those in heavy industry or mining). It was not surprising that they should turn out to welcome their liberators. Łódź's proximity to Warsaw and its proletarian and socialist

---

[1] Quoted in Janusz Gołębiowski, *Walka PPR o nacjonalizację przemysłu* (Warsaw, 1961), 135.

traditions as well as its apparent enthusiasm for Soviet liberation made it, for a time, the working-class capital of Poland.

With other major cities lying in ruins, Łódź in 1945 possessed the largest and most developed industrial base in Poland. The battle for Łódź had been brief, with much of the damage inflicted by the Germans as they retreated; most of the city's industry survived unscathed. Nearly one in twelve of the nation's workers in early 1946 worked in Łódź's factories; there were more than five hundred factories employing twenty or more people, the most of any city in Poland. (The surrounding province had nearly as many such factories.) More than three-quarters of the city's workers were employed in textiles (36 percent of all Polish textile mills employing twenty or more people were in Łódź) and clothing; many other factories primarily served the needs of the textile industry.[2]

This was a stable work force, mostly from in or near the city; in two sample factories, more than three-fifths of workers were born either in Łódź or in nine nearby counties. Slightly more than half lived in Łódź in 1939. One former worker recalled that until 1949–50 his small factory had no workers from outside Łódź. Numbers varied greatly (70 percent of the work force at the Gampe and Albrecht mill in 1946 were inexperienced repatriates from the eastern borderlands) but the labor community was generally more stable than the rest of the city.[3] Retired workers recall 1945–49 as years of strong community. One might still celebrate the name days of colleagues at work by decorating their machines or sharing a drink in the smoking room at break. If a colleague's machine broke down, one stopped work and helped her or him repair it. All workers knew their jobs and their place. "The atmosphere," recalled one, "was such that no one had to tell anyone anything [about keeping the work station clean], because that carried over from the pre-war era." It was a world of hierarchy and deference: older

[2]Adam Ginsbert, *Łódź: Studium monograficzne* (Łódź, 1962), 88, 162; *RS 1947*, 69–70, 77–88.

[3]Ginsbert, *Łódź*, 178, 190–91. For sample factories, see Sources. Interview with Stanisław S., 9 May 1990. On Gampe and Albrecht, see AAN KC PPR 295/IX/32, kk. 44–46. On neighborhood stability (measured by place of residence before and after marriage) in 1960, see Wacław Piotrowski, *Społeczno-przestrenna struktura miasta Łodzi: Studium ekologiczne* (Wrocław, 1966), 121–45.

Many workers lived in company tenements (*famułki*), like the Księży Młyn neighborhood, at Scheibler and Grohman Factory, Łódź. Katedra Etnografii, Uniwersytet Łódzki.

workers still stood up from their dinner when the supervisor entered the cafeteria.[4]

At the same time, the women who dominated these factories possessed a steely determination to defend their way of life. While women were just one-quarter of the nation's work force, they were more than half the workers in Łódź and dominated the textiles and clothing industries; in 1945, women outnumbered men in the twenty to thirty-four

<hr>

[4]Interviews with Stanisław S. and Wacław A., 8 May 1990, and Zdzisława G., 10 May 1990, Łódź. Quotation is from Stanisław S. While nostalgia certainly played a role, all interviewees seemed able to separate that period from later years with ease. Even Wacław A., who began work in 1949, was most emphatic in his description of work culture at that time.

age group by two to one.[5] Unlike women workers in many other cities, those in Łódź brought working-class experience into the postwar conflicts.[6] Duty to family and morality were the mainstays of the world of women workers, as captured in a song written by a young textile worker in 1948 to her year-old son:

> In Łódź on Sanok Street, on the second floor
> Where plaster was falling off the ceiling,
> My little son sat by me
> And this is what he said:
> Dear mother, where is my father
> Why doesn't he come back to me,
> Maybe you would be more happy, and richer
> And work would be more pleasant.
> Dear child, you have no father
> He lies in a dark grave,
> Let's go together to water the flowers
> And spend our free moments there.
>
> . . . .
>
> And now, son, we live together
> I love you more than life,
> I work hard to earn our bread, in Łódź in a state factory.[7]

This woman's goals were simple and clear; if thwarted, one could imagine her fighting to save both her family and the memory of her husband.

The postwar history of Łódź illustrates the conflict between the traditions of Polish labor and the norms of the emerging communist state. The war brought new players into Łódź society. Political and cultural life flowered, as government offices and national newspapers (such as the PPS daily *Robotnik*) located there while Warsaw was rebuilt; nearly everyone of political or literary note lived in Łódź. The war had destroyed most of the labor activist elite (although for the first time the government in Warsaw was ostensibly working class). They were replaced by newcomers to whom the city's traditions were foreign. The working class showed the strength of its community in resisting first economic, then political, and ultimately social incursions.

---

[5] *RS miasta Łodzi, 1945–1947* (Łódź, 1949), 303–5, 307; *RS 1948*, 165–66; Ginsbert, *Łódź*, 191.

[6] On women in prewar Łódź industry, see *Drugi powszechny spis ludności z dn. 9.XII.1931 r. Miasto Łódź* (Statystyka Polski, Seria C, Zeszyt 67) (Warsaw, 1937); AAN KC PZPR 237/XV/4, k. 1.

[7] Uniwersytet Łódzki, Katedra Etnografii, AZE 'B' 2320 (Józef D., interviewed 1979).

Searching for New Rules: Workers' Control and Conflict, 1945

As the Soviet offensive approached in January 1945, the workers of Łódź fought their own battles. Propaganda of the time celebrated their selfless devotion to class and nation as they prevented the Germans from looting or destroying factories and warehouses. A recollection of liberation at the Barciński woolen mill appeared in the PPR national daily one year later: "Shortly before their escape, the Germans did everything they could to destroy the factory completely. First they shut down the finishing and dyeing shops. Next they destroyed the turbines, dismantled the spinning machines and looms, partially packing them into boxes to take them away. The workers strove to frustrate these evil plans at all costs: 'We scattered machine parts to various corners. We conducted all sorts of sabotage. So they did not manage to evacuate the machines after all.' "[8]

Images of heroism and sacrifice dominated. At the Poznański cotton mill, PPR-member workers "scrabbled out coal from under the snow with their bare hands, and filled wagons pulled by other workers." At the Widzew manufactory, "No one ask[ed] about pay, but everyone st[ood] resolutely at his post." At the John metalworks, payment was strictly in kind; "but when, frozen and chilled after a hard day, [we] sat down at tables on which there was hot soup and bread [supplied by the factory committee], the wisecracks flew and bursts of laughter filled the cafeteria." The tram workers' union, like many factories, sent out volunteer "food-supply teams" to forage for supplies for its workers.[9]

As Loga-Sowiński's account of liberation revealed, nationalism was central to the politics of liberation: a city where the Polish language had been outlawed was now the heart of Poland. Thus, even a political rally could have symbolic value as a transmitter of Polish culture. More directly, workers asserted their Polishness by reclaiming their factories and expelling German state, military, or private management. Workers took great pride in their ability to outwit the Germans and run the factories themselves. Some took up arms to defend their factories against looters from the Soviet Army.[10] No doubt some accounts contained exaggera-

[8]*Głos Ludu*, 8 January 1946, quoted in Gołębiowski, *Walka*, 137.

[9]Wincenty Wysocki (factory committee representative), CRZZ Library memoir 644, 6–7, 13; Gołębiowski, *Walka*, 136–37; *Głos Widzewa*, 1 January 1946; Józef Kowarsz (tramworker), CRZZ Library memoir 589, 8–9. See also Bolesław Nowak (city parks worker), CRZZ Library memoir 478.

[10]Interview with Stanisław S. On Soviet attempts to confiscate factories, see Gołę-

tions, but the reach of civil authority in those first weeks was indeed limited. The stories were accepted by not just party leaders, for whom they were convenient, but many workers, for whom they were crucial to the reformation of working-class identity. For workers, the history of postwar Łódź began with a powerful citywide demonstration of worker control in ways important for the reformation of class culture. They evoked the wartime resistance, when sabotage and defense of the workplace had been the only means of anti-Nazi resistance. These forms of resistance were not easily directed from above; they offered the worker who performed them an individual way to oppose the enemy. They were a potential threat to the new state.

It was not far from these simple forms of self-organization to more organized worker control of enterprises. In Łódź, as across Poland, workers took the slogans of nationalization at face value and understood the state to mean themselves as they began reconstruction, restarted production, and elected factory management. One activist at the John metalworks described the mixture of workers who participated in this movement: "In the first day of freedom, the workers performed the functions of factory security and administration. Among them [were] old and young activists of the [prewar] 'class union,' members of the PPR conspiratorial groups, and many others. . . . Several foremen who had been working here for decades also showed up. . . . The workers looked on them with warmth and respect. . . . The workers assembled at the factory made up a sort of town meeting [sejmik], the first government of Łódź's metalworkers. . . . In the course of these chaotic general questions and answers, the worker government [władza] of the plant was born—one of the first in Łódź."[11]

In that first week, the John factory committee chose a director and heads of production departments from among the workers and foremen. A younger worker in a hosiery factory recalls how he was nearly chosen director by his co-workers: "There was a proposal that we choose from among those who worked there someone who would stand at the head of the factory, as an elected director. . . . There was even a suggestion that I stand at the factory's head, but I was a young man, and I didn't agree to this. So we chose a former foreman, a Pole of course. . . . Since he knew that factory very well before the war, because he was a fore-

biowski, Walka, 140. On nationalism in Łódź, see Feliks Tomaszewski, CRZZ Library memoir 33, 21–23.

[11]Wysocki, memoir 644, 3–4.

man, he chose some others, more enlightened workers, and they got the factory going."[12] Most often workers chose their own factory council; even after worker power subsided, these bodies often claimed the same powers that workers had exerted in those first days.[13]

The workers' control brigades were small, and almost exclusively male. At Poznański (where only seventy-nine workers showed up in the first days, and only 465 after two weeks), a list of noted pioneers mentions no women, although at least half the work force was female.[14] The leaders in this and other mills were likely the foremen, skilled workers from the mills' metal shops, and other skilled men. Most of the examples available are from male-dominated industries—metal, public works, and transportation—where the skilled, craft culture regarded the workplace as its own. The workplace was also emphatically community centered: "authentic" workers defended Łódź factories against "phonies" [*pyskacze*] from outside. But to the authorities, control looked like insubordination. "Discipline in the factories appears scandalous," declared the chair of the Łódź Regional Trade Union Council. "There can be no more cases where workers dismiss their director at a mass meeting."[15]

Each of these aspects of control—anarchic/syndicalist, nationalist, skilled, and gendered—reflected the traditions of working-class Łódź; over the next several years, they were replaced by other forms of struggle. The denial of workers' right to manage the workplace, and thus the elimination of independent labor organization, was a major source of working-class conflict in 1945–47. As the workers' control movement was eroded by the state, its meanings—pride in one's workplace and belief in class justice—remained. In resolutions and meetings in 1945, workers attacked management constantly, especially if a director that they or their factory council had chosen was replaced by a ministry appointee. Some felt that the appointed directors wasted workers' heroic efforts to save the factory, which had enhanced their sense of control and property. A speaker at a September 1945 meeting of postal workers recalled how the workers had organized and rebuilt their fleet: "trucks, tools, everything is [the workers']; they are co-owners, and will not allow

---

[12]Interview with Stanisław S. For another example of an elected director, see ŁAP Gazownia Łódzka 536, n.p.

[13]"Bolączki robotników Łodzi," *Trybuna Związkowca* 8, 1–15 August 1945; AAN MPiH 144, k. 176.

[14]Gołębiowski, *Walka*, 137.

[15]ŁAP WRZZ 6, k. 27. The terminology was explained to me by Henryk Szpigiel, son of a labor organizer and activist in the Łódź Jewish community of that time.

the wasting of their common property."[16] A representative of the Łódź railway workers protested threatened layoffs at the first congress of the KCZZ in 1945: "these people came to work to repair rail lines devastated [by war]. At that time, those who now work in administration stood on the sidelines; first the rails were reactivated, and only later did the administrative bureaus begin to form. Today, as winter approaches, they want to lay off these track workers as unnecessary."[17] Pioneers claimed special privileges based upon their service to the factory. The factory council at the Horak cotton mill complained in July 1945 that the new management had passed over the council—"which in its present makeup stands in defense of the factory from the first moment"—and all pioneers ("who by the sweat of their brow, with their own hard effort, laid the foundations under the restarting of industry in the period of cold and hunger at the dawn of Democratic Poland") in handing out bonuses.[18] Even in late 1947, paper industry workers pointedly contrasted their heroic labor of the liberation period with the wasteful practices of management: "after all, no one else but us defended these factories from the Germans. . . . And now elements which hinder us in our work have crept in."[19]

Through 1946, workers continued to contest the choice of administrative personnel, more often against an unpopular director than for a new one. A notable example was a four-day strike at the large Geyer mill in September 1945 against a newly appointed director. This strike was even supported by brief solidarity strikes in two nearby mills. Two months later at the Jarisch mill, strikers successfully argued that Director Gerson's actions harmed the workers as well as the state. By carelessly setting norms too high, without regard to the ability of the worker or of the machine, he made it impossible for many workers to earn bonuses (which often made up most of one's pay). He also offended workers' dignity by using them instead of horses to haul wagons. At the Łódź thread factory a year later, workers and the factory council announced plans to hold an election between two foremen for supervisor of the spinning shop.[20] Workers did not hesitate to accuse directors of crimes:

[16]A government spokesman responded that the state was in fact the owner, not the workers. ŁAP WRZZ 253, n.p.
[17]ARZ KCZZ WO 14, kk. 300–301.
[18]AAN MPiH 1025, k. 5.
[19]ŁAP WRZZ 66, n.p.
[20]ŁAP WRZZ 25, n.p.; ŁAP WRZZ 46, k. 63; ŁAP KŁ PPR 1/VI/69, kk. 69–71.

at the Poznański mill in 1946 they struck to protest the vice-director's refusal to submit to a search upon leaving the factory and called for the dismissal of the entire management for "systematic theft." At another factory, workers protested an attempt to hush up the red-handed thefts of the trade director.[21]

At three smaller Łódź factories in July 1945, celebrated strikes—the only strikes ever officially supported in communist Poland—protested threatened reprivatization. Workers struck for 1½ hours on 30 July to protest a court-ordered transfer of the factories to their former owners; the KCZZ passed a resolution in favor of state control over these firms. As a result, reprivatization was postponed. For the government, this (perhaps staged) victory showed that Polish workers had rejected capitalism. But in the context of the workers' control movement of the previous winter, another possible meaning emerges: workers expected the factory to return to their own control, not to the hands of the state.[22]

Strikes over nationalization reflected a continuity with prewar labor relations. Workers saw factory directors (who often made several times more than an average worker) as traditional antagonists like the prewar employers. That is, they perceived management, not the state or central economic administration, as having the greatest influence on their well-being. Workers contested wage scales, norm setting, and work rules to negotiate the parameters of the employer-worker relationship. Even when workers complained about problems outside the factory, such as high prices or shortages, they did so because they believed the factory director had the power to intervene. And while party or union representatives did intervene as well, the director was the one who answered the workers' charges. Similarly, when workers on rare occasions protested nationalization, they were seeking to retain the management they favored.[23] But despite their misgivings over what nationalization really

[21] AAN KC PPR 295/IX/32, kk. 7–10; AAN MPiOS 803, kk. 164–65, 191–93.

[22] Janusz Gołębiowski, "Rola PPR w przejęciu, uruchomieniu i nacjonalizacji przemysłu Łodzi," *Rocznik Łódzki* 6 (1962), 130–31; *W dymach czarnych budzi się Łódź: Z dziejów łódzkiego ruchu robotniczego, 1882–1948* (Łódź, 1985), 451–52. The Łódź PPR reported six antiprivatization strikes: ŁAP KW PPR 1/XI/29, n.p. See also "Przez uchyloną furtkę reprywatyzacji," *Trybuna Związkowca* 9, 16–31 August 1945. The unions may have played a role in organizing these strikes: ŁAP WRZZ 6, k. 30.

[23] Lucjan Motyka, at a January 1946 meeting of the PPS Economic Council, explained that such protests took place because small factory owners were paying workers additional money under the table. See Władysław Mroczkowski and Tadeusz Sierocki, eds., "Protokoły posiedzeń Rady Gospodarczej PPS (1945–1946)," *Z Pola Walki*, nos. 1–2 (1982): 248.

meant for workers' control, workers supported the policy. In June 1946, the citizens of Łódź bucked the national trend by approving referendum question 2, on nationalization, by a margin of three to two. In some worker districts the margin approached two to one.[24]

The other players in the factory were also bound by prewar models. Activists at the factory level had usually worked in the same factories before the war and knew the workers well. They strongly resented being ignored or mistreated by management as they had been before the war. Seeing all they had fought for taken away, they often took the lead in labor conflict. Young sociologist Hanna Świda met such workers in 1950; they spoke to her of "state capitalism" where added value was taken by the state as it had before by the capitalist, only now without a shadow of respect for the worker. PPS members before the war, workers now stayed away from labor organizations.[25] The PPR badly wanted these workers on its side. At the PPR's first congress in December 1945 Zofia Patorowa from the Poznański mill brought "joyful news. Our workers, PPR comrades, old veterans of work, have understood their duty to the state and our Party; there are cases that they themselves watch so that other workers do not waste too much, and do not leave work a few minutes early. This is joyful, because this is a healthy symptom, comrades."[26] Delegates interrupted her speech with applause eight times, relieved to hear a friendly voice from Łódź.

At the top, the unions of Łódź—first and foremost the powerful Textile Workers' Union (whose head, Aleksander Burski, was also in the PPR Central Committee)—quickly became an active arm of official labor policy. A strike protesting management's punishment of thieving workers at the Kinderman mill in August 1946 showed how the textile union could treat labor conflict. After negotiations with workers failed, union leadership recommended closing the factory and laying off all workers to rehire them under new conditions three days later. A similar lockout occurred a week later at a silk factory.[27] After such incidents, the textile workers of Łódź would be unlikely to turn to their union for support.

Similarly, the PPR leadership felt nowhere less at home than in this most

[24] AAN Referendum, II/29 (122), kk. 33–36.
[25] Hanna Świda-Ziemba, "Robotnicy 1950," in Hanna Świda-Ziemba, *Mechanizmy zniewalania społeczeństwa—refleksje u schyłku formacji* (Warsaw, 1990), 229–30.
[26] "I Zjazd PPR," *ARR*, 11:208.
[27] AAN KC PPR 295/XI/47, k. 67; AAN MPiOS 803, kk. 192–93. See also a union representative helping to arrest a worker accused of stealing at the Eitingon mill, June 1947: ŁAP WRZZ 66, n.p.

proletarian of cities. One subtext of postwar conflict, usually unrecorded, was the tension between workers secure in their class and community identity and outsiders at a cultural disadvantage among the urban proletariat. Soviet liberation notwithstanding, the people and leaders of Łódź owed least to the party, and the communists felt least welcome there—even (or especially) among prewar members.[28] Łódź seemed to Party leaders a foreign land inhabited by *baby* (the derogatory term used by frustrated politicians for women textile workers). Minister of Industry Minc attributed strikes to "the great nervousness of the Łódź proletariat, which is made up mostly of women."[29] Party inspector E. Kreczkowska reported from one mill in 1946 that party members actually avoided contact with nonparty workers: "When sometimes in the cafeteria nonparty [workers] sit and complain about the government, and the situation today, our Party members, instead of explaining [things], take their bowl of food and go to another table so as not to hear complaints." At Scheibler, reported another inspector, "it is hard to find PPR members at all during strikes, because they hide, and sometimes speak for the strike themselves." Indeed, it was more common to find party members in factories supporting strikes than working to crush them.[30]

Party membership was quite low in the city before 1948. While Łódź thereafter boasted one of the largest and most proletarian organizations in the country (by late 1948, 6.5 percent of the city had PPR membership, and nearly three-quarters of these were workers), its relative ability to recruit workers was not impressive.[31] In mid-1946 less than 6 percent of the workers in Łódź's twenty largest factories belonged to the PPR; even by 1948, the average in four large factories for which data are available had reached only 14 percent.[32] This was hardly the lowest

[28] See AAN KC PPR 295/V/6, kk. 2–3; AAN KC PPR 295/XI/10, k. 39.

[29] As proof of women's capriciousness, he cited a strike over the issuing of canned goods packed in flat, rather than tall, cans. September 1945, reprinted in *Życie Warszawy*, 22 November 1984.

[30] AAN KC PPR 295/XI/10, kk. 42–43; AAN KC PPR 295/IX/32, k. 19.

[31] *Partia w cyfrach*, sec. 3. See Zygmunt Pietrzak, "Rozwój organizacyjny PPR w Łodzi na tle sytuacji społeczno-ekonomicznej miasta (19.II–31.VII.45)," *Rocznik Łódzki* 19 (1974), 5–32; ŁAP KW PPR 1/XI/1, n.p.

[32] These statistics probably include office workers. Membership tended to be even lower at smaller factories because large factories concerned PPR leaders most. PPS membership averaged roughly two-thirds to three-quarters of PPR membership. 1946 figures: *W dymach czarnych*, 460; AAN KC PPR 295/IX/227, kk. 52–53, and other reports in this folder and in ibid. 295/XIII/18, k. 36; also ŁAP KŁ PPR 1/VI/141, k. 23. For 1947: AAN KC PPR 295/IX/30, kk. 29–32. For 1948, see ŁAP KŁ PPR 1/VI/142, k. 184 (Wima); ŁAP KŁ

percentage in Poland; the unindustrialized east had much fewer members. But in comparison to other industrial cities, especially in Silesia and the west (including Wrocław), this showing was very weak. A 1946 report for the PPR Central Committee explained that members were not good at recruiting because "not all PPR members love and understand the Party; they link Party membership with personal material benefits."[33]

Workers in Łódź did not feel that it was necessary to join the PPR in order to secure work or a better position. Stanisław S. remembers that it was not at all clear that membership guaranteed promotion; not until the PPR and PPS united (in December 1948) was there any obvious connection. And while workers knew the PPS well, no one knew just what kind of party the PPR was.[34] The factory council chair at one machine factory in 1946 was popular with workers because, as the personnel director complained, he did "not want to get involved politically with either worker party, because as he himself says, he agrees with their programs but does not trust the leadership."[35] In this work culture, the party was simply unnecessary unless it (or individual members) could help workers control their workplace and maintain the community.

The Moral Economy in Łódź

Workers' control as a symbol of the ascendancy of a class was broadly compatible with PPR ideology; its emphasis on skill and responsibility was undoubtedly valuable to economic reconstruction. Yet workers expected far more than the state was willing or able to give them. As a result, conflict between the regime and the working class of Łódź spread quickly to issues of food supply (aprowizacja), punishment for theft, the labor market, and the pay system before conflict came to a head over control of the work process in 1947.

Despite their constant talk of counterrevolutionary forces, the au-

PPR 1/VI/143, kk. 99 (Biederman) and 133 (Gampe); Wiesław Puś and Stefan Pytlas, *Dzieje Łódzkich Zakładów Przemysłu Bawełnianego im. Obrońców Pokoju "Uniontex" (d. Zjednoczonych Zakładów K. Scheiblera i L. Grohmana) w latach 1827–1977* (Warsaw, 1979), 446.

[33] AAN KC PPR 295/IX/32, k. 69.

[34] Interview with Stanisław S.

[35] The other four council members were also nonparty: "They are skilled workers and thus have some authority, and were therefore chosen to the factory council." AAN MPiH 171, n.p.

thorities had more reason to fear the consequences of not being able to provide for the people, because shortages made their political promises seem hollow. In April 1945, PPR Political Bureau member Jakub Berman told his colleagues of "alarming facts of hunger demonstrations by workers," including strikes, fainting at work, and demonstrations demanding "bread and work"; workers at the Gampe-Albrecht mill looted its food stores.[36] As would be expected from the role they had been assigned, union leaders especially feared hungry workers. Delegates to a mid-1945 postal workers' union conference in Warsaw pleaded that they could not return empty-handed to Łódź because the workers would "do them in." Shortages, explained a KCZZ representative, meant that "we really lose [workers'] confidence and their trust that we represent some force which is capable of giving something to the laboring class, as far as the establishment of social justice is concerned."[37]

Many basic necessities were beyond the reach of the average worker in 1945. The estimated cost of living for a working family of four in March was more than ten times the wages of two earners; 80 percent of these wages went for food. The introduction of ration cards in mid-1945 dramatically lowered food expenditures—when goods were available to cover the cards, of course. In May, workers received as little as 30 percent of the goods to which they were entitled.[38] Even as wages rose, they had far to go before reaching prewar levels: an early 1946 report estimated that buying power had fallen to as little as $\frac{1}{200}$th of the 1939 level.[39] Figure 1 compares the wages of textile workers with estimated family budgets through 1949. In the face of continued shortages through the winter of 1945–46, all the regime could do was appeal for workers' understanding.[40]

Payments-in-kind, or *deputaty,* made up much of the difference between wages and expenses; workers usually sold them on the black market. These deputaty might be factory products, such as cloth from a textile mill, or cigarettes (three thousand per month) at a tobacco factory; cou-

[36] AAN KC PPR 295/V/2, kk. 4–5; AAN MPiH 4200, k. 155.

[37] ARZ KCZZ WO 95, k. 90; ARZ KCZZ WO 141, k.168–69.

[38] Gołębiowski, "Rola PPR," 126; ARZ KCZZ WO 141, k. 161; AAN KC PPR 295/V/5, kk. 33–35. On ration cards, see Helena Gnatowska, *Rola Polskiej Partii Robotniczej w kształtowaniu i realizacji polityki socjalnej Polski Ludowej, 1942–1948* (Białystok, 1986), 124–34. Real wages fluctuated sharply through early 1947 (192–94).

[39] ŁAP WK PPS 22/XII/2.

[40] See PPR Political Bureau meeting of October 1945, AAN KC PPR 295/V/2, k. 21.

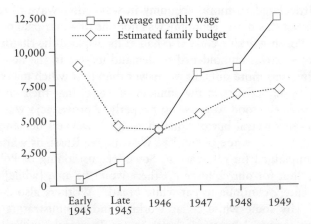

Figure 1. Wages in the textile industry and estimated family budgets

Note: For wages (except for 1946), see Puś and Pytlas, *Dzieje Łódzkich Zakładów,* 430–32. For typical 1946 wages, see AAN MPiOS 803, kk. 191–93 (Horak mill). See also Halina Wiśniewska-Bieniek, "Płace w przemyśle włókienniczym Łodzi w latach 1945–1949," *Rocznik Łódzki* 19 (1974): 141–57. Wages at first grew much more slowly in textiles than in metal or mining and began to catch up only in the second half of 1946: Gnatowska, *Rola Polskiej Partii Robotniczej,* 193. For budgets, see ARZ KCZZ WE 195 and (for Łódź in April 1948) AAN MPiOS 489, k. 63. For estimated prices in Warsaw of thirteen basic items in 1949, see *RS 1949,* 111–19. The apparent wealth of workers after 1948 is somewhat misleading, of course, because of the numerous hidden costs and inefficiencies of the system.

pons enabling purchase of factory goods; or simply goods the factory acquired for distribution. Workers thus had to take part in the free market to survive. The government estimated in late 1945 that payment-in-kind (presumably calculated at free-market value) accounted for 31 percent of a worker's monthly earnings, while ration cards provided 23 percent and actual cash wages 46 percent. Only when food production and distribution reached passable levels after the bitterly cold winter of 1946–47 could the government begin to phase out ration cards. As the złoty gradually stabilized, cash replaced payment-in-kind; workers seriously questioned, however, whether the proposed replacement was of equal value.[41]

Faced with the question of survival and acceptable living standards and armed with wartime and interwar traditions, the Łódź labor com-

[41]"Tam, gdzie powstaje papieros," *Robotnik,* 31 August 1945; ARZ KCZZ WO 141, k.10; AAN MPiOS 737, n.p.; *RS 1947,* 98–99, 148–54; ŁAP WUIiP 33, n.p.

munity articulated its moral economy in wave after wave of strikes in
1945–46. But this moral economy was not one of a marginal or ignored
class; the Polish working class also had at its disposal the rhetoric of the
new state, and was emboldened to demand its due in the new Poland.
No demand was more difficult to answer than that which many women
posed to union activists in the summer of 1945: that their children be
assured sufficient food to grow up properly. Aprowizacja was not just
a question of survival but of "quality of life": workers demanded "not
just bread, but . . . white bread."[42] "We can give Russians white flour,"
others complained (in reference to Soviet requisitioning of Polish production), "but for our children . . . there won't be any, [while] speculators will surely continue to eat white bread." Workers also demanded
to know why some white collar workers and administrators received
more than they.[43] A weaver's letter to the Poznański mill's biweekly
newspaper combined platitudes about productivity with remarks that
would be ominous to a contemporary management reader:

> In our section, we are working intensively. Our production is top-quality.
> We could produce more, if it weren't necessary to think about how to get
> some cash for books for Jadzia, or for a shirt for Stach, who is already a
> sophomore in high school and likes to study. The children will most likely
> get shoes in school. There isn't such a problem with underwear, since the
> points which I've now gotten three times allow me to see to that painful
> problem. . . .
> We were very happy when our delegate told us that now we would get
> more points for the same work. It will be possible to set aside a little of
> that for food, rent, and electricity. . . . We must end this note which we
> write for our little paper during our lunch break. We're in a hurry, because
> we have to get our coupons for meat and flour. On the way we'll find out
> when they'll be giving us points for last week. And one more thing: If our
> host will serve for lunch soup without potatoes, we'll serenade him like
> this:
> "We would really much rather not drink any more water!"[44]

Women such as that writer measured their work lives by the minute
details of aprowizacja—coal, bread, children's shoes, underwear. Moreover, they were willing to compare notes: "We are curious what it is like

[42]ŁAP KW PPR 1/XI/2, n.p.

[43]AAN MIiP 82, k. 30. ARZ KCZZ WO 125, k. 66.

[44]Here, as in many other sources used in this book, the Polish text makes plain that the
author is speaking about women. *Nasza Praca* 1, September 1945, ŁAP WUIiP 140.

in other factories. We would be very happy if [workers] would write to us from other factories about how women there work."[45] The Łódź PPR admitted that "achievements in the social sector, combined with a simultaneous raising of wages and a rise in productivity, lose their importance . . . and make little impression due to present difficulties with aprowizacja. . . . Women/mothers are the chief firebrands of dissatisfaction. . . . they do not understand political arguments; they demand food . . . for their children. To prevent strikes and ease the tense situation and the mood of the masses, [we must] win over the women."[46] Through their role as household managers, the women of the textile industry brought the concerns of the community into the factory. That is, their complaints were focused not just within the factory but across the community where they shopped with other women. They asserted their right to a living derived from their work, striking over management's quality control or demanding the right to buy their own production. Workers at the Union-Textil woolen mill struck in January 1946 when management sought to cut costs by ceasing distribution of a kilo of wool to each worker as agreed to after an earlier strike. A strike leader (the PPS secretary at the factory) explained: "We make the wool, the wool is ours, and we must get the wool."[47]

The first postwar strikes in Łódź occurred in early May 1945. Workers demanded better food in cafeterias and on ration cards or higher pay to compensate for high food prices. In July, there were twenty-three strikes; workers at "unusually boisterous" strike meetings shouted, "We've had enough politics—give us food!"[48] Government authorities generally took a dim view of aprowizacja strikes. "It is a bad thing to give [workers] what they are owed as the result of a strike," concluded a Ministry of Industry inspector in December 1945. "This results in the conviction that everything can be gained only through a strike; the strike could become a popular method not only to receive overdue benefits and services, but also to win conditions better than those which [workers] deserve according to the law and present agreements."[49] During the following sum-

[45]Ibid.

[46]ŁAP KW PPR 1/XI/2.

[47]Factory PPR leaders and foremen supported the strikers. ŁAP KD PPR Górna-Prawa, 1/VI/65. Also ARZ KCZZ WO 141, k. 31; AAN MPiOS 803, k. 146.

[48]There were at least eight strikes in May: ŁAP WK PPS 22/XIV/41; AAN KC PPR 295/XIII/28B, k. 400–401; ŁAP WRZZ 46, kk. 45–46; Andrzej Dysput, CRZZ Library memoir 630, kk. 4–5. July: AAN KC PPR 295/V/5, kk. 33–35.

[49]AAN MPiH 946, k. 23.

mer a PPR inspector blamed the newspapers "which print what goods are to be available on cards; [when workers] don't get that, this causes embitterment and arouses antipathy for the government which [they believe] is surely cheating them."[50] Workers waged a nearly continuous campaign of strikes through 1947. Eventually, authorities learned to give them what they demanded. After a series of strikes in the early spring of 1947, a Ministry of Industry representative discerned an "expertly agitated phobia of price hikes" and recommended that prices be held down at all costs.[51]

As much as they faulted the government for shortages, workers especially blamed speculators who took advantage of a poorly regulated free market. What workers could afford (on ration cards) was not always available, but what was available (on the free market) they could not afford. Prices in private stores were utterly out of reach. For example, while the metal industry was paying a maximum of 10 złotys per hour in March 1945, bread was 46 zł a kilo, beef 180 zł a kilo, and eggs 11 zł each. Explained a Ministry of Information and Propaganda secret report: "The lack of goods and inefficient distribution make for a lot of malcontents. The Łódź worker cannot accept the fact that his children can only gaze at cake from afar, and he is not satisfied that one like himself who works hard earns so little, while some parasite makes big money on the free market and the state gets nothing from him. In general, prices must be regulated."[52] The official press, by drawing attention to free market prices and shortages, shaped workers' anger toward independent dealers. Wartime memories of the black market made the emergence of a legal free market on the street and in private shops even harder to bear. Perceptions of injustice at the hands of private merchants would eventually strengthen the state's ability to pursue an anticapitalist political discourse.

---

[50] AAN KC PPR 295/IX/32, k. 20.

[51] AAN MPiH 41, kk. 464–65. The KCZZ estimated 209 strikes in the entire country from 1 June 1945 to 31 March 1946, with peaks in August, October–November and January–March. ARZ KCZZ WO 220. This estimate seems extremely conservative; brief work stoppages were probably uncounted. On strikes in Łódź in early 1946, see ŁAP WK PPS 22/XII/2 and 22/XII/7, n.p.; AAN KC PPR 295/XI/47, k. 62; AAN KC PPR 295/XIII/17, k. 5; AAN MPiOS 803, k. 7; AAN MPiH 214, kk. 10–11; ŁAP PZPB nos. 1, 2, k. 25.

[52] ŁAP WUIiP 29, n.p. See also ARZ KCZZ WO 125, k. 66. For examples of such anger in 1945 and 1947, see ARZ KCZZ WO 41, k. 40; ŁAP WRZZ 19, n.p. On the free market, see Gnatowska, *Rola Polskiej Partii Robotniczej*, 206–7, 214.

The moral economy of the Łódź worker justified theft from one's own factory as the most appropriate response to poor aprowizacja or low wages. As Kazimierz Wyka warned in his 1945 essay "Life As If," the practices of the war permeated postwar society. What had once been a weapon against the Nazis and a means of survival was then invested with renewed righteousness in the first years of reconstruction: stolen goods made up for the income withheld by the state. Railway workers accused of stealing in 1947 shouted down union activists with cries of "We will steal!" "Let us live!" "Give us coal!" Railway guards refused to detain workers caught stealing.[53] To steal was to exact justice, class justice, as a speaker at a 1947 conference of union representatives claimed: "Workers are thrown out on the street for the smallest offense, while directors who commit the greatest embezzlement are transferred to other posts without paying the consequences."[54] Speaking in early 1946, PPS activist Lucjan Motyka blamed government economic practice: "A worker who makes 1,000 zł monthly and must spend 1,000 zł monthly comes to the conclusion that he must steal, and the path he will follow will be the path of demoralization—and we have led him onto that path."[55]

Thefts increased steadily through 1945–46. In December 1945, theft accounted for 10 to 30 percent of production in Łódź (according to a poll of factory directors), compared to just 2 percent in 1939. At the Łódź thread factory, 31 percent of production, or about 18 kg of thread per worker monthly, was "systematically [stolen] by whole groups" of workers. It was necessary to steal significant amounts in order to support one's family. In November, the PPS estimated the amount stolen in the textile industry reached 200 million złotys, or 3,450 zł per worker, when the average salary was about 1,100 zł. If only half the workers stole, then each was taking home six times his or her wages—still only about 50 percent more than the estimated minimum budget for a family of four (see figure 1) and entirely plausible as families laid in supplies for the winter ahead. Stolen goods could be for one's own use but at such volume were more likely for sale on the black market to supplement a paycheck. Other workers produced goods for black market sale during

[53]Kazimierz Wyka, *Życie na niby* (Kraków, 1984), 175; ŁAP WRZZ, 64, k. 1.
[54]ŁAP WRZZ 19, n.p.
[55]"Protokoły posiedzeń Rady Gospodarczej PPS," 258–59.

work or used machines after work for this purpose. Theft continued unabated into 1947 when an estimated 17 percent of textile production was stolen—an amount far greater, given increased production, than the 30 percent of 1945. The value of goods stolen per worker was then approximately 4,000 zł.[56]

With the help of the UB, PPR and management reacted far more strongly to theft than to strikes. Arrests for theft increased steadily; in some cases, the entire factory was laid off, with workers screened and then rehired on new conditions.[57] Meanwhile, authorities searched for someone to blame. Some held that theft was the work of "a new element, made up of people who have not graduated from the school of the factory, from the school of the proletarian class struggle. [These] people came from various backgrounds, [and] brought to the factories their old habits, their ways of thinking—alien to the working class—consisting of 'snatch from the state and society as much as possible, and give as little of oneself.' "[58] Others saw in theft a counterrevolutionary activity; they told of thieves who boasted of underground directives to steal, the support of armed guerrillas, and gangs of profiteering workers who terrorized other workers into striking in their defense.[59] Nevertheless, it was not necessarily either the new workers or the reactionaries who stole. The Industrial Guard, which at most factories was made up of workers (usually with some factory background) whose membership in and service to the PPR won them the easier post, was often involved in theft— in fact, observers singled out guards as the worst thieves. The guards at Scheibler and Grohman, for example, were "mostly Party people . . . and are considered to be wholesale thieves." Factory, union, and party representatives were likely to be sympathetic to the plight of experienced urban workers.[60]

[56]ŁAP WK PPS 22/XII/2; AAN MPiH 1662; AAN CKW PPS 235/VII/169, k. 20; ŁAP WRZZ 6, kk. 76–77; *Życie Warszawy*, 22 November 1984. For 1947, see ŁAP WRZZ 7, k. 38; ŁAP KŁ PPR 1/XI/4, n.p.

[57]AAN KC PPR 295/XI/47, k. 67; ŁAP KŁ PPR 1/XI/1, kk. 1, 9.

[58]Cited in "Przegląd prasy," *Trybuna Związkowca* 13, 16–31 October 1945, 8. Also ŁAP WRZZ 7, k. 38; AAN MPiH 946, kk. 2–8.

[59]Gołębiowski, *Walka*, 268–70; *Głos Widzewa*, 15 October–1 November 1946; ŁAP WK PPS 22/XII/2; AAN KC PPR 295/XI/47, k. 62.

[60]AAN KC PPR 295/IX/32, kk. 18, 46; AAN KC PPR 295/XI/325, kk. 8–9. See also ŁAP WRZZ 6, k. 179; ŁAP KŁ PPR 1/VI/141, kk. 1, 18, 84; *Nasza Praca* 1, 1 September 1945, 4. For an account by an industrial guard member who relates with pride his actions in catching thieves, see Stanisław Baranowski, *Pamiętnik robotnika* (Łódź, 1974), 120, 134–38, 145–46.

Several strikes in the fall and winter of 1945–46 defended the right to steal. When a special police inspection in October 1945 caught ten workers at the Stolarów mill smuggling a total of five hundred spools of thread under their clothes, "the path from the factory to the gate was strewn white as snow" as other workers hastily dropped their loot. The whole factory struck when the ten were fired the next day. Even when management (with the UB) agreed to reinstate all but two, the strikers refused to back down and threatened to occupy the factory. "We all steal," they explained, meaning that the two workers were unfairly singled out for punishment. The strike became violent as a crowd of workers ejected the police from the factory, preventing them from conducting further inspections.[61] A similar incident at Gampe and Albrecht in January 1946 illustrated to what extent workers took their thefts for granted. When several people were arrested and fired for stealing, workers struck to demand not the freedom of their colleagues but a raise in pay. Reminded that their wages had not declined, they explained that they had made up the difference between wages and what they needed to live on through theft; if management intended to cut off their supplemental income, it should augment wages accordingly.[62] The authorities were helpless before workers' brazen defense of their rights. The PPR lamented that the lack of consequences for theft "demoralizes the workers; . . . the police and the courts don't react to such cases; those fired for stealing are immediately hired in other state factories, where they steal again."[63]

While sufficient wages and food might motivate workers to higher productivity, the largest obstacle to increased discipline was the labor market. On paper, the regime quickly took control of the labor market. The director at the Wima mill warned in May 1945 that workers who left for other factories would, "in the event of their new place of work being revealed, be conducted back to our factory and required to work here." Textile trade union chief Aleksander Burski called for work book-

---

[61] AAN KC PPR 295/XI/47, kk. 6, 62. For other examples, see ŁAP KW PPR 1/XI/2, n.p. In a February 1946 strike at the Zajbert mill, in response to an industry-wide circular mandating new punishments for theft, angry workers supported by factory PPR leaders stormed the gatehouse, attacked the controller, put a sack over the head of the Industrial Guard commander, and threw him out of the factory. AAN MPiH 214, kk. 3–7.

[62] ŁAP KŁ PPR 1/VI/141, k. 7.

[63] AAN KC PPR 295/IX/32, k. 46.

lets that would record workers' transgressions and follow them to new workplaces. Minister of Industry Hilary Minc urged a campaign to root out idle skilled workers engaged in black market trade and force them to return to work.[64]

Yet as long as workers had freedom of movement, management could do nothing for fear of turning workers against them—witness the problems of punishing theft. At the low wages available in mid-1945, many skilled or experienced workers avoided returning to the factories. They registered unnecessary skills at employment offices or openly refused work in factories they deemed unsuitable. Because the work force expanded seven times through the spring of 1945, large numbers of inexperienced workers were pressed into service. It was easy to find work or change jobs if one wanted to, and management was only too willing to comply with the demands of valued workers.[65] In May 1945, absenteeism reached 20 percent in some factories. The average Łódź worker worked 120 hours monthly of a possible 200 until the introduction of the bonus system and just 170 afterwards, often arranging to work for overtime pay as well.[66] Although employment bureaus throughout Poland continued to register tens of thousands of unemployed workers, demand for labor outstripped supply through 1947, while technological constraints prevented management from hiring workers to full capacity. A worker laid off could easily find work in another mill or factory, but some factories had to cut production for lack of personnel. "If there has of yet been no strike at John," concluded an investigation of the metal factory in mid-1946, "this may only be because there is the safety valve of escape to another factory if the director's promises of better conditions are not fulfilled."[67] Through 1947 at least, party and state organs regularly issued alarms about the state of discipline (tardiness, absentee-

[64]ŁAP Widzewskie Zakłady Przemysłu Bawełnianego "1-go Maja" 41, n.p.; "I Zjazd PPR," ARR, 11: 258–59; AAN MPiH 4200, k. 192.

[65]ARZ KCZZ WO 141, k. 131; ibid. 84, k. 91. According to one report, fewer than 3,200 of the almost 29,000 people registered as unemployed in the city in May 1945 claimed to be textile workers. Half of the unemployed, however, were Germans, whom factories presumably were refusing to hire. ARZ KCZZ WO 125, kk. 33–36. Also interviews with Stanisław S., and three workers from the John factory, 18 January 1990.

[66]AAN MPiH 946, kk. 2–8; AAN MPiOS 746, n.p.

[67]AAN KC PPR 295/IX/32, kk. 36–40. Also AAN KC PPR 295/IX/33, k. 90; AAN MPiH 1025, kk. 31–32. There were some 80,000 to 100,000 people unemployed in 1946, slightly less in 1947. Gnatowska, Rola Polskiej Partii Robotniczej, 185–86; ŁAP WK PPS 22/XIV/43; Życie Włókiennicze 10, December 1946, 3–4.

ism, and so on) in all industries; until the regime found new ways to control workers, it could not improve productivity.[68]

In later years repression would be the favored weapon; in 1945–46, however, both party leaders and management preferred to employ the carrot more than the stick. "The workers' endurance is facing a very serious test," Lucjan Motyka warned the PPS Economic Council. "The elections await us, and our older comrades are beginning to express themselves in opposition. This is because we have set ourselves the task in the economic plan of bringing our production to profitability in a very short time. I want to point out that even the wisest, well-devised plan might not be compatible with people's stamina. We must tackle the problem of workers' pay energetically."[69] In other words, workers' pay had to come before industry's needs. The foremost task was to revise the inefficient pay system to create incentives to produce. Some Łódź factories first introduced a system of piece rates plus bonuses (*akordowo-premiowy*) in July 1945. Over the next three years, bonuses came to represent a larger and larger part of the paycheck, with raises taking the form of bonuses more often than actual increases in the basic wage until the reform of January 1949 reversed this trend.[70]

While piece rates might raise productivity and restore discipline, they could also increase the worker's control over wages, allowing workers to decide how hard they needed to work. After some early opposition, workers generally came to accept piece rates for this reason, especially when they realized that hourly wages were not likely to grow to replace them. By late summer 1945, strikes were even reported in factories where the piece-rate system had not yet been introduced.[71] Piece rates might have even weakened labor discipline because they made time belong to the workers, not management. Reasoned workers at the John factory whom inspectors found lying in the sun during work, piece rates meant that workers could do what they liked.[72]

A piece rate, however, gave the worker control over wages only as long as she or he could control the rate of production. Higher produc-

---

[68]For examples, see AAN MPiOS 12, k. 130; AAN KC PPR 295/IX/32, k. 46; AAN KC PPR 295/XI/49, kk. 30–31.

[69]"Protokoły posiedzeń Rady Gospodarczej PPS," 258–59.

[70]Wiśniewska-Bieniek, "Płace w przemyśle włókienniczym," 151; Gołębiowski, *Walka*, 231–246; Gnatowska, *Rola Polskiej Partii Robotniczej*, 192–94.

[71]ŁAP KW PPR, 1/XI/2, n.p. For opposition to piece rates, see ARZ KCZZ WO 141, kk. 150–51; ŁAP KD PPR Bałuty 1/VI/36, k. 44.

[72]AAN KC PPR 295/IX/32, kk. 36–40.

tion norms did not necessarily bring higher production, only lower wages. Moreover, workers had little control over their standard of living as long as a large part of their earnings came in kind or on ration cards. Piece rates were not a way to become rich but, at best, a way to maintain the pace of one's work at an acceptable level. As norms rose, even this became impossible. Workers suffered from working at war-damaged machinery, from exhaustion and lack of proper nutrition, and from poor training. Because production was changed frequently to meet new demands, only the most skilled could keep pace; they might get almost nothing if production stopped for lack of raw materials or energy. Some workers at first earned less with piece rates than they had with daily wages—in one factory, norm setters had used wartime standards set for production in a technologically advanced German factory.[73]

For beating the norm, workers in 1945–46 received bonus points redeemable for goods at the factory; in textiles, one point was worth a length of cloth or a number of spools of thread. Workers could obtain cloth cheaply under this system and supplement their wages by selling their points on the free market. But the value of points ranged from 30 to 400 zł, depending on the quality of material made available by the factory. Because points came to be a significant portion of the worker's wages, those who could not produce enough and thus earned no points were unable to support their families.[74] When workers realized that they could not meet norms, they sometimes simply refused to try, as at Scheibler and Grohman in May 1945. Spinners slowed their machines, and the absentee rate increased sharply as management attempted to enforce norms. To avoid trouble, foremen accepted any excuse for absence and tardiness. Rather than reducing theft and absenteeism and raising discipline, the recently introduced piece rates and bonuses only increased worker resistance. That fall, a report from the same mill showed that, even though workers now accepted and met norms, they thought only about earning bonuses, not about improving productivity. In other words, norms became an end in themselves for both management and

[73]AAN MPiH 946, k. 15; also "Bolączki robotników łódzkich," *Trybuna Związkowca* 8, 1–15 August 1945; Grzegorz Sołtysiak, "Działalność socjalna związków zawodowych w Polsce w latach 1944–1945," *Kwartalnik Historii i Teorii Ruchu Zawodowego*, no. 2 (1989): 32.

[74]ŁAP WK PPS 22/XII/2, n.p.; AAN KC PPR 295/IX/32, kk. 21–23; ARZ KCZZ WO 292, kk. 8–9; ŁAP WRZZ 6, kk. 76–77.

workers. In October, the management at Scheibler and Grohman actually agreed to lower the norms for spinners and weavers.[75]

When management tried to achieve discipline with greater force, it was no more successful. At the Kroning Karolew manufactory in March 1946, the director (supported by the PPR and PPS) refused to negotiate with workers over bonuses and wages. Workers walked out, and on the fourth day of the strike, management announced it would cancel their contract and rehire workers on new terms. In response, strikers occupied the factory. When the city police supported the workers, management was forced to negotiate and brought in cotton-industry representatives to investigate workers' grievances. In this strike, both workers and management tested the limits of their power. Workers discovered that they could count on some support from even the police and that, even with management playing roles reminiscent of prewar labor relations, a strike could be both successful and unpunished.[76]

An August 1945 strike over the textile industry's second collective agreement in Pabianice (a smaller city connected to Łódź by tram) gives us a closer look at the way in which the moral community of 1945 resisted management and the state. Supposedly inspired by an agitator from a small textile town nearby, the strike began on the night shift at the Krusche and Ender mill, Pabianice's largest factory. Workers' complaint that the soup had gone sour—"which was not true at first," reported Pabianice officials, "since it was only moderately sour, and later . . . someone poured vinegar into it and ruined it"—gave rise to a whole range of demands, including an end to bonuses, wage raises, milk for children, white bread, vacations, and a return to two looms from four. Strikers' demands were rooted in a moral community: they concerned not only how well the community was supplied but whether it was paid fairly and equally. Angry workers protested the gross disparity in awarding bonus points: each worker received four points per month, while top management received eighty-six points each. Pabianice was ready for an excuse to strike: six other firms struck almost immediately, along similar patterns. Among complaints about food and fuel aprowizacja and the price of electricity, trams, and movie theaters, these strikers postulated that bonuses be either terminated or divided equally among everyone who worked for the same firm, even gatekeepers.[77]

[75]ŁAP PZPB No. 1, 2, kk. 9–11; ŁAP WRZZ 185, n.p.; For other cases, see AAN KC PPR 295/XIII/32, kk. 164–65; ŁAP KD PPR Górna-Prawa 1/VI/65, kk. 1–3.

[76]AAN MPiOS 803, n.p.

[77]AAN MIiP 301, kk. 40–41; AAN MPiH 41, kk. 418–19, 421, 424–29; ŁAP WRZZ

The determination of the strikers in Pabianice surprised local officials; they had not reckoned on the strength, even beyond the factory, of this labor community. Strikers were hostile toward management and PPR representatives. At Krusche and Ender, workers barricaded the gates against party members mobilized to work by PPR and PPS leadership and were able to hold the factory with the support of local police. Only on the fourth day, with the promise of worker delegations to Warsaw and Łódź, did the strike come to an end in Krusche and Ender. Strikers were also moved by emotional and sympathetic speeches given by young cadets from the Military Political Academy (probably from the Pabianice community) and stymied by the intervention of PPR members from the Information and Propaganda Bureau and the local PPR organization, who appeared at strike meetings in groups of eight or ten and prevented strikers from speaking.[78]

Efforts to punish or repress strikes in Łódź remained hesitant and ineffective throughout the first three years. While the Łódź UB boasted that it could prevent strikes by arresting the would-be provocateurs ahead of time, Chief Mieczysław Moczar admitted that, with only 260 agents in the entire province in late 1945, his department was rarely prepared. As late as 1947, a senior UB official counseled that interrogating workers after a strike might be counterproductive.[79] Even arrests could be inappropriate. In the Pabianice strike, the UB arrested a weaver named Głębicka at Krusche and Ender for her role in spreading the strike. Later, the PPR admitted that this arrest had been a mistake: "The arrest took place without the knowledge of the local Party organization, which even if it wanted to was completely unprepared to work against the solidarity strike which exploded at that factory. That strike was after all only partial: only two sections struck, and one of these returned to work after a time. At that moment Głębicka appeared at the factory and thanked the striking workers for taking up her cause."[80] Party leaders had learned their lesson and were thereafter more cautious with workers.

6, k. 30. One KW PPR member argued that, because the strike took place shortly after a "great workers' manifestation" in Łódź expressing similar demands in a legal manner, the Pabianice strike must have been externally organized: "After all, a strike does not erupt, it is organized." ŁAP KW PPR 1/XI/11, n.p.

[78] AAN MIiP 301, kk. 40–41.

[79] MSW MBP 17/IX/77 t. 1, kk. 2–3, 73.

[80] AAN KC PPR 295/X/5, k. 166; see also ŁAP WUIiP 57, n.p. Głębicka continued to be a problem for the authorities, as a report on a November 1946 strike at the same factory shows. ŁAP WUIiP 32, kk. 8–9.

"Every payday at large factories," reported Julian Kole in October 1946, "was discussed by Party and union leadership with great concern: will it go through, or will there be a strike? This is characteristic for Łódź after the introduction of almost every collective agreement."[81]

The Łódź strikes of 1945 and 1946 revealed the working class's resistance to its changing role in the Polish state—from heroic defender and rebuilder of industry to production unit. At one level, strikes over pay, food, or norms were simple demands for better circumstances. But in "democratic" Poland, they also meant defense or assertion of the power and privilege that workers imagined they would have in the new system. Having lost the battle for formal factory control, workers successfully gained control of the pay and supply agenda; the regime ceded control of the debate over wages as it denied their other demands. These strikes reflected the ambiguity of industrial relations and the confusion of government services and industrial wages. In the absence of a clear system, workers sought to set the rules themselves and communicate their sense of justice. In this way, they resurrected their version of the revolution of 1945 as one based on community values.

Solidarities and Divisions in the Łódź Labor Community

The phrase *moral community* does not mean that all workers felt solidarity with each other at all times. Such solidarity was the product of specific situations and often based on particular shared characteristics. The theme of solidarity across and between factories remained an important part of the labor culture in Łódź through the first years after the war, culminating in the great strike of September 1947. While the displays of community are most remarkable, those that cut across community are also important to note. Workers were hardly magnanimous in the difficult reconstruction years; rather, they feared that a meager pool of goods might be divided to their disadvantage. Like most moral economies, that of the Łódź labor community was both egalitarian and riven by jealousies. The bonds that linked Łódź workers were weakened by divisions rooted in craft, gender, skill, generation, and nation.

Solidarity, as expressed in labor protest against the arrests of workers,

[81] AAN KC PPR 295/XI/10, k. 25.

was often strong because workers were still willing and able to defend each other. For example, a spinner fired for theft at the Hirszberg and Birnbaum factory in October 1945 told workers as she left that she was being fired for no reason and that management planned to fire more. The spinners struck immediately, demanding unsuccessfully that she be reinstated. That same autumn, two successful strikes defended one worker arrested for leading a previous strike and another fired for insulting management and the factory council. The following spring, workers at a tobacco factory protested the hiring of three new workers while fifty veterans of the factory remained unemployed. In each case, the defense of a few was a means to assert collective rights—seniority, the right to one's job, and the right to a living.[82]

Yet workers sometimes did not seem to want to improve their lot so much as be sure that no one lived better than they. While they made it clear that they could not live on present wages and rations, they also hoped to ensure that no one got more than the community felt was fair; they particularly resented any hint of unequal distribution of wealth. "If Poland is poor," remarked a postal worker in explanation of the resentments behind one strike, "it should be poor for everyone."[83] Strikers in Pabianice announced that they would be willing to eat black bread and wash it down with black coffee if the same would be forced on all social groups. Others monitored the wages of their counterparts elsewhere in the factory and industry—striking, for example, to demand the same pay as similar workers at another factory. The Wima mill's newspaper bemoaned the "sneaky tactic" of fomenting conflict and distrust by "spreading false information about alleged high wages of workers at other factories."[84]

Resentments were also powerful across craft boundaries. A common theme of statements and resolutions from metal, energy, transport, printing, and chemical industries in Łódź through 1946 was their disadvantage compared to the textile workers, who had more access (through theft and the point system) to marketable goods than did workers in nonconsumer industries. If a factory did not produce consumer goods,

[82] AAN MPiH 41, k. 445; AAN MliP 82, kk. 9–10; ŁAP WK PPS 22/XIV/41 (cited in Władysław Stefaniuk, *Łódzka organizacja PPS, 1945–1948* [Łódź, 1980], 82); AAN CKW PPS 235/XV/44, k. 43.

[83] ŁAP WRZZ 253, n.p.

[84] ŁAP DPB 20, k. 41. *Głos Widzewa* 15 (26), 16 May 1946. See also, from 1947, ŁAP KŁ PPR 1/XI/1, kk. 38–39; AAN KC PPR 295/XIII/7, k. 99.

a worker could only receive what the factory was able to obtain on the black market. Metal workers felt particularly neglected and struck to express this feeling in at least seven factories in October–November 1945. This period was the height of protests in the Łódź metal industry and the only time in these years in which skilled workers as a group engaged in labor conflict in Łódź. The absence of conflict was itself a sore point: some workers resented textile workers' ability to win concessions through strikes.[85]

Skilled workers' anger was amplified by their memories of liberation in January 1945. They contrasted their earlier service to the nation with the treatment they now received and with the fortunes of the less skilled, less dedicated workers of the textile mills. The crews of Łódź's trams protested in January 1946 that, by carrying workers to factories at special discount rates, they contributed to the productivity of those factories. Nevertheless, they themselves received no bonuses whatsoever, while other workers received clothing, which tram crews also helped to deliver. Two months later, tram employees went on strike, justifying themselves as follows:

> Upon the retreat of the [Nazis] from Łódź, the workers of the city and suburban trams in Łódź rebuilt the company with their self-sacrificing labor and brought it to an exceptional level of technical efficiency.... It would seem that, as a result of such hard and fruitful labor, [we] would be treated materially if not better, then at least even with other workers in Łódź. [On the contrary], things have turned out quite the opposite.... Such an abnormal state of affairs has come to pass that every worker in the textile factories [can] give himself a good life, while our worker, in many cases, literally starves....
>
> We bore this difficult situation for a long time, guided by our feeling of civic duty—that it would be inadmissible for [city] transportation to interrupt its work. But when our workers see their starving families, they are overcome by such discouragement, apathy, and resentment that they simply do not have the strength to control themselves in order to carry on at their work.[86]

---

[85] ŁAP WRZZ 25, n.p.; ŁAP WK PPS 22/XII/2; AAN MPiH 1171, k. 71; AAN MPiH 41, k. 447.

[86] ARZ KCZZ WO 276, kk. 78–80. Other examples include city workers: ŁAP KW PPR 1/XI/2, n.p.; construction workers: AAN KC PPR 295/XIII/17, k. 14; and chemical workers and printers: "Bolączki robotników Łodzi," *Trybuna Związkowca* 8, 1–15 August 1945. See also AAN MPiH 1174, kk. 119–22; AAN MPiH 214, k. 8.

These workers, predominantly male, grounded their arguments in terms of service to the nation and society and invoked the rights of workers within their workplace. They assumed a hierarchy of labor (metal over textile) based on prewar relations, which they judged to be fair. Now they looked at other workers whom they judged to be inferior and felt cheated. Thus as social welfare issues redefined the place of the worker in society, gender and family roles were expressed as craft jealousies. Like party and state leaders, male workers thought of textiles as a female industry whose practices threatened their way of life, even though their families might depend on women's earnings. The subtleties of gender conflict were voiced by a PPR activist at the John metalworks: a worker could see the difference every day "when his wife and daughter come home [from work in the textile mills] with their paychecks." The less-skilled women in the textile mills, he implied, had not served Łódź and Poland so well as to deserve better treatment.[87]

But for the women of the textile mills the factory was a part of life; they did not necessarily leave it with marriage. They were more likely than men to live near the factory in which they worked. Nearly half of a sample at the Poznański mill were married, and one-third were over thirty. Their education was about the same as that of the men with whom they worked. Despite the resentments voiced by men, these women came to speak for all of Łódź; the war had feminized the city not only numerically, but symbolically as well.[88]

Women did not find it easy to act as a group. They were usually passed over for supervisory or political work: although women were a majority among textile workers, only a few mills elected more than two or three to factory councils in 1945—a reflection of the process of choosing candidates, prewar leadership traditions, and male-dominated proletarian politics.[89] Women's departments in party and union organizations were small and neglected. Above all, however, the nature of women workers' concerns *as women* constituted a challenge to both authorities and other workers; identification of their problems made their position in the factory even more vulnerable, because it exposed their challenge to the factory system. These workers simply wanted to control their work environment. The six objections that E. Rutkowska,

[87]AAN KC PPR 295/IX/32, kk. 36–40.
[88]Information on work proximity from Piotrowski, *Społeczno-przestrzenna struktura*, 137–42; other data from factory samples.
[89]See ŁAP KW PPR 1/XI/11, n.p.

a women's activist, raised about women's textile work would have threatened the drive for greater productivity had they been addressed: work in a standing position, work without breaks or variety, piece work, high productivity norms, excessive burden of work (for example, on too many machines), and work without a dinner break.[90]

When making complaints or engaging in conflict, the most effective women chose to represent themselves as mothers responsible for the health and continuity of the nation. As mothers, they cared for families and thus ought not to be laid off; they also knew best what their families needed and demanded payment in cash rather than in kind. At one factory, it had been a tradition to allow women to take off one day a month to catch up with domestic duties.[91] With a strong community behind them, women workers raised difficult questions. Why didn't the factory produce children's clothes? Why were nonproduction workers being fired when factory administration was growing? Why must even pregnant women exhaust themselves working night shifts? Why couldn't child care be more convenient so that women working the morning shift would not have to leave for work as early as 4 A.M. bringing their children to deposit at the factory day-care center?[92]

The most effective display of women's power in labor conflict came in the great strike of September 1947. No strike was more clearly gendered than this one, in which striking women, dismissed as "pious old biddies" (*dewotki*) by party leaders, deftly used their traditional roles as victims to their own advantage, creating rumors of beatings to spread a strike from one factory to the whole city. Rather than wage a hopeless violent struggle, they accepted the identity that a male skilled-labor culture had saddled them with. Frustrated male activists saw this approach as either pernicious feminine craftiness or proof that the workers of Łódź were indeed no longer proletarians and could not be dealt with using standard labor relations.[93]

Another effective role for women workers was that of consumer. Be-

---

[90]AAN MPiH 947, kk. 109–10. Rutkowska noted that many women preferred to have no dinner break or a shorter one so they could leave the factory as early as possible; these women, too, sought control, but in a different way.

[91]ŁAP WRZZ 185, n.p. For such rhetoric, see ARZ KCZZ WO 276, kk. 80–81; ŁAP WRZZ 188, n.p.; AAN KC PPR 295/XI/325, kk. 113–14.

[92]ŁAP WRZZ 2, k. 65; ŁAP WRZZ 65, n.p.; ŁAP WRZZ 68, n.p.; ŁAP WRZZ 186, n.p.; AAN KC PPR 295/V/2, k. 13; interview with Filomena and Stanisław S.

[93]For use of the term *dewotki*, see AAN KC PPR 295/XIII/18, k. 217. Another example of women who used accusations of violence in the factory against a superior is at the

cause women were generally the ones who shopped for the household, they were both more aware of the regime's economic shortcomings and more determined to resist threats to their livelihood. As workers, these women chose the factory as a locus for consumer protest. By waving crusts of bread or demanding that management give them good white bread, strikers strengthened the connection between their workplace and home and between power within the factory and power outside it. That striking as consumers could be successful was demonstrated by the near general strike of 7–25 May 1946, the largest postwar strike wave to that date in Łódź. Some 25,000 workers in thirty mostly textile factories in and near Łódź struck for up to nearly two weeks. In the largest strike, all 7,500 workers at the Scheibler and Grohman mill struck for seven days; the Geyer mill, with 3,700 workers, was shut down for nine. Surprisingly, the authorities failed to comprehend the role of consumer concerns in this strike. They claimed instead that the strikes began without any warning or organization over minor issues; therefore, the strikes were the work of outside "reactionary forces."[94]

At the core of the strike were wage-control issues. An industry directive had changed paydays from biweekly to monthly. This move toward efficiency was far from minor; it was both an affront to factory tradition and a blow to women who planned their family budget and shopped for food. Pay every second Thursday was convenient and logical for workers because it allowed them to plan purchases for the weekend. The requirements of accounting and not the needs of workers would now dictate monthly paychecks. In addition to the change in paydays, two Ministry of Industry directives provoked discontent. The first was a pay table that set a new range of basic hourly wages. Workers claimed that wages were too low to compensate for the rise in free market prices. The second change proposed replacing bonuses-in-kind with compensation of 100 zł per point. Strikers demanded 200 zł; because the average worker received nine to twelve points monthly, this was a substantial difference.[95]

Schweikert factory, against a foreman who pushed women in line for dinner and attacked them verbally: ŁAP WRZZ 185, n.p.

[94] Reports on the May 1946 strikes: AAN MPiOS 803, kk. 9–13, 139–53; AAN KC PPR 295/XI/48, kk. 13–14; AAN KC PPR 295/IX/32, kk. 7–12; AAN MIiP 927, kk. 22, 37–38, 42, and ŁAP WUIiP 32, k. 10. For an example of bread protests, see AAN KC PPR 295/IX/33, k. 65.

[95] AAN MPiOS 803, kk. 9–13. White-collar workers, incidentally, continued to receive

Officials were caught unprepared by worker-consumers' vehement objections. The strikers won all their major demands, costing the state a great deal of money. The ministry withdrew the new wage tables, established an exchange rate of 150 zł per point, and agreed to pay for involuntary work interruptions; the textile industry returned paydays to the biweekly schedule. But this new pay system was also unsatisfactory to workers who knew the market well. Several factories struck in June, including the Horak mill, whose 3,500 workers (almost alone in Łódź) had not struck the previous month. Strikers claimed that their points were worth not 150 but 250 or even 300 zł on the free market (due in part to strong demand in response to their impending cancellation); the difference cost workers 1,690 zł monthly. When the industry changed the system in July to a fifteen-day pay schedule instead of biweekly, workers struck again. The new system meant they might be paid on a Saturday after stores were closed, which had happened the first time this system was applied. This made planning the family budget all the more difficult, and pay still more troublesome to calculate. While the confusion compared unfavorably with the prewar system, this tradition was also a matter of survival.[96]

These same strikes also revealed divisions based on skill and generation. The bonus system widened gaps between bonused and unbonused workers, between those who beat norms and those who could not. It favored experienced workers who, if their machines were in good shape, could meet the norms much more easily than those who were just beginning, and make twice as much money or more than the lowest-paid workers. With a large part of their wages depending on bonuses, the experienced workers did not have time to teach new workers and resented their drag on production. The weaver assigned to looms with an inexperienced new worker or the foreman whose team included a high proportion of trainees felt wronged by the system.[97] Their resentment grew in the fall of 1946, when a new agreement imposed tighter restrictions on bonuses and thus lowered the earning potential of the highest-

---

their pay monthly under the new system: ibid., kk. 191–93. Tram workers, meanwhile, again demanded "bonuses for those who carry the ones who earn bonuses." AAN MIiP 927, kk. 37–38.

[96] AAN MPiOS 803, kk. 12–13, 164; AAN KC PPR 295/IX/32, kk. 21–23, 41–43.

[97] AAN MPiOS 803, kk. 187–93; ŁAP WK PPS 22/XII/2, n.p. On resentment of the less skilled, see also ŁAP PZPB 1 (Scheibler and Grohman), 2, kk. 8–11.

paid workers. Indeed, it was not the poorest workers who struck. During a strike at the Biederman mill, known as a stronghold of veteran workers, the PPR secretary observed sarcastically that those who began the strike were among the best-paid workers at the factory, earning 8,000 zł or more per month. In another strike, assistant spinners and weavers were the first back to work, while their experienced colleagues stayed out longest. Grievances in a third strike centered on the lack of difference between the wages of a spinner and those of her assistant.[98] Money was not the only reason experienced workers struck. They were more likely than unskilled or inexperienced workers to remain at the same factory—in one sample 51 percent of experienced and 38 percent of unskilled workers worked at the Poznański mill for three years or more. This commitment to one workplace (often located near their homes) made a strike the most effective means of protest.[99]

The experienced workers were feared and distrusted by the bureaucracy. A PPR Central Committee inspector's description of relations at the Geyer mill, where prewar workers made up some 60 percent of a 4,000-strong work force, exposed the PPR's insecurity: "Prewar workers are in the main people who have their little houses with small gardens; before the war, they were specially chosen by the [factory] owners to keep the peace in the factories, as a calmer element, less hasty to strike. However, that group is now disposed toward the reaction[aries] and takes the lead in all conflicts, [though] it is very valuable in the area of production."[100] Most unreliable of all were foremen. Both the trainers of new workers and a link to the cadre of experienced workers, they maintained an ambiguous position between workers and management. They were potentially a powerful tool for the regime—if they could be won over. A PPR Central Committee emissary blamed foremen at the Poznański mill (only 23 of 123 belonged to either major party) for a 1946 strike: they were "a hostile element, reactionary through and through. . . . [They] sow unbelief among the workers and work on their opinions, stubbornly persuading workers that it was better before the war, etc." Yet factory directors had to retain veteran foremen for their

[98] ŁAP KŁ PPR 1/VI/141, k. 21; AAN MPiH 41, kk. 456–68; ŁAP KD PPR Górna-Prawa 1/VI/65, k. 52. Also AAN KC PPR 295/IX/32, kk. 41–43.
[99] N=322 experienced and 125 unskilled. At John, 15 percent of skilled workers and only 4 percent of unskilled remained for this time.
[100] AAN KC PPR 295/IX/32, kk. 24–27.

experience; they attempted instead to undermine foremen's authority by limiting their power to determine and award bonuses.[101]

A new threat loomed before management at the same time: young or inexperienced workers appear frequently in strike accounts from 1946–47. Senior PPR activists were likely to be from an urban, skilled-labor background; for them, *youth* was a synonym for volatility and unreliability. They saw young workers as either falling under the influence of experienced workers or exhibiting irreverence toward all authority. Some young workers had grown up in the worker neighborhoods of Łódź; those at the Geyer mill "live mostly with their parents; having the assurance of material assistance from them, they do not care too much about work and are also inclined to cause conflicts." As a result, explained a PPR inspector, the factory was run at a pace decidedly unsuitable for either rapid reconstruction or a plan-oriented schedule. Lack of discipline was evident in "unnecessary strolls from shop to shop, standing around in groups during work, early exit and late beginning of work." These workers tolerated theft and were aggressive in opposing perceived injustice. At another mill the same inspector noted that many young workers were from outside Łódź (*napływowi*): "This is a stormy element, difficult to control and direct. They lack conscientiousness in performing their work, subordination, and work discipline. Young [workers] are mostly interested in sport, poorly understand youth slogans, and perceive themselves as 'the future,' in a future where everything is allowed." On balance, labor officials in 1945–47 preferred stable older workers who could exert positive authority in the factory; the most dangerous combination would be a strike, such as one reported at the Biederman mill in 1947, in which "reactionary elements drew around themselves demoralized youth."[102]

The most intense conflicts within the Łódź labor community, however, were with opponents who had by 1945 virtually ceased to exist. The prewar city was as much Jewish or German as it was Polish. Łódź had the second-largest Jewish community in Poland, totaling one-third of the city's population in 1931. Although most Jews in interwar Poland were workers, in roughly the same percentages as the Poles, the Poles remembered only the Jewish factory owners. It was easier to forget the

[101]MSW MBP 17/IX/77, k. 73. Poznański: AAN KC PPR 295/IX/32, kk. 24–27, 41–43. ŁAP DPB 6, n.p.; AAN KC PPR 295/IX/32, kk. 31–35.

[102]AAN KC PPR 295/IX/32, kk. 17, 24–27, 30. Biederman: ŁAP KŁ PPR 1/V/141, k. 21; also AAN CKW PPS 235/XV/86, kk. 10–17. See also ŁAP KW PPR 1/XI/2, n.p.

thousands of Jewish workers and artisans who in Łódź generally lived in the Bałuty district on the north side of the city. The Germans, in turn, had been much more numerous before 1918: they were 21 percent of the city's population in 1897 (and had still been a plurality a few decades earlier) to the Jews' 29 percent and the Poles' 46 percent. In 1931, nearly 9 percent—more than 53,000—of the city's residents still claimed German as their first language. This community of course quickly revived and expanded during the Nazi occupation. Many of these Polish citizens signed the *Volksliste*, which essentially required everyone to choose a nationality and offered many Poles of German extraction the chance—for which they would pay dearly after 1945—to declare themselves German.[103]

Many scholars have noted the Polish paradox of national antagonisms in a nearly homogeneous country.[104] The reasons for this paradox are not hard to understand. World War II destroyed Poland's social structure, eliminating long-time political and economic foes whose presence had shaped Polish social identity. As I noted in the introduction, national conflict in Łódź before the war often reflected social tension. By 1946, there were only 24,300 Germans and 11,500 of other nationalities (including Jews) among almost 500,000 city residents.[105] Postwar national conflict in Łódź was a way for workers to fill the holes left behind. Because a new Polish nation was constructed simultaneously with a new type of state, the authorities used the same populist-nationalist rhetoric as did the workers. Poles relieved their frustrations related to the war and the rise of communism with ethnic antagonism, expressing nationalism through opposition rather than solidarity. In other words, society was re-creating the axes of its identity.

German obviously had a different meaning than it did in 1939—not just an "other" now but a traitor as well. Still, very few Germans were left; most worked as unskilled laborers in some of the larger factories

---

[103]Julian K. Janczak, "Ludność," in *Łódź: Dzieje miasta*, vol. 1: *do 1918r.*, ed. Bohdan Baranowski and Jan Fijalek (Warsaw, 1980), 219; *Drugi powszechny spis ludności z dn. 9.XII.1931 r. Miasto Łódź*, 14; Ludwik Mroczka, "Skład wyznaniowy i narodowościowy robotników łódzkich w latach 1918–1939," in *Polska klasa robotnicza: Studia historyczne*, vol. 7 (Warsaw, 1976), 396–416; Szyja Bronsztejn, *Ludność żydowska w Polsce w okresie międzywojennym: Studium statystyczne* (Wrocław, 1963).

[104]Michael Checinski, *Poland: Communism, Nationalism, Anti-Semitism* (New York, 1982); Krystyna Kersten, *Polacy, Żydzi, Komunizm: Anatomia półprawd, 1939–1968* (Warsaw, 1992).

[105]*RS 1948*, 21.

(as at Scheibler and Grohman, where four hundred young Germans worked in mid-1946) or as forced laborers (as at the John factory).[106] Workers used the popular fear of Germans to their advantage. They accused factory management of collaboration with the Nazis, of hiding a German background or a Gestapo or capitalist past. Authorities took these charges seriously and investigated them, although the accused was not always removed. For example, workers at PZPB No. 9 wrote to the district PPS committee to report a foreman who had threatened to turn them over to the Gestapo for laziness: "So we the undersigned would like to know if he is back in the occupation [period], when he smacked Poles in the face and sent them to Sikawa? No. We don't want such people, who strike at the interests of the working class, here in our society. . . . This matter should be examined to uncover whether citizen Bilecki carries out such work consciously and purposefully, and whether he is a tool of the reaction."[107] These workers had learned the new language of political conflict and sought to use it to resolve labor disputes. Strikers at the Hirszberg and Wilczyński garment factory struck successfully to demand the removal of a supervisor who, they said, had sped up the machines during the occupation, thus forcing workers to sew faster. Management agreed to replace him with a candidate proposed by the workers themselves.[108]

A citywide strike in Pabianice in late October 1945 showed how nation could substitute for other tensions. By applying new labels to their opponents, workers at the Krusche and Ender and Kindler mills gave wage and aprowizacja demands greater force. The initial sources of conflict were actually among workers (or at least consumers) reflecting the egalitarian impulses noted earlier: at Krusche and Ender, outrage that the Pabianice police had received much more coal for the winter than they had; at Kindler, news that Krusche and Ender workers had better pay and aprowizacja. Workers' statements revealed many varieties of class, sectional, and national injustice. But Kindler strikers were most vehement in their attacks on factory director Herman, whom they

---

[106] At Scheibler, Germans' easy jobs, reported a PPR inspector, "cause indignation among worker-Poles." AAN KC PPR 295/IX/32, k. 17. Internment camp at John: AAN MPiH 972, k. 45.

[107] Sikawa, near Łódź, was the site of a small labor camp during the war. ŁAP DK PPS Śródmieście-Prawa 29/XIII/1, n.p. Other examples include ARZ KCZZ WO 141, kk. 41, 53; ARZ KCZZ WO 125, k. 19; AAN CKW PPS 235/XXVI/5, k. 29; AAN KC PPR 295/X/5, k. 33.

[108] ŁAP WK PPS 22/XIV/41, cited in Stefaniuk, *Łódzka organizacja PPS*, 82.

claimed was a German and should be removed for the harm he had inflicted on Polish workers. At open meetings, they charged him with numerous irregularities and malicious wrongdoing: that he personally swindled them out of coal; that he stole the socks and sweaters intended as bonuses for workers who had defended the factory in the last days of the occupation; that his son-in-law was served meat cutlets from the factory kitchen. They claimed that Herman favored both Germans and Jews (nonworkers) over the workers. "How can you say things are OK," shouted a glazier, "when that Jew Bork was sold 2400 meters of [cloth], on which he made over 3 million złotys, and a Pole isn't even sold 100m?" Complained another: "Poles [must] push carts, while Germans are taught to work the looms."[109] Management, then, was cheating workers both as workers and as Poles. This was a national as well as an intensely local conflict in which defense of rights to fair norms and bonuses reflected prewar and wartime relations.

Jews were a much more promising scapegoat for economic and political problems in Łódź, which was one of the strongest centers of Polish antisemitism. Older workers and PPR worker-activists denounced the imagined privileged position of Jews in Łódź society. While such activists claimed not to be taken in by "reactionary anti-semites," they claimed that, of twenty thousand Jews supposedly now in Łódź, not one worked in a factory except as white-collar employees; that young Jews were content to collect welfare rather than go to work; that still others had taken shops or jobs away from Poles. Finally, they claimed that half the numbers of the Security Apparatus were Jews who sat behind desks while Polish communists—the "real" party members—did the hard work "with machine gun in hand." Another aspect of the "Jewish question" was that Jews seemed to exemplify the foreignness to Łódź of many new elites. Those whom the PPR called "the most old-fashioned" (but whose views many party activists tacitly accepted) saw a conspiracy: "50 thousand Jews have been brought to Łódź [and are] specially favored in aprowizacja."[110]

[109]ŁAP DPB 20, n.p.; ŁAP WK PPS 22/XIV/37; AAN MPiH 41, kk. 435–43. Herman, in response to the last charge, noted that the Germans were being trained for the night shift on which no Poles were willing to work. Note similar use of Germans in Wrocław in Chapter 3. German workers at the related Biederman strike played a different role: they were the first to return to work from the strike: k. 446.

[110]AAN KC PPR 295/IX/29, k. 27; AAN KC PPR 295/X/5, kk. 99–102; ŁAP KW PPR 1/XI/2. See also AAN MIiP 82, kk. 5, 10.

In the factory itself, workers portrayed Jews both as shirkers and as oppressors. At Scheibler and Grohman, workers claimed that they had welcomed as colleagues Jewish workers in May 1945, but that of 120 Jews, only three remained one year later. According to a report sympathetic to such resentments, "the worker wants to see the Jew around him, but as a worker, not as a director. He says that there are still plenty of Poles to be made directors. The worker is outraged that all higher positions are taken by Jews who steal and then escape with the money abroad."[111] At the Biederman mill (known before the war for its strongly religious and "backward" work force), workers struck in June 1945 to protest the appointment of an engineer of Jewish background as factory director. The strike lasted for two and a half days, with only one demand: "we don't want a Jew-director." When Łódź trade union leader Aleksander Burski asked that party members at least return to work, they called him a "Jewish Wojtek" (a Polonized Jew). Meanwhile, a half-hour strike broke out at another factory over a similar issue, and conflict threatened a third.[112]

Whether desperate for worker support or reflecting common attitudes, party-member labor activists often took an active part in such conflicts and rumor spreading. In 1945, antisemitic incidents or statements appeared to express memories of prewar antagonisms. Thus, workers envisioned Jews (or Germans) primarily as economic exploiters— management or shopkeepers. They were not yet expressing as antisemitism hatred of the communists; attacks on Jews in 1945 at no time referred to the PPR, which for some would soon be synonymous with a Jewish conspiracy to control Poland. Neither the labor parties nor the state were cast as opponents in these strikes, nor in the Pabianice strikes in October (although PPR leadership opposed and organized against the strikes). Party-member workers, meanwhile, still played roles contained within the prewar labor culture of the city. Beginning in mid-1946, however, the party initiated a series of political conflicts that effectively excluded it from the Łódź labor community and broke open the limits imposed by working-class community traditions.

---

[111]AAN KC PPR 295/IX/32, k. 17.
[112]ŁAP KW PPR 1/XI/2, n.p. The protest was apparently successful in changing the director to workers' satisfaction: AAN KC PPR 295/X/5, k. 102. See also a threatened strike reported by an underground group: *Polska Walczy* 8 June 1945 (MSW MBP 41/229).

National Politics and Confrontation in the Factory

The PPR hoped to harness worker dissatisfaction by creating new targets to replace the traditional worker-management opposition. One such target was private industry—thus the reprivatization strikes mentioned previously, and the campaigns discussed in Chapter 4. Another was the armed underground. Clashes with the underground made effective propaganda and occasions for many resolutions and speeches in factories, as when four workers from a Łódź factory were murdered, ostensibly by members of an underground army, while en route to Silesia to get coal for their colleagues in September 1945.[113]

PPR leaders persisted in seeing the factory as a potential hotbed of anticommunist agitation. Yet while armed conflict continued through at least 1946 in the Łódź-Kielce region, (both during and after the war a major site of partisan resistance), this conflict was less evident in the city of Łódź itself. In one rare example, PPR officials in two factories reported that workers were passing stolen clothing and fabric to "the forest"—that is, to anticommunist partisans.[114] This artificial resuscitation of the class struggle, the PPR's raison d'être, was an attempt to deflect attention from the fact that the party itself now occupied the position of the prewar capitalist elite. The rhetoric of ongoing revolution was, of course, a precursor of the stalinist rhetoric of vigilance that emerged in 1948. It had the opposite effect: workers instead began to perceive the PPR and the state as their opponents, and responded to these threats to factory and community by shifting their demands from management to the party and the state.

Łódź saw its first political disturbances when the referendum campaign intensified. The first peacetime celebration of the labor holiday, 1 May 1946, became an important occasion for the state and the PPR to agitate in support of the three referendum questions. Some 200,000 people took part in or watched the May Day parade in Łódź, which stretched six kilometers and lasted for four hours. Factories spent lavishly on the parade, constructing floats on which workers "performed their normal work" on looms, printing presses, and lathes. One display, featuring bricklayers building a wall, carried the slogan: "Polish workers

---

[113]See ŁAP WUliP 29, n.p.

[114]There was no evidence to support this charge; it more likely reflected party distrust of older workers. ŁAP KŁ PPR 1/VI/141, kk. 12, 14. For political labeling of conflict, see, for example, AAN KC PPR 295/IX/29, k. 49; AAN MIiP 298, k. 52.

and peasants build up from its foundations the house of People's Poland."[115]

This impressive symbol of the importance of the worker in the new Poland—and also of the money and supplies the state and the factories really did have at their disposal—was followed two days later by an opposing political message. On the 3 May anniversary of the 1791 Constitution, students (mostly PPS members) of Łódź University, which had opened for the first time that year, organized an unofficial parade. Their shouted slogans were quickly met by a counterdemonstration that denounced the marchers as fascists. The efforts of the police to break up the demonstration resulted in two people wounded and seventeen arrested. The next day, the parties and unions organized meetings to protest the students' behavior.[116] While this protest may have been confined to students, the tension in the city—indeed, throughout the country—was not. Protesting workers never mentioned the politics of the referendum campaign nor the arrests of opposition activists. But the politically charged atmosphere, the state's evident weakness on economic and social welfare issues, and its apparent leniency toward recent strikes encouraged workers to oppose the regime.

The regime's worst fears were confirmed by a citywide strike that began the same week. Groups of students gathered at factory gates to agitate for the strike and issued leaflets calling for strikes at high schools and the university; three-quarters of the high schools struck. Partisan political conflict appeared for the first and last time in the factory. The PSL (with PPS support) made an unsuccessful attempt to register a party circle at the Łódź electric plant. Tram workers applauded Mikołajczyk's name and whistled down the communists. At Scheibler and Grohman, a courier was intercepted smuggling a strike fund into the factory; strikers sent a letter to PSL leader Stanisław Bańczyk. This strike was considered so threatening that three top PPR leaders—Gomułka, Minc, and Witaszewski—came to speak at the factory shortly before the referendum.[117]

After the 30 June referendum, with the parliamentary elections next

---

[115]AAN MIiP 804, kk. 74–75. May 1 did not become an official holiday until 1950.

[116]Ibid., k. 80. Note an earlier event with similar characteristics: the funeral of a student found murdered in a Łódź park in December 1945 apparently turned into a student demonstration with unspecified echoes in the factories. AAN MIiP 927, k. 5.

[117]AAN MIiP 927, kk. 37–38, 42; AAN MPiOS 803, k. 11; AAN KC PPR 295/IX/32, kk. 10, 12, 22.

on the political horizon, tensions only increased. They reached a boiling point with the pogrom of 4 July 1946 in which forty-two Jewish residents of one building in the city of Kielce were murdered by a crowd.[118] The politics surrounding the pogrom, which some people claim was a PPR-UB provocation intended to direct attention away from the fraudulent results of the referendum, were complicated indeed and may never be fully unraveled. If the PPR had encouraged such action, it was also quick to condemn it and, as was standard practice, organized worker demonstrations to protest the work of reactionary forces. Between 8 and 11 July, labor leaders called meetings in many factories to condemn the pogrom. They prepared resolutions and invited workers to sign them. The meetings themselves passed without incident, but few workers cooperated. In the Łódź thread factory, "the assembly accepted the proposed resolution indifferently and calmly, but supposedly [only] a small number of workers signed it." Only one shop in Scheibler and Grohman agreed to the resolution, and only some PPR members signed it. The next day, however, the daily newspaper of the Łódź PPR reported "in large type" that the workers at these and other factories had approved resolutions and demanded the death penalty for those found guilty of the pogrom. This attempt to propagandize the incident backfired, arousing workers' antisemitism and politicizing it by turning it toward the government and the PPR. Workers began to perceive the PPR and the government as "Jewish" in their opposition to the workers. When workers saw this report, strikes broke out at nearly a dozen factories, mostly cotton mills and sewing shops. The strikes' connection to the Kielce tragedy was clear; in one factory, there was even a spurious phone call informing workers that all of Kielce was on strike and asking for Łódź's support.[119]

Although the strikes lasted only an hour or so, PPR observers were taken by surprise at their vehemence. When the PPR secretary in one factory attempted to oppose the strikers, she was beaten by several of them. Warned a Central Committee report: "The situation in Łódź is serious, as evidenced by the mood among strikers, the strikes' swift leaps from factory to factory, and the aggression of striking women in all factories; they clawed and screamed ferociously. Slogans of revenge

---

[118]Bożena Szaynok, *Pogrom Żydów w Kielcach 4 lipca 1946* (Warsaw, 1992); Kersten, *Polacy, Żydzi, Komunizm*, 89–142.

[119]AAN KC PPR 295/IX/32, kk. 13–15, 23; AAN MIiP 927, k. 48; ŁAP WK PPS 22/XII/2, n.p.

and terror from the moment of execution [of the convicted killers of Kielce] were heard in the shops. [They] compare the alacrity of the Kielce trial with that of Greiser, who is still alive, though he is guilty of so many millions of victims.[120] Striking workers use such anti-semitic arguments as 'A pregnant Jew gets sixty thousand złotys, and what do I have?' [or] ... 'Why don't Jews work in factory shops? Po-land is ruled by Jews.' " Łódź Jews described a "pogrom atmosphere" in the city; there were rumors, for example, that Jews in the Bałuty district (a large worker district and the location of the Jewish ghetto during the war) had murdered a Polish child. While the strikes them-selves were easily broken up once the workers had made their demand (usually that a retraction be printed in the newspaper) the hostility lin-gered long after. The sentencing of the pogrom leaders sparked more protests.[121]

With the referendum and the changes in wage policy of that summer, the Kielce pogrom was a turning point in Łódź workers' perception of the government and the PPR. Workers made connections between the pogrom and the lowering of their wages in the recent collective agree-ment. At the John metalworks, which did not strike, the PPR secretary reported antisemitic agitation against bookkeeper Jung, a PPR member; in this way, workers linked the party, the Jews, and their low wages. But national association was indiscriminate; workers could also call PPR members "Gestapo" and *Volksdeutsche*, appellations unlikely a few months before.[122]

Hoping to deflect further unrest, the textile industry introduced on 15 September a new collective agreement that eliminated bonuses-in-kind and set the basic wage roughly equal to the previous earnings (including bonuses) of a worker who was producing at between 120 and 140 per-cent of norm under the old system. Now even workers unable to meet norms (20 to 25 percent completed no more than 110 percent of still relatively low norms) could earn a sufficient amount of money, and all could calculate their wages with greater ease. Nevertheless, this agree-

[120]Artur Greiser, commander of the Warthegau (the Polish lands annexed to the Reich) during the occupation. Greiser had not yet been executed, and workers clearly feared that his trial had only been for show.

[121]AAN KC PPR 295/IX/32, kk. 13–15. Jewish leaders in Łódź received reports of a planned pogrom in the Bałuty district and were able to prevent it. Information from Hen-ryk Szpigiel.

[122]ŁAP KD PPR Górna-Prawa 1/VI/65, kk. 32–33; AAN KC PPR 295/IX/32, kk. 44–46.

ment was also welcomed with a new wave of strikes, caused mostly by confusion over the new system and frequent errors by payroll departments. There were ten textile strikes in late September and at least seventeen in October, several as long as a week.[123]

To management, the October strikes, like those in May, seemed suspiciously organized. Workers at the Geyer mill (also a center of protest in May), disgruntled about poor raw materials that made meeting norms difficult, stopped work on Thursday, 17 October, after they received their second paycheck under the new collective agreement. Three other factories in the neighborhood struck the same day and two more on Friday. Strikers at Geyer told each other to hold out to the following Thursday when workers at nearby Scheibler and Grohman would be paid. Indeed, the strike was broken when workers heard that payday at Scheibler and Grohman had passed without incident. These strikes, marked by increased alienation between workers and their supposed representatives, reflected a deepening social and political conflict. Strikers refused to accept their factory councils (which seemed more like management to them) as negotiators on their behalf, or even struck to demand dissolution of their councils. They took advantage of the apparent weakness of management and labor institutions alike. At Geyer, some strikers claimed to fear that they would be beaten if they returned to work; local PPR leaders blamed PSL supporters. The strike at Gampe and Albrecht was a wild, angry protest. Frustrated strikers offered no delegation or strike committee and, at a meeting with the regional union leader Burski, offered no demands except one young woman's statement that "we don't want such a Poland." When a union representative asked for specific demands, strikers shouted that he should not pretend because everyone knew the strike's purpose. They then demonstrated before Geyer's gates, blocking workers from entering the factory. In retaliation, management arranged to blacklist all fired strikers to prevent the spread of discontent to other factories.[124]

Strikes virtually ceased in Łódź over the harsh winter of 1946–47; the

[123]There were also strikes in the mills of Lower Silesia at the same time. ARZ KCZZ WO 292, kk. 8–9; ŁAP KŁ PPR 1/XI/15, kk. 22, 93; ARZ KCZZ WE, uncataloged materials; ŁAP KŁ PPR 1/XI/2, k. 1; AAN KC PPR 295/XIII/18. See also Stefan Ciesielski, "Nastroje polityczne wśród robotników w Polsce w latach 1945–1946 (w świetle dokumentów Polskiej Partii Robotniczej)," *Dzieje Najnowsze* 21, no. 1 (1989): 118–20.

[124]AAN MPiH 41, kk. 456–58; ŁAP KD PPR Górna-Prawa 1/VI/65, k. 52. See also AAN KC PPR 295/XI/10, kk. 42–43. Related protests continued into November: see ŁAP WUIiP 32, kk. 8–9.

search for food and fuel left little time for protests. The labor conflict that reemerged in the spring and summer of 1947 was sharper and more politicized than before. As the influence of the PPR and the government became more evident in collective agreements, aprowizacja, wages, prices, and conflict management, the workers' anger became fiercer. Until now, the government's response to strikes had been to adjust the system and tighten its controls, which seemed only to heighten workers' perception of the government as in the enemy camp. The parliamentary election of January 1947 further separated workers and the state. Workers expected that the campaign would bring some improvements in their lives: they wondered "why the *aprowizacja* department had relatively rich supplies for workers at its disposal before the referendum, and now before the election has nothing but canned blood sausage." At a meeting at Krusche and Ender, agitators from the army and the PPS were drowned out by shouts for sugar and meat; no one took up the cheer "Long Live the Democratic Republic."[125] Given this reception, the PPR Central Committee reacted with alarm when the local PPR paper called on workers to double the established contribution to the national reconstruction fund. Party leaders reminded their Łódź colleagues that they had "set such [contribution] norms for the working class as would not pose a serious material burden nor provoke a worsening of moods in the pre-election period. In such conditions, [this] initiative can only cause a decline in Party popularity."[126]

Rather than easing the tension between workers and the state, the relative economic and political stabilization in early 1947 actually intensified conflict. Poland's leaders hoped their election victory and the new three-year plan would give them greater authority; the workers, however, now realized that the state was directly responsibility for working and living conditions. While they used the imagery of class conflict, workers were often imprecise about their enemy. Sometimes it was the government or political parties, other times a nameless "they," still other times speculators or swindlers; often, it seems, all three were the same. A May 1947 meeting of textile industry factory council representatives explored these links. Discussing the need for factory child care, speakers focused on the old magnates' mansions now occupied by new factory

<hr />

[125]ŁAP WUliP 31, n.p.; AAN KC PPR 295/IV/17, kk. 24–26; ŁAP WUliP 33, n.p.

[126]AAN KC PPR 295/VII/5, n.p. The secretariat called for a reprimand of those responsible and for a special meeting of the Łódź PPR to explain such a "leftish [*lewackie*] and sectarian" view.

management or by those who could afford them and had the right connections: "The palaces are occupied by people alien to us"; "They're making nightspots out of the palaces, while there aren't enough nurseries and kindergartens." One speaker drew another conclusion: "Most of all, the State is a speculator, since it raises the prices of some things by itself."[127] When 1,300 Łódź railway workers packed a union hall in February 1947, they angrily blamed working conditions on the regime. "Democracy," they argued, ridiculing the regime's own language, "is no blessing, but the cause of evil and injustice." They had been the first, they said, to join the struggle to rebuild Poland; but now, even though they were praised in the press, they were treated like "white niggers." While these complaints echoed those of 1945, workers now specifically blamed the state and its economic policies.[128]

Conflict within the factory bore evidence of a revival of prewar labor organization. PPR and UB observers noted with alarm instances of PPS or union support for strikers. In one strike in June, the Łódź Province PPR Committee alleged that factory PPS leaders obtained approval for the strike from PPS provincial headquarters, spoke on workers' behalf, and even picketed the factory gates encouraging workers not to return to work. The PPR demanded that the PPS expel these members from their party. Rumors of an impending fierce political battle spread among workers—for example, that the PPR and PPS had fought an armed battle in the city of Żyrardów leaving seven dead. Stanisław Mikołajczyk's assessment of the PPR's plight seems accurate: "Łódź after all is the cradle of the proletariat, yet even so the [government] bloc feared its own people and invalidated the PSL list there. So on whom can the PPR depend?"[129]

Neither the PPR nor management controlled the Łódź factory. While political stabilization allowed the PPR and labor organizations to become more aggressive in enforcing labor discipline and unity, they were not ready for such a role. Their inexperience, combined with their increased willingness to oppose workers, helped to fan the flames of frustration and discontent and sharpened the language of class conflict. The

[127] AAN KC PPR 295/XIII/7, k. 99.

[128] ŁAP WRZZ, 64, k. 1.

[129] AAN KC PPR 295/IX/436, k. 6. MSW MBP 17/IX/38, t. 1, n.p. (July 1947); MSW MBP 17/IX/103, t. 1, n.p. (April 1947). Other examples of interparty conflict include: ŁAP KŁ PPR 1/VI/141, k. 25; and AAN KC PPR 295/XI/49, k. 22. Other sources on strikes in the first half of 1947 include AAN KC PPR 295/XIII/18, kk. 93, 142; ŁAP CZPW 446, n.p.; and ŁAP KŁ PPR 1/XI/4, n.p.

disparate issues that motivated unrest crystallized in the late summer of 1947 into a larger conflict clearly embedded in national politics as well: the battle over multi-machine work. In this battle, the clearest articulation of the Łódź workers' moral economy, workers would defend both work process and their community traditions.

The Struggle over Control of Production and the Poznański Strike

The new three-year plan put additional pressure on the antiquated textile industry, still largely operating according to prewar production norms and methods.[130] As the huge mills expanded, renovating war-damaged production lines and starting night shifts, the industry sought new methods to help meet plan targets. The textile industry, with labor processes easier for unskilled labor to master, was an ideal target for a speedup of production. In the summer of 1947, the textile industry began to increase mechanization of weaving and spinning by forcing workers to work at more looms or spinning sides.[131] At first, these changes lacked ideological focus and were haphazardly organized. Management emphasized the economic reasons for the change; they tried directives and work rules, as opposed to propaganda and education, to encourage weavers and spinners to switch to a higher number of machines. Only in July did the Łódź PPR organization start a propaganda campaign to encourage individual, voluntary transition to multimachine work.[132] Elevated to the status of a political movement, it was christened *wielowarsztatowość* (multimachine work).

Unlike the administrative task of setting piece rates or norms, production campaigns—of which wielowarsztatowość was only the first—

---

[130]Much of the machinery at the Scheibler and Grohman mill had been purchased in the 1920s, and a substantial portion, including most or all of the machinery in some shops, dated from before World War I, even from the 1890s. Puś and Pytlas, *Dzieje*, 231–35. Information about the physical layout of the mills in 1947 is scarce; they were probably similar to those in the Soviet Union in the 1920s described in Chris Ward, *Russia's Cotton Workers and the New Economic Policy: Shop-Floor Culture and State Policy, 1921–1929* (Cambridge, U.K., 1990), 59–88.

[131]Before 1947 only a few participants in early labor competitions or selected workers in more modern factories worked on more than two spinning sides or more than four looms. ARZ KCZZ WO 125, k. 38; ARZ KCZZ WO 141, k. 10.

[132]AAN KC PPR 295/XIII/18, k. 215.

had ideological as well as economic aims. Competition and labor speed-ups required promoters—"transmission belts" in stalinist parlance. Thus, they unmasked the previously ambiguous roles of ostensibly labor organizations, bringing them explicitly into industrial discourse and on to the shop floor and putting pressure on trade unions to act as propagandists, not labor advocates. This change, much more than the organizational subordination of factory councils and trade unions discussed previously, ended the ambiguous position of those bodies.

Communist observers interpreted the violent strikes that this campaign provoked as due to poor organization by the party and provincial officials who had planned the campaign.[133] This explanation fails to appreciate the implications of the change for working-class identity and power. The factory relations with which workers were familiar had come under vigorous attack from a newly productivist state. Workers were being asked to give up hard-won victories; the new work rules ran counter to labor traditions. "Once [before the war] our class fought [for the right] not to work on more machines or spools," shouted a striking PPR-member worker at the Stolarów mill, "and today the state preys upon the working class."[134]

Multimachine work significantly expanded work space: three or four sides meant that a second aisle of spindles had to be watched, so a spinner could not possibly keep an eye on all her work at once. Increased mechanization heightened anxiety and physical exhaustion, and workers were alarmed by the proposed changes. Most threatening of all, some workers—those too old or methodical to adapt to faster work methods—became unnecessary as production sped up. "A bitter mood can be noticed everywhere," reported the PPR in April, "and the layoffs are the reason for this." Management used layoffs as a weapon: "workers who have been in a particular factory for thirty or forty years are being dismissed."[135] Factory administrators also began to promote a ten-hour day, with eight hours on Saturday and four on Sunday. When workers

[133]Helena Gnatowska, "Strajki w Polsce Ludowej w latach 1945–1947 w świetle dokumentów PPR," *Z Pola Walki*, no. 3 (1985): 110–11. See AAN KC PPR 295/XIII/18, k. 215; AAN KC PPR 295/IX/33, k. 2; AAN MPiOS 749, n.p.

[134]AAN KC PPR 295/IX/33, kk. 132–34; also kk. 1, 14. On the prewar struggle with rationalization, see Laura Crago, "Nationalism, Religion, Citizenship, and Work in the Development of the Polish Working Class and the Polish Trade Union Movement, 1815–1929: A Comparative Study of Russian Poland's Textile Workers and Upper Silesian Miners and Metalworkers," (diss., Yale University, 1993), chap. 7.

[135]ŁAP KŁ PPR 1/XI/4, n.p. Also AAN KC PPR 295/XIII/18, k. 124.

resisted, the PPS opposed the plan, followed by the PPR; trade union head Aleksander Burski condemned "fanatical" directors and "reactionary rumors." Nevertheless, the days of more work for the same money were clearly ahead: workers were asked to donate one free Sunday to work for the rebuilding of Warsaw.[136]

As the ruling institutions in Łódź joined together, so, too, the working class coalesced in a new way as younger workers entering the factories from rural areas supported their senior colleagues in resisting new work norms and practices. The result was the great strike of September 1947. Although the strike ultimately failed and brought increased state repression, it showed the labor community at the peak of its strength in communist Poland. Expressing their right to protest and their understanding of the workplace, the textile workers of Łódź forced a rethinking of communist policy.

On Friday morning, 12 September 1947, the spinners in one narrow-gauge shop at the Poznański mill shut off their machines. Over the following week, the strike spread to the rest of the factory and then to the rest of the Łódź cotton industry. By the time the last strikers went back to work on 25 September, some 40 percent of the city's workers, all in textiles or clothing, had struck in at least twenty factories.[137] The I.K. Poznański cotton mill (PZPB No. 2) had always been a center of labor conflict; it was the second largest textile mill in Poland, with approximately 6,500 employees compared to the 10,000 at Scheibler and Grohman. By 1947, its work force was a mix of experienced operatives, urban women new to the factory, and the first arrivals from the countryside. Party leaders considered it hostile territory: the religious devotion of its workers before the war had earned it the nickname "Częstochowa" from the site of Polish Catholicism's holiest shrine. Poznański was the focal point of a powerful community linking factory, home—especially the three-story brick tenements (*famułki*) across the street—and church.[138]

[136]ŁAP WK PPS, 22/XII/2, n.p.; Jaime Reynolds, "Communists, Socialists, and Workers: Poland, 1944-1948," *Soviet Studies* 30, no. 4 (1978): 530.

[137]Of approximately 105,000 workers in the city, 96,600 of whom worked in the textile industry (*RS 1948*, 166), about 40,000 were on strike at any one time. The highest official estimate was 26,000 (of 42,000) at seventeen factories on Saturday, 20 September. AAN CKW PPS 235/XV/86, kk. 33–34. This estimate seems, however, to omit brief stoppages and those workers who were mobilized to work but could not due to locked gates, shut-off turbines, or fear.

[138]AAN KC PPR 295/IX/33, k. 15. See also remarks by Łódź PPR leader Ignacy Loga-Sowiński at a KC PPR plenum shortly after the strike: "Stenogram Plenarnego Posiedzenia

I. K. Poznański mill, Ogrodowa Street, Łódź, 1930. Katedra Etnografii, Uniwersytet Łódzki.

The strike began with a conflict over work space.[139] Having recruited eight 'enthusiast' spinners to begin working on four sides (eight spools), factory management designated the best-lit and best-equipped shop in the factory for the volunteers' exclusive use. When management announced that all workers presently in that shop would be moved else-

---

Komitetu Centralnego PPR 11 października 1947r.," *ARR*, 11:295. Three churches are close to the factory; one, St. Joseph's, is directly adjacent to the *famułki* and was a focal point of opposition in the 1970s. The Church, however, played no role in the strike. Interview with a former priest at St. Joseph's Church, May 1990.

[139]This account is derived from these sources: AAN KC PPR 295/IX/33, kk. 1–3, 6–8, 11–14; AAN KC PPR 295/XIII/18, kk. 215–20; AAN KC PPR 295/XI/49, kk. 54–56; AAN CKW PPS 235/XV/86, k. 38; MSW MBP 17/IX/77, t. 2, n.p. See Padraic Kenney, "Working-Class Community and Resistance in Pre-Stalinist Poland: the Poznański Textile Strike, Łódź, September 1947," *Social History* 18 (January 1993): 31–51.

where, the affected workers refused to move; a crowd of angry spinners attacked the volunteers and forced them to quit work. The protesters feared that they would be transferred to poorer machines, limiting their ability to meet norms and maintain their wages, while a few women would now make substantially more. Some women were told they would lose their assistants as well. Workers were naturally suspicious of the term *volunteer*, which they (correctly) believed to be a prelude to more universal pressure to join the campaign. They claimed that these volunteers (whose eagerness was doubtful; only two dared to show up for their new duties on 13 September) would soon receive special treatment, while the rest of the workers would be forced to switch anyway.

The issue was not so much the specific change in labor process but control of that change and the labor process itself. Workers sought control of their work space, wages, and jobs. The physical connection between control and political and economic power was demonstrated when Kozłowski, Poznański's PPR secretary, switched on a set of forty looms in an attempt to convince weavers to return to work. It was the weaver's job to switch on her machine; Kozłowski's hand on the switch usurped that right, just as his party and factory management sought to force workers onto more machines. A group of weavers tried to attack Kozłowski in a crowd, shouting, "That's the one who started the looms!"[140] Workers displaced at Poznański and elsewhere walked among the shops to spread this news, thus marking the factory as a free territory. At the Horak mill, they raised the slogan "Each spinner must work on her own machine, since she is responsible for it." Sitting by one's machine, claiming it as one's own even when it was not running, was a way to make this point.[141]

The idea of physical control, also evident in the practice of the strike and in methods of strike breaking, was clearly gendered. While male workers in the metal factories or on the railroads, having rebuilt their workplaces themselves, expressed control of their entire environment, the women of the textile industry did not control the factory in the same way. Striking women did not occupy the factory around the clock; at the end of their shift or at the end of the day, they left the factory and

[140]ANN KC PPR 295/IX/33, k. 8.

[141]AAN KC PPR 295/XIII/5, kk. 11–12; MSW MBP 17/IX/38, t. 1, n.p. See also an earlier conflict at Poznański, when management ordered workers to begin work one-half hour earlier. In response, workers arrived at the earlier time and stood by their machines, waiting for the usual hour before beginning work. AAN KC PPR 295/IX/33, k. 7.

returned to their families. Their factory was a part of their life environment, and they could go to work without working; in other words, going
to the factory was a legitimate activity separate from the work performed—as much a part of their lives as the domestic duties that called
them home. This treatment of their workplace represented an even closer
relationship to the factory than that among male workers, for it disas-
sociated the workplace from work itself, unlike the male occupation of
a factory, which cut clear boundaries between the world of work and
the world outside. Women's labor culture encompassed their factory as
well as their home and their church.

When they left the factory, the women ceded control to management,
which could and did lock them out; eventually, this practice helped management and the PPR break the strikes. The preferred method of forcing
strikers back to work was to allow entry only upon signing a document
agreeing to return to work; this individual confrontation with workers
as they arrived was an effective challenge to the practice of occupying
the factory. Management could also use control of the machinery temporarily ceded by the workers to break the strike. At Scheibler and Grohman, several dozen trusted PPR members and foremen from both shifts
were assembled in a weaving shop at 4:30 A.M., an hour before the first
shift was to start. They spread out among the shops and began to work
with all the looms switched on. As workers arrived, they saw their workshops under control and in operation. In this way they were forced to
work because occupation would clearly be ineffective. By 5:30, about
one hundred workers had returned to work—enough to force the re-
mainder to work as well. Similarly, when the second shift began to waver
at the Barlicki mill, managers and foremen began to enter the factory to
start up the machines.[142]

Strikers' defensive attitudes toward pay reflected the moral economy
described previously. The only way to earn more through the piece-rate
system was to work more machines; by moving from two to four sides,
a spinner's monthly wages could rise from 5,000 to 12,000 zł, and a
weaver's wages, by a similar proportion. The experiences of workers at
other factories bore out this prediction. Yet the workers at the Poznański
factory were not convinced. "You can't fool us," they shouted. "We
know what this stinks of. You want to raise our wages temporarily, then

---

[142] AAN KC PPR 295/IX/33, kk. 97, 77. Another example, from PZPB no. 3: "I didn't
switch on my machine because I feared the others. Only when the foremen turned them
on did I go back to work" (kk. 104–5).

you'll cut them again."[143] While the UB pointed angrily to the lack of economic demands as proof of the strike's reactionary character, the strike was, in fact, economic: strikers felt that certainty about wages and control over the way they might increase were preferable to risk and incentive. They recognized that opening the door to new ways of increasing wages would destroy the relative equality that the present system maintained.

Finally, the issue of job security was central to this strike. Although the women in the spinning shop were only to be moved, that move cut their ties to their workshop and machine. It was easy enough to figure out that if more workers were switched to more sides or looms, many would have to switch to the night shift, as the administration at Poznański threatened, or even lose their jobs. Work at the same machine during normal hours improved wages and fostered a sense of security; work at a night shift or in a new production line was threatening. True, as one observer pointed out, "if we were to evaluate the incident at Poznański as [due to] fear of losing jobs, we would be mistaken; there are placards posted everywhere [saying]: 'Such and such a number of weavers are needed.' "[144] Yet women who had worked in the same factory all their lives, or who had lived nearby while their fathers and husbands went to work, had developed rhythms connected to their workplace and machine. Although finding a new job farther away was daunting, a move within the factory, away from one's own machine, might seem just as threatening.

Poznański's management stood firm, demanding that the spinners sign a pledge to accept the reorganization, and locked them out when they refused to sign. Encouraged by crowds gathered before the factory gates, the weaving shops (where some fifteen weavers had been working six looms since early August) joined the strike; by the fourth day, the strike spread to the entire factory. The strike by this time was well known across the city; hundreds gathered before the factory gates. When management tried a new tactic, allowing workers gradually back into the factory, the workers did not return to work but instead "wandered about." They were ready to return to work under the old conditions, plus full pay for the missed days, but these demands were unlikely to be met. As the PPR City Committee explained, "either we retreat, which will shake the multimachine movement and labor competition as well, or we break the resistance of back-

[143]Ibid., k. 20.
[144]Ibid., k. 142; AAN KC PPR 295/XIII/5, k. 12.

ward elements, organized and aroused by hostile elements."[145] Having long since lost their credibility, party, union, and factory council leaders were unable to find a common language with the workers. Siemiatycki, a long-time PPR activist in Łódź and an instructor in the trade union apparatus, subjected his party to scathing criticism after the strike: "Party committee secretaries in the factories have no authority; they are errand-boys, not co-managers. . . . There is no self-criticism, only praise, and people see the shortcomings and laugh."[146]

On the fifth day, the authorities began a new offensive. Management singled out ten unidentified leaders and announced they would be fired. The PPR, meanwhile, tried a tactic that had been used to great effect over the past two years. So far, other workers had been able to keep party-member workers from breaking the strike, but now trucks from PPR headquarters rounded up Poznański's PPR members from their homes in the middle of the night. They were brought to party headquarters where they were coached on their duties, then transported to the factory gates for the first shift. The plan backfired; the rumor mill quickly interpreted the roundup as mass arrests.

That same day, a local PPR activist and former member of Poznański's factory council came to the mill to agitate; surrounded by angry workers, he struck or pushed one. In the ensuing confusion some twenty-seven women staged a mass fainting—as PPR investigators suggested, probably simulated. This moment of unusual leadership electrified the strike. The women who fainted defused a tense situation, turning attention to reviving the "unconscious" women. At the same time, fainting had the effect of magnifying the incident, lending an aura of mass violence to what may have been a slap on the cheek. Fainting also asserted control of factory space by demonstrating workers' right to do as they pleased at their factory, even to lie unconscious. Finally, it expressed opposition to the intrusion of an unpopular outsider into the factory and the conflict and implied that all these women were victims. Indeed, someone obligingly called for an unnecessary ambulance, others spread the news throughout the factory, and the rumors began. By the end of the next day, stories of a pregnant woman kicked and one to four women killed had spread across the city. The following day at least six more factories struck, and on 20 September eighteen factories stood still, all expressing

[145] AAN KC PPR 295/XIII/18, k. 217.
[146] AAN KC PPR 295/IX/33, k. 142.

their solidarity with the women of Poznański. Railway workers conveyed news and rumors about the strike across Poland.[147]

The Poznański mill became the symbolic center of the citywide strike, and the events of the next days revealed just how strong and solidaristic the labor community could be. Colonel Józef Kratko of the UB later admitted that there should have been informers not just in the factories but in Poznański's tenements, "where more matters were decided than in the factory."[148] In most factories, the initial protest in support of Poznański quickly spawned other demands; while some demanded increased wages or better living conditions, the two main demands concerned multimachine work—even in factories where it had been successfully introduced—and support for the workers of Poznański.

Workers refused to trust the word of the PPR or management. Strikers at several factories demanded that a delegation of workers be sent to Poznański to verify the rumors of murdered women and find out whether workers had returned to their jobs. At Biederman, the delegation reported that "the women at Poznański begged us on their knees to support their strike."[149] The delegation did not dispute rumors of arrests and beatings, and workers at Biederman asserted they would only go back to work when Poznański did. In a city where rumors spread so quickly, everyone undoubtedly knew whether or not Poznański was still striking. Yet at the Dowborczyków section of the Eitingon mill, a delegation to Poznański was the only demand workers made. "It is obvious," commented the personnel director, "that no one could agree to that idea."[150] The workers and the authorities understood each other well. Workers advanced a seemingly innocuous demand, and their opponents unhesitatingly rejected it. For workers were asking for much more than a delegation; they were asking for the right to organize and communicate beyond the organizations set up for them. In demanding delegations, the textile workers emphasized their identity with a labor community and their wish to control and organize that community.

---

[147] MSW MBP 17/IX/77, t. 2, n.p. There were faintings at other factories: AAN KC PPR 295/XIII/18, k. 217.

[148] MSW MBP 17/IX/77, t. 2, n.p. Kratko added: "Poznański workers go in groups [on pilgrimages] to Częstochowa and are ideologically strongly tied to one another." The means by which rumors spread can only be guessed at; markets probably played an important role. At the Geyer mill, one worker explained that they were on strike "because their boarders had not gone to work." AAN KC PPR 295/IX/33, k. 111.

[149] AAN CKW PPS 235/XV/86, k. 30; also AAN KC PPR 295/IX/33, k. 3-4.

[150] AAN KC PPR 295/IX/33, k. 28.

Who led the Poznański strike and spread it to the rest of the city? The elites of the PPR and the UB debated this question and ordered dozens of reports. All assumed organized resistance by the usual "reactionary forces," although they acknowledged that the unidentified reactionaries took advantage of a charged situation. UB Colonel Julia Brystygierowa claimed that investigation had "led to the clergy as the source of ferment ... and it cannot be excluded that the clergy was the inspiration and the organizer of the strike." Another UB analyst, General Roman Romkowski, claimed to have uncovered strike tactics characteristic of the WRN, although the organization itself eluded discovery. There is, however, no evidence of the involvement of the underground or the clergy. Indeed, Romkowski referred to "the communication of single individuals and groups," which sounds more like the work of the community than an organization. Few workers were arrested (although many were interrogated as a way to encourage them to return to work) and the strike leaders, despite the UB's belief in the existence of such a group, were never found.[151]

Leadership meant rather that workers looked to certain respected workers to see how they would act in a tense situation. If such a worker, experienced in resistance techniques and familiar with strike traditions, switched off her machine, others would follow. The Łódź PPR City Committee blamed old women under the church's influence. "The show [*rej*] was run ... mostly by pious old biddies." The authorities underestimated these "pious old biddies," who knew how to provoke a strike and deal with strikebreakers by throwing pieces of metal into the looms of hesitant weavers or tossing a noose or a sack over a strikebreaker's head. Such methods of control could only be learned in the factory before or during the war; women with this experience now held prominent places in the shop-floor hierarchy and could influence the practices of workers in those factories. Factory community meant memory and continuity, sometimes imagined; continuity implied solidarity within the factory, in both work and conflict. Workers refused to turn each other in; at the Gutman mill, where older workers dominated, "the provocateurs returned to work first" as the strike was broken.[152]

In a city such as Łódź, it was common to find such workers in the

[151]In the first phase of the strike the UB arrested seventy strikers; most were released the next morning. MSW MBP 17/IX/77, t. 2, n.p. On the use of UB interrogations, see AAN KC PPR 195/IX/33, k. 110.

[152]AAN KC PPR 295/XIII/18, k. 217; 295/IX/33, kk. 50, 5, 64, 72.

PPR or PPS. In several factories, PPR members were leaders or organizers. "After all," explained the PPR secretary at the Gutman mill, "as a factory delegate, [I] could not betray the workers." At the Titzen mill, factory council chair Rzepecki from the PPS spoke up when strikers hesitated to voice demands. "Since the workers do not dare, I will explain," he said as he recited workers' grievances. Such a figure might be a respected prewar party member, such as one Oficzowa who was first to stop work at the Stolarów mill. As a striker at Geyer explained, "since the party women are stopping their machines, they know what they're doing, and so do we." A respected worker could also end a strike better than the authorities could; the same Oficzowa who had started the strike ended it, shouting at the other workers: "You all know what it means to stop the machines today! Before the war I couldn't get you damn fools out of the factory, and now you want to make trouble." She turned on all the machines, and the strike ended.[153]

But leadership in 1947 did not look the same as before the war. Lamented a PPS report: "When a strike broke out before the war, management almost immediately knew the names of the strike organizers; presently that can only be established with great difficulty, and then only the cases of the most aggressive individuals, not necessarily the actual organizers."[154] This claim was particularly true in bigger factories, where there had been a large influx of new workers participating in a strike for the first time. Although party observers in factory after factory lamented the damaging influence of the "difficult worker element" of older workers, it was just as obvious that "youth in general is the most enthusiastic to strike." The problem was really the combination—"one big melange"—which party agitators could not handle.[155] Younger workers created a different kind of strike from the one that observers expected. At the Eitingon mill, young workers "promenaded about the courtyards . . . [and] spent their workday [during the strike] in chatting and telling jokes." This strike was "simply a first," commented the personnel director. "[I]t has no comparison with any of the other strikes I've observed (including prewar strikes). People walk calmly about the factory

---

[153]Gutman: AAN KC PPR 295/IX/33, k. 50; Titzen: k. 66; Stolarów: kk. 132–34; Geyer: ŁAP DK PPS Łódź Górna 20/XIII/1, k. 8. Other examples include AAN KC PPR 295/IV/ 17, k. 48; AAN KC PPR 295/XIII/18, k. 217; and AAN KC PPR 295/IX/33, kk. 36–37, 42–42a, 72, 97–98, 107, 113, 120–21.

[154]AAN CKW PPS 235/XV/86, k. 39.

[155]Quotations from AAN KC PPR 295/IX/33, k. 72; AAN CKW PPS 235/XV/86, k. 35; AAN KC PPR 295/IX/33, k. 99.

courtyard, listening to what is said to them [by officials hoping to persuade them to end the strike], and they even admit that the strike has no tangible basis, yet they do not go back to work. There are instances in which people are led to their workplace, yet after half an hour can be found among the [strikers]. They cautiously explain that 'Nevertheless [we] would like to see how things are at Poznański.' " The Eitingon strikers did not voice any other demands; none brought up wielowarsztatowość, although management and the parties had earlier pressured workers to switch to more machines, and workers had resisted on the grounds that the machinery was too antiquated.[156] These workers, it seemed, wanted simply to be left alone.

The lack of traditional leadership was not just the result of poor information: there really was no leadership in many factories. Investigators found no strike leaders at the Gampe and Hoffrichter mill either: "On the day before the strike broke out, workers did not talk with each other. They were gloomy and grumbling; a calm before the storm." There were no angry demonstrations, no workers of great authority voicing demands. Workers claimed they had switched off their machines together, without any leadership. Traces of leadership by example did not crystallize into open opposition. Strike leaders were less bold and less experienced than at other factories. One younger worker who spoke up had a vague idea at best of what a strike was: "We know that it is written in the [collective] agreement that if you come to work and work two hours, the rest of the time you can protest, and the company [*sic*] must pay." This vague sense of rights was what emerged among more articulate workers as a moral community. An "old [PPS] Party member" said she would "hunt out those who move to more looms, because they taught [me] to fight for the improvement of the worker's life, and now the government is introducing [another] Bereza."[157]

The authorities had difficulty dealing with leaderless strikers, who refused to follow the rules of labor conflict. The workers of Eitingon claimed they were not on strike; this was just a protest. As with the young worker at Gampe and Hoffrichter who claimed that the right to protest was in the collective agreement, this attitude deflated the rhetoric of party agitators and precluded negotiation or discussion. Because the range of possible demands was limited, it was easier not to make any

[156] AAN KC PPR 295/IX/33, kk. 27, 148, 153.
[157] Ibid., kk. 70, 74. Bereza was a prewar prison camp for leftist political opposition.

demands at all and give the authorities no way to respond. Strikers refused to allow union and party leaders to address them. When management and the factory council attempted to defuse the conflict by leading the night shift in a rendition of the "Rota", the strikers dutifully sang the inspirational song (perhaps thinking of their own protest), and then continued to strike.[158] Strikers thus couched their protest in a strange form of civil disobedience, accepting symbols (the "Rota," or party discipline) while maintaining their protest. Just as the daily occupation of the factory asserted a kind of community control over the workplace, so this mode of conflict allowed strikers to adapt their protest to the limits of the communist state.

Not all workers in Łódź struck in September 1947. As remarkable as this strike was in the context of political change at the time, equally remarkable is the fact that the approximately 28,000 workers not employed in the textile industry in Łódź (most were in heavy industry or transport) did not strike in support of the women at Poznański.[159] They were certainly aware of the conflict. The John metalworks, the largest nontextile factory in the Łódź area, produced machinery for the textile industry; it was full of rumors about the events at Poznański. A group of workers began to complain loudly about the food at lunch on 19 September; when the factory council chair (a PPR member) intervened, they demanded to know "why you are murdering people at Poznański. They've beaten a woman and don't allow anyone to speak out; they just arrest them." On 22 September, posters announcing a 10 A.M. strike were found in the bathrooms and cloakroom. They called for higher pay, improved living conditions, and unity: "You don't have to be silent, but demand; it will be worse for those who hinder [us] and tear [this] down." Yet there was no strike. Even men in textiles were likely to continue work, as they did at Geyer.[160]

[158]AAN KC PPR 295/XIII/18, kk. 167–68. Workers at the Eisenbraun mill made the same claim: "We will not strike, only protest." The director agreed, but said a protest of more than one hour would be counted as a strike and workers would forfeit credit for work continuity. The workers refused to accept this declaration. AAN KC PPR 295/IX/33, k. 121. "Rota" incident: AAN KC PPR 295/IX/33, k. 138. On the "Rota," see chap. 1, n. 22.

[159]Figures for 1 January 1948, *RS miasta Łodzi*, 302–6.

[160]At John, the PPR suspected an underground organization of which there was no evidence. AAN KC PPR 295/IX/33, kk. 84, 89. On signs of unrest in other male-dominated shops, factories, or industries, see AAN KC PPR 295/XIII/5, kk. 13–14; AAN KC PPR 295/IX/33, kk. 44, 46–47. Geyer: AAN KC PPR 295/IX/33, kk. 104–5.

Why were strikes completely averted in the heavy industries and transport despite the fact that these workers believed their pay and working conditions were worse than those in textiles? The answer lies in the nature of skill and the problem of work control in heavy and light industries. Skilled workers were less likely to strike in September 1947 than were unskilled workers. Few workers in a textile mill were skilled; most of these were men employed in the machine shops. In Poznański and other mills, it was precisely those departments that did not support the strike. In a metalworks such as John, more than half the manual workers were skilled. In chemicals, the percentage was slightly lower (and the percentage of women higher); the ratio was comparable in the transport industries. The control that nominally un-skilled but experienced workers had over their work process was much weaker than that of truly skilled workers. Long-time spinners or weav-ers were not classified as skilled workers, although their work was not simple. Their jobs could be learned in a short time even though it might take years to reach the level of dexterity that experienced work-ers displayed. By contrast, the job of a lathe operator, a machinist, or a foundry worker required extensive training. A skilled worker could hardly be set to driving more locomotives at once or operating more furnaces. Thus, the skilled worker (who, again, was almost certainly male; only one of over 200 workers in the sample at the John factory was a woman) had a great deal of control over his position in the fac-tory and over the future of his job; this type of control was not yet threatened.

Therefore, to describe the conflict in textile mills as a struggle over "de-skilling" would be misleading. Experienced textile workers kept their jobs not through control of skill but through control of the work-place. While both textile and metal workers had enjoyed virtual control of the labor market until this time, textile workers lost this control in the summer of 1947 and thus felt an imperative not yet apparent to skilled craftsmen in the mills' metal shops and elsewhere. The relation-ship between worker and machine was no less strong in the textile in-dustry, as the Poznański strike showed. Increased machine/worker ratios meant an explicit reevaluation of the worker-machine relationship; the arbitrary movement of workers from shop to shop suggested that anyone could work any machine. Skilled workers, by contrast, could work as they liked or quit rather than strike. The contrast between textile and metal workers in Łódź thus demonstrates that erosion of job control was at the heart of the Poznański strikes.

The Poznański strike was a singular failure for the PPR and the UB. The role of PPR activists in the strikes was an embarrassment to the party, and the activity of its party circles declined markedly after September. Łódź PPR chief Loga-Sowiński had to admit that the party was "helpless," even when it knew about a planned strike a few hours in advance. Worst of all, it was weakest where it counted most, on the shop floor.[161] The UB, meanwhile, was no closer to its goal of a broad network of agents in the Łódź factories than it had been in 1946. In a typical large factory there might be half a dozen informers and an occasional resident agent. These people were of limited value, having given the UB little if any warning about the strike. During the strike, informers or agents went to work (as instructed by PPR leaders) instead of infiltrating striking workers, leaving the UB without any information about strike tactics or plans. For all the talk about the WRN, the UB really had no idea who the members of such a group might be. In the end, the UB had to admit that it was trying to cover up its lack of preparedness by interrogating workers in the search for provocateurs while the real culprits might be management, which frequently implemented new changes in pay or norms in an incorrect manner.[162]

Nevertheless, the PPR and management ended the Poznański strikes without overt concessions. Clauses in the collective agreement stipulated bonuses for continuity at work. Strikers were thus threatened with significant losses if the strike was counted as a break in employment and were given until 15 October to make up the lost hours. In many factories, workers—out of fear, poverty, or zeal—offered to make up the lost days.[163] Others stood by their strike and refused to surrender what ground they might have gained; the workers at Eitingon declared that "as long as the world has been turning, no strike has ever been made up, so neither will [we] make up this one." A strike was a normal part of labor relations, so strikers could not be punished; the demand that they make up the hours violated their traditions.[164] In earlier strikes, protesters had often gone back to work without their demands for fairer wages or better food having been met, while the state or management met those demands later,

---

[161] AAN KC PPR 295/IV/17, k. 53; *ARR*, 11:296–97.

[162] Colonel Kratko, in MSW MBP 17/IX/77, t. 2, n.p. In September 1947, there were 25 residents, 25 agents, and 374 informers in Łódź. September 1947 report, t. 1, n.p. Reynolds suggests that the army may have had a hand in suppressing the strike: Reynolds, "Communists, Socialists, and Workers," 534.

[163] AAN KC PPR 295/IX/33, k. 160; also k. 13.

[164] AAN KC PPR 295/IX/33, kk. 138–39.

as if independently. Strikers may have hoped that this strike would follow a similar successful course. In the long run, it did. The state could make no concessions to workers where production was concerned, for multimachine work was essential to the three-year plan, and a higher political value (as Chapter 5 shows) than worker support. The state found a way to respond to workers on its own terms—through the labor competitions that expanded rapidly soon after the Poznański strike.

The Poznański strike ended an era: no longer would there be great, community-wide strikes over issues of control. The official labor organizations learned to intervene early and (probably with some degree of intimidation) managed to avert most strikes. The battle over machines and norms was not yet over; there were at least seven strikes in the Łódź textile industry in the six weeks following the end of the Poznański strike. In November, a lack of raw materials again strained the productivity of the cotton industry and lowered wages. "That these protests did not transform into strikes," remarked the city PPR, "is thanks only to immediate intervention." Some spinners protested the switch to three sides, while others sought to return to two. Workers continued to use the strike to defend their community. In a strike at Wima in December 1947, workers favored by the pay system joined colleagues who were protesting pay inequalities within the plant. At Scheibler and Grohman in February 1948, one shop of spinners struck in support of another that had been shortchanged in calculating wages. In both cases, unaffected workers struck in solidarity with others in their community.[165]

Workers conceded, however, the larger terrain of control of production, an issue central to the strikes of 1947. This concession was as much due to the rise in state involvement and party discipline as to the decline in the workers' ability to unite in conflict. The winter of 1947–48 marks a significant step in the advance of state repression of labor. The Poznański strike was the last major conflict before stalinism in which the Polish working class actively resisted the threat to their work lives and asserted a different vision of Poland. After 1947, workers used more subtle methods in the battle against labor competition, internalizing labor tension and redirecting it to the safer private sphere of class identity. Such resistance, which posed a new set of challenges to the regime, could already be seen in Wrocław.

---

[165]Quotation from AAN KC PPR 295/XI/49, k. 90. Strikes: AAN KC PPR 295/IX/33, k. 141, 295/XIII/18, k. 182; AAN KC PPR 295/XI/50, kk. 6, 14; ŁAP DK PPS Zielona 33/XIII/2, kk. 73–74, 79–81; ŁAP KŁ PPR 1/XI/1, kk. 48–49; AAN KC PPR 1/VI/141, k. 133. See also MSW MBP 17/IX/38, t. 1, n.p.

3 Wrocław: Communism's Frontier

It requires a bit of optimism to expect workers to strike in a communist state. As two sociologists wrote shortly after Solidarity's defeat in 1981, "The more seriously you take available theories of Eastern European politics . . . the less likely it seems that workers in the state-socialist societies are capable of . . . collectively challenging state power."[1] But after examining Łódź in the years 1945–47, one should rather wonder why workers would *not* strike in early communist Poland. A favorable labor market, a state willing to go to great lengths to pacify workers and yet unable to exert any convincing force upon them, and pay, work, and living conditions far from ideal—all these make a strike seem perfectly natural. True, no other city struck quite as often as Łódź, but strikes were common in many industrial centers.[2]

In Wrocław, however, strikes were rare. There were no more than twenty in 1946–47, few lasting more than an hour or so. Conditions were ripe for large-scale protest: first, life was harder on the Polish frontier; second, the authorities were even less able to prevent conflict than those in Łódź; third, the Wrocław worker was not the kind one might expect to find accepting conditions in his or her new home. Most were

[1]Charles Sabel and David Stark, "Planning, Politics, and Shop-Floor Power: Hidden Forms of Bargaining in Soviet-Imposed State Socialist Societies," *Politics and Society* 11, no. 4 (1982): 439.
[2]See documents in *Aparat bezpieczeństwa w latach 1944–1956* and *Biuletyny informacyjne Ministerstwa Bezpieczeństwa Publicznego, 1947*, vol. 1 (Warsaw, 1993); and Kazimierz Kloc, "Strajki—pierwsza fala," *Res Publica* no. 3 (1989): 51–59.

peasants—but peasants in Poland had often in the past resisted noble landowners, imperial governments, interwar capitalism, and the Nazis. Despite all this, conflict was virtually invisible at the Wrocław factory, in marked contrast to other cities in Poland—Łódź in particular. Conflict with authority, as either Poles or workers, was utterly different from the patterns in Łódź.

How was this possible? Such a comparison shows that a blanket explanation of communist repression cannot help; the two cases are simply too different to make claims of a monolithic state seem plausible. Understanding their differences requires that we consider the geography, social structure, history, economy, and political relations of the local communities. Then we can explain the existence of two very different Polands in the years 1945–50: Łódź, an example of the Poland of the past, where prewar traditions strongly influenced social relations; and Wrocław, the Poland of the future, where social relations were reconstructed in a communist context.

Wrocław is essential to the study of the postwar era, for it shows how Poland was completely reinvented as a modern, Western, yet communist nation. This transformation was possible because of the acquisition of vast new territories to the west and north—32 percent of the new state's territory—through the Potsdam agreement of July 1945 in exchange for lands in the east ceded to the Soviet Union. The Recovered Territories were essential to Poland's future, both symbolically and economically. More advanced than the lost eastern lands, they allowed Poland to improve its industrial capability and standard of living. At the same time, they symbolized Poland's place among the victors of World War II, and cemented its relationship to another victor, the Soviet Union, which figured as guarantor of Poland's right to those lands. The success in integrating those lands with the rest of Poland was a test of the communist state's ability to manage what it had inherited. A Poland with this land could not be the same as the old Poland; control of the territory was a clear communist asset.[3] But the transfer to Polish hands

[3]Hugh Seton-Watson, *The East European Revolution* (New York, 1951), 172–73. On the postwar Polish-German border agreements, see Sebastian Siebel-Achenbach, *Lower Silesia from Nazi Germany to Communist Poland, 1942–1949* (New York, 1994), chaps. 5 and 9. Polish sociologists have studied the region as an example of social integration and modernization. Guides to this literature are *Ziemie Zachodnie w polskiej literaturze socjologicznej: Wybór tekstów*, ed. Andrzej Kwilecki (Poznań, 1970), and *Zachodnie i Północne Ziemie Polski w perspektywie badań socjologicznych*, Uniwersytet Wrocławski, *Prace Filozoficzne 64: Socjologia 5* (Wrocław, 1990).

was simple in comparison to the task of creating, physically and culturally, a Polish community in an alien land. As the Polish state and the Polish migrants to Wrocław took on this project, they eventually created a society much more hospitable to the communists than Łódź was.

"Ours, and Genuinely Polish": The Creation of Wrocław

The new Polish leaders began planning for the acquisition of the Recovered Territories well before the Red Army crossed the old Polish-German frontier in early 1945. The role of these lands in the new Poland was the subject of much debate in both communist and noncommunist circles. Early visions were not of a socialist planned city but of a symbol for a new Poland; the administrators of the region were more concerned with governing than with creating a new society.[4] Nevertheless, the communists took immediate control of the region. The Ministry of the Recovered Territories, headed by PPR Secretary Władysław Gomułka, oversaw repatriation, settlement, local administration, and the incorporation of the territories into Poland.

If the Recovered Territories were the "Wild West," then Wrocław was their Eldorado—a place where one might build a new future with one's bare hands. But in 1945 the sense of isolation was enormous among the oceans of rubble. Nowhere was there a feature that one could, without hesitation, recognize as Polish. A factory was a factory, perhaps, especially to those who had spent the war in forced labor in similar factories in Berlin and the Ruhr; but the surviving churches, schools, shops, and neighborhoods were all products of a different culture. Just as city blueprints were lost in the flames of the siege or taken by the retreating Nazi Army, so, too, were the cultural blueprints of this great city lost to those who came on the heels of the victors. The people who came to work in Wrocław's factories knew little more than the name of their destination. More than one new resident hopped off a stalled train headed elsewhere. A printer from Lwów recalled his first impressions of Wrocław: "Endless ruins, the stink of burning, countless

---

[4] See Tomasz Szarota, "Rada Naukowa dla Zagadnień Ziem Odzyskanych wobec osadnictwa miejskiego," *Polska Ludowa* 4 (1965): 83–99; Tomasz Szarota and Krystyna Kersten, eds., "Kształtowanie pierwszego planu osadnictwa Ziem Zachodnich w 1945r. (Wybór dokumentów)," *Polska Ludowa* 5 (1966): 127–89.

huge flies, the clouded faces of occasionally encountered Germans, and most important, the emptiness of the desolate streets."[5]

By 1949, Wrocław was again a city of some 300,000, filled with migrants who brought varied experiences to the new city. There were virtually no Polish natives in the Wrocław region.[6] Some migrants came to Wrocław on their way home from forced labor in Germany; without families to return to, they stopped in Wrocław or returned there after a quick reconnaissance of their old hometowns. Jan Kaniewski was one of these migrants. Forced labor in Hamburg gave him factory experience he had not acquired in depression-era Poland. In 1946, he came to Wrocław's Pafawag railway-car factory, where the technology now seemed familiar to him.[7] Many others had survived the war in the Eastern borderlands (the *kresy*), which had now been ceded to Soviet Lithuania, Belorussia, and Ukraine. They had witnessed Soviet power at close range and had been expelled from their homes. Assigned arbitrarily to new lives in the west, they arrived in Wrocław at the end of cattle-car journeys often lasting several weeks. Most migrants came on their own from the overcrowded farms and small towns of central Poland. Like many of their eastern counterparts, they had never been in such a large city, or such a Western one. The resulting mix of regional and social origins accomplished some part of what the social planners might have envisioned. Wrocław was a conglomerate of different communities not conducive to the formation of broader allegiances of class or even of nation; its residents had little in common with one another. This variety eventually shaped a city which was both a microcosm of Poland, yet unlike any other large city in Poland, or all Europe.

Those who migrated freely to the Wild West had many reasons. In an analysis of more than three hundred short autobiographies written as part of applications for work in two Wrocław factories, Jędrzej Chumiński has identified several dominant reasons for the move. More than half of the applicants gave two reasons: the desire to find work and difficult conditions—large families, destroyed homes, a lack of independence—in their previous home. They hoped to make some money and start their lives over. Both groups were as much forced from their pre-

[5]W. Kania, "Pamiętnik z lat 1945–1948," *Sobótka* 7 (1952): 229. See also Kazimierz Koźniewski, *Żywioły: Rzecz o ziemiach zachodnich Rzeczypospolitej* (Poznań, 1948), 342–49.

[6]See *Ci, co przetrwali: Wspomnienia Polaków z Dolnego Śląska*, ed. Karol Fiedor and Marian Orzechowski (Wrocław, 1959).

[7]Jan Kaniewski, *Było to na Pa-Fa-Wagu*, BPP 15 (Warsaw, 1949), 9–12.

Men clearing the rubble from General Karol Świerczewski Street (now Marshal Józef Piłsudski Street), Wrocław, 1947. A chain of workers is collecting bricks. Photograph by Adam Czelny. Muzeum Historyczne, Wrocław.

vious homes as drawn to Wrocław. These migrants were likely to be young, without families, and from small towns and villages. The average worker migrant in two sample factories was barely twenty-five.[8] These were the people who cleared the rubble and reconstructed the city. For them, migration was hardly unidirectional. In early 1946, a quarter of those coming from central Poland returned home, disillusioned by the atrocious conditions of life in Wrocław, while many others tried their luck in other Lower Silesian cities.[9]

The belongings left behind by the evacuating Germans proved a powerful attraction. City President Bolesław Drobner estimated that 60 percent of those who came to Wrocław in 1945 came to loot—for *szaber* (from the German *Schabernack*), as it became known.[10] Although the press decried szaber as the work of a corrupt minority, the desire to get back something from the Germans and make up for the difficult war years seems to have been universal. The director of Pafawag explained this need in a letter to the minister of industry: "Unfortunately, the moral level among the new personnel is unacceptably low; some clearly came not in order to work, but for so-called szaber! Upon completing their plans, they disappear from the area, leaving behind confusion and bitterness among those who remain. It should be pointed out, however, that the attraction to szaber is epidemic, and when the moment comes to leave [Wrocław], it is impossible to control these wild instincts. Even members of the factory council, whose task it is to maintain the order and safety of evacuated apartments have admitted their helplessness, as the mad desire to grab someone else's abandoned property is beyond all means of control."[11] Traders and shopkeepers also flocked to the region; driven by an "urge to trade," they saw an opportunity to make a lot of money with little effort.[12] Lower Silesia became legendary as a hiding

    [8]For sample factories, see Sources. The same was true of migrants as a whole: Mikołaj Jakubczyc, "Akcja osadnicza we Wrocławiu w 1945 i na początku 1946 roku," *Sobótka* 19 (1964): 284.

    [9]Jędrzej Chumiński, "Motywy migracji ludności polskiej do Wrocławia w latach 1945–1949," *Słupskie Studia Historyczne*, no. 3 (1993): 113–43; figures cited from 115, 135. Jędrzej Chumiński, "Czynniki destabilizujące proces osadnictwa we Wrocławiu (1945–1949)," *Acta Universitatis Wratislaviensis* 1512: *Socjologia* 10 (1993): 55–78. See also migrant biographies collected in AAN Główny Urząd Planowania Przestrzennego 549; nearly all display a sense of advance.

    [10]Stanisław Jankowski, *Przejmowanie i odbudowa przemysłu dolnośląskiego, 1945–1949* (Warsaw 1982), 223. On *szaber*, see Tomasz Szarota, *Osadnictwo miejskie na Dolnym Śląsku w latach 1945–1948* (Wrocław, 1969), 126–31.

    [11]AAN MPiH 31, kk. 14–15.

    [12]Szarota, *Osadnictwo*, 126. On merchants in Wrocław, see Zdzisław Zagórski, "Drob-

place for former partisans of the wartime resistance and others who hoped that the relative lack of trained police and civil administration would allow them to survive undetected. The authorities claimed to find evidence of enemy propaganda spread by these same people and accused them of szaber as well. Lower Silesia was full of "those destructive elements of Polish society which do not want to join in rebuilding the ruined fatherland [*ojczyzna*]."[13]

Unlike Łódź, then, Wrocław did not seem to newcomers a city of labor. Most larger factories were on the periphery; there were few company-built worker neighborhoods as there were in Łódź. Small workshops and garment factories were the only signs of industry in the center. The culture of the city was dominated by bureaucrats sent from Warsaw or transferred from now Soviet Lwów; they arrived first to organize administration and production. "In the literal sense there is no Polish working class in Wrocław," city officials admitted in September 1945. "There is only a bureaucratic class."[14] Given that the majority of the migrants who came to Wrocław in those first years were unfamiliar with both urban culture and the factory, it is not surprising that the experience of migration to Wrocław was framed not in terms of labor—as important as industry was to Wrocław's development—but as a move to the nation's frontier.

For Poland in 1945, the rediscovery of nation was an essential theme. Wrocław, destroyed as it had been, was not so much rebuilt (a term that might imply knowledge of its past and reclamation of that past) as it was discovered and claimed. Newspapers of the time continually trumpeted Wrocław "firsts"—first tram line, first newspaper, first cinema—without the adjective "Polish," as if such things had not existed in German Breslau scant months earlier. A Wrocław daily editorialized in

---

nomieszczaństwo wrocławskie," in *Struktura społeczna Wrocławia w 40-leciu Polski Ludowej*, ed. Zdzisław Zagórski, Uniwersytet Wrocławski, *Prace Filozoficzne* 60: *Socjologia* 3 (Wrocław, 1990): 99–116.

[13] AAN MIiP 550, k. 23. On evidence of underground partisans in factories, see WUSW WUBP 2/1, kk. 24, 34.

[14] Quoted in Jędrzej Chumiński, "Kształtowanie się środowiska robotników przemysłowych Wrocławia w latach 1945–1949" (diss., Akademia Ekonomiczna we Wrocławiu, 1992), 152–53. The bureaucrats have also dominated the historiography of Wrocław. See Anna Magierska, *Ziemie zachodnie i północne w 1945 roku: Kształtowanie się podstaw polityki integracyjnej państwa polskiego* (Warsaw, 1978). Most of the memoirs in *Trudne dni (Wrocław 1945r. we wspomnieniach pionierów)*, 3 vols. (Wrocław, 1960–62), are those of white-collar pioneers: organizers of the first newspapers, the first government administrators, and the surveyors of the city's industry.

September 1945: "We are rebuilding Wrocław—or rather we are building a new Wrocław—ours, and genuinely Polish."[15] Studies of the Recovered Territories speak of a distinct pioneer period through the spring of 1946, when the people who made the journey were still few and most came for the adventure.[16] Wages were scarce, and the only manual work available was clearing streets and repairing buildings. From that time have come legends of working all day for a bowl of thin soup, and for Poland. "Work here in the west was at that time [early 1946] a great risk, and very hard," recalled an electrician at a tobacco factory. "[It] began with the basics. I received an apartment in terrible state, without windowpanes or a roof. I didn't have the courage to go out on so-called szaber, because one could most often pay for it with your life. I have to admit that my family suffered terribly, because wages were very low, there wasn't any food. One had to work very hard, not counting the hours, because one thought only about rebuilding and restarting the factory as quickly as possible, to begin production."[17]

The peculiar resonance of the pioneer image reveals much about Wrocław's labor culture. While the theme of building was recurrent in propaganda of the time, the image of the builder was rarely revealed (in contrast to subsequent moments in Polish history when the image of the laborer in the act of building was clearly drawn and glorified). Wrocław's Pafawag (named from the first syllables of the words "State Wagon Factory") was one of the largest and most important factories in Poland. It began production of rail stock within six months of liberation, and soon employed some five thousand workers. But despite the obvious importance of skilled work, the emphasis in memoirs and historiography is on the tireless engineer, not on the talents of the machinist or electrician.[18] As Wrocław grew, the pioneer image faded, but the image of the city in its first year had great significance for the way in which its citizens would perceive their place in the new Poland.

The propaganda campaign to entice workers to the new western lands promised settlers great things. "You want bread—there's bread in the West!" promised an June 1945 article in *Trybuna Związkowca* entitled

[15] *Pionier*, 7 September 1945.

[16] See for example Zygmunt Dulczewski, *Społeczne aspekty migracji na Ziemiach Zachodnich* (Poznań, 1964), chap. 4.

[17] Wojciech Biernacki (born 1908, came from Zabrze January 1946), WAP Trade Union of Food Industry Workers 46, k. 23. Another example is Marian Kamiński (state hydrometer factory), CRZZ Library memoir 640, kk. 7–8.

[18] T. Oryński memoirs, Archiwum Towarzystwa Miłośników Wrocławia; *Trudne dni*.

"Go West for Prosperity." "Although already teeming with Poles, [the west] can take a lot more still," the union journal assured its readers in July. "Here there are great mines and industrial works, almost all of which are operating, from all areas of industry, even textiles. More—they are even digging up enough gold for wedding rings for all the newlyweds in Lower Silesia." The author amended these extravagant claims with a moral conclusion: "He who wants to work will find work there, and will have a guaranteed living, good living conditions, constantly-improving aprowizacja, and—after an initial difficult period—prosperity." A third article offered a paean to Wrocław itself: that 40 percent of the city's apartments were inhabitable with little or no repair; that ample food could be had in government cafeterias. As for fears of the Wild West: "Safety conditions are the very best . . . the Germans behave quite decently."[19] These articles were directed particularly at skilled or experienced workers less represented in the migrant population. For those with jobs already, the articles dismissed concerns about safety and promised a chance for a better home or a better job in a new factory.

In response to the shortage of skilled and experienced workers, the Ministry of Industry introduced a scheme of industrial sponsorship (matched by a system of city and regional sponsors). Individual factories in central Poland were assigned similar factories in the west and chose from among their employees the administrative, technical, and labor core of the assigned factory—often, however, choosing their worst employees. The work forces of several major factories in Wrocław were formed in this way from factories in Warsaw, Katowice, Poznań, and Łódź.[20] Like the organized migration plans, this program was dwarfed by independent, individual migration.

For those who did not come to loot or get rich, life in Wrocław was brutal and frustrating. Neither skilled workers nor young village migrants were prepared for the harsh realities of frontier life. The "Western bonus" that workers in the Recovered Territories received made little

[19]*Trybuna Związkowca*, 4 (1 June 1945), 6 (1-15 July 1945), 9 (15-30 August 1945).
[20]Anna Magierska, *Przywrócić Polsce: Przemysł na Ziemiach Odzyskanych 1945-1946* (Warsaw, 1986), 368-70; *Upaństwowienie i odbudowa*, 1:260; Irena Turnau, *Studia nad strukturą ludnościową polskiego Wrocławia* (Poznań, 1960), 214-28; Jędrzej Chumiński, "Formy werbunku pracowników przemysłu na tak zwanych Ziemiach Odzyskanych ze szczególnym uwzględnieniem Wrocławia (1945-1949)," *Przegląd Zachodniopomorski* 8, no. 4 (1993): 99-100; Stanisław Banasiak, "Udział Polskiej Partii Robotniczej województwa łódzkiego w zasiedlaniu Ziem Odzyskanych w 1945 r.," in *XX rocznica powstania PPR: Sesja naukowa Uniwersytetu Łódzkiego* (Łódź, 1963), 63-74.

difference; pay was still below that in central Poland, and costs of living were higher—9,600 zł monthly for a family of three in the fall of 1946 compared to about 4,200 zł for a family of four elsewhere.[21] The mad competition for apartments and shops left little for the average work seeker. Returning Germans claimed their apartments, often evicting Poles who had been assigned there. During the first year, Wrocław was a city without authority, one of the most dangerous places in Poland. As late as December 1946, there were reports of attackers in police uniform robbing passersby of money and clothing.[22] Whether the robbers were policemen or impostors, the message was that no one was in charge in Wrocław; there was no representative of the state upon whom one could rely.

Nor could state and city authorities provide a sufficient standard of living. There were no ration cards issued until November 1945, leaving workers to rely on the meager offerings of the factory cafeteria, if there was one. Railway workers had no cafeteria and in October received only ten kilos of bread and a kilo of lard each. State industry wages in the city ranged in November from 23 to 160 zł per day (German laborers made as little as 10 zł; private industry wages reached 200 zł), while a kilo of bread cost 23 zł, and a kilo of kielbasa 320 to 360 zł. There were no collective labor agreements in effect; construction workers had not been paid for three months and had no idea how much they were owed.[23] Skilled and experienced workers were particularly disappointed by what they found, and many returned quickly "to Poland," as Wrocławians described the homes they had left.[24] Even if conditions were acceptable, there might be no work: most factories did not begin operation until early 1946, and there were many other opportunities throughout Poland.

The lack of reliable pay, food supply, and housing; the absence of legal authority in the city; and the success of individual looters and shopkeepers all conveyed a message about individual resources and self-reliance. Patterns that hardships on the frontier encouraged among the pioneers lasted long after the economic and social situation stabilized

[21] See figure 1. Magierska, *Przywrócić Polsce*, 418–29; Siebel-Achenbach, *Lower Silesia*, chap. 7.

[22] AAN MIiP 552, k. 130; Chumiński, "Czynniki destabilizujące," 64–70.

[23] AAN KC PPR 295/XIII/28A, kk. 196–97. Workers were well aware that conditions were easier elsewhere in Poland. See, for example, construction workers' protests: AAN MPiH 1171, kk. 133–34.

[24] Chumiński, "Czynniki destabilizujące," 75.

and influenced the development of working-class culture. Workers learned to ignore the bureaucracies that could not provide for them. At one clothing factory in 1945, the director lamented the lack of apartment allotments, which meant that "individual workers have begun efforts on their own, pestering the relevant departments and demanding leave from work. Others, frustrated in their hopes, leave here or just don't show up for work again, or try for work where it is easier to get an apartment."[25]

Wrocław is perhaps unique in the history of urban expansion. Unlike boom cities during nineteenth-century industrialization or the new cities of the stalinist Soviet Union, Wrocław grew without an organizing force.[26] The state clearly had much less influence over Wrocław's Polish rebirth than might be expected in communist Eastern Europe. Although there were countless bureaucracies to distribute apartments, ration cards, and jobs, urban life in Wrocław developed on its own. The reach of the state and the parties was severely limited by the extensive damage to Wrocław's infrastructure by the war, the chaotic influx of people into Wrocław, and the city's distance from Warsaw.

Workers, indeed, had no one to turn to. Factory directors frequently acted as if the factories they had been assigned were their own and threatened to lock up workers who dared to object.[27] Workers' factory representatives lacked the long ties to community that made some Łódź activists so powerful and popular; as a result, accounts of factory disputes sound very different in Wrocław. Factory councils had little leverage and were helpless without management's cooperation. Factory administration clearly had the upper hand and violated pay and food supply regulations at will. A council member at a small Wrocław factory voiced his frustrations to union leaders: "We the factory council were chosen by [the regional union—that is, not by workers, perhaps because of the unstable work force] who gave us instructions about conducting business in this factory, but Citizen Director does not conform to these instructions and acts on his own, thus showing contempt for the law and the factory council; he does not want to meet with the workers,

---

[25]The apartments they had been assigned were eight kilometers from work in a dangerous neighborhood with no public transportation. AAN MPiH 1057, k. 317. Getting an apartment often meant paying a bribe as high as several thousand złotys. AAN MPiH 200, k. 50.

[26]For examples of labor on other frontiers, see David M. Emmons, *The Butte Irish: Class and Ethnicity in an American Mining Town, 1875–1925* (Urbana, Ill., 1989); Stephen Kotkin, *Magnetic Mountain: Stalinism as a Civilization* (Berkeley, Calif., 1995).

[27]Two examples appear in WAP KM PPR 30/V/3, kk. 20, 33.

regarding himself as a despot. . . . The director could lead the factory to ruin with such carelessness. . . . Wanting to extricate himself from this situation, Citizen Director accused us [to the police or the UB] of sabotage, of inciting the workers to revolt against him, and of committing various abuses."[28] As late as the spring of 1948, most factory councils seemed to have no idea where their powers ended and those of the director (or the party circles) began.[29]

The unions were no more satisfactory as worker advocates. As hostile as union activists could be in Łódź, the distance between worker and union was even wider in Wrocław. Like all Polish organizations in the region, the union apparatus was at first preoccupied with organizational tasks such as settling and feeding workers. The circumstances made Wrocław unions behave like state administrators, a role from which they could not extricate themselves.[30] "The work of the unions," reported Wrocław's regional labor inspector in 1947, "is weak, limited to secondary functions; [unions believe] the defense of the worker is the duty of the center [that is, the KCZZ and the ministries]. The lack of a competitive factory slowly creates an inevitable passivity, rather similar to bureaucratic activity. Cases in which unions do not support the worker in a dispute are not uncommon. Most painful for the worker is the lack of legal help which trade unions used to give their members."[31] Workers felt insulted by inaccessible, unresponsive unions, which did not even send representatives to local meetings to hear complaints. The Wrocław PPR was equally concerned, for as local union leaders isolated themselves from workers, they proved equally unreachable for the party.

[28]WAP WRZZ 50, k. 499. Other examples: WAP WRZZ 49, k. 255; WAP WRZZ 51, kk. 180–82; WAP WRZZ 20, kk. 19–20.

[29]WAP WRZZ 34, kk. 62–63.

[30]See Tadeusz Sierocki, "Udział związków zawodowych w zaludnieniu i zagospodarowaniu Ziem Odzyskanych w 1945 roku," *Biuletyn Biura Historycznego CRZZ*, nos. 2–3 (1964): 68–81; Szymon Goldman, "Z kroniki dolnośląskich związków zawodowych," *Biuletyn Biura Historycznego CRZZ*, nos. 2–3 (1964): 82–90.

[31]AAN MPiOS 750, kk. 3–4. Workers exacted their revenge when unions asked for money. Members of some union locals refused to contribute to a collection organized by the Wrocław OKZZ in November 1946 to rebuild its headquarters. Workers at the Klecina sugar refinery complained that, having already contributed 100 złotys each for the rebuilding of Warsaw, plus 0.5 percent of a half year's pay for rebuilding the country, with similar campaigns and the usual winter expenses on the horizon, they could not spare a full day's pay for the OKZZ. The printers' union local added that it had already approved a similar sum for the OKZZ cultural center. WAP WRZZ 52, kk. 86, 90. See also ARZ KCZZ WE 258, n.p.

Most union activists were incapable of shaping a disciplined union cadre; the best had "transformed themselves into union bosses of a sort, treating the trade union which they have organized as their own little fief [*kramik*], categorically resisting any kind of OKZZ [Regional Trade Union Committee] control.)[32]

The PPR succumbed to the same bureaucratic temptations as did the councils and unions. Delegated to Wrocław from Warsaw or another provincial organization, activists saw themselves as representatives of party leadership, neither responsive to nor responsible for the local situation. Mateusz Pastor, who took over the Provincial PPR Labor Department in early 1947, found his department completely moribund. Until now, he reported, "the trade unions were really a separate state, which did this or that. . . . One could not speak of basic work in the unions as we understand it. Our Party was interested in the unions only to the extent that in elections it tried to force [its candidates] into the regional section. That was the end of party work in the trade unions."[33] The PPR was "a typical pioneer organization," concluded another activist, "with all of the negative and positive consequences of that fact." That is, PPR activists, attracted to the heroic aspects of establishing a party foothold on the frontier, were ill-disposed to ordinary organizational work at the factory-circle level.[34]

Within the factories, the PPR's influence was hampered by an obsession with its membership strength and with the fortunes of the nominally allied PPS over which it was determined to maintain or achieve numerical superiority. Thus, a Ministry of Industry inspector explained the "hostile attitude" of PPS members in one Wrocław metal factory, where they slightly outnumbered the PPR and rejected proposals for joint meetings, by concluding that PPS members were in fact secret PSL members conducting "conspiratorial work."[35] Unlike PPR reports in Łódź, these reports rarely analyzed worker attitudes or addressed economic policy.

The PPS in turn was hurt by the fact, reported an inspector sent from Warsaw, that activists were usually the rejects from other provinces or

---

[32]WAP PPR 1/XII/2, k. 15.
[33]AAN KC PPR 295/XIII/2, kk. 21–23. See also AAN MPiH 128, kk. 60–61.
[34]AAN KC PPR 295/VII/2, t. 3, kk. 221–22. See also WAP KW PPR 1/VI/99, k. 182.
[35]AAN MPiH 173, k. 177. See also WAP KW PPR 1/X/4, k. 36. On PPR-PPS relations, see Marek Ordyłowski, *Walka z opozycją polityczną na Dolnym Śląsku w latach 1945–1948*, Akademia Wychowania Fizycznego we Wrocławiu, *Studia i monografie* 39 (Wrocław, 1994), 173–76.

the capital who found it hard to work together because of very different backgrounds; such problems were probably common to all organizations in the Recovered Territories. On the other hand, because PPS members were more likely to have been prewar party members, the party's more stable, conscious membership and greater focus on economics over politics (which this activist saw as a disadvantage in interparty relations) made the PPS a formidable opponent to the PPR.[36]

But politics, in the end, mattered most. Support from Wrocław was extremely important to the regime as a confirmation of the Polishness of the region; the 1946 referendum results were nowhere more falsified than in Lower Silesia. The real results (hidden until after 1989) gave a narrow defeat to question 1 (abolishing the senate), a narrow victory to question 2 (upholding the regime's major economic reforms), and a decisive victory to question 3 (on the new borders). Reported results, however, showed roughly 95 percent support for each question.[37] Opposition to the regime, while not threatening, was strong, especially among repatriates from the east. Wrocław voters, concluded party observers, were "hostile to People's Poland," "distrustful, and restrained."[38]

Just as the labor establishment was ill-prepared to manage the workers, the workers themselves were unlikely to submit to control. In Łódź, the experience of war contributed to a certain individualism. This attitude would be even more prevalent in a city created by migrants—a mostly self-selected group of individualists. Poles had been deprived of national and local institutions for six years and had in that time both resisted new (Nazi) structures and created their own—an underground army, underground schools, underground trade. Most of the people who came to Wrocław had probably had experience with these alternative structures or habits. Such habits were hard to unlearn—more so in a strange environment that did not evoke prewar social organization but only ruins to be picked over and looted. Out of this chaos came a society radically different from that in Łódź or the rest of central Poland.

---

[36] AAN CKW PPS 235/VIII/7, kk. 40–42. A PPR activist at the State Hydrometer Factory compared his party to the PPS: while the PPR "takes away the best activists [to non-factory administration], meanwhile the PPS is whole and is [made up of] conscious people." WAP KW PPR 1/XII/31, k. 64.

[37] AAN Referendum II/29, kk. 1, 49. These figures are from Lower Silesia. For some partial results from Wrocław, see AAN KC PPR 295/IX/362, kk. 47–48.

[38] AAN KC PPR 295/IX/49, k. 95; WAP WK PPS 36/VI/21, k. 10.

Collective Identities in a Fragmented City

Wrocław was understood by most who came there as a transitional city. It lies fewer than 150 kilometers from the German border, a border that in 1945 was far from certain. Fears that Poland's tenure in the West was temporary (that the Allies would give back the region to the Germans) were strong throughout the 1940s.[39] The Poles, moreover, were not the only ones to see the western territories as temporary possessions to be exploited. The Soviet Army saw these territories not as part of a fraternal country but of Nazi Germany and attempted to strip western Poland of much of its industrial capability, shipping machinery and raw materials to the Soviet Union.[40] Hard work, in this environment, could seem little more than a charade.

Had the administrative control of Wrocław been surer, the pioneer ethic and the idea of building Poland might well have contributed to a swifter evolution of a Wrocław patriotism. But as a police report on the political situation in November 1945 indicates, the pioneers of Wrocław felt deserted by local administration and unable to accomplish anything themselves. "As a result, their zeal has cooled," reported the Wrocław UB. "They return to central Poland or give in to the most varied pursuits—anything which will bring them enough to live. Of course they are embittered, and listen willingly to all kinds of reactionary rumors. In this way, a society convinced of the impermanence of the government and of the temporary nature of Polish authority in this region is slowly but surely being formed."[41]

The division between pioneers and later arrivals was also one of skill. Skilled pioneers kept separate from other workers; they also expected and demanded more from their factories than did workers unfamiliar with factory conditions. Management at Pafawag quickly learned that workers from Warsaw were the worst to control because they had high expectations. Pafawag's director reported that Wrocław's "grievous living conditions" worsened the mood of such workers: "More and more often they announce their intention of leaving; there is the fear that abandoning work could become a mass movement." At the same time,

---

[39]AAN MIiP 591, k. 55; AAN MPiH 173, k. 177.
[40]Chumiński, "Kształtowanie się," 47–54; Jędrzej Chumiński, "Przejmowanie przemysłu wrocławskiego przez władze polskie (maj-wrzesień 1945)," in *Studia nad społeczeństwem Wrocławia: Prace naukowe Akademii Ekonomicznej* 543 (Wrocław, 1990), 42–47.
[41]WUSW KWMO 146/10, kk. 71–72.

Women clearing rubble at the Dolmel factory, Wrocław, January 1947. Photographer unknown. Muzeum Historyczne, Wrocław.

those who had arrived later began to envy the pioneers, accusing them of profiting unfairly from their seniority. In fact, skill was not valued highly in Wrocław; unskilled tasks such as clearing rubble (300 to 700 zł a day) and rebuilding were at first more important, and better paid, than skilled factory work.[42]

Wrocław was also, as a frontier town, considered a masculine city, although there was actually a larger percentage of women working in the sample factories in Wrocław than in those in Łódź: 79 percent of the Wrocław clothing factory was female as opposed to 61 percent at Poznański; while the Łódź metal factory was more than 99 percent male, a similar factory in Wrocław had 20 percent women. Women also made up almost

---

[42]Chumiński, "Kształtowanie się," 177; AAN MPiH 31, k. 30. Szarota, *Osadnictwo*, 131–32. WUSW KWMO 147/50, k. 89.

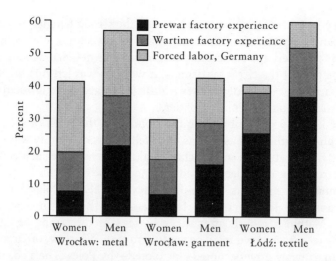

Figure 2. Gender and factory experience

Note: Data are from sample factories. Many workers listed *roboty* (labor, in a general sense) under the category "occupation during war," which could mean work in a factory, on a farm (sometimes identified separately), or in a camp.

57 percent of the city in 1946 and 54 percent a year later. But life in Wrocław was both dangerous and unfamiliar; memoirs of the time sound similar to those of the war. It was a city for the brave, where everyone feared walking alone after dark. Reports of rape by soldiers or bandits are a common theme in those memoirs. There was little room for traditional female gender images: as long as Poland's tenure in the west remained uncertain, to speak of child raising or housekeeping—issues that the women of Łódź used to great effect—could not be of much use.

Women workers in Wrocław lacked the resources that made the women of Łódź so powerful. A large proportion were single: more than three-fifths of those over fifty, for example, were unmarried, while less than one-quarter of the older men were unmarried. Many of these single or widowed women were also raising children and had come to Wrocław in a desperate attempt at independence and survival. They were also of rural origin and poorly educated (although not necessarily more so than men). Above all, women workers were hampered by their lack of factory experience. As figure 2 shows, women were much less likely to have any experience in a factory than were men, or than were women in the textile factory in Łódź.[43] The contrast between the strong female presence and Wrocław's masculine image contributed to a weak sense of community in that city: perhaps community formation was doomed as long as such a large part of the city's residents and workers was left out. At the very least, attention to gender makes it difficult to accept traditional images of Wrocław and the Polish frontier.

The key to social stability on the frontier, in the belief of state, party, and church authorities as well as the intellectual community was national identity. The situation in Wrocław ought to have made such consciousness strong, for its society shared common animosities that could unite a community of migrants. More than anywhere else in Poland, Germans, Russians, and Jews were important actors in the city through at least 1947. Within a month after the war, tens of thousands of Germans, mostly women and old men, began to return to Wrocław, often to houses and apartments now occupied—or looted—by Poles. The 110,000 Germans in Wrocław in early 1946 overwhelmed the 50,000 or so Poles.[44] Like the Poles, many Germans believed that the region would soon be returned to Germany. The returnees gave the city a distinctly German character for at least the first year. Street and shop signs remained posted in German through 1945; German was even used by Polish police and in official correspondence of the Polish administration. A poster advertising the "Recovered Territories Festival of Polish Culture" offered a wry metaphor for the thin veneer of Polish culture in Wrocław in the summer of 1946: it was printed over a German announcement from the war with the signature of the SS commander plainly visible, as if endorsing the Polish facade.[45]

Germans, however, were second-class citizens. Food was scarce, and Poles were given preference; Germans sold their possessions in order to buy food.[46] Those who remained in their homes did so at the price of

---

[43]Data from sample factories; Chumiński, "Kształtowanie się," tables 40, 44, 45, 60; Alina Woźnicka, "Przyczynek do dziejów aktywizacji zawodowej i społecznej kobiet we Wrocławiu w latach 1945–1948," *Klasa robotnicza na Śląsku*, vol. 1 (Opole, 1975), 381–401. Chumiński, "Motywy migracji," 121. See WAP KW PPR 1/XIV/24, k. 1.

[44]Ordyłowski, *Życie codzienne*, 26.

[45]AAN KC PPR 295/XIII/28, kk. 200–201; AAN MIiP 90, kk. 21–22; AAN MIiP 75, k. 88. A plan to have all Germans wear white armbands was quickly discontinued when it was discovered that this added to Poles' feelings of being outnumbered. Chumiński, "Kształtowanie się," 189.

[46]Germans in Wrocław staged a bread demonstration in late 1945: AAN KC PPR 295/X/5, k. 221

retreating to one room, leaving the rest to a Polish family. Poles associated all Germans with the Nazis and assumed that all were wealthy, concealing rich treasures in their attics and gardens. The Polish migrant in Wrocław guarded his or her apartment from the return of its German owners, bought essential supplies from Germans on the *szaberplac*, and worried about a rumored Nazi underground terrorist group called the *Wehrwolf*. Meanwhile, Polish and Soviet soldiers and police carried out frequent attacks on German civilians; no doubt many Polish civilians followed their lead. When Poland began forced expulsion of the German population in late 1945, some Germans left home with relief.[47]

The primary point of contact between Pole and German was at the workplace. In January 1946, there were almost 53,000 Germans in Lower Silesian industry, representing nearly three-quarters of those employed. Only in the second half of 1946 did Poles constitute a majority of workers. Wrocław, as the region's key city, was polonized more quickly than other areas; only a few hundred Germans were left in industry by the end of spring 1946. Although the Ministry of Industry created a Bureau of Labor Mobilization in September 1945 to promote swift polonization, industry could not afford to relinquish its workers until sufficient numbers of Poles came. As a result, some Poles left Wrocław for lack of work, while factories employed mostly less-expensive Germans.[48] City officials began to refuse permission to employ Germans, as factories were using highly skilled German workers for "dirty work" (such as clearing rubble) order to protect them "in anticipation of the beginning of production—since it is obvious that at the moment of beginning production the firm will not get a Polish expert on demand."[49]

Industrialists responded that Poles refused to accept work that was

<hr />

[47]On the German population and its expulsion, see Elżbieta Kaszubska and Jędrzej Chumiński, "Nastroje, postawy i położenie materialne ludności niemieckiej we Wrocławiu w latach 1945 i 1946," in *Kształtowanie się społeczeństwa i gospodarki na Ziemiach Zachodnich ze szczególnym uwzględnieniem Śląska*, Akademia Ekonomiczna, *Prace Naukowe* 608 (Wrocław, 1992), 93–106; Siebel-Achenbach, *Lower Silesia*, chaps. 6–7; Theodor Schieder, ed., *The Expulsion of the German Population from the Territories East of the Oder-Neisse Line*, trans. Vivian Stranders (Bonn, n.d.), esp. 228–36; Bronisław Pasierb, *Migracja ludności niemieckiej z Dolnego Śląska w latach 1944–1947* (Wrocław, 1969); Maria Podlasek, "W skórze Niemca," *Polityka* (15 May 1993): 17–22. On Polish attitudes toward Germans, see Edmund Dmitrów, *Niemcy i okupacja hitlerowska w oczach Polaków: Poglądy i opinie z lat 1945–1948* (Warsaw, 1987).

[48]WUSW WUBP 2/1, k. 54.

[49]WAP Zarząd Miejski 131, k. 53.

too hard or which they considered beneath them; if employers fired a German to hire a Pole, the Polish worker quit soon anyway, so it was safer to retain the German. Germans also worked more conscientiously in hopes of avoiding expulsion, industrialists claimed, while most Poles were unfamiliar with factory work and had to be trained.[50] German workers fell into two groups: a small cadre of skilled workers or technical experts, and a much larger group of unskilled laborers clearing rubble or sweeping streets. Basic pay was 75 percent of that of a Pole performing similar work, but Germans did not receive the 50 percent "Western supplement."[51] While some factories paid Germans less to encourage them to leave, the director of the State Hydrometer Factory (which employed one of the largest percentages of Germans) nearly started a riot among Poles by giving German workers extra food to make up for their lower pay. Workers at the cast-iron foundry struck over preferential treatment of German workers: "The Poles were downcast . . . : even though they were good, experienced skilled workers, the worst German was better than them. This discouraged them, and was a painful addition to their low wages."[52]

In Polish eyes, Germans were acting like victors, biding their time until Poland was forced to surrender Wrocław. At the Klecina sugar refinery in early 1946, a factory council representative used stark imagery to protest discrimination against Polish workers: "German workers rest on couches, with down quilts for covers. Poles bunk on the floor, with nothing to cover them." "The work of Germans looks like mockery and sabotage," charged another. "One sees lines of Germans on road work, handing back and forth a bucket in which there is literally half a brick." In this speaker's opinion, the murder of 6 million Polish citizens should be avenged by finding six hundred German saboteurs and "punishing them appropriately."[53] As in Łódź, Polish workers tried to retaliate by accusing German skilled workers in particular of a Gestapo or Nazi past. But here it was not so easy because the accusers had no knowledge of

[50] AAN MPiH 200, kk. 24–25; AAN MPiH 1057, k. 333.

[51] AAN MPiH 113, k. 45; Chumiński, "Kształtowanie się," 188–90, 193–96, and tables 26–28. There was also a labor camp for Nazi party members. Stefania K. recalls that Pafawag crews did not begin clearing rubble from streets until 1947; it is likely that only Germans and other forced laborers performed this work in 1945–46.

[52] Chumiński, "Kształtowanie się," 180–83, 198–99. See also Kaszuba and Chumiński, "Nastroje, postawy, i położenie," 105; WAP PPS 36/XIV/40, kk. 124–28.

[53] WAP WRZZ 49, kk. 398–99.

the workers' pasts and management was unlikely to sacrifice skilled workers.[54]

In the Wrocław factory, both employers and workers sought simply to exploit the unusual opportunities that the rebuilding of a new frontier city provided—or ought, in their view, to provide. While many migrants to Wrocław hoped to start a new life in the land of freedom and opportunity, employers saw an opportunity to benefit from cheap labor that, because it was from a defeated nation, could be exploited without limit or fear of sanction. They did not recognize a common agenda based upon a shared nation any more than did their Łódź counterparts. The apparent contradiction between official nationalism and actual management policy worked against national identification among Polish workers. In other words, workers' Polishness was, unlike that in Łódź, not cemented by experience in the factory or neighborhood: Polish Wrocław was a nation without community.

Poles also faced uncomfortably close contact with the Russians in the Soviet Army. As elsewhere, the Soviets in Wrocław played an ambiguous role, one that neither they nor their Polish hosts ever resolved. They acted officially as caretakers of formerly German territory and industry until (often reluctantly) they relinquished control to Polish authorities. Yet for obvious political reasons, their role as advisors to the new tenants was far greater. Soviet Army advisors were involved in key decisions in vital factories and local government. As even the PPR leadership was forced to admit, Polish-Soviet relations were beginning to look like that of an "occupied country."[55]

The semi-demobilized soldiers of the Soviet Army were a ubiquitous feature of the western territories landscape and became synonymous in the Polish mind with looting and robbery. Even today, jokes about illiterate soldiers' fascination with watches and bicycles are common in every repertoire; at the time, the humor was darker. The Polish migrant had reason to fear uniformed Soviet soldiers met on the street; city archives are filled with reports of muggings, burglaries, rape, and murder attributed to Soviet soldiers. Polish workers, on the street after dark or in the early morning on the way to or from the factory, were particularly

---

[54]An example of Gestapo accusations appears in AAN MPiH 203, k. 51. See 1949 letter from the wife of a Wrocław textile worker to the magazine *Przyjaciółka*: "If you ask Director Kołacki for something, . . . he responds 'I would explain it to you in German.' What kind of a Pole is this?" AAN KC PZPR 237/VII/96, k. 168.

[55]AAN KC PPR 295/V/5, kk. 40–44.

vulnerable. The director of Pafawag reported two murders in October 1945 of workers who returned home late. Evidence, he wrote, pointed to "marauders in Red Army uniforms." Soviet soldiers employed at a flour mill were reported to be attacking workers from nearby factories. The Polish police seemed powerless. "Every case of robbery or theft," noted the Provincial Information and Propaganda Bureau in 1946, "has been ascribed to the soldiers of the Red Army, towards whom hatred and distrust has grown." Nevertheless, there were no recorded protests by workers against the Soviets, either in the factory or on the streets. Although the Poles feared the Soviet Army, they did not respect it; a grudging calm emerged only in the second half of 1946.[56]

One other national group shared the Polish experience of transience in Wrocław. Lower Silesia was home to the largest concentration of Jews in Poland between 1946 and 1949, when a new wave of emigration began. There were 47,000 Jews in Lower Silesia in early 1947—20,000 in Wrocław alone. First from the concentration camps of eastern Germany, then in waves from the east, Jews were among the first arrivals in the area. Purged of the Germans, this territory reminded them of neither Germany nor Poland; here, one could even open a shop with Yiddish signs or speak Yiddish, practices less welcome in the Poland of the late 1930s. More than half the members of the Jewish *Bund* were in Lower Silesia. Jewish engineers helped to rebuild Pafawag, and Jewish cooperatives were common. Thousands of Jews worked in Lower Silesian industry. Yet there were no examples of anti-Jewish demonstrations like those in central Poland. Because this was home for no one, it was perhaps more difficult to feel threatened by the Jews.[57]

[56]WAP Zarząd Miejski 126, 127; AAN MPiH 31, k. 25; WAP KM PPR 30/V/3, k. 25; AAN MIiP 549, 550, 552. Until military archives are opened, the role of the Soviet Army in Polish industry and society, especially in the Recovered Territories, will remain a difficult issue.

[57]Lucjan Dobroszycki, "Restoring Jewish Life in Postwar Poland," *Soviet Jewish Affairs*, 3, no. 2 (1973): 58–72; Arnold Goldsztejn, "Ludność żydowska na Dolnym Śląsku w latach 1945–48" (diss., Uniwersytet Wrocławski, 1968). Goldsztejn suggests that another reason for the lack of open antisemitism was that migrants from the East saw Jews as familiar—"their own"—and valued their contribution to the economy: interview with Arnold Goldsztejn, 11 August 1993. Józef Adelson questions this assumption: "W Polsce zwanej Ludową," in *Najnowsze dzieje Żydów w Polsce w zarysie (do 1950 roku)*, ed. Jerzy Tomaszewski (Warsaw, 1993), 392. Bund (data for early 1949, just before the Bund was dissolved): AAN KC PZPR 237/VII/12, k. 5. The PPR at first had some difficulty getting factory directors to hire Jews: AAN KC PPR 295/IX/370, k. 41; WAP KM PPR 30/VI/6. On echoes of the Kielce pogrom in Wrocław, see Ewa Waszkiewicz, "Ludność żydowska

In either a positive or a negative sense, it is difficult to speak of a national community in Wrocław in the late 1940s. The difficult, sometimes starvation conditions and the disorganized administration did not foster a national identity. Even the threats posed by German workers and Soviet soldiers and the lure of antisemitism could not compete with the power of the frontier to dissolve national ties. Those who felt their Polishness challenged simply left the Recovered Territories quickly, returning "to Poland" with either a sackful of loot or sad stories of hardship. But many more stayed and sought in the fragmented identities of regionalism some connection to the homes they had left.

Wrocław in the first two postwar years was not a city to which one moved and settled but a camp filled with migrants from all over Poland and Europe. Everyone either had somewhere to return to or (if from the kresy) thought mostly of the home left behind. As one parish priest recalled: "There was no one group which would give direction to the life of the parish. [It was] a pastiche of people of different habits, customs, and traditions, torn from different communities, of diverse levels of education, professions, trades, and groups, with sharply evident regional antagonisms. . . . *Centralniacy* [those from central Poland] called all people from the East 'Ukrainians,' while the faithful from the East looked with distrust and disbelief at the so-called *centralniacy*. At family celebrations—christenings, weddings, or holidays—one invited mostly 'one's own.' "[58] The divisions and animosities that arose from this mixture were decisive for the development of a labor culture in Wrocław. All these groups brought their own traditions and cultures to Wrocław and attempted to order their environment in ways with which they were familiar.

The most extensive survey of the regional origins of the inhabitants of Wrocław was conducted by Irena Turnau in 1947–48. Map 3 compares her survey of 25,600 registration cards from the City Administration with data compiled from the personnel archives of two Wrocław factories—a metal factory and a clothing factory. Migrants were fairly evenly distributed from across Poland, in both the general population and among factory workers; no one regional group dominated. In each sample, five or six regions supply at least 9 percent of the population;

---

na Dolnym Śląsku w latach 1945–1948," in *Z badań nad dziejami Dolnego Śląska po II wojnie światowej*, ed. Stanisław Dąbrowski (Wrocław, 1993), 50.

[58]Quoted in Bp. Wincenty Urban, "Archidiecezja Wrocławska w latach 1945–1965," *Nasza Przeszłość* 22 (1965), 65.

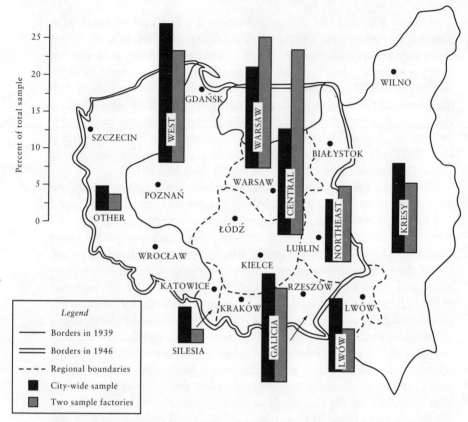

Map 3. Poland in 1939 and 1946, with regional origins of sample populations in Wrocław

Note: Irena Turnau, *Studia nad strukturą ludnościową polskiego Wrocławia* (Poznań, 1960), 31. On sample factories, see Sources at the end of this book. "Other" includes migrants from Western Europe and autochthons.

no single region was the source of more than 26 percent of the population. Migration to Wrocław was overwhelmingly uncontrolled, the trickles of organized transports lost in the flood of independent migration. While the State Repatriation Office (PUR) attempted to organize transports and provide temporary shelter and food, the task of resettling millions of Poles (and Germans) was more than the new administration could handle. Wrocław society thus looked nothing like what any planner had envisioned. The variations among regions are important for understanding the weakness of national consciousness because regional origin was the dominant social identity in Wrocław. A brief sketch of the general characteristics of each region, based upon the two sample factories, will illustrate this diversity.

The single largest group from any one province came from the capital region, nearly two-thirds of these migrants from Warsaw itself. Warsaw's destruction at the end of the war scattered its inhabitants, including many workers whose factories were destroyed, across the country; a large proportion had spent the war in Germany. In addition, Warsaw delegated skilled workers, and white-collar personnel formed the core of many Wrocław factories. Since workers from Warsaw often came because of their work experience, they were among the oldest migrants, with an average age of twenty-nine in 1945.[59]

The largest regional cohort came from the central region. This group is much larger than Turnau's study shows, for central-region migrants were overwhelmingly workers. They were also younger and usually from rural areas (56 percent, the second-highest in the sample). This area has historically been Poland's agricultural heart and among its most over-populated and depressed areas—a hotbed of partisan army activity during the war. The smaller group from northeastern Poland was similar in most ways.[60]

The west region, source of roughly 15 percent of the workers, was strongly influenced by German culture and Prussian rule. It was generally more industrialized and had a denser road and rail system than the rest of Poland, while the countryside was more prosperous and stable. The barriers between village and factory were thus weaker than elsewhere; a villager from this region (47 percent of this region's migrants to factories were from villages) would not be unfamiliar with urban culture. Breslau had historically been a natural destination for these migrants. Development in the region in the interwar years further enhanced the region's sense of superiority to "Russian" Poland. "Poznaniaks" were often characterized by others as arrogant and scornful of their less civilized neighbors to the east.[61]

---

[59]Turnau, *Studia*, 41. See also Zofia Szepajtis, "Załoga Państwowej Fabryki Wagonów we Wrocławiu," *Studia nad rozwojem klasy robotniczej*, part 2 (Łódź, 1962), 20. Interview with Tadeusz S., a young welder from a Warsaw railway factory who came to Pafawag in 1945.

[60]See S. Iwanik, *Migracje chłopów kieleckich, 1945–1949* (Kielce, 1988). Central region includes Kielce and Łódź provinces; Northeast includes Lublin and Białystok provinces.

[61]See interview with Stefania K. later in this chapter. West region includes Poznań and Pomorze provinces. The small group from Silesia was rather similar.

The most rural group of migrants came from Galicia, which had been part of the Austrian Empire before 1918. Galicia's overpopulated villages and small towns were the source of most of the migration: two-thirds came from villages and barely one-tenth from the largest cities. Because of Galicia's proximity and good rail connection to Lower Silesia, official migration plans had called for the surplus population of this region to be directed toward Wrocław and the surrounding countryside. Fewer workers came from Galicia than in Turnau's citywide sample, because Kraków had sent many white-collar workers to Wrocław.[62]

Some planners had hoped to transfer the entire Polish population of Lwów (lost to Soviet Ukraine) to Lower Silesia. The personnel of many Lwów institutions—for example, the university, the trams, and the rails—were in fact transferred, officially and unofficially, to Wrocław.[63] For this reason, popular memory traces Wrocław's origins almost exclusively to Lwów, giving the city a white-collar, professional pedigree that it does not truly merit. The lesser place of the worker in Wrocław and the importance of establishing prewar heritage for the city have encouraged this tradition, as has Lwowiaks' anticommunism. Migrants from the eastern borderlands had witnessed the Red Army's invasion of September 1939 and the mass deportations of Polish citizens over the next two years and had then lost their homes to the Soviet Union in 1945; they could hardly be expected to view the PPR or the Soviet Army favorably.[64] Lwów province migrants were rather older (average age, twenty-seven years in 1945) and more urban than others; 64 percent came from the city of Lwów itself. The last major group of migrants came from the other six provinces of the kresy. This was the most undeveloped part of interwar Poland, with few cities of any size beyond Wilno; however, given the directed nature of their migration, a surprisingly high percentage (62 percent) came from towns. It was simply not easy to migrate from an eastern village to a city in the Recovered Territories. These migrants were even slightly older than those from Lwów and less represented among workers than in the general population.

Within the factory, each group possessed a distinct culture that they

[62]Szarota, *Osadnictwo*, 89–96. Galicia region includes Kraków and (post-1945) Rzeszów provinces.

[63]Ibid., 98–99; Turnau, *Studia*, 45.

[64]See Jan Gross, *Revolution from Abroad: The Soviet Conquest of Poland's Western Ukraine and Western Belorussia* (Princeton, 1988).

felt separated them from other groups. This perception of difference is hard to pin down, in part because the intervening years have fostered a myth of social integration from the very start. An exchange with Stefania K., a young widow from a Kielce village who worked in the kitchen at Pafawag, reveals both the persistence of that myth and the reality underneath.[65]

> Q: Did you feel any difference between yourself and the other women?
> SK: No. Everyone was equal. . . . Almost everyone was from a village. . . . And there were some from Warsaw . . .
> Q: The ones from Warsaw—did they put on airs?
> SK: Oh yes, they put on airs—terribly—that they were from Warsaw.
> Q: What did they say?
> SK: Well, that we are 'Kongresówka', and they're from *Warsaw*. . . . [66]
> Q: Were there people from the *kresy*, and from Lwów?
> SK: A lot. . . . They were second-class [*na drugim planie*]. We paid no attention to them—and to this day.
> Q: Why?
> SK: I don't know. . . . That's the way it was.
> [Later in the interview, the topic returned, in an exchange about conversations at the workplace]
> Q: [Did] people talk about—"I'm from those parts," and "I'm from there"—that "here it's better, there it's worse" . . . ?
> SK: Yes! If someone was from Poznań province, then they were from *Poznań province*! Because if [one was] from Kielce or Lublin province, it was all the same.

Real differences in age, experience, education and culture among regional groups were magnified in a city foreign to nearly everyone. Suspicious of those from other backgrounds, migrants relied upon ties that were easiest to recreate. Thus, a young Silesian worker (in an interview conducted in 1947 or 1948) said: "In general, I hang around with mates who came from my part of the world [*z moich stron*], and whom I knew before. Sometimes I even like people from elsewhere, but I sense regional differences."[67] Turnau points out that this caution was remarkably com-

---

[65]Interview, 4 June 1990. Stefania K. was twenty-eight at the time of her arrival in Wrocław in the fall of 1946. She worked at Pafawag until 1949.

[66]"Congress Kingdom" or pre-1918 Russian Poland. The term is used derogatorily here, to mean outside of Warsaw.

[67]Irena Turnau, "Tworzenie się wielkiego miasta z różnorodnej ludności napływowej (Wrocław—miasto przemian społecznych" (diss., Wrocław University, 1950), 149; other examples, 138–52.

mon among younger migrants, whom one might expect to have fewer qualms about meeting strangers. Older migrants, meanwhile, often explained their reason for keeping a distance in terms of morality. A bricklayer from Lwów said: "I keep in touch with old acquaintances from Lwów who live nearby. I have nothing to do with my neighbors, because they are from central Poland, and don't even go to church."[68]

Regional ties were the glue that helped to form neighborhoods. One might find a place to live through one's factory or through an organization like a political party, but most migrants found an apartment on their own. Stefania K. first found a room in a workers' hostel by joining the PPR, which then arranged a job as well. She later moved to the apartment of a friend from back home before finding an apartment in an outlying villa district controlled by Pafawag. Neighborhood ties in outlying areas (the semi-villages which surrounded the city core) were especially likely to be constructed along regional lines. Here migrants could in effect re-create their home villages within the city. The family of Stanisława J., a young migrant from near Lwów, chose such a neighborhood in order to tend the cow and chickens they had brought from home.[69]

Peasant migrants tended to choose apartments downtown in neighborhoods built for the German workers of the first industrialization several generations earlier. Commented one worker at the time: "The largest number of those from villages live in the city center, in ruined buildings. Country people don't mind—it was dank in their huts too, and the windows didn't open." A dark, damp, one-room apartment in a half-ruined building could be an advance if there were electricity and running water. And in the unfamiliar city, such migrants undoubtedly preferred to live close to others of similar background. As a result, Wrocław's social geography was the reverse of the traditional urban arrangement: the center was dominated by new workers of peasant background, while the white-collar workers and intelligentsia generally lived in villa neighborhoods around the periphery.[70] Workers of urban background, in turn, were the most likely candidates for factory-controlled housing. These allotments were often distant from the factory at a time when there was little or no public transportation. For example, two-thirds of the workers in the tender shop at Pafawag lived in factory

[68]Turnau, *Studia*, 277–80. See also memoirs in *Trudne dni*.
[69]Interview conducted 18 August 1990.
[70]Turnau, *Studia*, 250–52; Turnau, "Tworzenie się," 126–29.

neighborhoods; Pilczyce, one of the largest of these neighborhoods, was more than an hour's walk to work.[71]

Within neighborhoods, the most important institution was the church. Groups of settlers from the eastern borderlands often traveled with the local or village priest. Upon arriving in Wrocław, Stanisława J.'s family first sought out their parish priest, who lived in another neighborhood; he helped them navigate local bureaucracies. Churchgoers frequently crossed parish borders to attend other churches in which the organist was from Lwów or the priest was of a particular familiar tradition.[72] Even in the city center, most parish priests reported distinct dominant regional groups in their parishes in 1945. For example, repatriates from the east and migrants from Poznań province dominated the parish of St. Boniface, the first Polish parish in Wrocław; Lwowiaks and reemigrants from Bukowina stood out in St. Elizabeth parish; the priest at the Redemptorists' mentioned migrants from Poznań and Upper Silesia. Some parishes were more working class, while others were dominated by the *inteligencja*. Although the church, led by Apostolic Administrator Bishop Karol Milik, sought to unite the Catholic faithful as Poles, it was no more successful than state officials were.[73]

The most important public institution in the lives of the workers ought to have been the factory. In a transient society, work tied migrants to the city; the sponsorship scheme described previously indicates the role that factories were supposed to play in social organization and integration of the individual migrant into Polish society. Indeed, a kind of "factory patriotism" emerged in the largest "flagship enterprises." Factories housed, fed, and clothed their workers; factory cooperatives were often the only place where necessities could be acquired at affordable prices. Even the available entertainment was provided by the factory: the largest ones organized and supported the city's first cinemas, theaters, and sports teams. Pafawag's social and cultural programs were among the most developed in all of Poland. In April 1946, Pafawag published the

---

[71]Turnau, "Tworzenie się," 126–29 and charts 2–4.

[72]Interview; Turnau, "Tworzenie się," 131–33; Ks. Tadeusz Budziński, "Zażyłość z miastem," in *Kościół na Ziemiach Zachodnich. Ćwierćwiecze polskiej organizacji kościelnej*, ed. Ks. Jan Krucina (Wrocław, 1971), 273–79.

[73]Bp. Wincenty Urban, *Duszpasterski wkład księży repatriantów w Archidiecezji Wrocławskiej w latach 1945–1970* (Wrocław, 1970), 27–30. Parish priests saw distinct differences in belief and worship styles among migrants. The groups listed here were considered the most religious; migrants from Kielce were the "most difficult." Urban, "Archidiecezja Wrocławska," 12, 18–21.

first factory newspaper in the country, an eponymous biweekly with a press run of about three thousand; a factory radio broadcast in the cafeteria. Pafawag had three *świetlica*s (cultural centers) in districts where the factory owned apartments; from 5 to 9 P.M., workers could play chess or ping-pong or read magazines. Many workers participated in the drama circle (which presented two plays in May 1946 to poor reviews from the factory paper), band, or choir. Many more played for the factory soccer team (Pafawag was then building its own stadium) or the boxing, cycling, and track-and-field clubs. Pafawag even owned two vacation houses and organized summer camps for children.[74] However, the factory was only effective so long as it could keep its workers. As we will see, this was a nearly impossible task.

The paeans to the pioneer spirit and the support for initiatives such as the university or Pafawag's sports teams, revealed an official commitment to a local patriotism in Wrocław. This policy culminated in the Recovered Territories Exhibition of the summer of 1948. Hundreds of thousands of people came to see exhibits showing the economic and technological potential of Poland's west. After 1948, however, the party made a conscious decision to retreat from local patriotism and return to slogans emphasizing the unity of People's Poland.[75]

Identities in Wrocław worked differently from those in Łódź. In settled Poland, identities such as regional origin, skill, gender, and nation might well be the basis for conflict, but differing groups were nevertheless recognized as belonging to the same community. Workers in Łódź felt they belonged and stood their ground to fight for better conditions. In the manifestly transient environment of the frontier, the dissatisfied could simply return "home." As in Łódź, the people of Wrocław sought to redefine what it meant to be Polish; yet here they could always come to the simple conclusion that they were not in Poland and leave, thus breaking their frail ties to the city.

Wrocław, in sum, was deeply fragmented by distrust between skilled and unskilled, worker and nonworker, pioneer and newcomer, and among those from different regions. Equally important was the tension between the migrants to Wrocław and the state. The new citizens of the

[74]AAN MPiH 4260, kk. 104–15; also Zbigniew Tempski, *Trzy sylaby: Rzecz o Pafawagu* (Wrocław, 1960). Chumiński, "Kształtowanie się," 205.

[75]Koźniewski, *Żywioły*, 423–36; Małgorzata Wawrzyńska, "Miasto Wrocław i jego mieszkańcy w pierwszych latach powojennych 1945–1948," *Rocznik Dolnośląski* 10 (1987): 293.

city had been misled about the riches that awaited them; they felt isolated from the rest of Poland; they were neglected, underfed, and treated
as mere token Poles by both Germans and Russians. In time, an identity with Wrocław would emerge among the generations born there.
Before that time, the common ground that linked, however tenuously,
Wrocław's workers also held them apart: the experience of the physical
frontier, which was also an ideological frontier at the forefront of the
state's transformation of Poland. That frontier profoundly affected the
way in which workers saw themselves, one another, and the authorities;
it was at the heart of the differences indicated previously, and it shaped
patterns of resistance and accommodation.

The PPR and Suppression of Labor Conflict in the Wild West

Given the potential for class conflict on the Polish frontier, why did the
workers of Wrocław not strike? Why did the national tensions, indifferent bureaucracy, and desperate living and working conditions not
provoke a collective response? Despite the multitude of social conflicts
in Wrocław, it had far fewer strikes than Łódź. Railway and tram workers struck at least five times in 1945–46. There were brief strikes in
the summer of 1946 at the cast-iron foundry (over delayed paychecks,
new norms, and the director's apparent preference for German workers) and at Pafawag, sparked by a mixture of "pseudo-economic demands" and political tensions. Other strikes, all protesting wages in late
1946, included a six-hour protest by the entire work force at the Ko-
perta paper factory, a brief protest by twenty-five workers at the Archimedes metal factory, a one-and-a-half-hour strike at a lathe factory,
and a near-violent incident at a tin and enamel factory in which workers threatened to throw out the director for withholding paychecks.
There were even fewer strikes the following year: a railway workers'
protest in September, a protest against a pay cut at the electric plant in
May, a one-hour strike over wages and norms at the shipyard in June,
and a protest against the dismissal of a popular clothing factory supervisor in July.[76]

[76]On rail and tram strikes, see WAP PPR 1/XII/31, k. 64; AAN MPiH 591, k. 61; ARZ
KCZZ WE 142, n.p. On the cast-iron foundry, see WAP WK PPS 36/XIV/40, kk. 124–
28. On Pafawag, see WAP WK PPS 36/XIV/20, k. 46; AAN CKW PPS 235/XV/59, k. 25.
On late 1946 strikes, see AAN MPiH 196, kk. 9–10; WAP KW PPR 1/X/37, k. 439; WAP

All but three of these strikes occurred in the metal industry or in transport where one might expect to find a cadre of skilled workers. Thus, the contrast with Łódź, where strikes took place in industries dominated by experienced but unskilled workers, is all the more remarkable. Yet these skilled workers (if indeed they led the strikes) were unable or unwilling to make a greater impression. Their strikes were almost unremarked (which says as much about the inefficiency of Lower Silesian party organizations as about the workers and the strikes themselves). In short, there were barely a dozen brief, limited strikes in a city of several hundred thousand people over two and a half years, although workers faced perhaps the worst conditions in Poland, distant party and union structures, an invisible local government, and industrial managers desperate to rebuild and get production going as quickly as possible. While unskilled labor might have been plentiful, skilled labor certainly was not, as the constant complaints of factory officials attest. Even with this advantage, workers did not protest.

Lack of conflict was not influenced by any close, paternalist relationship within the factory; the half-ruined factories were hardly welcoming, despite attempts to make them so. Another plausible reason might be the availability of alternative means of formal protest or resolution of potential conflict. There were certainly other means of formal protest available to the Polish factory worker. An endless stream of meetings (factory councils, unions and parties; technical conferences; ceremonial gatherings; and so on) afforded numerous opportunities to voice discontent, and indeed workers were often as angry at these meetings as they were in Łódź. Yet workers in Łódź found that such meetings, at which instructors from the PPR and other organizations implored them to "talk freely" about their problems and complaints, accomplished little; a strike was the only way to get demands heard. While union officials in Wrocław noted frequent angry protests about poor work conditions and wages, such anger did not lead to organized protests.[77]

The lack of protests can not be ascribed to the strength of the

---

KW PPR 1/X/5, k. 135. On strikes in 1947, see WAP Związek Zawodowy Kolejarzy WO 1, k. 71; AAN MPiOS 750, n.p.; WAP WRZZ 34, k. 66; AAN MPiH 168, n.p.

[77]Examples from 1946: clothing industry: AAN KC PPR 295/VII/52, k. 109; ARZ KCZZ WO 79, kk. 2, 10–11. Printers: ARZ KCZZ WO 271, k. 47; WAP WRZZ 50, k. 484. Tram workers: WAP WRZZ 51, k. 179. Railway workers: Aleksander Druszcz, "Na spółdzielczym froncie," in *Taki był początek: Wspomnienia działaczy PPR Dolnego Śląska*, ed. Henryk Smolak (Wrocław, 1962), 77.

Wrocław PPR or UB, although in a city where they did not have to contend with an established community, their power ought to have been impressive. One might expect to find the PPR acting swiftly to resolve disputes and mobilizing its membership against dissent. But there is no evidence that the Wrocław PPR organization was more powerful than elsewhere; rather, as shown previously, the PPR suffered the same problems as other labor organizations when attempting to implement its policies. Wrocław was farther from Warsaw than any city of comparable size; it was hardly a prized destination for party bureaucrats, although it might mean a promotion.

Yet large numbers of workers did belong to the PPR. While the PPR's obsession with numbers may have weakened its message, it did ensure that a large proportion of the work force came into frequent contact with the party or its members. From 1,181 members in January 1946, the PPR grew to 18,808 in the city by August 1948; 64 percent were workers. The PPS, meanwhile, claimed 4,570 members in Wrocław in September 1946 and 14,377 a year later. The ratio of PPS to PPR in factories was roughly similar; one can estimate that between 50 and 60 percent of the workers in Wrocław were PPR members in 1948.[78] This percentage was among the highest membership rates in the country. Nationwide, 18 percent of those employed in factories belonged to the PPR in January 1948; the 22 percent in Lower Silesia formed the third-highest rate of any province, while only 14 percent of workers in Łódź city belonged to the PPR. Numbers were often much higher in Wrocław itself: 70 percent of the work force at the hydrometer factory, for example, and 59 percent at the garment factories.[79]

Who were the workers in the so-called working-class parties? To some

---

[78]Anastazja Kowalik, *Z dziejów Polskiej Partii Robotniczej na Dolnym Śląsku w latach 1945–1948* (Wrocław, 1979), 41; Karol Boromeusz Janowski, *Polska Partia Socjalistyczna na Dolnym Śląsku w latach 1945–1948* (Wrocław, 1978), 36; 52 percent of PPS members in Lower Silesia were workers, and the number was probably higher in the regional capital. Number of workers in Wrocław: estimated from Chumiński, "Kształtowanie się," tables 30, 34. As in Łódź, it is difficult to know whether totals included white-collar workers, a larger percentage of whom usually belonged to the PPR (because party patronage was more important in the assigning of white-collar jobs than it was for production workers). Lower Silesia had the second-highest percentage of office workers among PPR members in the largest factories of any province: *Partia w cyfrach*, 37.

[79]*Partia w cyfrach*, 34. Of Wrocław's total population, 8.5 percent, again one of the highest totals in the country, belonged to the PPR in August 1948 (in Łódź, 6.5 percent): *Partia w cyfrach*, fig. 19. Factory numbers from WAP WK PPS 36/XIV/20, k. 130 (May 1948), and WAP KW PPR 1/XII/28 (June 1948), respectively.

extent, the profile in Wrocław supports the hypothesis that communism is strongest in underdeveloped areas.[80] While Wrocław was hardly underdeveloped, its proletariat certainly was. There was, of course, no party tradition in Wrocław. Almost 85 percent of Lower Silesia's PPR members in late 1946 joined the party after arriving in the area.[81] In the two sample factories, a comparison of the economic and social backgrounds of party-member and nonparty workers helps to explain both why workers joined and why they did not protest. Party members in Wrocław factories were quiescent, not because they were forbidden to strike or were successfully indoctrinated. Rather, high membership indicated the extremely low level of political and organizational culture among Wrocław workers.

As will be evident from the following figures, membership in the socialist party was different from membership in the communist party. Some PPS members were familiar with that party's traditions in their home cities because they or their parents had belonged to it or to PPS youth organizations before the war. Tadeusz S., a welder at Pafawag, belonged until 1947, as his brothers had in Warsaw before the war.[82] The PPS did not pursue recruits nearly as avidly as did the PPR; its members were more likely to belong by choice. Some workers, pressured to join a party and wishing to be left alone or hoping to advance, may have chosen the PPS as a lesser evil; or, unfamiliar with both parties, they may have assumed that a prewar pedigree was more respectable. Among workers with no knowledge of political traditions, the PPS stood little chance.

Most workers joined a party when they began work. While data on entry into a party are unavailable, it was common practice among personnel directors, most of whom were members of the PPR, to make membership a virtual prerequisite for employment. A comparison of two small wood factories in Wrocław shows how effective a personalny could be. In one, the personalny belonged to the PPR: there were thirty-seven PPR worker-members and only three in the PPS. The other had a PPS personalny, and fourteen PPS members among the workers against only one PPR member.[83] A Wrocław metal worker retells in his memoirs

[80]R. V. Burks, *The Dynamics of Communism in Eastern Europe* (Princeton, 1961), 65–66.

[81]AAN KC PPR 295/VII/2, t. 3, kk. 221–22.

[82]Interview, 15 July 1990.

[83]State Carpentry-Construction Products Factory No. 8 employed ninety-six; State Barrel and Tub Factory No. 9, forty-four. In both, the factory director was of the same party as the *personalny*. Interestingly, in May 1948, eight months later, the personnel directors

the story of a semiliterate peasant named Koń. When Koń came to the factory, "the PPS and PPR secretaries were on duty in the personnel bureau; [Koń] happened to be received by the PPR Secretary, [who said] 'If you want work, join the PPR.' He joined."[84] A potential worker could join even sooner in order to find work. Stefania K. found work in Wrocław in this way:

> SK: When I was living in that [workers'] hostel, two men came—they also lived there. But they were some sort of, how can I put it—they were armed, you know? . . . They asked what we're [she and a friend] doing. We say that we don't have work yet, that we had worked on the trams, but there you had to come home from work very late at night, and that we're afraid, and we can't work like that. And they say that they'll arrange work for us in Pafawag. And they arranged it. We went there, and they hired us.
>
> Q: Did they tell you to join the party to get that job?
>
> SK: I was already in the party, I had already signed up. Because when we hadn't anything to eat, you know, there wasn't any money, and we went to the [PPR City] Committee, they signed us up right away, and that's why they gave us two weeks' worth of food, for free. . . . Because there was no other way.[85]

The practice of tying work to party membership was so common that in early 1947 the Ministry of Labor and Social Welfare issued a circular forbidding the practice. But little changed; the party personnel departments continued to act as employment bureaus.[86] As factories rapidly expanded their work force, they could hardly require membership of every new worker; these workers were targeted later. Within the factory,

---

were still of the same parties, but the party membership in the PPS factory had switched: twenty-four in the PPR, two in the PPS. The change indicates the PPR's overpowering strength by this point, with unification nearly a fait accompli. WAP KW PPR 1/X/36, kk. 210–11, 233–34. Direct information on this practice could come only from party personnel files, which are still closed. It is impossible to tell from the sample data whether a worker recorded as a member in 1948 joined in 1945 or began work in 1945 but joined later.

[84]Later Koń became the factory's PPR Secretary himself, having "learned the multiplication tables and some simple economic rules." Marian Kamiński (State Hydrometer Factory) CRZZ Library memoir 640, 3–4.

[85]Interview.

[86]Chumiński, "Kształtowanie się," 184–85. One PPR factory representative explained the practice rather differently: "No force at all is used on those entering party ranks; neither is it made too difficult [to join]. New members are subject to observation for a long time, and are made politically aware." WAP 4th KD PPR 34/VI/11, k. 145.

as clothing factory worker Stanisława J. recalled, recruiting went on during work. Those who joined, young and inexperienced, did so partly to get some peace from the recruiters as well as out of fear. Some hoped that membership in an organization was a way to feel a part of the city and the factory. Like Stefania K., many joined to get an apartment and a job, although the party could also take away these gifts from those it deemed undeserving.[87]

Most Wrocław workers were similar to these women. Nearly half the workers in the sample factories had been living in villages in 1939; less than a third (in Łódź, nearly half) had lived in medium-sized or large cities, where most political activity would have been concentrated. And the vast majority of all workers—seven out of ten in the two sample factories—had been in school, on a farm, or not working at all in 1939; more than half of these inexperienced workers were from villages. Peasant-origin workers were as much as five years younger, on average, than their urban counterparts. In both sample factories, more than three-fifths of the workers were under thirty when hired.[88]

Most of these workers—about three-fifths—were also single when they began work; workers from villages, especially women, were most likely to be single or widowed. Although the countryside was, of course, politicized before and after the war, these workers were still least likely to have been affected by labor party organization and propaganda before their arrival in Wrocław. Figure 3 shows the different paths to party membership in the PPR and the PPS; the former were as likely to come from villages and small towns as were nonparty workers, while PPS-member workers were more urban than other workers. Figure 4 shows a similarly low level of experience with a factory or craft in 1939 (with the exception of PPS members in the metal factory). Figure 5 reveals a generally low level of education. In each case, the Łódź PPR, and especially the PPS, were able to attract the more qualified workers: those more urban, more experienced, and more educated. (Łódź workers overall were, of course, more urban and more experienced; their lower level of education perhaps indicates a more traditional connection to the factory, which made education seem superfluous [see Chapter 6].) When combining the first two variables, we see that 40 percent of the PPR members and 29 percent of the PPS members in the Wrocław factories had no factory experience and came from a village. These migrants, then,

---

[87]Interviews; Chumiński, "Czynniki destabilizujące," 60–61.
[88]Sample factories; Chumiński, "Kształtowanie się," 269–73, 279–83.

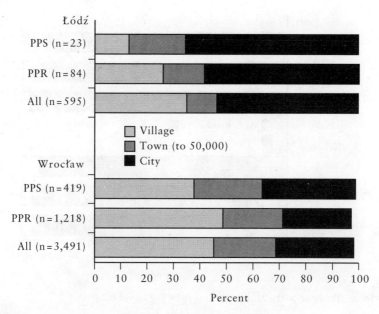

Figure 3. Postwar party affiliation and prewar (1939) residence

Note: Data are from sample factories. Many workers listed *roboty* (labor, in a general sense) under the category "occupation during war," which could mean work in a factory, on a farm (sometimes identified separately), or in a camp.

were particularly likely to become party members, especially of the PPR. PPR members were not the urban, experienced cadre that the party may have wanted, but they were better than the shortage of members in Łódź.

Why did workers join the party if they were not attracted by experience of prewar capitalism? One factor surely drove them away: workers who lived in the kresy in 1939 and experienced both the Soviet invasion of Poland and forced migration after the war were unlikely to join either party. In the sample metal factory, 36 percent of these belonged to either party, as compared to 43 percent of other workers. In the clothing factory, the difference was even greater: 22 percent and 58 percent, respectively. In the latter factory, nearly all kresy party members were from Lwów, a city of strong prewar leftist traditions; few other workers from this region were party members. Most were like Stanisława J., from a village near Lwów: she recalled May Day parades in 1940–41 as "forced marches." While she took part in the first such parades in Wrocław, she later stopped going, even as a brigade leader whose responsibility was to check attendance. For

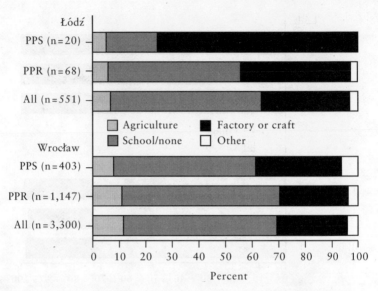

Figure 4. Postwar party affiliation and prewar (1939) ocupation

Note: "Other" includes army, commerce, and office work; the totals exclude workers for whom there is no information. "None" could mean farming or housework.

the same reason, she never joined the party, hiding in the bathroom whenever recruiters appeared.[89]

One might expect workers who spent part of the war in Germany or other European countries, most of them in forced labor (both industrial and agricultural) or in German concentration camps, to join a party: they were likely to have a very different perception of the war and the meaning of Soviet liberation than those from central Poland or the kresy. However, party membership among this group was, in both sample factories, nearly the same as that among workers without German experience. As was the case with prewar labor experience, familiarity with German terror and gratitude for the Soviet liberation—which might be termed a positive reason (that is, one consonant with an ideological model of party membership) to join a leftist political party—are not a significant factor.

The absence of experiential differentiation between PPR and nonparty workers stands in contrast to the image of the PPR at the time. Official histories of the PPR emphasize the party's proletarian character. The

[89]Interview.

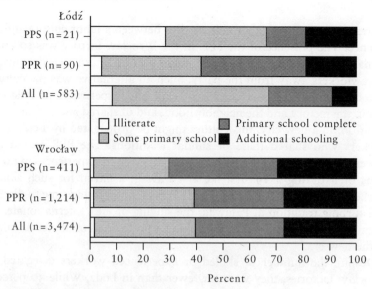

Figure 5. Party affiliation and educational level

data presented here suggest otherwise. The party was strong, not in the factories of Łódź, a traditional working-class city, but in Wrocław, where most workers had neither factory nor urban experience.

The workers in Wrocław were something of a blank slate—rural, young, poorly educated, and inexperienced. Communist party membership in Wrocław did not indicate strong labor or class identity but was in fact a manifestation of the lack of a labor culture. Workers joined political parties, especially the PPR, because there was no alternative method of making one's way in the city and the factory. While the party organization itself was not particularly powerful in Wrocław, its membership was far easier to recruit, organize, and control than that in Łódź. The same phenomenon that led Wrocław workers to join the party also made it unlikely that they would strike. Although their conclusions exaggerated the PPR's popularity, the party's provincial leaders could boast in late 1946 that "strikes in Lower Silesia are a rarity, immediately liquidated as a rule. The workers are in a fighting mood, and it is easy for our Party to mobilize them."[90]

The contrast between Łódź and Wrocław, then, was not so much a

[90]AAN KC PPR 295/IX/362, k. 48.

contrast between two labor cultures but between a labor culture and its absence. The presence of the PPR in the Wrocław factory was so great primarily because, unlike in Łódź, there was no alternative that might draw workers away from the party. Such an alternative was the culture that dominated Łódź—a culture of skill and experience, of relations within the factory and the neighborhood, and of shared and remembered tradition. In a new city, this culture might be propagated by a cohort of workers who shared these or similar traditions. The PPR feared the power of such a cohort—naturally enough, given its experiences in Łódź. Signs of it during a 1946 strike at Pafawag, a haven for such skilled workers, worried both parties. The PPR Secretariat found time to discuss a disturbing tradition at Pafawag: the singing of the "Internationale," a "remnant of the past"—that is, evoking a proletarian militance unsuited to the new era.[91]

Despite the number of skilled or experienced workers delegated to Wrocław factories, they were far fewer than in Łódź. While 30 percent of workers in the Wrocław metal factory and 22 percent in the garment factory had factory or craft experience before the war, the factories of Łódź had nearly twice as many: 50 percent in metal, and 40 percent in the textile mill had worked in a factory before 1945. More important, skilled workers in Wrocław came from a dozen different cities and hundreds of factories. In Łódź, nearly all were from Łódź, and many had worked in the same factory before 1939. The working-class culture experienced workers in Wrocław remembered from before the war was actually made of many cultures that were further weakened by the move to Wrocław. The traditions of skilled labor, moreover, did not necessarily translate into experience in the Wrocław factory. In a small factory such as the Wrocław shipyard, experienced workers might dominate, but their sense of displacement was strong. A shipyard worker recalled his first years in Wrocław: "It is true that the work force was made up of metalworkers, smiths, and machinists, . . . but each of us encountered a shipyard for the first time. . . . For each of us it was something new; this was not shoeing a horse or fixing a lock. We immersed ourselves, complete novices, in the mysteries of the building of floating objects. This was, at the same time, a good school. Taking apart a hulk, we truly learned the construction of barges from the very basics, quickly familiarizing ourselves with the professional terms for various parts, [as

[91]WAP KW PPS 36/XIV/20, k. 46; AAN CKW PPS 235/XV/59, k. 29; AAN KC PPR 295/VII/2, k. 226.

taught by] the only foreman, Pawłowski, who had worked in a shipyard before the war."[92] Unlike workers in Łódź, most of whom stayed in their city, and even their factory during and after the war, the experienced worker in Wrocław, even if he or she had spent the war at home in Warsaw, Kielce, or Łódź, had now moved to a foreign city that lacked even an existing labor culture that one could join.

Such experienced workers could not play an important role in the factory because the factory community so strong in Łódź was virtually absent in Wrocław. For example, the practice of leaving work together at the end of the day for a drink in a nearby tavern, so common in Łódź, was unknown (or at least not memorable) in Wrocław. A group of metal workers in Łódź enthusiastically recalled the camaraderie of those days:

Worker 1: [Workers] went to restaurants more often than today, because there were very many restaurants, and they were cheap, you could go there; one usually went to stand [at the counter] for five minutes, or one went to stand for two hours, or to sit. . . . For some herring, for example, there was a restaurant on the corner of Obywatelska [Street]. . . . The foundry workers went to that one on Końska, or on Obywatelska—and the supervisor, and one or two foremen [went too]. . . .
Worker 2: Listen, mister, when one of the guys had his nameday, then he bought rounds for everyone in Obywatelska like you wouldn't believe. . . .
Worker 3: People worked together . . . when a group was [leaving work, someone would say] "Let's go to the restaurant [*knajpa*]."

Metal workers in Wrocław, in contrast, were equally emphatic that they had never done the same:

Q: Would you go to a *knajpa* [after work]?
Worker 1: No, because you didn't have the cash—we made pennies. It was like this. You go to your garden plot, you don't meet your acquaintances, and you won't say anything. . . .
Worker 2: There was nowhere to go. . . .
Worker 3: If there was a nameday, or a child's birthday, . . . then you had a family gathering, and a few neighbors, because that was cheapest.[93]

[92]Izydor Tomaszewski, "Jak się rodziła wielka Wrocławka" in *17 opowieści prawdziwych: Wspomnienia dolnoślązaków*, ed. Janina Wojtanowicz (Wrocław, 1968), 63–66. The author recalls that many soon left for easier work in Wrocław's large metal factories.
[93]Łódź: workers at John metal factory, 18 January 1990; Wrocław: workers at Pafawag, 8 February 1990.

Despite Wrocław's hundreds of restaurants and bars, the divisions among workers by age, region, and experience and those divisions caused by labor turnover were too strong to allow such a community. Other sources suggest drinking was even more common in Wrocław than in Łódź; however, one drank because there was nothing else to do, not as part of communal rituals.[94]

The result of this lack of a labor community was the indifference—lack of discipline, as it was framed by official observers—of most Wrocław workers, which simply took the place of formal resistance. The numerical and organizational power of the PPR did not truly suppress resistance in Wrocław but allowed it to emerge in less confrontational ways. A closer look at the Wrocław work force finds, in fact, that workers were as troublesome to the authorities as they were in Łódź. There were alternatives to open conflict available in postwar Poland that were appropriate to Wrocław's highly fragmented work force; they require us to reconsider the nature of protest and consent between the working class and the state employers at the birth of Polish stalinism.

For workers from villages and small towns, strikes were an unfamiliar tool; their resistance traditions, whether violent partisan warfare or individual passive resistance to taxes or work requirements, were very different from the modes of resistance common among urban workers.[95] Individual means of expressing grievances replaced the collective protests in which workers in Łódź engaged. Because of poor living and working conditions in the first few years, most workers' unfamiliarity with factory conditions, general expectations that life in general ought to be better after the war, and the weak ties among workers and between workers and supervisors, the inclination to work hard and become part of a factory community was weak. The lack of labor discipline was "the most burning issue in Lower Silesia," in the words of a PPR inspector in late 1946: "One of the best [disciplined] factories is [Pafawag], in which labor discipline also still leaves much to be desired. Workers wander about the buildings and courtyard in large groups. The worst factories that I visited were PZL in Psie Pole [Wrocław; an aircraft engine

---

[94]Julian Cierpisz, "Na 'Dzikim Zachodzie,' " in *Mój zakład pracy: Wspomnienia*, ed. Wiesław Szyndler-Głowacki (Warsaw, 1965), 204; Urban, "Archidiecezja Wrocławska," 44–45. Pafawag had a beer kiosk: Tadeusz S., interview.

[95]For introductions to this topic, see Charles Sabel, *Work and Politics: The Division of Labor in Industry* (Cambridge, U.K., 1982), 132–36; Barrington Moore, *Injustice: The Social Bases of Obedience and Revolt* (White Plains, N.Y., 1978); Moshe Lewin, *The Making of the Soviet System: Essays in the Social History of Interwar Russia* (New York, 1985).

factory] and the State Lathe Factory in Wrocław. These factories are headed by people who do not care about rebuilding and raising production. For more than a year, there have been 1100 workers and six directors in these two factories, and they still produce nothing. At PZL . . . I found workers resting and sleeping at 1330—that is, during the workday."[96] In a tin and enamel factory, a Ministry of Industry inspector blamed the "lack of subordination to the factory council's orders" on a work force consisting of a "migrant element . . . demoralized by easy money early on and by the general lack of discipline."[97]

The meaning of discipline, of course, is subjective: solidarity and collective resistance could easily seem like disorder to a production-oriented state. Pafawag exemplifies the tension between still-unenforceable planning goals and propaganda, on the one hand, and workers' indifference, misbehavior, or stubbornness, on the other. Amid national fanfare, the still-under-reconstruction factory produced its one-hundredth wagon in January 1946. This moment was portrayed as a symbol of Poland's rebirth, implicitly a sign of the adaptation of the migrants to their new home. "Since that ceremony," the factory's director wrote just a few weeks later, "we have observed apathy, lack of enthusiasm, and lack of a sense of responsibility to one's work. Employees complain about low wages, claiming that the Western bonus does not even the difference in prices of basic necessities; moreover, the approaching spring brings the promise of the start of construction work, in which there are no set pay tables and wages tend to be several times higher than in [manufacturing]. Inexcused absenteeism has risen in several departments to 20.3 percent. The threat of being fired generally makes no impression, given the ease of finding employment in other industries."[98] Older skilled workers and foremen at a Pafawag technical conference later that year also saw a divide between them and new workers. They lamented the latter's contempt for work rules and regulations and recalled the good old days of 1945 when most Polish workers at Pafawag were the skilled cadres sent from Warsaw or Silesia. Now "a worker says he's done his job because he's met the norm, that is, 100 percent." Such workers refused to accept alternative tasks assigned during work delays caused by power failures or material shortages. Many were finished, washed, and

[96] AAN KC PPR 295/IX/49, k. 124.
[97] AAN MPiH 4260, k. 28. See also WAP KW PPR 1/X/4, k. 26; AAN MPiH 173, k. 177; WAP ZZB WO 1, n.p.
[98] AAN MPiH 31, k. 61. See also WAP WK PPS 36/XIV/20, kk. 69–70.

dressed by 2:30, an hour before the end of the shift, although the porter would not unlock the gates. Some broke open their lockers in their haste to leave. "A large part of our work force has never worked in large groups before," explained one speaker, "and does not understand the necessity to work together and to assume joint responsibility for their work."[99]

The authorities associated workers' lack of discipline with criminal activity such as theft, looting, and the black market. These, too, were part of the arsenal of protest methods available to Wrocław workers, alternatives that obviated the need to protest in a more formal way. A chemical industry official inadvertently made this connection in 1947. While "the Lower Silesian chemical industry can boast that nowhere until now have there been any serious conflicts," he wrote, thefts were often on a mass scale: "workers steal both products and small tools. Party members and even guards steal, too." Indeed, workers were less likely than those in Łódź to defend theft collectively.[100]

The Wrocław worker's strongest weapon was the labor market, which in Wrocław and the Recovered Territories was advantageous for the worker—the best in Poland, in fact.[101] This was a land of opportunity for the migrant, filled with jobs for the taking. Until management could control the market, there was little anyone could do to discipline the worker—although management probably preferred poor discipline to strikes. Without the sums of money that labor competition would offer (Chapter 5), attempts to control workers were comic at best. Management at a Wrocław chemical factory introduced a schedule of incentives in October 1946 that gave workers points for reporting faulty work, hauling rubble, helping to rebuild the factory, teaching new workers, using their own tools, and "conscientiousness." Points were subtracted for tardiness, beginning lunch early, inexcused absence, "starting quarrels with older workers," smoking in the cafeteria, standing idle, playing chess or taking a bath during work, or improper fulfillment of certain tasks. The range of sins tells us as much about what workers were getting away with as about management's goals.[102]

Workers recognized that there was no need for them to do more than

[99] WAP Pafawag 173, k. 3.
[100] WAP KW PPR 1/X/4, k. 37; WAP KW PPR 1/X/36, kk. 15–19; WUSW WUBP 2/27, k. 9. Tadeusz S., interview.
[101] Chumiński, "Kształtowanie się," 152–60.
[102] WAP Chemitex 58, kk. 23–25.

necessary; both authority and incentive were insufficient to change work habits. The small wage increase that beating the norm might bring was insufficient compensation; it was as easy to find similar or better work elsewhere. Workers also left for farming, for private industry and crafts, to clear rubble—anything that gave them a chance to survive or prosper on the frontier. The dream of making it rich in the Wild West was still powerful.[103]

Unlike many similar workers in Łódź, these workers had no family with them—no "anchor," as the director of Pafawag put it. About two-thirds of the workers in each of the two sample factories were single or widowed. In April 1946, there was only one family member for every three Pafawag workers; numbers were not much higher elsewhere—roughly one family member per two workers at the garment factories. The future for these workers was distant, and the need to settle in one place small. With the German Army widely expected back any day, workers preferred to spend what they earned or send it back to families in central Poland.[104]

Labor turnover in all Lower Silesian factories throughout the 1940s was more than one and a half times the average for Poland as a whole.[105] From the fall of 1945 (when most factories began production or were finally turned over by the Soviet Army) through mid-1946, the effort to revive Wrocław and its industry meant more than enough work; migration to the city was both uncontrolled and experimental—that is, many came for a few days or weeks to test the waters. Even with competition from German workers, there was more work than there were candidates. By March 1946 Pafawag, which employed at the time about 3,000 workers, had employed 15,000 workers in ten months.[106] The labor market in Wrocław stabilized somewhat through 1947 as positions left by evacuating Germans were filled and factories reached initial capacity. A police report in the spring of 1947 noted a rise in unemployment when some factories laid off office and unskilled workers; the PPR reported the first signs of factory patriotism and work-force stabilization. Still,

---

[103]AAN MPiH 200 kk. 24–25; ibid. 271, k. 118; WUSW KWMO 147/50, k. 89; WAP WRZZ 33, k. 8.

[104]Pafawag director quoted in Chumiński, "Kształtowanie się," 280; *Pafawag: dwuty-godnik pracowników P.F.W.*, 10 April 1946; Chumiński, "Kształtowanie się," 282; AAN MPiH 126, k. 9; sample data.

[105]Chumiński, "Kształtowanie się," 177–78, and table 21.

[106]WAP KW PPR 1/XII/31, k. 63; WUSW KWMO 146/10, kk. 54, 61, 92; Magierska, *Przywrócić Polsce*, 392.

Posters such as this one, from 1946, probably did not do much to make the Wild West more inviting or less alien. Text reads: "Textile Worker! More Working Hands are Needed in the West." Designed by Roman Szałas. Muzeum Niepodległości, Warsaw.

turnover was reported up to 100 percent yearly in some factories.[107] Finally, in 1948 and 1949, the labor market expanded again under the pressure of the three-year plan. New workers poured into the city, and labor turnover remained high: the yearly rate at Wrocław metal factories in early 1948 ranged from 26 percent (at Pafawag) to 85 percent.[108]

An early proposal to control workers by means of work permits or identity cards failed. Factories resorted largely to market controls, offering higher wages than those specified by collective agreements and even raiding other factories, particularly in the metal industry, in search of skilled workers.[109] As in Łódź, a skilled metal worker could make more money working in his craft in another industry than in a metal factory. The highest pay at the Archimedes factory in late 1947, for example, was 25 zł per hour for a skilled craftsman—about 5,000 zł per month. In the construction industry, the same worker could make three times as much, even with the winter layoff. The Archimedes director complained that "a cleaning lady [elsewhere], who uses such 'precision' tools as a rag and a mop, is equal in pay to a skilled worker in the metal industry, who . . . works at piece rate. . . . And thus the migration of workers from factory to factory, the mass exodus of unskilled workers in the spring to the building industry, to demolition and assembly companies, etc. The result is the demoralization of skilled workers."[110] The essential difference between the skilled worker's search for work in Wrocław and in Łódź was that the Wrocław skilled worker was isolated. There was no network or community of experienced labor as there was in Łódź. In a vicious circle, labor turnover also made community formation more difficult; the chance for labor traditions to take root in Wrocław was slim.

Skilled workers would normally be more stable than others; this was the case in Łódź. But as figure 6 shows, skilled workers in Wrocław

[107]WUSW KWMO 148/19, k. 238; WUSW KWMO 148/5, k. 1; AAN KC PPR 295/IX/ 362, k. 120; WAP KW PPR 1/X/4, k. 37. On unemployment, see Jędrzej Chumiński, "Możliwości zatrudnienia w przemyśle na tak zwanych Ziemiach Odzyskanych ze szczególnym uwzględnieniem Wrocławia (1945–1949)," *Przegląd Zachodniopomorski* 8, no. 3 (1993): 43–47.

[108]WAP KW PPR 1/X/7, k. 24. Archimedes, a factory of two hundred to seven hundred workers, had employed four thousand by 1948: WAP KW PPR 1/XII/24, k. 80. On the influx of workers, see WUSW KWMO 150/10, n.p.

[109]AAN MPiH 1057, k. 333; WAP KW PPR 1/X/7, k. 9. See also AAN MPiH 173, k. 88.

[110]WAP WRZZ 66, kk. 44–46.

were actually more likely than unskilled workers to change jobs. Unskilled workers were one and a half times more likely to work for at least three years in the factory than were skilled workers. Overall, nearly three-fifths of those employed in the metal factory at some time between 1945 and 1949 worked for less than one year. This is a fivefold turnover in just over four years, given a total of about 2,500 workers. Party membership was thus positively correlated with job stability. Party members or affiliates were more likely to remain at work for a longer period than were nonparty workers, although more than half still left within one year. Worker members may have considered, or been told, that it was their duty to stay. Those who joined a party expecting to advance would certainly stay longer than other workers. Finally, many recognized that it would be difficult to leave without facing an inquiry from the party, as Stefania K. found out when she quit her job on the trams.[111] The culture that could take root in the factory, then, was more likely to be invented by the PPR—or, rather, by the workers, less urban and less educated, who were PPR members. The Wrocław factory—and to a great extent, Wrocław society—was their creation.

But enlisting a large proportion of the Wrocław work force was not the same as developing a disciplined party cadre. Rather, the party was able to grow precisely because of the inexperience of the workers who came to the city. This point requires us to reexamine our understanding of the role of communist parties in Eastern Europe. The PPR in Wrocław did not create relatively docile factory relations through repression or agitation; instead, its success was a *product* of those relations. Search for explanations for the lack of strikes leads beyond the PPR to the demographic and cultural shifts associated with the Recovered Territories and the great migration west. As community was central in Łódź, so the lack of community in Wrocław proved to be its defining characteristic. While the workers of Wrocław did have the individual ability to resist the state, their resistance would be easier to break.

The workers of Wrocław were not entirely different from the workers of Łódź. They lived in the same political system; the newspapers they read, the films they saw, and the lectures they attended conveyed the

---

[111]At the electric power plant in Czechnica just outside Wrocław, eighty-six of ninety-eight workers in 1947 were PPR members. Conditions in this small community were particularly harsh; workers swore that "if they weren't PPR members, and if not for the PPR circle, everyone would quit." WAP KW PPR 1/X/7, k. 111.

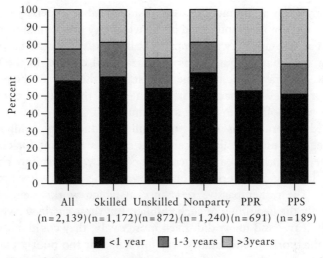

Figure 6. Career longevity in metal factory

Note: Because of the method of selection, data from the textile factory are not usable for this analysis.

same messages. Nevertheless, the relationship between worker and state was profoundly different. A labor or factory culture usually develops within a community well before the evolution of formal labor politics and organizations. In Wrocław, the two arrived at the same time. The creation or establishment of working-class traditions in the new city, therefore, was hindered and altered by the simultaneous creation of labor institutions by the state. Two modes of culture—a transmitted culture of labor and tradition and an organizationally generated culture of membership—competed in a way unique to Wrocław and Poland's Recovered Territories. The former culture lacked the resources of the latter, no matter how poorly those resources may have been employed.

Unlike new workers in Łódź, the large mass of unskilled or inexperienced workers in Wrocław were from villages and small towns; they were not likely to be sons and daughters of workers. They came from all over Poland and created social identities in ways that would lend stability or logic to their lives after six long years of war. The most powerful community, based on regional allegiances, was also the most divisive. The shopkeeper or priest from the same district in Lwów province was more important than the workmate from Poznań who spoke and acted differently. The result was a citywide work force that could not easily form a community around shared labor experience or class, and that did not seem interested in the wider city or national community either. Factory culture was completely alien. So was organizational culture for that matter; but it was organizational culture, in the form of the PPR, that met workers at the train station, the door of the personnel office, or the sewing machine. It was the party that offered a job and a home—which offered to create a community.

Shared experience is most powerfully produced by conflict. Class struggle, or conflict easily perceived as such, is a means for class consciousness to form. The ingredients for conflict were certainly present in the harsh living and working conditions and the illusory freedom of the frontier. The rather passive resistance in which workers engaged was potentially the beginning of such conflict. But these single workers could as easily leave, and many did. Even more easily, they could find another job. If the work in one factory was too harsh or too poorly paid, there was always work in another factory or on a construction gang in Wrocław and beyond. To strike when there were so many jobs available elsewhere was senseless. It might also be ineffective because there were always new workers arriving. (Wrocław had in a sense both a constant labor surplus and a constant labor deficit.) One could instead get one's due by stealing, looting, coming to work late, leaving early, or just leaving.

Wrocław was not typical of Poland in the years 1945–47; most industry was still performed in old centers of Polish industry such as Łódź, where relatively stable communities returned to the same labor and neighborhood relations—and conflicts—as before the war. But Poland was only beginning to change. As new workers flooded into Wrocław, they were also arriving in another destroyed city, Warsaw. Soon migrants like these would be arriving in the new centers of industry: in the expanding coastal industries of Szczecin, Gdynia, and Gdańsk; in the mines of Silesia; in the new factories of Poland's future. Much of this expansion and migration took place on the other side of the stalinist divide, in the early 1950s and after. Wrocław was the first example of the new migrant city in postwar Poland, and its experience says much about the worker culture of the future.

In laying the foundations of stalinist society, the state had two tasks. First, it needed to address the causes of worker unrest in Łódź and turnover in Wrocław: problems of wages and food supply, representation, and politics. Second, it needed to create a new factory culture to harness the potential of the new workers like those in Wrocław. The next three chapters will look at a series of initiatives that addressed these two goals and formed the bases of the stalinist social and political system.

Part II

The Party's Revolution, 1948–1950

4 The Social Foundations of the Stalinist System

The autumn of 1947 marked a transition between the revolutions of 1945 and 1948–50 and thus a movement toward the establishment of the system commonly called "stalinism." At the same time, this moment highlights the complex ties between the politics of stalinism and social forces. On one side there was the beginning of the cold war. At a meeting in the Polish mountain town of Szklarska Poręba, Stalin's delegation pushed Poland and its neighbors to strengthen their "people's democracies." In Warsaw, the Moscow communists led by Bolesław Bierut rejected PPR leader Władysław Gomułka's "Polish road to socialism," which, "nationalist in form, socialist in content," had adapted the Soviet model to Polish conditions.[1] Nevertheless, while this sequence of events helped to establish the era of stalinism in Poland (which ended only with the death of Bierut and the return of Gomułka to power in 1956), it does not account for other events of that same year, such as the great strike of September, the Battle over Trade, or the birth of labor competition. Thus, it can say little about what the system looked like and how it operated. As with the revolution of 1945, we must understand society, and especially the working class, to understand stalinism. Life in the working-class community went on unchanged in many ways, regardless of the events reported in the newspapers. But stalinist Poland was very different from what most people, even those untouched by repression, would have imagined in 1945. Class rhetoric became ubiq-

[1]On the periodization of stalinism, see Andrzej Werblan, *Stalinizm w Polsce* (Warsaw, 1991), 8–9.

uitous and was turned against the workers themselves, while the communist party became a nonclass, all-embracing social organization. The end result was a system in which boundaries between public and private were severely eroded, and people were mobilized into obligatory participation in the charades of stalinism.

It should be clear from the preceding chapters, however, that the construction of such a political system did not occur in a vacuum but in response and relation to social actions and social pressures. The regime did not simply impose its will on a passive population; in industry, it had to cope with major strike waves, endemic labor turnover and insubordination, often hostile prewar traditions, and serious economic shortcomings. The PPR and its allies had tried to build a new Poland without class conflict in 1945–47. This state of affairs could not be stable, at least not in a system whose ideology was based upon the key concept of class struggle. Eliminating class struggle—that is, denying conflict over the means of production—while at the same time promoting the rhetoric of revolution raised too many thorny questions. In what ways, as workers asked in the strikes of 1945–47, were factory directors different from capitalist owners? Why were strikes not an appropriate means of winning concessions or drawing attention to grievances? Who stood behind the new managers, and what exactly did they have the power to accomplish? And if there were no class antagonisms, then what was the workers' place in the ostensibly workers' revolution? In short, who were the workers supposed to blame for their troubles, and just how could they achieve what they believed the revolution was supposed to bring about?

The social revolution, so evident and probable an outcome of the war, had by 1948 become something quite different; and the components of a state socialist—or stalinist—revolution began to fall into place. This is not to suggest that workers had controlled the revolution at the beginning and then lost it to the state and the PPR over the course of three years. No one was truly in control of the direction of social change; only during 1948 were the communists able to gain the upper hand in the factories and working-class communities. As they did so, the shape of Polish stalinism was determined by negotiation based upon the positions that workers, both in Wrocław and in Łódź, had staked out. In the end, the communists were able to impose their interpretation of change on the course of events.

Whether or not communist hegemony was foreordained, the authorities could and did draw some important lessons from the events of the previous years, using popular desires to appeal specifically to working-class opinion. This chapter will focus on the communists' attempt to secure a postrevolutionary legitimacy and impose some kind of order in society, the factories, and the party itself. It did so in part by responding to workers' concerns—for example, the enormous potential of popular anger over prices, speculation, and trade in general, or the lack of trust in labor organizations. Subsequent chapters will consider the consequences of the pressure for higher wages and social advance, but the legal-political measures examined here were crucial building blocks of the new system.

Law, Discipline, and the Rhetoric of Class

As the previous chapters have shown, strikes in Łódź and discontent in Wrocław were often intimately linked to extrafactory economics: prices on the free market and supply on the state market. Indeed, it was not the state but the workers who introduced anti–free-market rhetoric into public discourse, calling for punishment of speculators, fair prices for working people, and wider availability of staple goods. Well before the First Congress of Trade Unions issued demands for punishment of speculators in November 1945, there had already been two strike waves sparked by workers dissatisfied with prices and aprowizacja. Obviously, the state-controlled economy was as much to blame as the free market, but the latter made a politically expedient target. For example, a resolution passed by a July 1945 open union meeting at the Łódź electric plant called for an end to price speculation by private shopkeepers and proposed "flying controls" to combat price gouging.[2]

Workers expected management and the state to answer their demands for more equitable distribution of goods, yet there was little at first that cash-strapped authorities could do. The crackdown on speculation and the free market certainly had its own ideological impetus, and one can argue that it was inevitable regardless of what workers wanted. But PPR ideology here coincided—or appeared to coincide—with worker demands; moreover, both the PPR and the workers shared a belief in the use of law to force discipline on a class. This was an important moment in worker-PPR relations, telling us much about the impact that worker

[2]ARZ KCZZ WO 41, k. 140. Similar regulations can be found in ARZ KCZZ WO 14, 18, 19, 40, 41.

protest had on the conduct of PPR and state policy before stalinism. The state chose a quasi-populist weapon to combat economic problems. Officially prompted by an appeal from the KCZZ, the government formed the Special Commission for the Struggle against Abuses and Economic Sabotage in November 1945. In its first year, the Special Commission was given the power to confiscate goods and arrest, try, and sentence speculators (a category continually broadened during the commission's tenure) to short terms in labor camps.[3]

Until 1947, state economic policy—advocated even by PPR hard-liner Hilary Minc in early 1945—was the one championed by the PPS, which called for a mixed or three-sided (state, cooperative, and private) economy with an important role reserved for private enterprise.[4] Emboldened by the PPR electoral victory in January 1947 and searching for a response to the lengthy and threatening strikes across Poland during the fall and winter, Minc launched a new attack in May of that year, which came to be known as the Battle over Trade (*bitwa o handel*). Briefly, this campaign privileged state-run trade and manufacture and tightened control over the other sectors. In supporting this reversal of state policy, PPR leaders pointed to the continuing difficulty with aprowizacja and prices and to the renewed worker protests in Łódź and elsewhere. They blamed private agriculture for failing to supply sufficient goods and private trade for unnecessarily driving up prices, and they claimed that state-run commerce could assure a decent standard of living more efficiently and honestly. The PPS (and the Central Planning Bureau, dominated by PPS economists) saw the fault in monetary policy and problems in the state sector itself, although the party acknowledged the need for closer control of the private sector. But the PPR's diagnosis had political appeal, because it identified scapegoats who were both easily recognizable to workers and a convenient target for the state. The PPR used this campaign to attack the very idea of private trade; the battle quickly became a war *against* trade, climaxing in late 1947 and early

[3]Dariusz Jarosz and Tadeusz Wolsza, "Komisja Specjalna do Walki z Nadużyciami i Szkodnictwem Gospodarczym (1945–1954)," *Biuletyn Głównej Komisji Badania Zbrodni Przeciwko Narodowi Polskiemu Instytutu Pamięci Narodowej* 36 (1993): 7–36. See also Grzegorz Sołtysiak, "Komisja Specjalna do Walki," *Karta* 1 (January 1991): 81–97. The appeal from the KCZZ and key government decrees are in *Komisja Specjalna do Walki z Nadużyciami i Szkodnictwem Gospodarczym (1945–1954). Wybór dokumentów*, ed. Dariusz Jarosz and Tadeusz Wolsza (Warsaw, 1995), 15–25.

[4]Jaime Reynolds, "Communists, Socialists and Workers: Poland, 1944–1948," *Soviet Studies* 30, no. 4 (1978): 526.

1948. It was the PPR's first major conflict with the PPS and the first to involve society as well; the result was the fulfillment of a basic tenet of the communist economic vision and a victory for the hard-line wing of the PPR.[5]

As with the formation of the Special Commission, this chain of events was formally preceded by, or coordinated with, populist appeals from the trade unions. In May 1947, the KCZZ called for the "mobilization of our material, financial, and human reserves and the maintenance of social discipline" and noted that speculative price rises caused a drop in real wages. As it had in 1945, the KCZZ called for use of the death penalty if other measures (labor camps and heavy fines) proved insufficient. On 4 June, the KCZZ further pledged to mobilize workers to cooperate with and participate in this battle. It resolved to hold regular meetings in factories to report on the progress of the battle and "to organize Committees for the Struggle with High Living Costs [*drożyzna*] in factories and trade union sections, chosen, if possible, at meetings devoted to the struggle with speculation and high living costs." These factory committees would delegate some 15,000 social monitors and inspectors "to monitor local stores for abidance by established prices."[6]

The KCZZ's statements were echoed by similar ones at the local level, probably orchestrated from Warsaw. The members of one Wrocław union passed the following resolution: "We construction workers . . . appeal fervently to the government of the Polish Republic for the most severe punishment of profiteers, speculators, and dishonest merchants, in connection with an increased monitoring of the prices of staple goods. [We] demand for the above-mentioned strict jail terms and even the death penalty, in order to eliminate unjustified price hikes completely." In Łódź, a conference of factory council representatives warned: "The speculators have come out into the open and are getting fat at the expense of the working class. . . . Workers demand sharper measures towards speculation. . . . Don't stop at inspection of private stores, but liquidate them if they do not conform to official price tables."[7]

The legal structure of the campaign was erected quickly. First, the

[5]Andrzej Jezierski and Barbara Petz, *Historia gospodarcza Polski Ludowej 1944–1975* (Warsaw 1980), 56–57; Janusz Kaliński, *Bitwa o handel* (Warsaw, 1970); AAN KC PPR 295/V/3, kk. 55, 58–63.

[6]"Udział związków zawodowych w walce ze spekulacją i procesie normowania sytuacji rynkowej w latach 1944–1948," ed. Julian Krupa *KHRZ* no. 2 (1977): 47–53.

[7]WAP Związek Zawodowy Budowlanych WO 5, k. 35; AAN KC PPR 295/XIII/7, kk. 97–99.

Special Commission's powers were significantly expanded in June 1947; while its earliest work had focused on szaber and the uncovering of large-scale economic sabotage, it now joined the battle over speculation and high prices. Second, the Ministry of Industry and Commerce created a central Price Bureau, which established standard base prices on some goods and an acceptable range for retail prices. At the local level, some three hundred Social Price Monitoring Commissions (the name, of course, suggested representation of the people's will) conducted direct inspection by mid-1948 of stored goods, account books, bills, and prices in stores and warehouses. They were authorized to report illegalities to local Special Commissions and recommend appropriate punishment.[8]

Rhetorically, the emphasis shifted from actions that harmed the state, such as the production of bootleg liquor or unregistered slaughterhouses, to actions that harmed workers: high prices in stores or speculation that prevented goods from reaching the market. The Special Commission and the bitwa were concrete political and economic responses to workers' real frustrations about food prices. They were also part of a propaganda campaign: a play for popularity and an attempt to provide a scapegoat to appease an angry, hungry population that had endured a severe winter. The tenor of the commission was provided by its PPR members, led by ideologist Roman Zambrowski; the idea of punishment for those who harmed workers, however, was widespread in society. In arguing its case, the PPR could draw on workers' statements about private trade—for example, "one lived better under the sanacja regime, and [now we are] white slaves."[9]

The Battle over Trade introduced a new, safer kind of class conflict, aligning the parties and the PPR-allied state employers with the workers against newly outlined class enemies. A PPS instruction on the battle with speculation called for "creating a better climate in workshops, factories and institutions by means of a mutually loyal relationship between employee and employer." Calling for its members to explain the real reasons for price hikes, the PPS sought to redirect the class struggle away from the employer and the shop floor to the community and the shop-

[8] *Komisja Specjalna do Walki,* 37–51. Kaliński, *Bitwa o handel,* 101, n. 17; AAN CKW PPS 235/XV/2, kk. 212–13.

[9] ŁAP WRZZ 68, n.p.; see examples of workers' anger in Chapter 2; Stefan Kalinowski, "Z działalności Komisji Specjalnej do Walki z Nadużyciami i Szkodnictwem Gospodarczym (1946–1947)," *KHRZ* no. 2 (1976): 54.

keeper. The PPR's instructions were similar but placed greater emphasis on the "moral-political mobilization of the working masses." The success of this war, the PPR admitted, called for honesty in propaganda—an end to "official optimism." As an earlier PPR directive had remarked, "The working masses should see clearly that our Party is ready to condemn abuses."[10]

For the average Polish worker and consumer, the operation of the Special Commission was evident in well-publicized scandals of embezzlement or hoarding and in the highly visible efforts of its regional and local representatives to monitor and control prices on the free market. In a society overflowing with righteous anger from the war and postwar shortages, the latter function of the Special Commission could find an enthusiastic response; in Wrocław, a large part of the denunciations received were from workers.[11] Responding to the moral economy workers had expressed (for example, in Łódź in 1945–46) organizers framed the campaign in gender terms. Led by those in Łódź, women workers were among the most vocal, even violent, in demanding change. That the campaign sought to cast wives and mothers as vigilant heroes is another indication of its intended social bases. A KCZZ document of 12 June 1947 outlining factory participation stated that "working women, and the wives and daughters of workers and employees, should be drafted into all committees."[12] The propaganda behind a price commission formed at the Wrocław spirits factory in August 1947 played effectively on the image of shopkeepers as threatening family livelihood—"parasites of society and especially of working people," in the factory PPS Secretary's words. A representative of the city PPS at the spirits factory meeting remarked that "the main agent [in this plan] will be the wives and mothers of employees, since in running a household and making purchases of food items" they would be aware of differences in prices between stores. For workers seeking a scapegoat for their problems—and work at this particular isolated factory, in a divided, ruined city was especially thankless—the power to stop high prices could be attractive.[13] But a

[10]AAN CKW PPS 235/III/3; AAN KC PPR 295/IX/382, kk. 13–20; AAN KC PPR 295/XI/12, kk. 48–50. See also *Komisja Specjalna do Walki* , 65–66.

[11]Barbara Rogowska, "Delegatura Komisji Specjalnej do Walki z Nadużyciami i Szkodnictwem Gospodarczym na Dolnym Śląsku w latach 1945–1947," in *Z badań nad dziejami Dolnego Śląska po II wojnie światowej*, ed. Stanisław Dąbrowski (Wrocław, 1993), 76.

[12]"Udział związków zawodowych w walce ze spekulacją," 49–53.

[13]ARZ KCZZ WE 258, n.p. The dominance of the PPS at this meeting is worth noting.

few months later, the Wrocław trade union organization reported that "the anti-speculation campaign has weakened; committees created and organized in work places show no activity, with some exceptions."[14]

The bitwa enjoyed some early successes as an outlet for class anger. Workers and consumers in general liked the get-tough slogans and an early proposal for people's courts to try speculators. Early, well-publicized convictions in economic *afery* (scandals), followed by positive economic effects, satisfied popular expectations. While few people's courts materialized, more than one-quarter of the denunciations received by the Special Commission in 1946 came from individuals. Although the percentage declined sharply the next year, the number of such reports remained roughly constant through 1948.[15]

But workers expected much more from the Special Commissions than they got. Except for the price of bread, which declined substantially, there was little change in free-market prices in Warsaw between late 1947 and late 1948.[16] Just three months into the Battle over Trade, the Wrocław PPR reported that "lately one can sense the masses' ever greater embitterment; they expected a tougher waging of the battle and a subsequent improvement in their lives. The panicked fear which consumed merchants at the very beginning of this campaign has long passed."[17] Workers especially feared that the war with private trade would only mean less food in the shops; some went so far as to warn shopkeepers of impending inspections.[18] Pending an improved standard of living, one response to workers' fears was not long in coming: the Special Commission's activity increased markedly beginning in 1948. Spurred on by official class rhetoric, many local commissions overran their mandates, conducting hasty investigations or issuing excessive pun-

[14] WAP WRZZ 68, k. 2.

[15] Tomasz Żukowski, *Związki zawodowe i samorząd pracowniczy w polskich zakładach przemysłowych w latach 1944–1987* (Warsaw, 1987), 32–33; AAN MIiP 82, k. 26; Jarosz and Wolsza, "Komisja Specjalna do Walki," 25. On *afery*, see reports throughout MSW MBP 17/IX/38, t. 2. There were fifty-eight citizens' courts with 450 total members: *Partia w cyfrach*, sec. 20.

[16] AAN MPiOS 489, n.p.

[17] AAN KC PPR 295/XIII/25, k. 93. See also AAN CKW PPS 235/XV/78, k. 17.

[18] AAN KC PZPR 237/XXXI/132, k. 61. In Wrocław in September 1948, there were rumors among workers that, in connection with the search for speculators, all apartments would be searched and reserves as small as two kilos of flour would be confiscated. WAP KW PPR 1/VI/99, k. 85.

ishments, taking bribes or practicing extortion. Officials in Warsaw found it necessary to rein in activists in the provinces.[19]

The Battle over Trade marked a transition in the communist regime's struggle with real and imaginary opponents. In 1945–1946, the villains in official rhetoric had been war destruction, departing Germans, and untrustworthy Western allies. Now the slogans of battle with the reactionaries, capitalists, and saboteurs replaced the former enemies in the official class war. The foundations of that war were the leading parties' ideologies and working-class frustrations; the *bitwa* was as much a response to the threat of the latter as it was to the dictates of the former.

Yet workers discovered that the battle's imagery of class conflict offered new tools for labor conflict in ways that the authorities had hoped to eliminate. Workers and labor organizations incorporated terms such as *speculator, reactionary,* and *red bourgeoisie* into their protests. Because the battle had formally begun with the trade unions, labor representatives felt emboldened to issue calls to management to join the cause. "Messrs. directors and higher bureaucrats have not yet joined the battle [with speculation]," protested a textile factory representative in July 1947. "[They] smash up automobiles, when it would be better if they took equal part with the workers in this battle."[20] Councils, unions, and party organizations also portrayed management as political opponents who persecuted PPR members for politicizing the factory, discriminated against party members in promotions within management, or attempted to control the council or even the local union. Even the party itself was labeled (during the Poznański strike) as "the red nobility."[21] In this confusing era of worker-management relations, both sides tried out any new tool that came to hand. Workers had learned a great deal over the past three years and did not express support for the state or the PPR when they adopted official terminology. The official campaign against speculators only confirmed a pessimistic view of "the authorities," even as those authorities strove to win support through their campaigns. As a Łódź PPS member charged shortly before party unification,

---

[19]Jarosz and Wolsza, "Komisja Specjalna do Walki," 24–25; Kaliński, *Bitwa o handel,* 99–104.

[20]ŁAP WRZZ 19, n.p.; WAP KW PPR 1/X/5, kk. 158–59.

[21]AAN KC PPR 295/IX/33, k. 83. See also WAP KW PPR 1/XII/34, k. 5; WAP KW PPR 1/XII/36, kk. 161–62; ŁAP KW PPR 1/XI/1 n.p.; and, from late 1949, ŁAP WRZZ 2, k. 53.

the PPR itself had simply become management, bringing about "the exploitation of worker by worker."[22]

One area where authorities' and workers' use of class imagery conflicted was in the knotty problem of private industry. On the one hand, private employers were hostile to unions and factory councils; on the other, private employers paid better.[23] Even the Battle over Trade sometimes seemed to be no match for the private sector. The authorities' confusion surfaced in fights over reprivatization like that in a small cardboard factory in Zgierz (near Łódź) in early 1948. For party activists, this issue should have been black and white: the return of the prewar owners symbolized capitalism's relentless assault on socialism. But who were capitalists and who were communists? At an emergency meeting of the factory's workers, one PPR representative warned that workers who had saved and rebuilt the factory were now "exposed to the temptations of capitalists pretending to be communists. . . . We must defend ourselves against exploiters who are now attacking the working class across the whole world. We cannot tolerate capitalist lackeys, neither in the party nor in the factories. We will defeat them in every part of the factory." He denounced the "negative activity of some individuals who poison everybody's lives and who should be excluded from worker society." On the one hand, incidents like this were grist for the party's propaganda of vigilance against the enemies of the working class victory, and so on. But they also sent workers a confused message. Speakers implicated party members, the state, and the courts, which allowed capitalists to continue their attack quite legally. Others blamed workers and even the "passivity and gullibility of the Polish people, who are taken in by cheap baubles and promises." The lesson that workers drew was that all authorities were in it together.[24]

The economic scandals that were the bread and butter of the national press in 1948 only encouraged this impression. One of the first such scandals of national significance was the Dolewski affair, the trial of a paper-industry magnate accused of fixing prices and paying bribes to high government officials. The trial of Dolewski and his associates began in Łódź in the second week of January 1948—matched conveniently by

---

[22]ŁAP WK PPS 22/VII/93, n.p.

[23]ARZ KCZZ WO 417, n.p.; WUSW KWMO 148/19; MSW MBP 17/IX/77, t. 2, n.p. (October 1947); MSW MBP 17/IX/38, t. 2, n.p. (January 1948).

[24]ŁAP WRZZ 260, n.p. Another case appears in ARZ KCZZ WE 82, n.p. (24 June 1948).

the trial of the Krupp family and other German industrialists in Nuremberg at about the same time. Among other things, said the prosecutor, Dolewski's manipulation of the paper market had made it difficult for the children of working Poles to buy notebooks for school. But according to the Łódź UB, "in worker circles one encounters the conviction that Dolewski will be freed no matter what, since everything can be hushed up with money."[25]

Before the war, workers had complained about the lives that the factory owners led in their great palaces. In this supposedly egalitarian age, they compared money; the Wrocław police reported in June 1948 that workers frequently complained about the gap between their wages and management salaries. As a PPR activist-worker at the Barlicki mill in Łódź said, "The scum which ground us down before the war make 20–30 thousand, and we who build Poland get 5–6000 [monthly]."[26] Labor activists retreating from the use of strikes also learned the value of the new language of class conflict and adopted it to attack management. Factory council members at a Zgierz cotton mill complained that the director "should have his office on this side of the street, where the factory is, to be more closely tied to the workers. . . . [He] complains to the woman who brings him dinner from the kitchen that he won't eat from such a bowl, that the dinners are not good, the kielbasa isn't tasty, the lettuce should be served with cream; he orders coffee to be brought five times a day. And this has an effect on the workers; there are some whispers, and dissatisfaction, and we as the Factory Council cannot allow this, and must put a stop to it. . . . The Chief Director asks the councilors if the matter of ordering coffee, and those dinners, is such a great crime? He got the answer that as a proletarian he should not behave in this way or any other."[27] This director was probably a PPR member, since the councilors admonished him in their version of party language. In early 1949, a union activist summed up the problem this way: "Today we do not have that democracy of which we dreamed. The aristocracy is creeping in among us. Directors smash up cars, and do not know how to drive. The lowest worker makes 8000 *złotys*, and directors make 28–34,000. Yet they have the same stomachs. The gentlemen directors don't do anything in cooperation with us, and black-

[25] MSW MBP 17/IX/10 t. 2, k. 2.
[26] ŁAP KD PPR Górna-Prawa 1/VI/65, k. 88; see also WUSW KWMO 149/16 n.p.
[27] ŁAP WRZZ 288 n.p.

mail us. [We have to] bow low, and be obedient. The trade unions [union leadership] should come to us and see how the situation looks."[28]

The image of the speculator—someone profiting from the hardship of the people—was an important part of how workers came to view authorities, and how the authorities came to characterize opposition. This type of class identity proved quite versatile throughout the communist era as a weapon of both the regime and the opposition. During the three-year plan, even as the private entrepreneur was almost extinct by late 1948, the perceived enemy was never vanquished. His symbolic endurance could be seen in both Wrocław and Łódź—the former known for szaber, the latter full of myths about the exploits of the rich since its earliest days. The Wrocław police reported that workers in one downtown district "claim that rich people occupy the 1st and 2nd floors [of apartment buildings] and the villas, while workers live on the upper floors, and usually in older buildings, where the apartments are cramped and uncomfortable." There were small riots or disturbances in that district in the summer of 1949 in which Jews accused of speculating were attacked and beaten.[29] In Łódź, Cecylja Sierakowska made similar allegations to union delegates in late 1949:

> As a *przodownica* [leading worker] . . . I speak in the name of 4,850 women. I am a worker. I've had conversations with women on the housing issue. They complain that it is difficult for a worker to get an apartment. There are still many apartments where two people have one room with a kitchen. . . . The looter has rooms, and the worker, basements and attics. (applause) . . . Women tell me that when there are inexpensive goods, only looters get them—supposedly on their identity card [that is, a card identifying one as a worker, allowing purchase of certain goods]—and in an hour there's nothing left, and those goods are on the Bałuty Rynek [an outdoor market]. Isn't there any inspection there? Obviously not, for if there were inspection, it would surely turn out that almost all [sellers] have no workbooks [that is, proof of employment], since a worker who has a job won't stand in line six or seven hours for some goods.[30]

Sierakowska was surely a party member, and her remarks were probably approved beforehand; nevertheless, many workers shared her senti-

[28]ŁAP WRZZ 297, n.p.
[29]WUSW KWMO 150/10 n.p. In June, rents had been raised by 100 percent.
[30]ŁAP WRZZ 2, kk. 49–50. Another speaker identified specific apartments where doctors or lawyers had more rooms than they should (k. 66).

ments. This made the authorities uneasy, for any dissatisfaction was hazardous to encourage. "We must be vigilant in the factories," concluded a Łódź union report, reviewing some of the rumors heard in the city in the summer of 1949.[31]

Not until 1950, indeed, would the vigilance of the state be turned on the workers. For example, the Special Commission's labor camps—the term suggesting a place where one who had not performed honest work would be forced to do so—remained largely outside the workers' experience; they were a place where managers and merchants, less often workers, were sent. Labor camps (there were thirty during this period) were created in early 1946; by 1949, just over 20,000 people had been sentenced to these camps for periods from one week to two years. The vast majority were punished for "office crimes," "speculation," or "actions against the state monopoly." Less than 7 percent of those sent to camps in 1946–48 were charged with "plunder and appropriation of public property"—that is, theft, the only major crime in which a worker could participate as a worker. While the number of workers targeted grew from 12 percent of those sent to camps in 1946 to 20 percent two years later, these numbers were tiny: the latter equals just 1,071 workers.[32]

Worker crime remained a minor issue for the police through 1947. The Security Apparatus pursued just 534 cases of property crimes in all of Polish industry in June through August 1947. Of these, just eighty-two concerned theft, and the UB made only 164 arrests. Numbers were not significantly higher in 1948 but began to rise in 1949.[33] Despite frequent entreaties for vigilance by Security Apparatus chiefs, police activity in the factories was insignificant. Even in December 1949, the Łódź UB complained of an "insignificant agent network in the largest factories ... and there is absolutely no one in the smaller ones." Overall, the agent network in industry was "very weakly used." Workers seemed less of a threat (whether symbolic or real) than managers, technicians, or merchants. The energetic pursuit of sabotage crimes in 1948–49 rarely

---

[31] ŁAP WRZZ 19 n.p.

[32] Jarosz and Wolsza, "Komisja Specjalna," 28; AAN Komisja Specjalna 18, kk. 149, 184, 202–3; AAN Komisja Specjalna 21, passim. Tomasz Grosse et al., "Szarzy ludzie zaplątani w codzienności komunizmu," *Przegląd Historyczny* 84, no. 3 (1993): 335–50. On labor camps, see also Sołtysiak, "Komisja Specjalna," and *Komisja Specjalna do Walki,* 125–61.

[33] MSW MBP 17/IX/38, t. 1 (September 1947); tt. 2–4. There may also have been arrests by civilian police, of course, but the latter were less likely than the UB to take action in factories.

identified workers as culprits; rather, workers were victims prevented from accomplishing their tasks by politically hostile supervisors.[34] In 1950, workers abruptly joined the category of potential enemies of the system; that year, there were almost 2,200 *convictions* for crimes against social property in Łódź alone; roughly two-thirds of these were for theft.[35]

Strikes also continued to be a problem. The great Poznański strike was by no means the end of labor conflict in Łódź. Indeed, in some ways strikes were even more likely in 1948 than the previous year because workers now had no other avenue for protest. While workers could no longer openly defend their community (as they had in many aprowizacja strikes of 1946) or control of their jobs (as in the control strikes of 1947), they still sought a minimum of security and basic rights, expressing expectations that shaped the nature of the stalinist party and state. A (almost surely incomplete) survey shows some sixty-two strikes or threatened strikes (a term often used for brief action in which workers actually stopped work for a time and threatened to walk out of the factory) in Łódź from November 1947 to November 1948, most in the summer and fall of 1948. Most strikes were brief, ad hoc protests against declining conditions; some workers even avoided the word *strike* in order to avert an escalation of the conflict beyond their control.

Zdzisława G., a young worker at the Łódź thread factory, discovered in early 1949 just how dangerous it could be to strike. When workers were told to work eight hours one Saturday, older women in the factory planned a two-hour protest in front of the factory gates during their shift. Because she lived near the factory, Zdzisława G. joined in. As a result, "They fired me for disciplinary reasons, and told me that I was the provocator of the protest. But I only listened to the older women, and they said that they would come at eleven, but came at one. And I walked in front of the factory from eleven to one. There were a few of

[34] MSW MBP 17/IX/38, t. 4, n.p. See other reports in tt. 2–4. On sabotage, see Zdzisław Albin Ziemba, "Prawo karne Polski Ludowej w latach 1944–1956," in *Stalinizm*, ed. Jacek Kurczewski (Warsaw, 1989), 119–25. The category of sabotage emerged as an important party concern only in late 1949, from which time it was a category regularly covered in provincial reports. See, for example, WAP KW PZPR 74/VIII/6, passim.

[35] The 1950 estimate is based on thirty-five convictions per ten thousand inhabitants; the national rate was 9.8 theft convictions per ten thousand. AAN Ministerstwo Sprawiedliwości 2713, kk. 54–59. See also Witold Świda, *Wpływ zmiany ustroju na przestępczość (w świetle przestępczości w Kaliszu i powiecie kaliskim)*, Prace Wrocławskiego Towarzystwa Naukowego, series A, 67 (Wrocław, 1960), 1:35–42.

us there—exactly nine. . . . They took us away. . . . I began to cry—I was young. . . . They ordered me, and two others, to make up the hours, but it still didn't help us much—they fired us." Older workers, apparently unafraid of the consequences, protested to management on her behalf. "They said they would strike, that if they don't hire me back they would call a strike. 'The girl is innocent,' they said, 'because . . . we didn't come.' " This protest failed, too, and Zdzisława G. was forced to find work at another factory farther from home.[36]

As Zdzisława G. discovered, strikes in 1948 and after could be as divisive as they had been unifying before. Bereft of the solidarity afforded by a trusted factory council, union, or party leader, workers both old and new were left to fend for themselves against each other and management. This unstable set of relations gave rise to situations like that at the Horak mill. Management announced that Good Friday would be a holiday if workers made up the lost hours beforehand. All departments did so except the weaving shop, which declared that it would "break with this German tradition and work on Friday normally." All assumed that Saturday would also be a holiday, but management then ordered that workers wishing to take Saturday off should work four hours on Friday—leaving the weavers to work eight on Friday and four on Saturday. Instead, the weavers left with the rest of the workers after four hours on Friday.[37]

In mid-1948, labor unrest still was not repressed consistently. Clearly, the PPR had yet to establish control over the Łódź factory. Most workers were still the same ones who had struck the year before, although their room to maneuver within the system was steadily shrinking. The first anniversary of the Poznański strike, in September 1948, was a somber occasion. New pay tables had drastically equalized wages, and aprowizacja problems and rumors of impending war fostered a "food panic." The PPR and the unions were able quickly to suppress any action in observance of that anniversary; only one brief related strike was reported.[38] The Poznański strike slipped into obscurity, never to enjoy the fame of later worker unrest in People's Poland.

---

[36]See Chapter 5. Interview, May 1990.

[37]They later agreed to make up the lost hours after Easter. ŁAP KŁ PPR 1/VI/143, k. 30; ŁAP CZPW 447, k. 10.

[38]ŁAP CZPW 447, kk. 3, 11; ŁAP KŁ PPR 1/XI/1, kk. 105, 131–34; AAN KC PPR 295/XI/50, k. 109; ŁAP CZPW 448, k. 9; ŁAP WRZZ 66, n.p. On 1948 strikes in general, see monthly reports in MSW MBP 17/IX/38, tt. 2–3.

A PPR report on workers at Poznański in November 1948 reveals more about how the party and its estimation of the workers had changed than about the nature of working-class protest:

> Among the workers employed in our factory, a relatively large percent is not conscious about today's reality, thanks to the former education of the working class by the old *sanacja* [the prewar dictatorship] regime. Among those employed, a religious upbringing and an anti-semitic attitude still show themselves. . . . The activity of hostile elements on our turf appears in various forms. Workers' paydays . . . pass with relative difficulty, as they are taken advantage of by an element which is not awakened to us, in order to sow confusion and dissatisfaction among the worker masses which we have not yet succeeded in winning for the present reality. . . . a very large percent of our employees is under the influence of the clergy, which strives to spread anti-semitism and propaganda hostile to the USSR.[39]

Although strikes might be almost a thing of the past, disorder in the workplace—in particular, labor turnover—was as great as ever. The authorities searched desperately for ways to control discipline from late 1947 through 1949. A factory in Wrocław experimented with colored pins to keep workers in their place during work. One Wrocław union proposed taking away the union cards from workers who were more than ten minutes late. The employment bureau in Łódź introduced a system of blacklisting workers who had quit without giving notice: when they showed up to work somewhere else, they were identified and sent back to their original employers.[40] Party leaders in Łódź conducted a propaganda week in June 1948 under the slogan "Let's make our work more effective!" Besides organizing factory meetings featuring speeches on the monetary cost of poor discipline, they planned radio and newspaper announcements, short films in cinemas, and even slogans to be printed on cigarette packages.[41] Yet party and industry reports from Łódź in late 1949 still spoke of "mass absences" at many major facto-

[39]ŁAP KŁ PPR 1/VI/142, k. 28.

[40]WAP KW PPR 1/X/36, kk. 4–5; WAP WRZZ 2, k. 76; ARZ KCZZ WE 146, n.p.; ARZ KCZZ WO 496, k. 5.

[41]AAN KC PPR 295/XI/50, kk. 98–99. See also comment by a Łódź railway official in May: "If each worker leaves his job for only one minute in the course of the day, the losses resulting . . . yearly would reach nine million zlotys. . . . These figures should be used . . . in propaganda campaigns." ŁAP KW PPR 1/X/2, k. 23.

ries; administrators reported drunkenness on the shop floor and found that even registration could not stop workers from quitting.[42]

The solution was a dramatic rewriting of the relationship between workers and their employer to incorporate a moral code in the workplace. The party's opponents had once been capitalists, reactionaries, and clergy; now they were lazy or insubordinate workers and bureaucratic or (conversely) syndicalist labor organizations. Whether or not any of these labels were in some sense real, they spoke volumes to the PPR as it renewed the revolution both internally and externally. Thus, the PPR factory committee during an October 1948 strike at Geyer warned workers that "we will pay only those who work, and we will give no credit (*bonifikaty*) to loafers."[43] Activists in the Łódź transportation union called for the consideration of moral character in naming avantgarde workers; competition regulations in Łódź's textile warehouse called for points to be subtracted for "neglect of outward culture" such as impoliteness, unfriendliness, or unkempt dress.[44]

After the PPR and PPS joined to form the Polish United Workers' Party (Polska Zjednoczona Partia Robotnicza, PZPR) in December 1948 (to be discussed later in this chapter), there was also, for the first time, mention of firing workers not for specific crimes such as stealing or striking but for being the wrong element. The Łódź PZPR announced in February 1949 that " 'labor malcontents' would be dismissed, non-experts first. This is an element recruited in large part from small liquidated private initiative, unhealthy [for] production, looking for employment only with an eye for social benefits ([cheaper] apartment rent and electricity, fat coupons, etc.)."[45] This was the language of the Battle over Trade—indeed, the party admitted that some of these workers were the victims of that campaign. Now, they were being pursued in the factory as well—for their past as much as their present. The implication was that the division in society was not just between those who worked and those who did not but between those who deserved the work they had and performed it honorably and those who did not deserve it. By late 1949, talk of saboteurs in the workplace was becom-

---

[42]ŁAP KŁ PZPR 34/VIII/79a, n.p.; ŁAP Zakłady Przemysłu Wełnianego "9-go Maja" 297, n.p.

[43]ŁAP KŁ PPR 1/VI/142, kk. 109–10.

[44]ŁAP WRZZ 19, n.p. (August 1949); competition regulations: ŁAP WRZZ 68, n.p.

[45]AAN KC PZPR 237/XXXI/132, k. 30. In another case, a committee including party and union representatives at the state tobacco factory in Łódź decided to lay off sixty workers "who do not carry their share of the work." ŁAP WRZZ 68, n.p. (November 1949).

ing common. In a very different way from 1945, the factory once again became a location of class struggle.

The June 1950 law on socialist work discipline marks the official beginning of the open battle with worker crime and the dawn of stalinism in the factories. The major crime targeted by the law was absenteeism, although drunkenness and leaving the factory during the work day were also addressed. Missing four days in the course of a year made a worker subject to criminal proceedings. The usual punishment was 10 to 15 percent of one's pay for one or two months, during which time the worker lost the right to quit. The law virtually ignored workers' behavior during work, dealing only with their physical presence in the factory. Nevertheless, all workers were potential culprits; whether they struck or showed up late, they "lowered the effectiveness of the self-sacrificing work of their comrades and exerted a negative influence on the further constant growth of the working masses' living standards and culture," as the law's preamble explained.[46] What was once a matter for the worker's supervisor or the factory director now became the business of the state. In just seven months in 1950, 42,443 workers were convicted under the law; this represented 21 percent of *all* convictions in Poland that year and (with other crimes included) pushed industrial workers to more than half of those convicted in Poland that year.[47] While the law stressed punishment, PZPR leaders tried to steer the focus toward education through the trade unions, youth organizations, and mass media.[48] Workers reacted with disgust, and sometimes even with strikes, but their protests were entirely ineffective.[49] Stalinism had finally come to the fac-

[46] Najnowsza historia polityczna Polski: Wybór źródeł, Part 5: 1949–1956, eds. Wiesław Kozub-Ciembronowicz and Jacek M. Majchrowski (Kraków, 1993), 51–55. Jadwiga Kalinowska, Postawy robotników wobec pracy (Warsaw, 1978), 33–34.

[47] AAN Ministerstwo Sprawiedliwości 2713, kk. 107–10, 149–51. In 1951, convictions on this law were 35.5 percent of all convictions. Not surprisingly, a high percentage of these convictions were in Wrocław province. In Łódź the number was smaller, but these convictions were almost three-quarters of all convictions in the province—the highest percentage in Poland. At the same time, other crimes applicable to all of society increased dramatically in 1950. Convictions for whispered propaganda (rumor-spreading) were more than two and a half times higher than in 1949 and five times the number in 1948. Convictions for insulting authorities (znieważenie władzy) rose more slowly but were twelve times more common. Ibid., 121.

[48] See AAN KC PZPR 237/VII/93, kk. 207–8, 237/XXXI/5, kk. 44–45; Antoni Czubiński, Najnowsze dzieje Polski, 1914–1983 (Warsaw, 1987), 349.

[49] Janusz Tomaszewski, "Zadania 'produkcyjne' związków zawodowych i ich realizacja na Dolnym Śląsku w latach 1945–1950," in Z badań nad dziejami Dolnego Śląska, 37–38.

tories. Workers had hardly expected that their desires for greater law and order would be thrust back upon them in this way; they found, moreover, that they no longer had any advocates in the factory.

The Party Takes Over the Factories

Redefining the individual worker as potential criminal and economic saboteur was only one part of the stalinist subordination of the working class. The PPR also had to take control of the factory itself. As Chapter 1 showed, subduing the factory councils and unions was relatively simple; but these organizations, spineless and distrusted by workers, had no power. In 1948–49, the councils and unions were finally transformed into agents of factory control in conjunction with the simultaneous drive for worker productivity (discussed in Chapter 5). The campaign to transform the labor organizations often used the language of conflict perfected in the Battle over Trade. It was a response both to the evident shortcomings of labor organizations revealed by the persistence of labor unrest and to their lack of credibility. The PPR sought simply to use effectively those bodies upon which it felt it should be able to rely. Whatever the reach of its propaganda, the party could not mobilize workers effectively until it established itself within the factories. This process of streamlining labor organizations was another aspect of the political and social campaigns of early stalinism. Party control of labor meant a removal of politics (in the sense of democratic representation) from the workplace, and the state control of the work of social organizations.

Factory councils, which in the strikes of 1945–47 had proven to be one of the raw edges of the new factory system, were the first problem. Their ambiguous relationship to management and the PPR had certainly not endeared them to the workers; they were able neither to ensure peace in the factory nor to answer workers' complaints. It was workers' distrust of and indifference toward the way the factory councils operated, as much as the momentum of stalinism, that made their statization possible. The PPR used the nationwide council elections of March 1948 to secure the councils into the party-state apparatus, where their functioning—if not their effectiveness or popularity—would be more certain. One industry proposed an "election quadrumvirate" that would agree upon a slate of candidates under the union's aegis, and try to prevent the appearance of wild slates that might be "put forward by part of the nonparty work force, or by those dissatisfied with the union list." Com-

munists would dominate a committee composed of the personnel director, a representative of the old factory council (preferably from the PPR),
and the secretaries of the PPR and PPS factory organizations; the committee was to work with the district-level PPR, even in issues involving
PPS candidates. The factory council would then be a PPR organization
in the sense that membership in the party was important for a council
member. The role of the union, the ostensible parent body, seems more
of an afterthought; neither was it important that this proposal was from
a management organization because party allegiance was expected to
outweigh labor relations.[50]

The labor departments of the PPR and PPS issued instructions calling
for PPR-PPS equality (with some agreed-upon nonparty members) on
common lists.[51] As in the Battle over Trade, the labor parties attempted
to summon popular support for their election strategy. Factory *masówki*
(mass rallies) critiqued the performance of outgoing councils. According
to the Łódź-Górna PPR Committee, these latter were very popular with
workers, perhaps because they gave workers a chance to express their
disappointment openly. Workers' complaints, as the PPR reported (and
probably arranged), suggested what kind of restructuring, in response to
what shortcomings, would be important in the new councils. PPR council candidates led the critique, faulting the old councils for insufficient
support of multimachine workers and lack of interest in increasing
worker productivity and decreasing waste as well as issues such as day-
care and cafeterias.[52]

The PPR left little to chance in the actual elections. Election committees,
probably like the quadrumvirate described above, formed groups of agitators (at some cost to production) to campaign among nonparty workers.
The campaign was conducted not only at work but at workers' homes:
party politics thus became community politics, too. In Łódź's textile mills,
"our [PPR] comrades reported lists of nonparty workers, especially
women, who were known to them for their aggressiveness and a bad attitude toward our Party. For example, at Eisenbraun we had one hundred
such [names]. . . . Our comrades from the League of Women [*Ligówki*]

---

[50]AAN MPiH 142, n.p. PPR discussions of the upcoming elections used language such
as "we have to conduct elections," or "the [PPR] Labor Department conducted the election
campaign." See WAP KW PPR 1/XII/3, passim.

[51]Examples in "Dokumenty PPR i PPS dotyczące działalności związków zawodowych,"
211–12; and AAN KC PPR 295/XIII/9, k. 102.

[52]ŁAP KŁ PPR 1/XI/7, kk. 1–6. In addition to material cited in preceding chapters, see
WAP WRZZ 58, kk. 6, 17; ŁAP WRZZ 66, n.p.

went to the indicated addresses, especially to the women, and at [their] homes engaged in conversations on their concerns and personal problems—and there were several who needed help; then they turned [the discussion] to their workplace, and the factory council elections. The results of this campaign were generally good, since those elements were neutralized during the campaign, and [some] even voted for the slate of our candidates."[53] Party, League of Women, and youth organization members also brought nonparty workers to vote, conducting them to the voting urn and, ideally, ensuring that they cast ballots for the PPR.[54]

The council elections were marked by bitter interparty fights. There were virtually no nonparty candidates except for those vetted by the party and marked (internally) as "PPR" or "PPS" candidates.[55] Accusations flew on both sides—from the PPS, that PPR leaders were encouraging workers to vote only for PPR candidates, even campaigning within polling places; and from the PPR, that PPS members were not voting as agreed on for PPR candidates. "Where there is no common front cooperation," reported the Łódź City PPR, referring to the policy of working together toward eventual unification, "and no tendencies to switch to our side, the PPS does not vote for us, and its leadership doesn't hand out our numbers [to voters] at all. Most (90 percent) of our comrades voted for the PPS. It should be pointed out that those in the PPS whom we vote for get the majority of votes. In some factories, there was a rough battle for victory. . . . The decisive moment in the elections was the last day, meaning the method of leading [voters] to the urns. At Horak, our Party organization took insufficient control of agitation, and could not lead [voters] to the urns, while the PPS conducted a sudden campaign in the last days."[56]

The PPR, however, won impressively. Across Łódź, it lost only three elections in textile mills. In the Górna district, it won more than 80 percent of the council seats, even in factories considered PPS strong-

[53]ŁAP KŁ PPR 1/XI/7, kk. 1–8. The Horak mill sent out 26 home agitators, who talked with 800 workers, and 120 factory agitators who reported contact with 2600 workers. Scheibler and Grohman had 24 home agitators and (on paper, at least) 485 factory agitators. ŁAP KŁ PPR 1/XI/8, kk. 68–70.

[54]This was a tactic practiced with success in the referendum of 1946 and the Sejm election of 1947. See sources in note 53, and also AAN KC PPR 295/XIII/7, kk. 169–70, and, in Wrocław, WAP WRZZ 3, k. 192.

[55]WAP KW PPR 1/XII/27, k. 9.

[56]ŁAP KŁ PPR 1/XI/4, n.p.

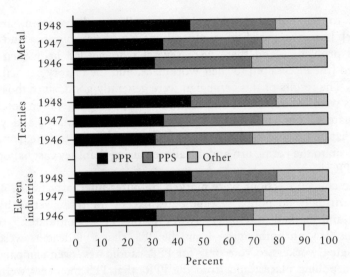

Figure 7. Party membership in factory councils, 1946–1948

holds.[57] The party did well in Wrocław, too. The 1948 elections reversed the balance, which had stayed relatively even through 1947, in the PPR's favor nationwide, particularly in key industries, as figure 7 illustrates. In Wrocław, where the PPR was strong numerically, the party was also stronger in the factory councils. Nonparty or other-party council members made up 59 percent of all members in 1946; PPR members were 24 percent and PPS members 18 percent. In 1948, PPR dominance was abruptly complete, more so than elsewhere in the country; its members formed 69 percent of Wrocław council members, while the rest belonged to the PPS.[58] The Wrocław PPR was still not satisfied:

> We must evaluate the course of elections to this point . . . negatively. In preparing the election *aktyw,* we repeatedly stressed that it was necessary to bring common-front PPS-ers into the factory councils alongside PPR members through mutual voting for identified candidates; this did not enter the consciousness of some County Committee Secretaries, and as a result no PPS-ers at all got into many factory councils. . . .

[57] ŁAP KŁ PPR 1/XI/7, kk. 1–6.; ŁAP KŁ PPR 1/XI/4, n.p.
[58] WAP KW PPR 1/XII/24, k. 88. These data cover fewer than twenty councils in 1946–47, however. Other data on Wrocław factory councils are in ibid. 1/XII/19 and 1/XII/31. Similar statistics are not available for Łódź.

The PPS at the present moment shows no activity at all in the election campaign. The rank and file of the PPS in the factories spread the word that they prefer to vote for PPR candidates, because in the near future there will be one Party anyway. If in some factories the PPS got a relatively larger percentage of seats, it is only because a considerable number of PPR votes was cast for PPS candidates.[59]

In both cities, the PPR was clearly looking ahead to party unification even as it celebrated its new supremacy over the PPS.

One opponent that the PPR was unable to master was the indifference of the workers. Many workers in Łódź—50 percent of female and young workers at Horak, for example, despite intensive home and factory agitation—chose not to vote at all. Many others voted "without interest in the political aspect" or cast votes only for the two or three candidates they knew. As an activist at the Poznański mill said, many workers thought: "What do the elections matter to me? I'll drop my blank card [thus supporting the official slate] and that'll be the end of it."[60] Participation was higher, generally between 80 and 90 percent, in Wrocław, where the higher party membership among workers was easier to organize.[61]

Regardless of the indifference, the factory council was now available to be used as the PPR had envisioned from the beginning, as a weapon in the struggle for the building of a socialist economy. Some workers had imagined something of the sort, too, but their ideas of mobilization, control, and management were quite different from those of the PPR. The party had re-created the councils as its own organ. But the councils quickly lost any influence or worker support they had had. PPR and union investigators reported that councils were unable to perform the duties expected of them and were not doing anything at all. The PPR discovered, having filled the councils with worker-members drafted into service rather than volunteers, that the councils were worse than ever. Councilors were "workers taken away from their machines, and their heads spin from all that paperwork." "Though they are our comrades,

<hr>

[59] WAP KW PPR 1/XII/2, kk. 13–14.
[60] ŁAP KŁ PPR 1/XI/8, k. 70; ŁAP KD PPR Górna-Prawa 1/VI/66 k. 132; ŁAP KŁ PPR 1/XI/7, kk. 7–8. In the Geyer mill, turnout was probably lowered because the list of candidates was not posted so as not to upset the workers. AAN KC PPR 295/XIII/7, kk. 169–70; also ŁAP WRZZ 66, n.p.
[61] WAP KW PPR 1/XII/26, 27, 28, 29. A year later, after the PPR–PPS merger had removed any politics from the election process, turnout in the Wrocław construction industry was as low as 50 percent. WAP ZZB WO 16, k. 41.

honest and eager to work, . . . because of their lack of consciousness, matters are often left unattended."[62] As before, the councils lacked contact with the workers, were unable to function, or were "relegated to the role of an agent which graciously accepts the actions of management or personnel directors. Some . . . receive, for a favorable position or for taking no position, a luxuriously appointed office, courtesy of management, and they lock themselves in it, neither seeing nor hearing the voices of those who elected them."[63] The language the PZPR used in 1949 to criticize councils reveals their intended place: they were accused of "solidarism" or of having "a narrow understanding of their defense function"—that is, they sided with workers instead of working as part of the state machine.[64] The battle for the councils had come full circle, with the same rhetoric used to attack these bureaucrats as had been used against the activists of 1945–47.

The PPR devoted almost as much energy to elections for union governing boards as it did to the factory council elections. President Bierut himself weighed in on the importance of unions as an educational tool. Despite early setbacks and intense rivalry with the PPS, the PPR was able to gain firm control.[65] The unions did not become the masters of the factory, even on behalf of the state; subordinated to the communist party, they became simply would-be mobilizers, while labor became just another group to be mobilized. But if unions could deliver the goods, then workers would accept them; when they could not, workers were not interested in being mobilized, and unions were helpless. The leather workers' union reported in September 1948 that, as a result of disappointing collective agreements, factory workers were "losing faith in trade union representatives, treating them as if they saw before them the lords of [interwar] Poland." Warned another union activist: "The union rank-and-file accuses [union leaders and factory councils] of neglecting to enforce the collective agreements and to look after workers. There is

---

[62]ŁAP WRZZ 2, k. 64; AAN KC PPR 295/IX/34, k. 13.

[63]ŁAP WRZZ 2, k. 53. See also WUSW KWMO 149/16 n.p.; ARZ KCZZ WO 535, kk. 61–67, 90–92; WAP WRZZ 2, kk. 130–31.

[64]Żukowski, *Związki zawodowe*, 24.

[65]On Bierut, see Salomea Kowalewska, "Wzór osobowy i pożądane postawy pracowników w przemyśle," in *Przemysł i społeczeństwo w Polsce Ludowej*, ed. Jan Szczepański (Wrocław, 1969), 221. On PPR union strategy, see Kazimierz Kloc, *Historia samorządu robotniczego w PRL, 1944–1989*, SGPiS: Monografie i opracowanie, 351 (Warsaw, 1992), 60–63; AAN KC PPR 295/V/3, k. 9, 295/XIII/8, kk. 33–36, and "Dokumenty PPR i PPS dotyczące działalności związków zawodowych," 198–200, 209–10.

serious danger that ... union members will not pay their membership dues."[66]

Meeting this threat head on, the KCZZ proposed in June 1948 a plan to improve its contact with the workers by switching from an automatic system of collecting dues (by paycheck deduction) to voluntary payment in which shop stewards would collect dues directly from members. Union leaders hoped that the new system could strengthen contact between activists and membership and further centralize union administration.[67] In the context of the concurrent unification of the PPR and PPS, this change could only ensure the superiority in the factory of the new party (with disciplined members) over the unions (with voluntary members). Voluntary dues brought an end to the closed shop—except that the door was now open, not for other unions, but for the PZPR. Unions were relegated to the background, behind the party and behind management.

KCZZ leaders probably envisioned voluntary dues as progress toward a renewed relationship with the workers; in the short term, they feared a massive departure of members and that many others would simply refuse to pay. To determine its chances of survival, the KCZZ sent unions a questionnaire on their plans for switching to voluntary dues and their assessment of workers' likely reaction. It asked unions to explain how their present system worked and report progress in implementing the change. Most unions reported that under the old system members only signed a declaration of membership; at most, a model declaration of consent to automatic deductions was signed by two members for the whole factory. A few, like the miners and steelworkers, had had a voluntary system from the beginning.[68]

Some unions apparently hoped the change would be easier if they targeted the most reliable workers first. The sugar refinery workers' union announced it would begin in January 1949 with the seven refin-

---

[66]WAP KW PPR 1/XII/37, k. 49; WAP WRZZ 24, kk. 21, 23; ŁAP WRZZ 64, n.p.; WAP WRZZ 1, k. 6.

[67]Halina Jakubowska, "Rozwój i działalność związków zawodowych w Polsce w latach 1944–1948," in *Ruch robotniczy w Polsce Ludowej*, 2d ed., ed. Janusz Gołębiowski and Władysław Góra (Warsaw, 1980), 145.

[68]Completed questionnaires from late 1948: sugar refinery workers, ARZ KCZZ WO 464, kk. 43–45; miners and steelworkers, 473, k. 11; garment workers, 484, kk. 25–26; wood industry and forest workers, 485, kk. 24–25; metal workers, 486, kk. 99–100; postal and telecommunications, 491, kk. 108–9; municipal and public utilities, 500, kk. 37–40; food industry, 506, kk. 95–96; and others.

eries that won the labor competition in the current sugar-beet season. The municipal and public utilities workers' union also planned to begin with the best departments. The chemical workers' union attempted to capture the KCZZ's twin goals of democracy and greater worker responsibility with a poster popularizing the new system: "Your 12 Basic Responsibilities as a Member of the Chemical Industry Employees' Trade Union." This poster reminded workers that "to be a member of the Union is the responsibility and honor of every employee . . . [and] regular payment of membership dues is proof of your attachment to the union, and proof of your organizational discipline." It exhorted workers to "be a monitor of your own pennies which have been handed over for the union's purposes."[69]

The results, at least in some unions, were not what the KCZZ had hoped. In November 1948, 87 percent of Poland's nearly 4 million workers belonged to a union.[70] The metal workers' union predicted that "during the introduction of the new system . . . , the departure of a certain percentage of members is expected." In July 1949, the Łódź section of this union conducted a study of dues payments in large factories and found that while 80 percent of the approximately 21,000 metal workers (including office employees) in the province still held union cards, only 60 to 65 percent of the members paid their dues, a figure that remained roughly constant from January to July.[71] No doubt part of the difficulty was the new dues-collecting bureaucracy. Nevertheless, around half the metal workers chose not to pay dues, turned in their union cards, or were dropped from the union rolls.

Workers showed even greater apathy toward the elections held in the spring of 1949 for delegates to the Second Trade Union Congress. Of some 29,000 workers at eight chemical plants across Poland, for example, only 30 percent took part. Even many of those who voted were tricked into participation when the factory gates were locked. Attendees seemed uninterested in the election or union matters, preferring to dis-

---

[69] ARZ KCZZ WO 463, n.p.

[70] Halina Jakubowska, "Udział związków zawodowych w życiu publicznym i społecznym w pierwszych latach Polski Ludowej (1944–1948)," *Z Pola Walki*, no. 2 (1979): 161.

[71] ARZ KCZZ WO 486, k. 100. Data compiled from tables on forty-four factories (thirty-seven in or near Łódź) appear in ARZ KCZZ WO 487, kk. 4–5. While there are some inconsistencies in the data, the percentages range consistently from a high of 69.1 percent dues paid in April to a low of 55.2 percent in July. Also see WAP Pafawag 252, k. 10. In the textile union, 40 percent of the 22,000 members in Łódź were late in paying their dues: ŁAP WRZZ 68, n.p.

cuss labor competition or the lack of meat.[72] Workers and party spokes-people alike now attacked unions in language similar to that used against management or speculators. They were aristocratic, cut off from the workers, reactionary; they were "remnants of the reactionary union lords" and "people who are hostile to the ideals of the reborn labor movement in Poland, people from the old workers' aristocracy." They practiced "dignitary-ism" and "do not inculcate [the workers] politically in the spirit of class struggle."[73] A delegate to a Łódź union meeting spoke of betrayal by former comrades: "We chose people from our ranks, and they ought to take care of us, and not look on egotistically." Another added: "How is it that those who [worked] with me [now] have bellies and new suits, and I have nothing, and look like a tramp? (applause)"[74]

At the Second Congress in June 1949, the KCZZ finally broke away from the remaining traditions of trade unionism, formally acknowledging the unions' subordinate position to state and party. Renamed the CRZZ, or Central Trade Union Council, it echoed the PZPR, denouncing tendencies toward union autonomy, independence, anarcho-syndicalism, and neutrality. At the highest levels, the party and the union were nearly synonymous: while 28 percent of union rank and file were party members; more than 80 percent of members of central union administrations belonged to the PZPR.[75]

Union leaders fought to maintain their standing among workers but did so at a price that workers were not always aware of. When a Łódź union official named Czernik came to conduct a postcongress meeting at a Łódź garment factory in late June 1949, he announced that "everyone has to speak out emphatically and sincerely about what hurts and worries them. [You] should not be afraid, since there is no Security Apparatus here to lock [you] up or something like that. Really, nothing

---

[72]ARZ KCZZ WO 588, kk. 94–95. The turnout was even worse in Łódź textile mills: only 14.2 percent of the workers at the three largest mills. In Wrocław's artificial silk factory, 21.2 percent participated. ARZ KCZZ WO 591, kk. 369, 405–7.

[73]ARZ KCZZ WO 495, kk. 14–16; WAP WRZZ 34, kk. 120–21.

[74]ŁAP WRZZ 297, n.p. See also meeting of railway union delegates in Łódź, November 1949. After a speech on trade unions and the international situation, "a chaotic discussion began, having nothing in common with the [topic]. Repeated efforts by the chairman to bring the discussion to order had no effect." During the singing of the "Internationale," people "rushed the exits." ŁAP WRZZ 68, n.p.

[75]Władysław Ratyński, *Partia i związki zawodowe w Polsce Ludowej* (Warsaw, 1977), 183–86, 188–89; Kloc, *Historia samorządu robotniczego*, 64.

will happen to [you]; [you] won't be fired or locked up."[76] Although the workers were suspicious of such appeals and doubtful of the usefulness of taking part, a strong current of dissatisfaction ran beneath the seemingly calm, productive atmosphere at the factory. When news of the meeting spread, "first the cutting rooms began to stir, [saying] that they earn too little; they began to mutter that they weren't going to work for such pennies. . . . Two lines of young workers also revolted; they did not want to sew pillowcases instead of sheets, because they considered this work too hard for them."[77] Only 250 of 1,600 workers in the morning shift attended the meeting, which was then called off, provoking further outrage among the workers. The afternoon shift's meeting was more successful. Workers complained about wages, bread, and clothing. But the contrast between the political, internationalist language of the union activists and the concerns of the workers was abruptly exposed in the discussion of the Second Congress: "Aksler [a CRZZ representative] explained that there were representatives of other countries at the Congress, among them one from France, who said that if a worker reveals his complaints, no one wants to hear him, and if he speaks loudly and openly they arrest him, and [they use] bullets against strikes (stormy applause from the auditorium, shouts, etc.), but when [Aksler] added that this is how it is in France, [there was] consternation, silence, and murmurs in the hall. One could hear: 'what, is it better here?' [and] 'and what happened at Poznański?' Then women began to shout that they didn't fight before the war so that now they would have to string up their stomachs; they fought for the improvement of the worker's life, and what do they have for all that now."[78]

These union representatives were torn between their duties as messengers of the party and industry to the workers and their old role of worker advocates. But they tried to win popularity for the unions by pointing the blame at others and carefully encouraging workers to oppose management. First, they blamed low pay (a sore point after the January wage reform, discussed in Chapter 5) on management's poor organization of work. Then at another meeting the next day, when a group of workers complained that they were not paid for stoppages caused by mechanical breakdowns, "Aksler told them that if management did not want to pay for stoppages, then kick up a fuss, damn it! Block the factory gates,

[76] ARZ CRZZ WO 631, k. 5.
[77] Ibid.
[78] Ibid.

don't let the director in, go to him and break his doors down, because management shouldn't feast on the stomachs of the workers, and should go to jail if he does."[79] The delighted workers shook Aksler's hand. This was the kind of union response they wanted, even if they had to endure speeches on the international situation in the bargain. But what they did not know is that Aksler reported next to local PZPR headquarters, where he supplied the names of those workers who had "a certain influence among the work force, and who spoke up the most" during the factory's PZPR chairwoman's speech.[80] Party discipline came first for union leaders, and many of the loudest protesters were PZPR members.

The problem of official unions in state socialist Poland is of interest because of the clash of two rhetorics, evident in both the issue of dues collection and the incident at the Łódź garment factory. One was the idea, inherent in the concept of a union, of democratic expression of ideas, and the workers' right to monitor their superiors. Union leaders, of whatever allegiance, continued to express faith in this idea, which surfaced mainly in campaigns to provide workers with food, housing, and education. The other was that the unions were an organ of the state. Leaders of the KCZZ often became high government officials and vice versa. The union's involvement in raising production from the very beginning linked it implicitly to the goals of the state itself and thus to the goals of the employers. KCZZ leaders imagined that this official role would give the working class a voice in the centers of power, but there was one fundamental problem with the idea: there already existed a nominal voice of the working class in the centers of power—the communist and socialist parties, especially the PZPR. The unions as allies of the state were relegated to a marginal role because the parties were more important in both government and the factory. If one wanted to obtain something or seek redress, the PZPR factory committee exuded more power and influence than did the union or factory council.

On the eve of the PZPR's creation, the PPR Secretariat prepared a resolution on the work of party members in the labor movement. This document outlined the most urgent tasks of the unions: they should develop worker contact with the peasantry, mobilize workers to vigilance in the fight against sabotage, strengthen ties between leaders and masses, steer qualified workers to administrative posts, conduct socialist education, and spread information about the Soviet Union. There was

[79] Ibid., k. 6.
[80] From Aksler's report: ARZ CRZZ WO 690, k. 61.

no mention of traditional union functions, some of which were assigned to the factory councils in this schema; instead, the unions were now clearly "transmission belts" between party and masses.[81] The prestalinist era of the trade unions ended with the law of 1 July 1949, approved at the Second Trade Union Congress and quickly passed by Parliament. As a result of this law, workers were explicitly denied the right to organize freely, except as approved by the CRZZ itself. The tasks of the unions were defined as follows: they were to "cooperate with authorities and institutions in the area of public administration, national economy and supervision [*kontrola*]." As regulated by the government, the unions became part of the government hierarchy.[82]

The PZPR and the New Mobilization Politics

By mid-1948, the PPR was beginning to feel more at ease in the factory. Even the habitually nervous UB felt more comfortable: in April, Minister Stefan Radkiewicz argued in a meeting of the ministry's upper echelon that it was no longer necessary to have an agent or informer in every factory—that was a practice useful "in unstable times." Now, he felt, contacts with "honest citizens, PPR members, etc." would usually be enough.[83] Radkiewicz's optimism (which would soon seem out of place as stalinist paranoia gripped the communist elites) was due in part to the PPR's success in taking control of the factory. But control of the factory meant little as long as the party had minimal control over its own ranks.

Until 1948, the PPR had been content simply to avoid conflict with nonparty workers in Łódź or to sign up huge numbers of workers regardless of their attitude and background in Wrocław. Now it realized how tenuous its hold was over workers and began to redefine membership, eroding the boundaries between public and private life. The com-

[81]AAN KC PPR 295/V/7, kk. 97–110.

[82]Reprinted in "Pierwsze dokumenty normujące podstawy prawne tworzenia i działalności związków zawodowych w początkach Polski Ludowej," ed. Andrzej Nieuważny, *KHRZ* no. 4 (1986): 63–65. Kazimierz Grzybowski, "The Evolution of the Polish Labor Law, 1945–1955," in *Legal Problems under Soviet Domination: Studies of the Association of Polish Lawyers in Exile in the United States*, vol. 1. (New York, 1956), 84–86.

[83]MSW MBP 17/IX/77, t. 4, k. 123. See approving comments by Colonel Brystygierowa and others.

munists certainly faced a tough task. As few as one-quarter of the party's members throughout Poland paid dues in 1947.[84] Most regarded membership as merely a necessary step to a job or other benefit; just as they spurned the unions that were unable to deliver, so they ignored the party, which was just another trade union. This was particularly a problem in Wrocław, where the PPR had grown precisely because of its ability to deliver. Membership did not make trust in the party any less fragile.

The vast majority of Łódź workers, of course, did not belong to any party; secure in their communities, most workers had little fear of the PPR. Concerned about the indifference toward the party, the Łódź PPR inquired in the fall of 1947 why workers were turning in their party cards. Workers readily gave a variety of reasons for quitting the PPR: that they "earn too little, so they don't want to be PPR members"; "lack of time, and lack of interest in issues discussed in the circle"; old age, or exhaustion; "the PPR did not help in finding work"; "doesn't want to be hanged [for PPR membership] later"; "she had joined only under strong persuasion by her girlfriend"; "it's best to be nonparty, for then you have no responsibilities"; "PPR members forced her to work during the [September 1947] strike, so she doesn't want to belong to such a party." Some even claimed that they had no idea they were party members. This free expression at the beginning of stalinism is remarkable: so many were still willing not only to leave the party but to give frank reasons for doing so. Perhaps the presence and perceived strength of the PPS was one reason that workers were unafraid to voice their challenge to the PPR. Some workers admitted this: that "if they switch to the PPS they'll get better work"; "they have more faith in the PPS"; "their husbands belong to the PPS, so they'll switch to that, and it is all the same, PPR or PPS."[85]

In Wrocław, the PPR began to discover the potential of its mass membership. A conflict in December 1948 illustrates how much control the PPR now had as well as the remaining limitations on its power. Garment factory no. 1 (one of the factories sampled in Chapter 3) employed about 3,700 workers, 75 percent of them women and more than one-third (although "completely unformed politically") members of the PPR. In division E, where the incident took place, half of the 400 workers belonged to the PPR, with another 20 percent in the PPS. It was a situation typical for Wrocław: a high degree of party membership with, as it

[84]AAN KC PPR 295/V/3, k. 20. The numbers in 1946 had been as low as 7 percent.
[85]AAN KC PPR 295/IX/228, kk. 89, 105, 134, 154.

turned out, a low degree of appropriate political consciousness. In 1947, the workers of Division E had collected money to buy several religious pictures to hang in each workshop of the division.[86] The September 1948 PPR plenum apparently prompted the lax PPR factory organization to crack down on these displays.[87] On 30 November, after the workers had gone home, PPR Secretary Błażejewski ("known as a 'crazed' anti-cleric"), with the personnel director and a PPR activist-seamstress named Rdzanek, removed the pictures. A report filed by two Central Committee inspectors best describes the scene:

> On December 1 at 6:30, at the moment of beginning work, the [women] workers noticed the pictures were missing. A roar arose, and shouts of "someone took the pictures," "they're taking God away from us," and "we want God." At the shout "Rdzanek did it," most of the workers ran to the shop where Rdzanek works and threw themselves on her, shouting "give up the pictures." Rdzanek, terrified, escaped to the sorting room, with a frenzied crowd of *dewotki* [pious biddies] after her. In the sorting room, [they] began to beat comrade Rdzanek; members of the PPR and PPS led the attackers, pushing aside nonparty [workers], [saying that they] "must settle accounts themselves, and would not be punished for it [as Party members]."
>
> At this moment, comrade Błażejewski entered the factory; the whole crowd threw itself at him. [They] began to beat him and tear at him, shouting "give up the pictures," and "you burned them." Błażejewski, terrified, led them to his office and gave back the pictures.
>
> During the whole incident, substitute pictures and medallions appeared and were hung in the place of those which had been removed. After receiving the pictures, [the workers] hung them back in their place, and they returned to work. The entire fracas lasted about two hours.[88]

Relations in this factory were, to say the least, confused. The PPR appeared completely out of contact with the workers, most of whom were party members. While the Wrocław party organization blamed the

[86] Neither the national seal nor portraits of state leaders were hanging anywhere in the building. The PPS secretary, meanwhile, was alleged to have a picture of the Virgin Mary in his office; for good measure, one PPR official had purportedly been a PSL member until 1947. This account is based on AAN KC PPR 295/IX/51, kk. 365–70; AAN KC PPR 295/IX/370, kk. 43–45; and WAP KW PPR 1/XII/2, kk. 85–86.

[87] This plenum saw the ascendance of the Moscow faction of the PPR. Gomułka was forced to engage in self-criticism, the first step toward his removal from power. Kersten, *Narodziny systemu władzy*, 346–49.

[88] AAN KC PPR 295/IX/51, kk. 367–68.

incident on outside organization, the Central Committee inspectors noted that Błażejewski had guilelessly tried to pave the way for the removal of the paintings by remarking, in conversations during the previous weeks, that the PPR planned to take them down. "Instead of laying a foundation, this on the contrary mobilized all the dewotki to be vigilant. The supposition is that they consulted with one another at home and in church about how to act if such a thing were to take place—and thus were organized and ready to react."[89] Perhaps such a conflict could take place in a city like Łódź. The outcome there, however, would be quite different from that in Wrocław; it could not be otherwise given the mass party membership in most Wrocław factories. Such peculiar worker-party relations, in which the party was determined, dominant, and distant from the workers while the workers were equally distant from a factory culture and ready to defend values important to their church-based or regional communities, was more typical of the future of Poland than of its past. In Łódź, 1948 strike leaders were still often PPR members who believed "the time was ripe" for them to make demands.[90] With the community behind them, they could be excused for believing that they dealt from a position of strength.

The suppression of the garment-factory incident revealed that, however uncontrollable the membership may have seemed, the PPR ultimately could mobilize its members and impose party discipline. A factory PPR and PPS joint meeting that afternoon issued a resolution prepared by the parties' executives, expelling a number of workers from both parties and promising a further vetting of the ranks; a speech on the local activities of the church followed. Next, some workers spoke up and explained that there would have been no altercation had they been properly informed; indeed, they would have taken the pictures down themselves. While this claim sounds a bit disingenuous, the workers did in fact remove the pictures the next morning. The PPR, however, reacted quite severely. A representative of the city PPR committee threatened to close the factory and lay off all the workers; foremen and brigade leaders in Division E were degraded to ordinary workers, and several workers and administrators were fired.[91] The party, in other words, used this moment to make clear to workers what their obligations were as party members: contrary to rumor, they could certainly be punished for

[89]Ibid., k. 367.
[90]MSW MBP 17/IX/38, t. 3, n.p. [August 1948].
[91]AAN KC PPR 295/IX/370, k. 45.

beating a party activist, and party membership meant not immunity but certain sacrifices if one were to retain the party's trust. Workers in Wrocław had not joined the party for ideology and were unlikely to leave it for ideology either. Rather, they would remain in the party and follow its rules.

The lax attitude toward membership had to change with unification of the parties; a new direction began with tests of members' worthiness. In mid-1947, both the PPR and PPS pledged to purge their ranks of reactionary elements (as they had in previous purges stretching back to mid-1945); serious housecleaning began as the unification of the two parties approached in late 1948. The PPR was to clean itself of opportunists; the PPS, of opponents to unification—the right wing of the party. The purge fell more heavily on the less pure PPS, judged to be more riddled with elements unsuited for membership in the new whole. In total, some 13 percent of the PPS was purged, compared to only 3 percent from the PPR.[92] The purge was meant to be a sort of cleansing ritual intended to make the party worthy of participation in a new, purer organization—the PZPR. The drive to unify the PPR and PPS did not merely suppress political diversity. The Polish United Workers' Party (PZPR) was a fundamentally new presence in the factory, much more than just a larger PPR. It was dedicated to mobilizing its members, and even nonmembers, to active political participation.

The theoretical struggles within each party found no echo among Łódź and Wrocław workers except that some were now purged by their party organizations. In Łódź, 35 percent of the four thousand expelled from the PPS (about 10 percent of the city organization) were workers.[93] Expelled workers were branded differently from other purge victims. Of the thirty-one PPS members expelled at the Scheibler and Grohman mill in Łódź for whom reasons are given, thirteen were workers. Only one was accused of being "hostile" and "right wing"; five "did not accept the merger." The most common reasons were drunkenness and theft. In contrast, all eight expelled foremen were accused of being rightists, as were most of the ten office workers.[94]

[92]Kersten, *Narodziny systemu władzy*, 351; on unification in general see 125–35; Bronisław Syzdek, *Polska Partia Socjalistyczna w latach 1944–1948* (Warsaw, 1974), 437; Norbert Kołomiejczyk and Marian Malinowski, *Polska Partia Robotnicza, 1942–1948* (Warsaw, 1986), 505.

[93]Kersten, *Narodziny systemu władzy*, 351.

[94]Ninety-seven PPS members were expelled; thirty-six were workers, and twenty-four foremen or other labor supervisors. Only two were women. In many cases, two or more

This fit the PPR's portrayal of the PPS as the party of the privileged, the labor aristocracy, and the technical elite. For example, at the Łódź electric plant, long a PPS stronghold, the PPR alleged that the PPS-dominated bureaucracy gave bonuses only to office employees and even conducted sabotage, shutting off power to whole neighborhoods.[95] The PPS was similarly demonized in Wrocław; a UB report in early 1949 claimed that "one of the circles engaged in the spread of hostile propaganda is that of expellees from the PPS, who are ever more clearly crystallizing into groups, and keep in constant contact with one another. These groups [the report identified fourteen] are independent, connected by workplace [or] regional background, and make use of legal organizations."[96] The PPR knew better, of course; one PPR activist in Wrocław admitted that the PPS had significant influence among workers in many industries.[97] But the characterization conveniently put the PPS in the same category as earlier enemies of the workers' state.

The PPR viewed itself in no less harsh terms, although the consequences were less dramatic while the party was busy directing the evisceration of its rival. In communities and factories across the country, the victory of the new line was, for the moment, likely to be just another speech at a party meeting. Nevertheless, the change in political culture was evident. The PPR seemed to take care to present the purge as a victory for popular values if not of populism itself. Thus a litany of "rightist and nationalist" sins that a critic detected in the Łódź PPR included "lack of attention to the interests of the workers"; "an often contemptuous position toward employees in lower positions"; "insufficient activity in the struggle with speculation"; "toleration of theft, indifference to the signs of reaction"; and antisemitism.[98] With such rhetoric, party leadership positioned itself as more populist than discredited local officials and sent the message that local activists would neither encourage nor tolerate the tendencies that workers had shown

---

reasons were given for expulsion. ŁAP KD PPR Fabryczna (Scheibler and Grohman) 3/V/1, kk. 44, 49–50.

[95] The PPS had five hundred members at the plant, the PPR two hundred—most of whom, admitted the PPR secretary, were opportunists who had little understanding of ideology. ŁAP KD PPR Śródmieście-Lewa 1/VI/100, kk. 46–47.

[96] WUSW WUBP 2/37, k. 11. An example of such accusations appears in AAN KC PPR 295/IX/447, k. 39–40.

[97] WAP WK PPS 36/VI/3, k. 47. On PPS purges in Wrocław, see Ordyłowski, *Walka z opozycją polityczną*, 176–83.

[98] ŁAP KW PPR 1/XI/1 n.p. [October 1948].

in past years. (On the other hand, while verification might have made the party cleaner, it raised questions about the suitability of the party for administration. The sight of continuous internal purges could only be unnerving, even for the nonmember.)

For the first time, workers had to reckon with the responsibilities of being a party member. Consider, for example, the "self-criticism" meeting (that is, devoted to exposing members' sins) of the Klecina (Wrocław) sugar refinery's PPR circle in late 1948. Speakers' confessions about drinking habits revealed conflicts between party discipline and community pressures in which imposed ideas of class began to squeeze out organic ones: "I've been working in the sugar refinery two years," explained one worker. "There were cases where someone came with vodka, and it was 4 P.M., so I drank. There were four such cases where someone came and offered me a drink. But drinking all the time—no. My father [was] a shoemaker, I myself was a shopkeeper before the war. I am 61 years old."[99] This speaker tried to defend his relationship to other workers (in part by depicting himself in a passive role in social relations) and reconcile that relationship with the duty of belonging to the party.

Whether or not workers accepted the right of the party to censure their social habits, they did attempt to state their cases in the language of the party. "I joined [the PPR in 1946] out of conviction," explained a member of the Industrial Guard. "Only now am I learning to write and read. . . . I will never forget that my father wielded a scythe all day for 90 groschen; I will always be a proletarian."[100] In another self-criticism session ("on the matter of purging our ranks of alien elements") at the Piast brewery in Wrocław, a speaker revealed himself to be caught between two constricting models of behavior. He was accused of stealing beer; his remarks addressed his reasons for sneaking out of the back of the factory, where he was caught: "I went out the back gate . . . because that day I had gotten a large amount of money for overtime work, and my mates were waiting for me at the [front] gate so I would drink with them, and I wanted to avoid them, since I had no intention of drinking vodka, which I avoid, with them. . . . I am the son of a worker, and have sincere intentions toward the PPR and the world of labor. I have been negligent in Party work because as the only welder, I am not spared

[99]Another employee explained that he had gotten drunk only once, so it was not a habit. As for joining the party: "Others signed up, so I signed up, too." All speakers were reprimanded. WAP 3rd KD PPR 33/VI/6, kk. 56–57.
[100]Ibid., k. 57.

during the season, and I have never refused work after hours."[101] This speaker's explanations can hardly be taken at face value; neither he nor others would be likely to admit to a fondness for drinking (even at a brewery!), or to antipathy toward the party (which was possible in Łódź). The wooden language of allegiance to the "world of labor" nevertheless indicated a desire to remain accepted by the PPR and a willingness to conform at least outwardly to its rules, even while feeling torn by allegiance to the informal rules of his work mates.

As it taught its worker-members to behave properly, the PPR also attempted to raise the productive element in its ranks. As figure 8 shows, the percentage of party members who were workers fell by nearly two-thirds by early 1947, to just over one-half. The "verification campaign" of 1947, intended to clean the party of those who were not paying dues, disproportionately eliminated workers.[102] In the spring of 1948, the PPR still had only 7 to 9 percent of all textile factory employees in Łódź, and only 4 to 5 percent in the central production shops. In some railway shops, numbers were as low as 1.5 percent. Pointing to numbers like these, the PPR Secretariat issued a directive in March 1948 calling for "constant, systematic growth of our Party in the ranks of the working class."[103]

With factory councils and unions now reliable tools, the party could recruit production workers with greater success. But while, as before, the party happily accepted any new members, it now wanted those members to be worthy. This meant members who could reliably be mobilized for the tasks ahead. The Secretariat's directive previously quoted provided the following guidelines for finding new members: "At a [factory] circle meeting, each Party member ought to supply names of the best workers in the shop, of leading workers [*przodownicy*], of multi-machine workers, of those who are conscientious and disciplined in work, who are skilled in their craft, who are respected by the body of workers, of those who are readers of the PPR press, of those who are systematically present [or] who speak at meetings." Such workers, the

---

[101] WAP 2d KD PPR 32/VI/8, kk. 124–25.

[102] The campaign of 1 June 1947 to 1 January 1948 resulted in very few expulsions, perhaps a thousand or so (of some 800,000); most members removed from party rolls were not counted as expelled. AAN KC PPR 295/IX/379, k. 4; AAN KC PPR 295/IX/476, kk. 13–23. Payment of dues jumped to 51 percent after this campaign; AAN KC PPR 295/IX/388, kk. 1–3.

[103] AAN KC PPR 295/VII/6, kk. 117–18; numbers in ŁAP KŁ PPR 1/XI/7, kk. 1–6; AAN KC PPR 295/VII/7. In 1949, the percentage of workers in the PZPR rose slightly to 56.8 percent. Leszek Grzybowski, *Robotnicy w PZPR, 1948–1975* (Warsaw, 1979), 32–33.

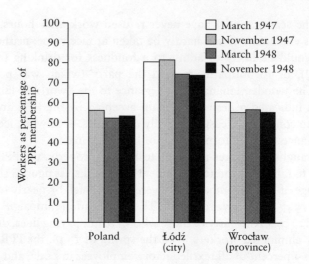

Figure 8. Workers in the PPR during the purges, 1947–1948

Note: Between 1 October and 15 November 1948, 23,162 people were expelled from the PPR across Poland; 32.4 percent of these were workers. In the city of Łódź, 55.4 percent of the 748 expelled during this period were workers, as were 25.9 percent of the 923 expelled in Wrocław. Much of the purging, however, took place in the last weeks of the campaign (late November to early December). AAN KC PPR 295/IX/476, kk. 7–8, 24, 31, 77, 80; *Partia w cyfrach,* Section 9, Table 4. For Wrocław city, there are partial data from five four-day periods in November and December; in these periods, expellees from the city were 30.8% of expellees from the province. AAN KC PPR 295/IV/7, kk. 226, 237; AAN KC PPR 295/IX/390, kk. 188, 208, 213.

directive continued, should be invited to special open party meetings at which several workers who had been coached in advance would publicly announce their intention to join. But, cautioned the Secretariat, there could be no mass enrollment campaign; use of administrative pressure to join the party would be punished. These new members, the PPR leadership hoped, would be *real* members.[104] One factory committee proposed attracting members by popularizing the achievements of the USSR and Marxism-Leninism using folk performances.[105] Such tactics would have seemed ludicrous a year earlier; in the stalinist era, they would be standard fare. The PPR was coming into its own as the vanguard of the working class and had adopted a proprietary tone toward workers.

The party's new interest in the quality of its members was above all aimed at workers, who satisfied statistics on proletarian membership but

[104]AAN KC PPR 295/VII/6, kk. 117–18.
[105]ŁAP KŁ PPR 1/VI/142, kk. 109–10.

Reasons for expulsion from the PPR, 1948

Reasons	Poland All N= 19,476	Łódź (city) Workers 414	Non-workers 334	Łódź (province) Workers 521	Non-workers 844	Wrocław (province) Workers 702	Non-workers 1,532
Ideologically alien	29.7%	31.9%	23.4%	10.2%	14.7%	23.9%	20.8%
Of an alien class	19.0	0.0	30.8	0.0	18.0	1.9	17.8
Drinking habit	12.5	13.3	8.7	23.0	13.0	24.6	19.5
Enemy propaganda	7.3	6.3	3.3	4.8	6.4	8.0	7.2
Collaboration with enemy	8.0	1.7	3.9	6.0	11.3	9.1	6.5
Economic harm	4.6	4.1	6.0	1.2	4.6	2.8	4.8
Theft	4.6	10.4	1.8	20.5	2.5	9.8	4.4
Immoral life-style	3.8	3.4	1.2	16.5	10.9	7.3	6.0

Note: For national data (early October to mid-November), see AAN KC PPR 295/IX/389, k. 3. For Łódź (18 October to 15 November), see AAN KC PPR 295/IV/6, k. 274. For Łódź province (15 October to 1 December), see AAN KC PPR k. 298. For Wrocław province (1 October to 1 December), see AAN KC PPR 295/IV/7, k. 220, and 295/IX/390, k. 217. See also Łódź data on individual expulsions in AAN KC PPR 295/IV/6, kk. 295–97, and ŁAP KD PPR Fabryczna 3/V/ 2, k. 5.

often did not live up to ideological standards. The Łódź Party Control Commission listed twelve crimes for which one could be expelled from the party. The list illustrated the new emphasis on the morality of the average member. Being "ideologically alien," for example, could mean having joined for material reasons or continuing to attend church; another category was for those who gave up their party cards themselves, saying that they had received nothing from the party. One could be expelled for theft, excessive drinking, an immoral life-style, or lack of party discipline such as failure to pay dues or attend meetings.[106] The table above compares reasons for which workers and nonworkers were expelled from the party during the preunification campaign. Party obligations meant different things for the worker and the nonworker. Moral reasons for expulsion—drinking, immorality, and (to a lesser extent) adherence to ideological precepts—were more often used against work-

[106]The meaning of *immorality* was not defined in these documents. AAN KC PPR 295/ IV/6, kk. 305–6.

ers; in the economic sphere, theft was almost exclusively a charge against workers while economic harm covered roughly the same private-enterprise ground as the Special Commission. Workers' class allegiance, on the other hand, was generally taken for granted; even as it sought to discipline them, the party still assumed that all workers were proletarian, and gave them the benefit of the doubt.

Even with the new moral requirements, it was easy to be a party member before the autumn of 1948. PPR membership meant only a general obligation to attend party meetings more or less regularly and to be certain to appear at major events such as the May Day parade. It was a path that many workers in Wrocław chose. The duties of a non-party worker were even less taxing. Social mobilization—that is, extra-party mobilization—had meant a few collections for the rebuilding of Warsaw, the occasional optional mass meeting to condemn reactionaries at home or abroad, and a stroll through the city on 1 May. But as party unification neared, even attending a meeting brought greater responsibility. Locking gates to keep party members at a meeting was a recurrent motif in PPR reports of late 1948. Distress over worker indifference represented genuine apathy as well as a raising of the stakes by the party. And as strong as the concern was in Łódź, Wrocław was the PPR's city, where it should have been easy to shape a new, disciplined party.[107] Yet everywhere the party turned, its members were in disarray, uninterested in showing a higher degree of discipline at work or at meetings than their nonparty colleagues. In one factory, the popular PPR Factory Committee leader was planning to quit work and open a store. In another, the party had 360 members (about 22 percent of the factory); yet high turnover, "lack of class militancy," and indifference to the problem of sabotage marked the party circle. In a third factory, only four of one hundred PPR members had completed a party course, leaving the rest unable to "take appropriate positions" on labor issues and "militant feelings."[108]

Debate at a PPR meeting in one ceramics factory exposed the clash between the party's call for discipline or agitational militancy and the rank and file's desires. A report presented to the meeting, at which just half of membership was present, raised the locked-gates refrain: "If we are Party men [*partyjniaki*], then we should come to meetings voluntarily, and it should not be necessary to stand by the gate and tell each one

---

[107]Example: ŁAP WRZZ 66, n.p. [no. 2 garment factory, November 1948].
[108]AAN KC PPR 295/IX/51, kk. 39–40; WAP KW PPR 1/X/5, kk. 152–54.

to stay because it is a party meeting." Added another: "Comrade Party members are not disciplined at work; they leave their job to go into the city during work." This brought a heated response from the floor: "there's a lot of gab at this meeting about discipline, [yet though] my husband works, we don't have an apartment—how can we work; it'll come to the point that we'll have to quit work and leave Wrocław." In response, members were admonished to speak with a party sense [*poczu-cie partyjne*] and speak only when given the floor; although there was no sign of general protest, it was clear that members were not taking the call for greater discipline easily.[109]

Having taken control of Poland with relative ease, the party could be forgiven for assuming that Poles would quickly become active participants in communism. Confrontations like this one showed that imposing party culture on such a disaggregated, apolitical society was not so simple; complaints about workers' lack of political activity or consciousness became a standard feature of communist activism. The untested workers who flocked to the cities were willing to join the party in large numbers and attend meetings. But as the model of the mass organization evolved from one of sheer numbers to an activist regime, Wrocław workers, so adaptable to the first model of party membership, proved much more reluctant toward the second. The tacit support that workers sometimes seemed to offer did not mean willingness to join in displays of joy such as shouting slogans. They lacked—indeed avoided—the collectivity essential for small party campaigns such as collections or volunteer work. Like many revolutionaries before them, the Polish communists discovered that, at least in relatively peaceful times, workers never seem to be as excited by political goals as the leaders are. After all, they could, like the woman at the ceramics factory, simply leave the city or open a store if work was unsuitable or the party too harsh. The hold of the party over society was simply not yet strong enough to impose models of behavior reliably.

The campaign to build a new party building in Warsaw—a new home for a new type of party, built with the contributions of the Polish people—exemplified the new burdens placed on workers. The participation of nonparty workers was as important as member contributions because it might indicate the support the PZPR had in society. PPR reports carefully monitored the average amount given by workers of different in-

[109]WAP 2d KD PPR 32/VI/7, kk. 292–94.

comes, by PPS members, and particularly by nonparty workers.[110] As the same people conducted dozens of other collection campaigns, they were constantly disappointed. The personnel office at a Wrocław ceramics factory complained of workers' reluctance:

> The worker element in our [Industrial] Association is incredibly difficult, unintegrated, and little developed from the civic point of view. The best proof of this is the fact that in October, a collection was conducted in the factory for a banner for the City Command of the Civil Militia, the result of which was that 120 workers gave "as much as" 900 *złotys*, thereby showing a "model" example of generosity and civic advancement.
>
> Up to now, it has been impossible to call any sort of meeting to which a larger number of workers would come; . . . "as many as" 20 percent came to a meeting of the TPPR [Polish-Soviet Friendship Society], and "as many as" 18 percent to an organizational meeting of the Collegial Self-Help Fund [*Kasa Samopomocy Koleżeńskiej*]. . . . Management was forced to resort to the ultimate method of locking the gates when it called a meeting for 9 November. At that meeting, thanks to management's authority, a resolution was passed to devote four hours on Sunday, 21 November, to cleaning the rubble, trash, and junk from the beautiful building on Kołłątaj Street assigned to us for offices. This action was conducted with positive results.[111]

Aside from the startling spectacle of workers' performing chores for management for free, this irony-laden report reflects a significant interpenetration of party and nonparty spheres. All workers, not just PPR members, were expected to contribute to the police banner or join the TPPR (whose name itself recalled its political patron), both of which would have been the burden alone of party members not long before.

The PZPR was not only a mass party but the *only* mass party, for its partners—the peasant and merchant parties (the Unified Peasant Party [ZSL] and the Democratic Party [SD]) and until 1950 the Labor Party— were much smaller organizations of limited constituencies. In its totality, the PZPR merely made official what the PPR had accomplished in practice. Party unification hardly went unnoticed, especially as the new moral requirements became evident. The general popular indifference was certainly marked by some apprehension. In Wrocław, attachment to political organizations had been shallow; workers had joined in great numbers from the very beginning, making parties a de-ideologized stan-

[110]Example: AAN KC PPR 295/IX/34, k. 8.
[111]WAP KW PPR 1/X/37, k. 281.

One example of a political contribution campaign. Workers at an unknown factory sign pledges for the National Loan for the Development of Polish Forces, 1948(?). Banner reads: "Pledging for the National Loan for the Development of Polish Forces Is the Patriotic Duty of Every Pole." Archiwum Akt Nowych, Warsaw.

dard feature of the labor community. They continued to join in 1948 but still without any evident enthusiasm. The PPR City Committee noticed a certain reluctance to make political statements for fear of running afoul of the current campaign against rightism and nationalism. Many chose not to join political organizations at all but to keep a safe distance.[112]

In Łódź, where the parties (especially the PPS) had meant something, the atmosphere in the factories was fatalistic and resentful. While the PPS had still been able to draw supporters in 1947, by early 1948 PPS members could see the writing on the wall. The PPR's advantages in factory administration and its successful manipulation of the factory council elections made it clear who would control a future united party. A UB informant overheard the following comment from a woman worker to a friend: "I'm curious when they will unite; they'll surely chuck out all the PPS-ers, and you too probably won't get anything, for they are nasty people—it's better to give in, for the [PPR] at our factory are impossible, it simply makes me sick to work."[113]

As had happened before the parliamentary election in late 1946, apprehension about political change was sublimated or reflected in anticipation of war. Workers' letters opened by the UB often discussed these fears. The cold war was now well underway; what workers distilled from the front pages pointed to increased international tension at least. One wrote in September: "You hear a little too much about war now. Supposedly they will mobilize up to 42 years old. In some places this has already started. . . . Men are preparing to [escape to] the forest. . . . People at work talk of nothing else but the war, and lament it already." Another expected the outbreak of war by 15 September; this war, he felt, would bring "justice and peace" and the end of "the old world of wrongdoing."[114]

The certainty of impending cataclysm and obsession with external threats did not revive interest in domestic politics. Letters from Łódź inspected by the UB revealed that such antipathy was tinged with familiar animosities. "In Poland," wrote one person to friends in the

---

[112]Cited in Małgorzata Wawrzyńska, "Miasto Wrocław i jego mieszkańcy w pierwszych latach powojennych, 1945–1948," *Rocznik Dolnośląski* 10 (1987): 292.

[113]MSW MBP 17/IX/10, t. 2, k. 65; also kk. 66, 266, 277. At an April 1948 briefing of WUBP chiefs, Zabawski, the Lower Silesian UB chief, reported: "Workers . . . accepted [unification] slogans [presumably for 1 May] of unity with great satisfaction." He was echoed by the chief of the Poznań UB. MSW MBP 17/IX/77, t. 3.

[114]MSW MBP 17/IX/10, t. 2, kk. 87–88, 129–30, 149; quotations: k. 174.

United States, "you work only to eat—there's no hope of [earning enough to] buy some clothing. Jews have it very good—they don't work at all, but rule the Poles." Another wrote: "Here in Poland, instead of getting better, it's worse and worse. It's supposed to be a workers' paradise, and legal equality, but those at the trough, who shout that things are good in this country, have 40 thousand [złotys] and more a month, while an ordinary worker has barely five thousand, [and] when he has a large family he must eat black bread and potatoes with borscht."[115] This worker imagined the party not as a political organization but as a quasi-state umbrella group responsible for national welfare. In this way, his understanding of politics coincided with that of the PZPR itself.

The party, however, expected more. Judging from its discourse, nothing actually changed with unification: party ranks in Łódź were still full of opportunists, prewar strike breakers, and toadies uncommitted to the problems of raising production.[116] In Wrocław, society as a whole was still stolidly indifferent. Noting the lack of reaction to a March 1949 letter from Polish bishops, a Wrocław administrator unwittingly got to the heart of the problem: the shaky border between public and private in stalinist Poland. "Society's passive attitude suggests that people unwillingly engage in matters which are not part of their professional duties, and the only possibility of interesting society in these problems lies with the political parties and all the labor organizations."[117] As the example of Wrocław shows, it was one thing to desire the total mobilization of society; it was another thing entirely to mold even the party ranks, let alone the nonparty work force, to a new activism. The creation of the PZPR was a significant step toward this goal. Membership in this organization no longer implied adherence to a particular political idea—

[115]Ibid., k. 107. On the other hand, two workers with longer memories wrote more optimistic letters to France, where they had worked before or during the war (k. 264): "Don't hesitate and don't believe anyone—none of the propaganda. Come to Poland and come to me in Łódź, you'll get work in a factory, or wherever you want, immediately." "You ask if you can come back to Poland. You can come back boldly, nothing will happen to you. Who wants to work, finds work. There is enough work here in Poland, 100 percent better than before the war."

[116]See ŁAP KD PZPR Widzew—WZPB 1 Maja 43/X/4-1, n.p.

[117]WAP Zarząd Miejski 134, k. 110. See also a report of May 1949: "The most numerous masses . . . very often do not understand the point of existing bureaus and authorities, and of decrees issued. That population does not think about the authorities' decrees at all, and is neither negative nor clearly positive towards them. . . . The participation of society in political and social life is significant, but is concentrated overwhelmingly in the workplaces" (k. 121).

as might membership in the PPR, PPS, or PSL—but an obligation to join the front ranks of the communist revolution.

As workers tried to retreat from the political arena, the rhetoric in politics and the factory continued to sharpen. The one-party state found itself in an ideological trap of its own making. In the Battle over Trade, the state had sought to create a new opposition or new axes of class conflict. Its efforts found some echo among workers, for it was easy to blame speculators or bad party members. But the battle drew workers' attention to the state's role in the economy; if the state could not deliver, it would fill, in workers' minds, the slot left behind by the jailed profiteers. Thus, workers came to associate poor living standards or repression with the PZPR and the state. An anonymous letter one worker sent to Minister of Industry Hilary Minc in January 1949 laid out these charges clearly:

> Citizen Minister!
> Do you think that your game is not transparent to us workers, who have had enough of your democracy based on demagogy and your charlatan's road to socialism? Do you think that we, the working people, don't see your limousines, beautifully furnished apartments, and in general your private rotten life. . . . You announce that the factories in which we work are our exclusive property, only ours—and how does it turn out but that we are only miserable servants with a lower wage rate than in private factories. And after all, if this is our property, then the income which the factory gives should be divided among the workers, and we would pay a tax like the private factories pay. You don't like it, do you? for then there wouldn't be money to build you palaces in which there are dozens of square meters of space for each bureaucrat. . . . I'd like to write to you more and tell you about your mistakes and cheating moves, if you'd like, and if you'll read them carefully. If you agree, say so in *Trybuna Ludu*, which I read. For now, so as not to get in trouble, I won't sign my name.
> A follower of the Teachings of Marx and Engels[118]

The myriad resentments and associations in this letter were the product of the influences and experiences of an educated worker comparing the hopes in 1945 with the apparent results of 1949. The writer no longer saw the state and the party as invincibly progressive nor believed that he and the communists shared a common purpose of revolution for the

[118]AAN MPiH 91, n.p.

working class, yet still he believed that one could explain it all, man to man, and improve one's lot.

The purpose of creating the PZPR was not to reach out to society but to include all of society within the party's grasp. Whether this was successful is a topic for the next two chapters. But the party's language and its concerns became increasingly foreign to the average Pole, especially after the PZPR plenum of November 1949. Beginning shortly before, party documents suddenly and for the first time adopt a Soviet-style rhetoric of vigilance and attack. Condemning Gomułka and other leaders, the PZPR searched for enemies everywhere, in the party and without, and conducted propaganda about the more violent purges taking place in fraternal countries. But party leaders found to their dismay that even the PZPR rank and file was uninterested and refused to take the campaign seriously. Perhaps, however, no amount of vigilance or seriousness could ever be enough for party leaders. The workers were no longer perceived by the PZPR as allies or even potential colleagues; workers were instead potential enemies prone to sabotage and needing strict discipline. The November plenum even rejected the idea of the mass party, although without calling for a drastic reduction of the PZPR's size.[119]

The political and institutional changes of 1948–49 created what may be called the foundations of stalinism. These changes bore some relation to the desires or aspirations of the working class: that speculation be curtailed, that councils and unions be empowered, and that politics as such not interfere with one's life. Except for the first aspiration, these needs were hardly met; rather, the opposite occurred. The party-state addressed these issues with its own aims in mind, reflecting back from a twisted mirror a picture of popular demands that bore little relation to real needs. But popular dissatisfaction had been addressed and manipulated to contribute to the rise of a stalinist state. The campaigns that accomplished this also succeeded in imposing new kinds of class rhetoric on factory and national politics. The enemy was no longer without but within the working class and the factory—even within the party itself. The simpler polarization that workers had understood was no longer

[119]See reports from Wrocław in AAN KC PZPR 237/VII/89, k. 31, 66–67. On the plenum and the campaigns of late 1949, see Andrzej Paczkowski, *Pół wieku dziejów Polski, 1939–1989* (Warsaw, 1995), 261–63. On the language of the PZPR, see Werblan, *Stalinizm*, 11.

tenable; the enemy was everywhere, and only the party knew where to find it.

The stalinist political system would be incomplete, however, without a collectivist, mobilized, integrated society organized toward production. This was obviously a much more difficult task; indeed, it seems next to impossible when one looks at the Polish working class and its ability to express discontent in Łódź or its sheer disintegration in Wrocław. The next chapters will look at the efforts to stalinize the Polish working class through the imposition of a new collectivism based on labor competition and at how workers both resisted and accommodated themselves to these changes.

5 The Rise and Fall of the Labor Hero

Having mastered politics in the campaigns of 1946 and 1947, centralized and nationalized the economy, and made public language an agitation tool by infusing it with a new class rhetoric, the Polish communists still had not created stalinism. Stalinism, after all, was a social as well as a political system. The problems with food supply and wages, the workers' evident recalcitrance, and the impracticality of Soviet-scale mass terror meant that the cooperation of the Polish worker was absolutely vital to the economic success of the country, upon which, in turn, political success rested. In the years 1948–50, the regime sought to obtain this cooperation on its own terms.

Gaining such participation was, to judge from the two cities we have studied here, a formidable task. On the one hand, experienced workers like those in Łódź had shown their willingness to protest state economic policy. Strikes might be suppressed, but suppression would not in itself improve productivity; as long as the state was unable to furnish a sufficiently attractive standard of living, the worker remained the weakest link in the factory regime. Although strikes were much less threatening after 1947, the workers of Łódź were hardly content. Yet no more reliable, surprisingly enough for party leaders, were the inexperienced workers who dominated the factories of Wrocław. While they joined the PPR in satisfyingly large numbers, they appeared to be even less productive (although it is difficult to make such a comparison) than those in Łódź. They had no attachment to their job, the factory, or the city and worked in a wide-open labor market. Thus they were harder to discipline, even within the party. If these workers were a blank slate, the

PPR had been slow to inscribe its creed on them. Still, the absence of open conflict offered hope that these workers would, in time, be amenable to the political system now being created if their energies could be channeled in ways beneficial to the regime.

Chapter 4 looked at ways in which the state attempted to subordinate workers to an emerging stalinist political system. This chapter will show how the state worked to resolve two pressing social problems. The first was Poland's dire economic situation after the war; the second was the failure to win the active support of the workers. The solution was the mobilization of workers to greater (and higher-quality) production. At the same time, workers like those in Wrocław had to be motivated to greater allegiance to their jobs and the party, while communities like Łódź needed to become more like Wrocław, a place where party culture was dominant and the factory clearly controlled by management and the state, not by working-class tradition. In other words, productivity had to be made both predictable and politically useful. Labor competition, the solution to these problems, was a regime of forced intensification of labor and, as essentially a new kind of progressive piece rate, was surprisingly conciliatory toward workers' demands for a higher standard of living. Borrowed from the Soviets, labor competition had become by 1949 a central feature of the factory regime throughout Eastern Europe.[1] Political agitation became a part of labor mobilization only in late 1948; until then, the state invoked the economic and patriotic necessity of rebuilding Poland.

Youth Labor Competition: A Confrontation of Cultures

One may question how successfully labor competition raised productivity or attracted workers' enthusiasm. It was nevertheless crucial to the creation of a factory culture radically different from that fostered by the established working-class community. Labor competition was nothing less than a wager on the enthusiasm of new workers because it offered them a chance to earn more money, gain advance in the factory, and see their names in the newspaper. In this way, the communal power of labor conflict was not so much repressed as defused. The mobilization

---

[1] François Bafoil, "Adolf Hennecke, un Stakhanoviste allemande ou les fondements de la RDA," *Cahiers du Monde Russe et Soviétique* 30, no. 1 (1990): 5–25; Lewis Siegelbaum, *Stakhanovism and the Politics of Productivity in the USSR, 1935–1941* (New York, 1988).

of labor transformed labor relations, replacing tradition and experience with a new work ethic of individual competition against norms and other workers. As labor competition moved from the limited arena of party enthusiasm to the larger working community, it changed the boundaries and shape of the working class and subjected most workers to direct state control. But the economic, political, and cultural results of labor competition remained ambiguous throughout the 1940s and were not always advantageous to the state.[2]

Given its history of labor conflict, Łódź was an appropriate, if challenging, site for the first attempts to promote Soviet-style productivity. First, labor competition, or any positive representation of labor, was an obvious way to generate contrary publicity about workers' attitudes toward the regime and thus counteract from above the strength of Łódź labor culture. Second, the dominance of a continuous labor community had made the city resistant to economic change or expansion; labor competition provided an opening for those who came to the factory or city for the first time. Third, Łódź in 1945 attracted many young people who were enthusiastic about revolutionary change and eager to tackle the city's problems by creating the new methods of work and politics that the regime required. Łódź's temporary position as the seat of many government and other central offices made it the place to seek guidance from and rub shoulders with the new leaders of Poland. It also boasted a new university, the first higher-education institution in the city. Its very presence in a proletarian city made this university a haven for "progressive" politics.[3] Finally, labor competition focused on the unskilled industries; while its rhetoric might champion skill, promising success for those who knew their jobs and their machines best, in fact the less skilled a worker's job, the more it could be sped up to beat norms and win competitions. The heroic names in labor competition appear in construction work, mining, foundry work, and textiles; a 1948 survey of adult competition in six industries found that more than three-quarters of the

---

[2]Labor competition (*wyścig pracy* or *współzawodnictwo*) took many forms. There were three kinds of competition (with victory usually judged by the percentage of production norm achieved): between workers, groups of workers, or factories. Other forms of labor mobilization (included here under competition) were the multimachine campaign (*wielowarsztatowość*), the "savings movement," in which workers were encouraged to use less material input and energy and produce less waste, and the "inventor movement" (*ruch racjonalizatorski*). At least through 1949, the term *socialist competition,* standard in the Soviet Union in the 1930s, was not common.

[3]See the memoirs in *Tranzytem przez Łódź* (Łódź, 1964).

participants worked in textile mills or foundries. Within those industries, more complex tasks were discouraged by labor competition.[4]

The idea of a Youth Labor Competition (*Młodzieżowy Wyścig Pracy*, MWP) was formally proposed by the chairman of the Łódź section of the PPR youth organization Union of the Youth Struggle (ZWM) in June 1945. Neither the local PPR, which doubted the competition's chances of success, nor the PPS, which recognized the threat to workers, gave the project its support; national leadership—in particular PPR General Secretary Gomułka—provided the backing necessary to begin the campaign.[5] Some skepticism is appropriate when approaching such claims of grassroots origins, but neither the state nor any of the parties was really in control of the economy or society in 1945. The PPR ranks did at this stage contain many enthusiasts—like those in the Łódź ZWM—excited about building socialism. Nevertheless, as these enthusiasts began to organize their competition, their efforts looked anything but grassroots to most workers.

Youth activists were motivated by two problems. One was the difficulty that young people had in finding work in the factories, which hired experienced workers first; the MWP was a way to get young workers noticed and hired. The other reason was purely monetary. ZWM reports about the competition prominently mentioned the rewards available to the winners; indeed, competition planners began by surveying factory pay and bonus policies.[6]

This campaign was decidedly premature. The ZWM was only just in the process of organizing; moreover, production competitions were impossible in many factories where production norms and piece rates had yet to be introduced. A PPR Central Committee inspector remarked in

[4]*Partia w cyfrach, 1944-1948*, (Warsaw, 1948), 117. One example of intra-industry differentiation was in woolen weaving: weavers producing blankets on cord looms could not work more than two looms or make more than ten thousand złotys in 1948, while an ordinary weaver might work six looms and make 15,000 with little trouble. A similar gap existed between woolen and cotton mills. MSW MBP 17/IX/10, t. 2, kk. 16–17, 59.

[5]Wiesław Wolski, "Narodziny i przebieg Młodzieżowego Wyścigu Pracy w Łodzi i województwie łódzkim w latach 1945-1949," in *W 35-lecie Młodzieżowego Wyścigu Pracy: Materiały i wspomnienia na spotkanie przodowników MWP*, ed. Andrzej Lech and Tadeusz Wojtkowiak (Łódź, 1980), 19–22; Halina Batorowicz, *Młodzież we współzawodnictwie pracy, 1945–1975* (Łódź, 1975). On the start of competition in one factory (Scheibler and Grohman), see ŁAP PZPB No. 1, 2, k. 5; a representative of PPR provincial leadership proposed joining competition and was seconded by a PPS leader.

[6]"Wyścig pracy łódzkiej młodzieży robotniczej," *Walka młodych*, 8 August 1945, reprinted in *Związek Walki Młodzieży: Materiały i dokumenty* (Warsaw, 1953), 329–32.

First national ZWM rally in Warsaw, 22 July 1946. Members of the Łódź ZWM display their labor on a parade float. Side banner reads: "With Labor and Struggle We Will Build the Edifice of the Future"; rear banner reads: "Struggle, Study, Labor." Archiwum Akt Nowych, Warsaw.

the third week of the campaign that "if the ZWM had looked at matters realistically, it would not have come out with such an initiative in the factories."[7] The MWP was at first a rather modest movement of greater political than economic impact: just 3,600 young workers in twenty-nine factories in Łódź and the province took part; half of the competitors were ZWM members. Originally planned for just the month of August, the competition lasted for six weeks until mid-September 1945.[8]

The PPS youth organization soon withdrew its original support, leaving the MWP strictly a communist program.[9] Organizers also faced resistance from management and foremen. At the PPR's First Congress, Eugeniusz Szyr of the Ministry of Industry rejoiced in this resistance as proof of workers' revolutionary quality.[10] The greatest resistance came from older workers who found the combination of political and economic slogans either incomprehensible or ominous. The first round of the MWP welcomed the political symbolism of intergenerational conflict, portraying prewar workers as trapped by their past and unable to accept the new slogans. Propagandists used the same arguments that they had used against strikes—that the rules were different under capitalism. Halina Lipińska, Youth Labor Competition's most famous participant, showed in her 1950 autobiography the arguments used against workers like her mother:

---

[7] AAN KC PPR 295/X/5, k. 99. With the exception of the labor competition movement, youth organizations played a minor role in factories. The ZWM was much more powerful than its PPS counterpart, the Youth Organization of the Workers' University Society (Organizacja ·Młodzieżowa Towarzystwa Uniwersytetu Robotniczego, OMTUR), which joined with the ZWM in 1948 to form the Union of Polish Youth (Związek Młodzieży Polskiej, ZMP). Even in 1949, workers made up just one quarter of ZMP membership; most members were high school students or peasants. Barbara Fijałkowska, *Ideowo-polityczna działalność związków młodzieży w Polsce w latach 1944-1957* (Warsaw, 1978), chap. 4; AAN KC PZPR 237/VII/116, k. 75; AAN KC PPR 295/VII/51, k. 166.

[8] Wolski, "Narodziny i przebieg," 24; Czesław Kozłowski, *Związek Walki Młodych i Organizacja Młodzieżowa TUR w Łodzi i województwie łódzkim (1945–48)* (Łódź, 1972), 136–39. On competitions before the MWP in Łódź, see Janusz Gołębiowski, "Rola PPR w przyjęciu, uruchomieniu i nacjonalizacji przemysłu Łodzi," *Rocznik Łódzki* 6 (1962): 123–24; Lucjan Kieszczyński, "Moja działalność w łódzkiej dzielnicy PPR-Górna Prawa (styczeń–czerwiec 1945)," *Z Pola Walki*, no. 2 (1974): 290; ŁAP KW PPR 1/XI/2 n.p.; and Eugeniusz Gudziński, "Związki zawodowe wobec problemu aktywizacji produkcyjnej załóg robotniczych (1945–1948)," *KHRZ*, no. 4 (1981): 24–27.

[9] Kozłowski, *Związek Walki Młodych i Organizacja Młodzieżowa TUR w Łodzi*, 139.

[10] "Dyskusja na I Zjeździe Polskiej Partii Robotniczej nad sprawozdaniem organizacyjnym Komitetu Centralnego i referatem KC w sprawach gospodarczych (8–10 XII 1945 r.)," *ARR*, 11:205–6.

Many unenlightened workers, men and women, read the labor competition as an organized attack on their rights.

"We've worked so many years," they said, "and we've never heard of any competition!"

"The youngsters want to take our bread away!" others added.

Even my mother shared these fears. "If you do the work of two," she said, "they'll throw that second worker out in the street!"

"But, Mama," I explained, "not only don't we want to take anything away from anyone, but on the contrary: we want to give to everyone! The more material we produce, the more shirts workers will have. That's clear, isn't it? And no one will throw anyone in the street. Unemployment exists only in the capitalist system. It does not threaten us. There's no lack of work here, and there never will be."[11]

The Youth Labor Competition thus helps to explain the major strike wave of autumn 1945 as one over worker-employer relations, especially negotiation over norms and rates. Against a background of mounting aprowizacja troubles and the decline of worker power in the factory came a wave of young agitators (some were teenagers) exhorting those whom older workers might consider apprentices to join a production campaign that might smash norms only just established. The respect suddenly accorded these beginners and the sight of fresh-faced agitators roaming the factory must have been galling to many experienced workers, especially if the technical accommodations made for the novices or the meetings called by enthusiasts interrupted the rhythm and practice of work. Workers everywhere have always had names for those who break ranks to work longer or harder; that a PPR-linked campaign encouraged such behavior could not endear the party to those who valued such solidarity. Labor competition was still a small, relatively isolated movement, however, and physical attacks on participants were not as common as in later years.[12]

The regime's attachment to youth increased over time, reaching maturity around 1948. During its first years, a large but quickly declining leadership faction identified with the prewar traditions of the labor

---

[11]Halina Lipińska, *Mój awans* (Warsaw, 1950), 14–15. See also Wolski, "Narodziny i przebieg," 25, and Stanisław Jankowski, *Odbudowa i rozwój przemysłu polskiego w latach 1944–1949* (Warsaw, 1989), 301–2.

[12]One example was the beating of two PPR member–workers at the Stolarow mill who began work on four instead of two looms in 1945. Janusz Gołębiowski, *Walka PPR o nacjonalizację przemysłu* (Warsaw, 1961), 268. For a contrasting memory, see Julian Kaczmarek, memoir in *Łódzkie Zeszyty Historyczne (Ruch młodzieżowy—tradycje i współczesność)*, no. 5 (1985): 140.

movement and with the skilled, experienced workers who were the traditional base of the labor parties and its most favored constituency. But with the ascendancy of the Moscow wing of the PPR and the decline of the PPS, youth was increasingly seen not as a group of incorrigible louts or thieves but as the future of industry and the nation. In July 1948, the Łódź PPR worried that labor competition's large awards only for the very best "excludes workers who are weaker in qualifications, whose advance [*podciągnięcie*] we seek most of all."[13] For the party and the state, the value of the young workers lay in their lack of experience with factory life and practices. They were vulnerable, believed party activists, to either progressive or reactionary forces, while an older worker's consciousness was already formed. Bolesław Bierut's official patronage of the MWP and the support of many other dignitaries underscored the importance of this campaign for the PPR. Much more than productivity was at stake. The enthusiasm of young workers would symbolize the progressive, future-oriented nature of the PPR and the social transformation that the party hoped to represent. Assessing the new regime in 1948, Aleksander Janta observed: "Only the youth are truly important. No one will cure the old of their habits, traditions, memories, or attachments; [the regime] waves its hand at them [saying], 'let them live as they can and know how—it's not worth it to persuade them to the new convictions. They'll have to yield to them anyway, sooner or later. Or rather sooner.' "[14]

The first Youth Labor Competition ended with a ceremony in the Textile Worker cinema in downtown Łódź. Guests from the provincial PPR, the army, and the local government and representatives of socialist labor from Yugoslavia, Romania, Bulgaria, and the Soviet Union gathered beneath banners reading "Long live the heroes of labor!" and "Long live the ZWM, Organizer of the Labor Competition." Industry and state officials sponsored the awards. For example, first place in the knitwear section was sponsored by Gomułka and industry director Ignacy Tybor; other awards were named after Prime Minister Edward Osóbka-Morawski and Minister of Information and Propaganda Stefan Matuszewski.[15] After the first competition, the idea spread to the rest of

[13]AAN KC PPR 295/XI/50, kk. 112–13.
[14]Aleksander Janta, *Wracam z Polski 1948* (Paris, 1949), 149. See also ŁAP KŁ PPR 1/VI/141, k. 5.
[15]Wolski, "Narodziny i przebieg," 26; Małgorzata Rutkowska, "Włókniarze w Młodzieżowym Wyścigu Pracy," in *W 35-lecie*, 72.

the country as the ZWM prepared for the next round. In the political geography of the period, only Upper Silesia's coal mines surpassed Łódź in importance. In October 1945, seventy miners representing nearly all Poland's coal mines came to Łódź with forty wagons of coal extracted on Sunday and overtime hours as a gift for the textile workers. The miners visited several mills and pledged further to work one unpaid Sunday a month for the next four months and send the extra production to Łódź. Textile worker representatives pledged to increase their productivity as well and send the surplus goods to the miners. Another delegation of "young Silesians," presumably ZWM members, came to work temporarily in the Łódź cotton mills "to get to know methods of operation."[16] The frequent symbolic linkage of the two industrial centers helped to emphasize the national importance of the young textile workers' efforts.

The next round of competition did not begin until the summer of 1946, when it became an element of the national referendum campaign. The competition began on 30 June, the day of the referendum; the MWP Organizing Committee announced that "The Youth Labor Competition will be the response of the young generation, thrice 'yes' to the questions in the referendum." Participants from Łódź now made up less than 10 percent of the more than 42,000 participants nationwide in this four-month round.[17] As in 1945, strikes frequently interrupted the competition in Łódź. Amid the economic and political crises of 1946, the success of the MWP became increasingly vital to the regime as both propaganda and a promise of economic revival. Participation thus became a virtual obligation for ZWM members. "In no factory where there is the ZWM," resolved Łódź youth leaders, "can youth not take part in the second round of the Youth Labor Competition. Not one of us may be missing. Participation . . . is the duty and honor of every young worker-Pole." To achieve this goal, participation was opened to workers not on piece rates, who were to be judged on days worked, conservation of materials, attentiveness, cleanliness of work station, skill improvement, and pro-

---

[16] *Trybuna Związkowca*, 1–15 November 1945; Wolski, "Narodziny i przebieg," 27.

[17] Wolski, "Narodziny i przebieg," 28; Zbigniew Studencki, "Młodzieżowy Wyścig Pracy w województwie śląsko–dąbrowskim," in *W 35–lecie*, 83–84. On the competition in Wrocław, see Julian Cierpisz, "Na 'Dzikim Zachodzie'," in *Mój zakład pracy: Wspomnienia*, ed. Wiesław Szyndler-Głowacki (Warsaw, 1965), 211–12; and Szymon Goldman, "Z kroniki dolnośląskich związków zawodowych," *Biuletyn Biura Historycznego CRZZ*, nos. 2–3 (1964): 87. Documents appear in *Związek Walki Młodzieży: Materiały i dokumenty*, 350–52, 369–75.

duction.[18] The third round—which, in further indication of the MWP's urgency, began immediately upon the close of the second—was in turn linked to the approaching parliamentary election, with the slogan: "We cannot speak up for popular democracy with the ballot [being too young to vote], so let us answer with the strength of our shoulders."[19] Intended to last three months, this round lasted for six, until May 1947, and in Łódź until October, when the fourth round began (followed immediately, in May 1948, by the fifth and final round, which continued until it merged with the adult competitions that December).

Those who joined the campaign were promised only a badge. Why a hundred or so young workers, some as young as fifteen, joined the campaign in each factory can only be surmised. Some may have hoped to impress the foreman, believing that their jobs depended on it. A few were likely taken by the revolutionary symbolism and sought to belong to the new world. MWP propaganda even appropriated the imagery of experienced workers' finest moment: the heroic defense and rebuilding of the factories in early 1945. When in December 1945 many Łódź factories found themselves without coal to heat the workshops, the ZWM paper gave a stirring account of competitors soldiering on in freezing temperatures.[20]

Most participants saw competition as an individual challenge. Thus, they broke decisively from traditional ways of viewing work, skill, and career progress. They created new labor collectivities to replace the old which had excluded them. A garment worker who participated in the early MWP recalled that her competition group "not only mobilized to more productive labor, but also consolidated itself internally. It not only achieved better productive results, but also raised its qualifications. It also gave an appropriate retort to those who mocked, or dared to criticize, the competitors [*wyścigówki*]." Another clothing worker, participating in a "youth production line," explicitly recalled the athletic nature of the event: the "whistles and shouts when the *sportowcy*, that is, those taking part in the [Youth] Labor Competition, appeared in the workshops." A metal worker remembered that "some machinists and welders

---

[18]Łódź ZWM quoted in Rutkowska, "Włókniarze," 73; Wolski, "Narodziny i przebieg," 29.

[19]Quoted in Wolski, "Narodziny i przebieg," 30. Note the athletic imagery of this slogan; such imagery will be further discussed.

[20]"Wyścig pracy młodzieży łódzkiej trwa nadal," *Walka Młodych*, 25–31, December 1945, reprinted in *Związek Walki Młodzieży: Materiały i dokumenty*, 332–33.

from our shop looked on us with an unfriendly eye, calling us Communist puppies whose heads are spun around with foolishness, and don't understand anything."[21]

The athleticism of the MWP was captured in a slogan popular in the second round: "Who will do more, who better?" [*Kto więcej, kto lepiej?*][22] While individuals tried to beat norms and won high bonuses, medals, recognition from important national leaders, and publicity, they came to see their work as an athletic contest. As a Wrocław union activist explained after the second round, the MWP was "a sporting feat; each competitor tore for the finish line, and thus the youth labor competition yielded high scores."[23] In both the second and third rounds (1946–47), this individualism caused problems for organizers: young participants frequently showed up late on Monday, left early Saturday, wasted material, and shunned cooperation with older workers.[24] The solution, a union activist implied during the fourth round, was to make competition a permanent feature of labor, for "youth is enthusiastic but not persevering, so it is appropriate to devote more work to youth in this direction in order to awaken it appropriately."[25]

Breaking the Collective: Heroism in Labor Competition

The general factorywide competition movement (*współzawodnictwo*) that emerged in 1947 used the same individual imagery as the youth campaigns despite its evident drawbacks. Like the MWP, adult labor competition began with a semimythic individual initiative. On one day in July 1947, miner Wincenty Pstrowski, whose name was to become synonymous with the movement, extracted 273 percent of his daily norm and issued his famous appeal: "Who can extract more than I?"[26]

---

[21] Łucja Skowronek, Julian Kaczmarek, and Jerzy Miścicki, memoirs in *Łódzkie Zeszyty Historyczne* 1, no. 5 (1985): 137, 139–40, 131.

[22] Kaczmarek, in *Łódzkie Zeszyty Historyczne*, 1, no.5 (1985): 140; Jerzy Miścicki remembers it as "Who will be faster, who better" (131).

[23] WAP WRZZ 19, k. 3.

[24] Kozłowski, *Związek Walki Młodych i Organizacja Młodzieżowa TUR w Łodzi*, 145–46.

[25] LAP WRZZ 19, n.p.

[26] Although the story is rather hazy, Pstrowski was most likely a willing participant in a propaganda effort organized by local party or union activists—like the orchestration of Mateusz Birkut's bricklaying feat in Andrzej Wajda's film *Man of Marble*.

In its first eighteen months, adult labor competition grew enormously. By June 1948, almost seventy thousand workers were participating in forty-four of Poland's largest factories and mines; by that September, roughly one-third of foundry, metal, and textile workers were involved in labor competition, with participation among miners and railway workers nearly twice as high. Even these numbers meant that more than 80 percent of Poland's workers were not participants; yet in key industries and factories, labor competition was a universal fact of life.[27]

Mass labor competition—which from early 1948 was formally under union direction—was a gamble, bringing with it larger versions of the problems that the MWP had faced. The authorities hoped to encourage a mass movement from below rather than organize productivity by force. The idea was to encourage workers to perceive that they were both a part and a beneficiary of the new system. "Now one speaks differently to the worker," remarked a UB colonel to his colleagues. "One does not call upon [workers] to commit sabotage and break tools [as during the Nazi occupation]; instead, one even talks about raising productivity, and labor competition of course. But first one must improve living conditions. Such propaganda best reaches the worker."[28] At the same time, the PPR engaged in the same contradictory thinking that it had displayed toward the factory councils. On the one hand, it wanted industrial administration to be a co-organizer of labor competition; on the other, it feared the bureaucratization of the movement. The party seemed to believe that the problem could be solved and labor competition made more natural through greater involvement of provincial PPR leadership in the organization of labor competition.[29]

But competition once unleashed was not easily managed. The Ministry of Industry concluded in October 1947 that "it does not seem that the development of the labor competition campaign could be accelerated by removing its features of a movement from below and giving it features

---

[27]*Partia w cyfrach*, 117; Jankowski, *Odbudowa i rozwój*, 303–5; Gudziński, "Związki zawodowe wobec problemu," 39. As with the MWP, adult competition started in Silesia and Łódź, and much later in Lower Silesia and elsewhere. Jankowski, *Przejmowanie i odbudowa*, 250–52; general numbers on labor competition in Łódź are in *RS miasta Łodzi, 1945–1947*, 322–27, and ŁAP WRZZ 42. Some large factories in Wrocław had not yet implemented any competition by late 1948. WAP KW PPR 1/X/17, kk. 232–39; WAP KW PPR 1/VI/99.

[28]MSW MBP 17/IX/77, t. 3, n.p. (April 1948).

[29]June 1948 circular, in "Dokumenty PPR i PPS dotyczące działalności związków zawodowych," *KHRZ*, nos. 2–3 (1964): 201–2.

of a movement directed from above through administrative decrees."[30] Nevertheless, it was easy for management to use competition to balance the books, getting more output for the same money. Managers prepared the new system without worker or factory council input and made no provisions for the workers displaced. Corrected (that is, raised) norms and tighter supervision often outweighed the competition bonuses, resulting in lower wages for some workers. In the construction industry (later the flagship of labor competition), workers for this reason preferred in 1948 to work for a daily wage rather than work to norms or try to beat them.[31]

Workers, in turn, tried to square labor competition with their desire to control how they earned their wages. Some believed that now everyone would receive equal reward for work above the norm. They saw competition as part of a contract; transport workers in Łódź explained that if "the collective agreement secured their wages, we will for our part work honestly and productively in labor competition."[32] Others complained that management got larger rewards than they for rises in production or consciously discriminated against competition participants. There were charges of fixed competitions and controversies over the announcements of winners.[33] Between or within factories, wage differences resulting from labor competition provoked conflict in Łódź. Workers in departments or factories where work could not be sped up for reasons of precision or technology saw their wages decline relative to those of movement participants and accused management of depriving them of their right to earn more. When the MWP was submerged in the general movement, the participation of young and inexperienced workers declined. The new movement at first favored those who were already well off and better skilled; thus, those who could be sure of winning were most likely to take part.[34]

---

[30] AAN MPiH 1020, k. 137.

[31] ŁAP KŁ PPR 1/XI/18, k. 65; WAP KW PPR 1/X/7, k. 609; AAN KC PPR 295/XI/50, kk. 88–89.

[32] ŁAP WRZZ 66, n.p.

[33] WAP WRZZ 19, k. 2; ibid. 2, k. 6; AAN KC PPR 295/IV/17, k. 64; MSW MBP 17/IX/38, t. 1, n.p. (December 1947).

[34] AAN KC PPR 295/XI/50, kk. 84–85, 112–13. The latter report proposed two solutions to the discrimination against inexperienced workers: rewards based on improvement, and brigade or group competitions. A group of workers from the John metal factory interviewed in Łódź in January 1990 also recalled that competition favored experienced workers, not new rural migrants; see also ŁAP WRZZ 275, n.p. (December 1949).

Disappointed with the rewards or fearful of the results, many workers resisted competition. They felt that participants in labor competition were hoodwinked by the regime, which was sure to trick the workers by raising norms, lowering awards, or increasing physical exertion. Pstrowski's challenge was followed immediately by a competition—ostensibly a spontaneous challenge from below—between the miners of Upper Silesia and the textile workers of Łódź. PPR and union organizations quickly lent official support, but "a rumor spread all across Łódź," acknowledged the PPR Central Committee, that "it will be necessary to work twelve hours a day and on Sundays too, and that such a bill [on work hours] has already been drawn up by PPR members in the Sejm [Parliament]." Fearing a shortage of raw materials, workers across central Poland talked of slowing production.[35] "The labor competition movement has encountered hostile activity from the moment of its inception," admitted the UB in February 1948, reporting "sabotage both covert and less so; . . . anonymous letters and threats are commonly sent to leading miners (Pstrowski, Ratajczak) and to labor avantgardists in the textile industry (Łódź, Lower Silesia); rumors are spread that all workers taking part in the labor competition movement are losing their health. Moreover, conventional wisdom says that in the near future wages will be lowered and there will be layoffs (Łódź), and that one should give up [more] productive work since management will take and waste on drink the money a worker earns (Żagań, Lower Silesia). Graffiti against competitive work appeared on the walls in the Cegielski Works in Poznań." Graffitists in Bydgoszcz used a turtle symbol to call for a work slowdown. Competitors in Łódź and Silesia were pelted with spools or beaten. There was even, reported the UB, an underground band in the Piotrków area that frightened workers out of joining competition.[36]

Who were the protesters? Putting a different spin on Aleksander Janta's analysis, Stefan Jędrychowski of the PPR Central Committee blamed resistance on "the backward element of the working class, which does not understand the whole meaning of that movement for raising the

[35] AAN KC PPR 295/XIII/5, kk. 11–14. See also AAN KC PPR 295/XI/49, k. 43.

[36] Quotation and Piotrków information are from: MSW MBP 17/IX/38, t. 2; report from Bydgoszcz in MSW MBP 41/234, k. 42 (see also k. 38). Other examples appear in MSW MBP 17/IX/77, t. 2, n.p. (October 1947); "Stenogram plenarnego posiedzenia Komitetu Centralnego PPR 11 października 1947 r.," *ARR*, 11: 297; MSW MBP 17/IX/38, tt. 1, 2, n.p. (December 1947, June 1948); and ŁAP WRZZ 74, n.p. (October 1948).

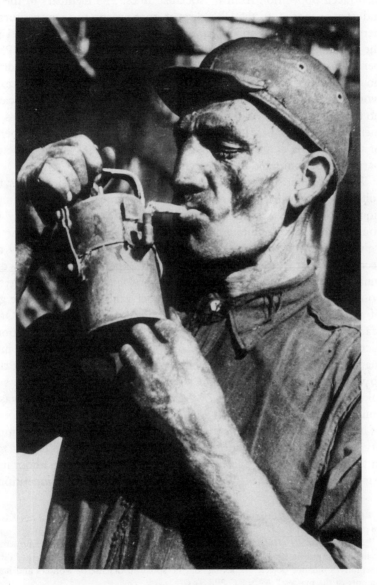

Miner and hero-worker Wincenty Pstrowski, 1948. Archiwum Akt Nowych, Warsaw.

prosperity of the working class and of society in general."[37] The PPR also faced opposition from its socialist allies. PPS members in the coal industry proposed, to the UB's disgust, that prospective competitors undergo a medical checkup and that youth and women be excluded. Under the headline "The Human Element in Labor Competition," the PPS paper *Robotnik* remarked: "The best work safety and hygiene conditions do not lessen the weariness . . . ; the work of such a [female textile] worker resembles a mad dance among the machines. . . . There can be no thought of such work effort over the long term."[38] Nevertheless, PPS members still took part in competition in significant numbers; 35 percent of the socialists at forty-four factories in June 1948 were competition participants, compared to 44 percent of PPR members.[39]

Where the factory was dominated by older, experienced workers, their solidarity and belief in apprenticeship led them to discourage competition participants. A multimachinist at the Widzew manufactory who sought advice on technique from older workers complained that they "give no answer, or answer that they do not want to give away their secrets, for that [comes with] many years of experience, and each worker must get there on her own. Explanations . . . that they wrong their younger colleagues, that they should understand that it is for the good of all and of the state, did not help—they gave no answer."[40] Others feared the threat to workers' jobs and control of their own labor. A factory council chairman at one Łódź mill angrily confronted a multi-machine volunteer: "What, are you crazy? We are fighting for [the right] to work on only one loom, and you want to work on two looms and take bread away from others."[41] Mistrust of labor competition was encouraged further by the illness and death, rumored to be from overwork, of hero-miner Pstrowski in early 1948. While Pstrowski was sick, miners at one Silesia mine announced: "We want to live, we don't want to lie in the hospital like Pstrowski. We don't want to be written about in the papers like other mines. We'll work, but without any competition."[42]

[37]December 1947. Jędrychowski claimed that resistance was declining. AAN KC PPR 295/XI/2, kk. 15–16.

[38]Quoted in MSW MBP 17/IX/38, t. 2, n.p. (February 1948). When a PPS representative at the Wima mill in Łódź spoke against labor competition in September 1948, PPR representatives did not object, "believing that he spoke in defense of workers and has the support of the masses." AAN KC PPR 295/IX/34, k. 11.

[39]*Partia w cyfrach*, 117–18.

[40]ŁAP KW PPR 1/IX/20, kk. 80–82.

[41]ŁAP WK PPS 22/XII/11–12, t. 2. See also AAN KC PPR 295/XIII/18, k. 246.

[42]MSW MBP 17/IX/38, t. 2, n.p. (January 1948; see also April and May 1948); WAP

To some, labor competition confirmed their darkest fears about Soviet "Stahanovite" labor; others—PPR members in particular—were reminded of prewar experiences and claimed there was no difference between private and state capital. As a graffito in a Łódź woolen mill put it (presumably commenting on the removal of a crèche): "The Virgin Mary has gone to the Women's League, St. Joseph to the PPR, the straw to the Peasant's Self-Help, and the donkeys and sheep to labor competition."[43]

Indeed, the authorities looked not just for "conscious" workers to join the movement but opened it to all comers. At its height in 1948–49 individual labor competition was not about politics, but about workers' concerns regarding material welfare and job control. Although reports of the movement's popularity seem dubious, the authorities could not easily retreat without wreaking economic chaos in workers' lives.[44] The material effects of the campaign will be discussed later; the greatest immediate impact of competition was on the models of labor and skill because it opened up the factory to a new generation of workers shepherded by the PPR. Reinterpreted through communist propaganda, individual achievement became a central feature of the new factory culture. Labor competition heroicized work life and created a pantheon of heroic models in the factory.

Who was the labor hero—the *przodownik*? As I noted earlier, experienced workers had a better chance of success in early competitions. Like those who resisted competition, they were survivors from the old labor community, succeeding through experience rather than zeal or strength. As knitwear worker Stanisław S. recalled, "If someone wanted to make money and was careful, he could have good results without labor competition."[45] Before labor competition, indeed, models of productive labor had been quite different. To be a *przodownik pracy* (literally "work leader" but "labor avant-gardist" better conveys the term's

---

KW PPR 1/VI/99, k. 51. The Pstrowski case remained one of the classic unsolved mysteries in popular lore throughout the communist era.

[43]ŁAP DK PPS Łódź–Zielona, 33/XIII/2, k. 87. Also WAP KW PPR 1/X/7; AAN KC PPR 295/XIII/7, kk. 152–53; Janusz Tomaszewski, "Zadania 'produkcyjne' związków zawodowych i ich realizacja na Dolnym Śląsku w latach 1945–1950," in *Z badań nad dziejami Dolnego Śląska po II wojnie światowej*, ed. Stanisław Dąbrowski (Wrocław, 1993), 30–31. Aleksei Stakhanov was the Soviet Union's first hero–worker. See note 1.

[44]For an example of such official optimism, see (from early 1948, Łódź), MSW MBP 17/IX/10 t. 2, k. 59.

[45]Interview, 9 May 1990.

propaganda sense) connoted experienced leadership, as in a series of sketches in a factory paper in early 1946. In one, citizen Helena Gajda commented not on new work methods but on the changes she had seen in the factory since 1925, on food supply problems, and on the factory's daycare system. Another sketch began as follows: "One of the leading [*przodujące*] workers in the [Egyptian Spinning Shop] is citizen Maria Gawrońska, who has worked with us very long—24 years already. Twenty-four years is a long time; one can see and hear a lot. Citizen Gawrońska knows very well how difficult the situation in this country is, and therefore the situation of workers. In the matter of supplies, it is very difficult for the worker, and even though we are aware that the difficult material conditions are the result of huge wartime destruction, we must mobilize all our means to improve the life of the worker." Gawrońska offers not incredible productivity but wise observations on the nature of work and hardship, from the perspective of a long-time community member in both factory and neighborhood. As an experienced worker, she could also express common grievances.[46]

Ideology was not a prime motivator for these workers. Skilled metalworker participants polled at Pafawag talked not about the future or the party but about nation, pride in their skill, and personal well-being. One of these workers, Dionyzy Dylewski, wrote:

> The main reason for joining labor competition was the desire to show my colleagues a model of productive work, and to spread my work methods to other lathe operators; I knew that this would contribute to the acceleration of the rebuilding of the country and the improvement of life for the working masses.
>
> I also read in the papers about the privileges and high earnings of a work leader in the coal industry; this encouraged me to organize and join labor competition in my department.
>
> I achieved my results in labor competition thanks to my high lathe-operator's skills and long years of work.[47]

But one purpose of labor competition was to allow young workers to make their way in the factory without having to rely on their seniors; PPR propaganda accomplished this goal through the use of sport and heroic images. Newspapers, pamphlets, songs, and ceremonies all pro-

---

[46] *Głos Widzewa*, 7 (18) and 8 (19), 24 February and 3 March 1946.
[47] WAP Pafawag 77, k. 36; see other declarations in same folder, especially that of Stanisław Mrożek, k. 35.

mulgated an image of labor competition that soft-pedaled politics and highlighted the glory of the individual and his or her team—the factory. The model of heroic youth that had first appeared in the MWP reached its peak in 1949–50. A ditty entitled "A Mason's Date," which appeared in a ZMP journal in 1949, showed youth single-handedly rebuilding the country, in a manner reminiscent of John Henry:

> Once by a ruin stood a bricklayer
> Waiting for his sweetheart.
> He waited hour after hour
> Until finally fury overcame him. Ech!

> Thought the chap to himself
> "He who wastes time goes backward,"
> He forgot all about the girl
> And took up his pickaxe.

> After the pickaxe came the trowel
> He spat hard upon his hands.
> Wiped the sweat and mightily began
> To lay the foundation down. Ech!

> When he had laid the ninth floor
> He remembered his dear one.
> He looked down at the street
> But she was not there.

> Higher and higher rose the walls
> Suddenly he heard a voice from below.
> Someone's running up the stairs
> And lamenting aloud. Ech!

> "Stop, wait, my dear!
> Why do you torment your poor darling so?
> I've been chasing you for two hours
> And can't catch up to you!"[48]

In this verse, with its allusions to folk tunes, the social nature of the bricklayer's act is absent. His is an entirely individual, personalized feat, its apolitical nature suggested by the casual way he achieves it. He is a master of a world in which work is as worthy of adulation as sports.

---

[48] "*Młode ręce budują . . .*": *W naszej świetlicy ZMP* (Warsaw, 1949).

Similarly, a labor avant-gardist recalls in his 1949 autobiography that as a youngster "I was involved with sports with my whole soul. I kicked the ball around, boxed, and trained for the 100-meter run. I dreamed of the successes of Kusociński."[49] He implies that labor competition helped him to fulfill those athletic dreams.

The team, the central metaphor of labor competition, is a dynamic image that is as hard to square with a disciplined, faceless system as it is with the traditional labor community. The factory became a competitor with fans and rivals (and the PPR secretary as coach), and the top avant-gardists became star players, as shown in the following article from the Łódź PPR newspaper. Note the use of the old names for the factories to give the contest a more popular flavor:

Summit Rivalry of Colossi:
Who Will Come Out On Top, Szajbler or Horak?

It's true that the weavers and avant-gardists from Ruda [Pabianicka, the location of the Horak mill], and comrade Łęgosz, director of the factory, had Pabianice [cotton mill] in their sights when, in the last days of April [1948], they switched to working ten looms, but—as so often happens—fate has played them a trick. As the most unexpected thing on earth, Szajbler [Scheibler and Grohman], with its "twelvers" [weavers working twelve looms] has appeared as the main rival. This sensational news was received in Ruda like a bolt from the blue. "Aha, so that's how it is? They couldn't forgive us for being first in the May labor competition?! But no problem, comrade, we aren't afraid of them . . . we've already heard a little bit about their 'twelvers.' " . . .

What do the main heroines at [Scheibler's] New Weaving Mill say about their feat? . . .

Easily, with a sense of their own power, they strode the long gallery [between looms], like tamers of wild animals. And the "animals" are as obedient as sheep in the skilled hands of the weavers. "They go like gold," says Comrade Korzeniowska joyfully.

"Is work on 'twelves' much harder than on 'sixes'?"

Comrade Korzeniowska looks at me with pity, and explains in my ear: "Oh, not at all, not at all, comrade . . . but this is a secret. . . . Maybe it's better not to write that in the paper . . ."

[Next came a portrayal of another "twelver," Genia Ossendowska, twenty years old.] Like a good, conscious ZWM-er, she understands what

---

[49]Włodzimierz Gmitrzykowski, *Za przykładem Matrosowa*, BPP 6 (Warsaw, 1949), 7; see also 32. Janusz Kusociński was a Polish track star, a medal winner at the 1932 Olympics.

this means for the country, and like a single girl, independently earning her living, she is happy with her upcoming payday. "Please just don't think," she adds, "that I made out poorly until now on the 'sixes.' No, I lived just fine with my 15–16 thousand monthly [about twice the average paycheck]. And now that it will be more, that's even better. . . .

What will the earnings of these weaver pioneers be? This is not yet known at the moment. The comrades are calm, however. They were not cheated when they switched to six looms, so they shan't be wronged now either, when they are working twice as many looms. And the fact that their pioneering work goes for the good of the whole working class—this they understood long ago.[50]

Patriotic loyalty to a people's democracy is here just an afterthought to the main themes of money and individual accomplishment. The off-hand way in which a relatively large amount of money is mentioned is surely calculated to surprise. Ossendowska is a "single girl, independently earning her living"; money, labor, and the ZWM organization give her the independence and freedom of a lion tamer, calmly turning wild beasts into sheep. Her portrait blends modesty and power, emphasizing the satisfaction that these heroines find in their recreation-like work. Ossendowska explains that for a while in 1945 or 1946 she worked in an office, but "I was terribly bored there—after all, there were three of us when one could do the work perfectly." In the PPR paper's version, ordinary workers could find it in themselves to become heroes and participate in a historic battle of titans.

A curious, brief strike in early 1948 suggests that some workers recognized the value of such images as an expression of class identity. Fifty-two workers in the sorting room at a Łódź woolen mill interrupted work to protest an article in the Łódź PPR newspaper entitled "Weak Development of Labor Competition at PZPW No. 4." Strikers demanded that the article be retracted, shouting: "That's the pay for our work!" and "If the editor is so smart, let him come to work himself." They demanded, in short, that their productivity be duly recognized. Management agreed to convene a meeting with worker representatives at which a letter was composed to the newspaper.[51]

Although they might be a part of a team, labor heroes were meant to take very personal paths to success, achieving their results through self-examination and self-knowledge. Their autobiographies offer precise

[50]*Głos Robotniczy*, 6 May 1948.
[51]ŁAP CZPW 448, kk. 4–6.

technical explanations of how they analyzed their work motions and materials and improved them to make higher production possible. This approach directly challenged traditional ways of getting training and knowledge in the factory from one's elders and superiors. The autobiography of a young machinist from Poznań, Mieczysław Łykowski, was an example of the idea that the new method of self-training was superior to the old. Łykowski was frustrated by being unable to beat his norm by more than 30 percent, and realized the problem was the knife used with his lathe. In a technical handbook, he read about a superior hard-alloy knife. The shop supervisor, however, refused to allot him such a knife. Writes Łykowski,

> I didn't give up. I decided to get a Vidia knife at any cost. I bought one on the free market with my own money, and reported it to brigade leader Bińkowski. The results of this correction were not long in coming: in the next month I doubled my production, and reached 276.64 percent of norm.
>
> But now something happened which I did not expect. Instead of words of praise, charges and reproaches flew. Shop supervisor Engineer Gruszczyński announced publicly that my [results] are pure nonsense. Brigade leader Fabisz wore a look as if I had personally insulted him by beginning to work differently than had been done until now. . . . Voices were heard saying: "Łykowski is a fraud. We know all about such trick results [*lewe normy*]." . . . They were still stuck in the old concepts, and maintained the position that only the way they were taught, the way one worked in their time, was good, and that one should not shake those "sacred facts."

When management summoned a special commission to observe him, the confrontation was an athletic challenge for the 24-year-old machinist:

> I was pleased, as if someone had sat me on seven horses. At last they would be convinced. I was absolutely certain of victory, for I had already conducted tests several times, had put the machine on the highest speed— it went fine. . . . So I laughed to myself, imagining the faces on those un-believers when they saw the results of today's control check. . . .
>
> I started the machine. With stopwatch in hand, like at a sports contest, they watched my fingers. In forty minutes—that is how long the commission checked me—I achieved 600 percent, while less than an hour before my result which was half as high had been suspect.

The hero was now redeemed: management helped Łykowski and called a Poznań newspaper to come and write about his success. Łykowski was

Poster, 1947. "Through Labor Competition to a Poland Strong and Rich." Designed by Włodzimierz Zakrzewski for the Central Trade Union Commission. Photograph by Julia Pirotte. Muzeum Niepodległości, Warsaw.

satisfied with this vindication but admits that "maybe if everything had gone swimmingly from the beginning, my success would not please me so much." Like a true socially conscious competitor, he claims that even his recent record-breaking totals of more than 500 percent are not enough; he pledges to achieve 650 percent in honor of 1 May.[52]

Łykowski did not claim to have succeeded due to his acquired skill; "I Only Improved It" is the title of his story. Instead, he claimed to have broken records by going *against* the skill traditions of more knowledgeable workers, who were now foremen and supervisors as a result of their experience. His feat was a challenge to them and was fueled (in his retelling) by love of the challenge. His willingness to stand up to his old-fashioned superiors and the substantial rewards he earned were meant as an inspiration to the young, ambitious worker.

The concept of service to one's country, let alone service to one's party, is remarkably muted in these examples. Łykowski, the young mason, the older avant-gardists, or even Scheibler's "twelvers" portrayed their duty as primarily to themselves and secondarily to other workers or the consumers in need of goods. Thus, while the political implications of labor competition were evident from the beginning—for example, when competition was tied to May Day or national elections—even then ideology remained subordinate to the idea of work for Poland or one's class, not for the party. Within the factories, party leaders were closely involved in the organization of labor competition. At awards ceremonies, PPR leaders and PPR themes were prominent. Yet three months after such a ceremony in February 1948 at Pafawag, management decided that "in the present stage of development of labor competition, it would be more advisable to distribute prizes not at specially arranged ceremonies, but only normally, during payment of advances."[53] The lack of ideological commentary in early labor competition is striking, even allowing for Polish communism's relative subtlety. For the prestalinist state, the construction of new social ideals—interest in the economy and the factory's welfare, belief in the opportunity to advance—was in itself more important than the propagation of socialism.

---

[52]Mieczysław Łykowski, *Ja tylko usprawniałem*, BPP 5 (Warsaw, 1949), 30–37. See also Gmitrzykowski, *Za przykładem Matrosowa*, 20–21.

[53]WAP Pafawag 77, kk. 18–19, 34.

The Economics of Labor Competition

If we leave aside the intangible propaganda benefits, was the dramatically improved production of a few workers profitable for the state? Because many workers did not participate and the authorities' sponsorship of the movement was for inspirational as much for economic motives, statistics cannot tell us very much. A great deal also depends on perspective; some people in Poland benefited more than others. Any answer must attempt to balance the economic needs of all the actors against the political and cultural aims of the movement. In the long run, however, labor competition made high wages (and worker satisfaction) a priority, regardless of actual production.

The authorities hoped at first that labor competition would improve production. Postwar production was at intolerable levels: for example, with employment at 55 percent of the prewar total in the second quarter of 1945, output was just 30 percent of 1938 levels.[54] As the aprowizacja strikes of 1945–46 showed, factories were hampered by a multitude of nonproduction obligations. Party leaders realized that it was imperative to focus workers away from the revolution onto production goals. To this end, more and more factories began in 1947 to call "production conferences" at which workers (or a workers' delegation or only the factory council) took part in discussions of ways to resolve production problems. The PPR Central Committee constantly searched for ways to bring workers into the technical planning process. They hoped not to increase workers' control but to mobilize workers into a party-controlled campaign for higher production. An early party document instructed factories that issues such as aprowizacja, child care, and culture were inappropriate topics.[55]

From the workers' perspective, the question of economics was somewhat easier: for most participants competition was profitable through at least 1948. As Wrocław unionists realized, in most factories "labor competition is treated like a progressive piece rate."[56] Of all the potential motives for participation in labor competition, by far the most important

---

[54] AAN MPiH 946, kk. 2–8. Hilary Minc in September 1945 gave a figure of 70 percent of prewar production—with wages at only 25 percent of prewar levels. *Życie Warszawy,* 22 November 1984.

[55] AAN KC PPR 295/IX/382, kk. 71–71a. See also AAN KC PPR 295/VII/5, kk. 161–64; AAN KC PPR 295/XI/12, kk. 26–28, 53–55; WAP WRZZ 66, k. 27.

[56] WAP WRZZ 66, k. 27.

was pay. Real wages climbed almost 60 percent from 1946 to 1949, with the greatest rise coinciding with the onset of labor competition in late 1947 and 1948. Korzeniowska, the star weaver at Scheibler, made 14,566 zł in 1947; the following year, another weaver at Scheibler made 25,000.[57]

But as the Poznański strike showed, the promise of higher pay was often offset for experienced workers by the fear of losing control over their jobs, mistrust of management's motives, and knowledge that norms were likely to be raised anyway. Management and the PPR worked to break this mistrust and prove that labor competition paid off. Better working conditions, medals or other symbolic awards, clothing, and above all pay would entice workers into the movement and prevent strikes and labor turnover. Taking this approach was often how labor competition was created in a factory: first attract a few workers and give them better working conditions (as in the Poznański strike) if possible; then reward them handsomely.[58] *Drogowiec*, the road workers' union monthly, published a poem meant to illustrate this purpose of competition:

> A labor competition poster
> was hung upon the wall.
> Wacek Brona read it carefully
> and all the workers laughed.
>
> The very next day the pickaxe flew
> and sweat poured down Wacek's face.
> And all the other workers
> stared and shrugged their shoulders.
>
> Wacek became a labor leader
> and when payday comes on Saturday,
> He hefts the pile of money he's earned
> (those fools aren't laughing any more).
>
> All the workers gathered 'round
> to hear what Brona had to say,

[57]Stanisław Jankowski, "Warunki bytu ludności," in *Gospodarka Polski Ludowej 1944–1955*, 3d ed., ed. Janusz Kaliński and Zbigniew Landau (Warsaw, 1986), 65–66; Wiesław Puś and Stefan Pytlas, *Dzieje Łódzkich Zakładów Przemysłu Bawełnianego im. Obrońców Pokoju "Uniontex" (d. Zjednoczonych Zakładów K. Scheiblera i L. Grohmana) w latach 1827–1977* (Warsaw, 1979), 430–32. Also ARZ KCZZ WO 417, kk. 13–15.

[58]See discussions of such strategy in WAP KW PPR 1/X/64, kk. 36–38; WAP KW PPR 1/XI/22, k. 234; ŁAP WRZZ 19, n.p. (January 1948); and AAN KC PPR 295/XIII/5, k. 11.

And he told them "Comrades!
Only with labor will we reach our goal!"

His words reached their hearts
and soon work buzzed all around.
The pickaxe and the shovel flew
and beads of sweat moistened every brow.

And on Saturday when they're paid
the cash flows by the thousands.
Everyone has a joyful smile
as you can see for yourself.[59]

But labor competition could not reward everyone handsomely. Throughout 1948, workers and management seemed to be trying to understand what labor competition was, whom it was for, and whether or not it was advantageous. The promised benefits were not always forthcoming. If management failed to reward workers properly, using only token prizes, they removed the one incentive workers had to participate. Some workers recognized that labor competition was not in fact a system through which they could control their earnings; instead management retained that control. At the Mewa chemical factory, for example, workers claimed there was a 50 percent bonus ceiling no matter what their production.[60]

These rewards soon became an integral part of the state-worker relationship. Labor competition was the material manifestation of communist ideology about workers' privileged role in society. This idea proved to be impossible to back away from, for workers came to expect rich rewards for their labor—and for increasingly ordinary labor, too. As the excitement and the voluntarism disappeared from the movement, expectations of a certain standard of living remained. Economist Czesław Bobrowski warned of this danger as early as 1946; the combination of labor conflict and workers' reaction to labor competition helped to keep industry's social obligations at the forefront.[61]

[59] Wojciech Laskowski, "Przygody Wacka Brony," *Drogowiec*, nos. 10–11 (October–November 1948): 16.

[60] ŁAP WRZZ 66, n.p. See also ŁAP DK PPS Łódź–Górna 20/XIII/1, k. 15.

[61] "Protokoły posiedzeń Rady Gospodarczej PPS (1945–1946)," ed. Władysław Mroczkowski and Tadeusz Sierocki, *Z Pola Walki*, nos. 1–2 (1982): 246–47. On wages and incentives in state socialism, see J. Wilczynski, *The Economics of Socialism: Principles Governing the Operation of the Centrally Planned Economies in the USSR and Eastern Europe under the New System*, 3d ed. (London, 1977), 103–12; and János Kornai, *The Socialist System: The Political Economy of Communism* (Princeton, 1992), chap. 10.

Bonuses and prizes were a central part of early labor competition. A competitor in the fifth round of the Youth Labor Competition, Warsaw, May 1948, poses with diploma and radio. Photographer unknown. Archiwum Dokumentacji Mechanicznej, Warsaw.

The authorities measured their success in two ways. First was satisfaction of workers' needs. Wrocław PPR leaders, for example, condemned in late 1948 the "complete indifference toward the masses" of local economic administrators, for whom "workers' needs [came] last," and criticized factories' attempts to save money by cutting social programs.[62] The second measurement of success was participation in competition. In Łódź, the cradle of competition, 30 percent of the factories participated in competition by February 1949, yet production was still just half what it had been before the war. Despite the cotton industry's leadership in competition, by May 1950 (on the eve of the law on socialist labor discipline) most factories had recorded no real improvement in production over 1947. In fact, this industry and others saw a continuing decline of productivity reaching desperately low levels.[63] Because authorities nevertheless continued to laud labor competition, one must conclude that the propaganda and social-engineering benefits were more important than real economic achievements.

Figure 9 shows how tenuous the link was between increased competition and improved productivity, whether measured in terms of productivity per worker or percentage of monthly plan completed. While factorywide productivity rose 10 to 15 percent during 1948, this change was bought by a near doubling of wages (measured in constant złotys); similarly, average worker norm completion rose by 50 percent (reaching an improbable *average* per worker of 276 percent in November 1948), yet productivity measured in złotys somehow remained nearly level. Management had set norms so that the plan was reached if each worker achieved 150 to 180 percent of his or her norm. According to these measures, labor competition was no success at all. By the early 1950s, Pafawag's production plans sometimes proved hard to meet because devotion to production records detracted from overall productivity.[64]

The PPR at Pafawag had little to boast about: although its member-

---

[62] WAP KW PPR 1/X/4, k. 67.

[63] ŁAP WRZZ 19, n.p. AAN KC PZPR 237/V/3, kk. 83–92. Tomaszewski, "Zadania 'produkcyjne'," 30. At Widzew manufactory, workers achieved 141 percent of the norm before labor competition, and the plan was met at 102 percent. With 1,200 of 7,620 workers participating in June 1948, the average result was 143 percent, yet only 90 percent of the plan was achieved. AAN CKW PPS 235/XV/90, k. 14. Other data appear in ŁAP WRZZ 66, 68, 69, 341.

[64] Zbigniew Tempski, *Trzy sylaby: Rzecz o Pafawagu* (Wrocław, 1960), 93–94. See also Tomaszewski, "Zadania produkcyjne," 27.

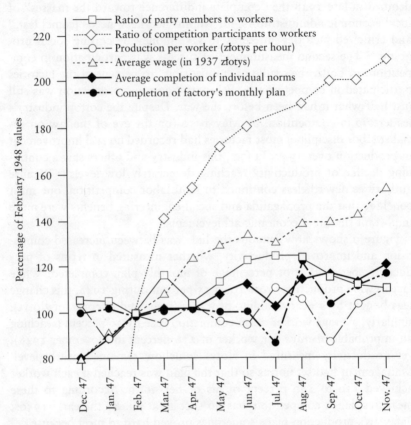

Figure 9. Labor competition and productivity at Pafawag, 1947–1948

Note: February 1948 = 100. February 1948 values: 44.6 percent of workers were in the PPR or the PPS; 11.5 percent participated in competition; the average production per worker was 12.84 current złotys per hour; the average wage was 47.9 (1937) złotys; the average norm completion was 226 percent; 104.4 percent of the factory's plan was completed.

Data were compiled from WAP KW PPR 1/X/39, passim; WAP WK PPS 36/XII/6, k. 245, 36/XII/34, kk. 11–15, 36/XIV/2, kk. 208–9; and WAP Pafawag 77. See WAP KW PPR 1/X/40 and 42 for similar but less complete information on other Wrocław factories. Note that in July 1948 the largest shop in the factory was closed for repairs. Group competition began with 2,116 workers in August, rising to 3,011 by October. A factory-wide competition with the Victoria steel mill in Wałbrzych began on 15 June.

ship increased by 40 percent, from 1,000 to 1,400, and most of these members participated in competition, party membership did not translate into more productive work. The shop with the highest participation rate (no. 7, which produced coal wagons and was the first in which group competition was introduced) was also known as the part of the factory "least developed politically" and where most workers were new to factory labor. Only the workers benefited from labor competition at Pafawag. The winner of the January 1948 competition took home 39,346 złotys—3.2 times what he had earned in December. Most received much less, yet still the average wage nearly doubled (not including overtime).[65]

Workers quickly found ways to adapt to the new system. Just as before the war, a special relationship with a foreman or supervisor who would fix results could be beneficial, as those who doubted Mieczysław Łykowski's feat (discussed previously) well knew. What worked before, such as having one's production counted twice or producing smaller sections of cloth, would work now. Because of the emphasis on results, a few minutes of intense work might be enough to achieve avant-garde status.[66] Labor competition could also reduce cooperation on the shop floor because some workers looked to win prizes any way possible. In Łódź, a PPS subforeman in a textile mill noted "small, infrequent cases where weavers do not help each other or give appropriate advice to one another; for example, when a weaver notices that his workmates' threads are tearing, or that a tangle is forming, and doesn't tell him about it, so that the other could avoid further spoiling of the material; as a result it looks as if he himself is able to complete more meters [of cloth] than is his friend."[67] This state of affairs led management at Poznański to put multimachine workers together, thus provoking the great Poznański strike. The arrangement was logical for technical and some propaganda reasons, but it defeated the larger propaganda purposes of the campaign entirely: avant-gardists could advertise multimachine work better if they were scattered among other

[65] WAP KW PPR 1/VI/36, k. 101; WAP Pafawag 77, kk. 77–79.
[66] AAN KC PPR 295/IX/31B, kk. 177–78; ŁAP WRZZ 66, n.p. (August 1948); AAN KC PZPR 237/VII/116, k. 171; WAP Pafawag 77, n.p. (April 1948). Competitors at Pafawag often achieved identical results month after month, which also suggests some friendly collusion, possibly with the help of the foreman.
[67] ŁAP WK PPS 22/XIV/40, n.p. (October 1947). On the other hand, competitors at several textile mills reported in 1947 that they frequently helped one another adapt to multimachine work. ŁAP DK PPS Łódź-Górna 20/XIII/1, kk. 16, 28.

workers. What helped production might not make sense ideologically and vice versa.

There was, in fact, little in labor competition, an externally-dictated solution to the postwar decline in worker output, for management. Competition was a poor substitute for better technology and worker training and often distracted from the business of production. Typical interfactory competitions awarded points for not only percentage of plan achieved and productivity but work attendance, savings, safety, job training (in students per worker) and social or cultural programs (expansion of the factory library, new apartments for workers, and so on).[68] Labor competition could pit the party and the hero-workers against management. For example, competition discouraged changes in product lines because workers engaged in setting records did not have time to learn new systems.[69] Another obstacle to higher productivity was the increased likelihood of accidents—which in Wrocław rose by almost 7 percent between August and September 1948—as workers participating in competition skipped breaks or worked overtime. Material and time losses due to damaged machines and tools offset higher profits and output.[70]

But for the resourceful manager, labor competition increased power over norms and piece rates and offered a way to show some success on the balance sheet to satisfy the central planners in Warsaw. The factory thus regained some of its autonomy: good numbers could be enough to keep the plan setters and organizers at bay. Armed with these numbers, some factories became powerful kingdoms, just as some workers became the new royalty.[71] Indeed, because workers in 1948 often restricted their demands to specific norm inconsistencies or delayed paydays, and now that management had somewhat deeper pockets in the second year of the three-year plan, a dialogue of sorts (although considerably less advantageous to workers than in the past) was reestablished. Management seemed inclined to grant workers' relatively modest demands. As one Łódź manager put it, "[I'd] rather go to jail for lowering norms than

---

[68]Example in WAP Pafawag 77, kk. 1–9.

[69]WAP WRZZ 66, k. 28.

[70]WAP WRZZ 24, k. 34; WAP Pafawag 173, k. 141. See also AAN MPiH 271, k. 118.

[71]See Michael Burawoy, *The Politics of Production: Factory Regimes under Capitalism and Socialism* (London, 1985), chap. 4.

for a strike."[72] To prevent a strike in another factory, management paid the hardest-hit workers on six production lines 800 złotys each and lowered norms, in consultation with the Łódź PPR. Management lowered norms again one month later when workers struck to protest new production changes, claiming they could not beat norms by the accustomed margin.[73] The result of this collusion between workers and management, according to the Łódź PPR in June 1948, were

> disturbing signs of strike tendencies among certain factory work forces in the cotton industry. . . . The focus causing this inflammation is PZPB No. 5 [Wima], where for some time a criminal procedure of artificially boosting workers' salaries through improper interpretation of the collective agreement has been practiced, with application of norms lower than in other factories, and mainly, recording of fictitious delay hours. As a result, spinners achieved 200 and even 260 percent of the norm, which is evident nonsense since in practice the maximum excess of production norms should not come to more than 160–170 percent. . . . externally (in data for the factory director and the industry chairman), norm beating is shown in the limits of probability, that is, no higher than 170 percent; the fantastically high norms circulate only within the [factory's] pay and labor department. This caused spinners' wages to reach more than 18,000 złotys monthly. News about such high wages had perforce to reach the work forces of other factories and provoke there understandable bitterness.

Suppression of these practices only brought more strikes, at Wima and several other factories.[74] The confusion in the factory, as each department tried to get the best deal for its workers and avoid sudden protests of this kind, could not have helped production.

Labor competition also helped management to control workers in several ways. First, it broke the vicious circle in which low wages increased the likelihood of low productivity from untrained or indifferent workers, which in turn kept wages low.[75] Second, labor competition gave management a weapon against workers' lack of discipline and labor turnover. Through at least 1945–49, the supply of workers outpaced

---

[72]MSW MBP 17/IX/38, t. 3, n.p. (August 1948).
[73]AAN KC PPR 295/XI/50 kk. 124, 132, 135–36.
[74]Ibid., kk. 84–85, 109; also ŁAP KŁ PPR 1/IX/1, k. 105; ŁAP CZPW 448, k. 9; and MSW MBP 17/IX/10 t. 2, k. 124.
[75]ARZ KCZZ WE 146, n.p.

demand. In cities such as Wrocław, where the need for labor was rapidly expanding, precompetition wages were too low to attract and keep good workers. Even in 1948, most factories in Wrocław were said to be running at a deficit; as a result, workers often refused to take jobs offered to them, despite the existence of a 1946 law on the duty to work. At the same time, overemployment swamped many factories. "Wherever you look," noted a union official after a mid-1947 visit to the Widzew manufactory in Łódź, "women are sitting and chatting for hours. Next to one mechanic installing a roller there stand another six. And there are a lot of supervisors and foremen on the floor."[76]

Despite Halina Lipińska's assurances quoted earlier, one could certainly be laid off in noncapitalist Poland. Unemployment increased significantly in late 1948 and early 1949; the most obvious cause was the expansion of labor competition. In Wrocław, unemployment increased from 1.4 to 3 percent from January 1948 to February 1949; over the same period, it climbed from 1.2 to 4.2 percent in Łódź. Smaller cities such as Tomaszów Mazowiecki or Żyrardów (likely sources for the waves of migrants needed for massive industrialization) saw unemployment rates higher than 20 percent.[77] Although the communists may have felt ambivalent about unemployment, a favored tool of capitalist economies, they nevertheless found it extremely convenient by 1949.

For all its odd divergences from communist ideology, labor competition was the way the Soviet Union had resolved the socioeconomic challenges of building communism. To say that it was simply an import, however, is only part of the story because labor competition cannot be understood separately from the social pressures it sought to address. In this sense, the economic outlines of stalinism were as much negotiated as they were imposed. For a time, at least, some workers benefited from the system as much as did the state. This process of negotiation was the other side of labor competition and of the communist system as a whole. Ultimately, labor competition was one of the most successful strategies that the state employed in the development of a stalinist society. The personal and material rewards that labor competition promised were significant, and the way in which the movement glorified the individual

---

[76]Hanna Jędruszczak, *Zatrudnienie a przemiany społeczne w Polsce w latach 1944–1960* (Wrocław, 1972), 142–48; WAP WK PPS 36/XII/23, k. 129; WAP WK PPS 36/XIV/2, k. 88. ŁAP WRZZ 66, n.p.

[77]AAN MPiOS 571, kk. 4–5. For other unemployment statistics, see ŁAP WK PPS 22/XIV/43; ŁAP WRZZ 74, n.p.; and WAP Urząd Wojewódzki VI/42, kk. 63–67, 117–19, 246–47.

was vital in shaping its reception by many Polish workers. Although it is perhaps imprecise to call competition for such rewards voluntary (many no doubt felt they had no choice if they were to support their families), workers could refuse. Worse for the party, participation often carried no political meaning. In March 1948, the PPR Central Committee noted with alarm that few competitors were party members; in June, only 6.4 percent of all *przodownicy* in surveyed factories belonged to either the PPR or the PPS.[78] Rather than creating new enthusiasts of communism, competition was only enriching the apolitical masses.

Discipline and Acceleration, 1948–1950

With the approach of the new type of party, the PZPR, there also emerged a new world in the factory. Slowly, against the will of both management and worker, the system of relations within the factory was altered and set into a larger regime of party-orchestrated productivism, propaganda, and social engagement promoted by the PPR/PZPR. The worker lost further control of the work process, which passed from management to the state-party apparatus. Eventually labor competition became a forced, ritual campaign and lost its earlier attraction.

A year after its initiation, labor competition had reached a critical point as its original heroic-national image increasingly fell victim to factory politics. Explained a PPR Central Committee inspector, local or factory PPR leaders considered labor competition an administrative problem and became involved only when it was time to award prizes. Management, meanwhile, was not the party's best ally. Workers and factory councils charged that foremen and directors claimed all the credit for successful competitions and fixed results so that prizes were won by favored workers. Factory control of labor competition might improve management's standing among workers, but factory directors could not be relied upon to give the movement the necessary ideological content.[79] Labor competition, after all, had to do more than just produce good numbers; it should transform the very meaning of work and its environment to match the needs of the stalinist state.

[78] AAN KC PPR 295/VII/6, k. 117; *Partia w cyfrach*, 117–18.
[79] AAN KC PPR 295/IX/31B, kk. 177–78; ŁAP KŁ PPR 1/XI/2, n.p. (July 1948). On management's unreliability, see also AAN KC PPR 295/XI/50, k. 53; WAP KW PPR 1/XII/34, k. 5; and WAP WRZZ 19, k. 22.

The decline of the Youth Labor Competition anticipated the trend toward a more tightly focused movement. Beginning with the fourth round, which commenced in November 1947, youth organizers tried to control the way that enthusiasts worked and contain the deleterious effects of heroism and poor discipline—wasted material, lack of cooperation with older workers and foremen, and excessive absenteeism. They placed new emphasis on work discipline, conservation of materials, and quality; participants began more actively to agitate fellow workers to join the campaign. The fourth round also stressed cooperative competition among groups, brigades, shops, factories, and even industries.[80]

As youth and adult competitions merged in late 1948, group competitions replaced most individual contests. A group competition lent itself to improving discipline, ideological diligence, and sociopolitical participation—especially in Wrocław, whose work force was of symbolic importance to the new state and where lack of discipline remained "a terrible plague" even in late 1948.[81] At the Wrocław garment factory, competition between shops was introduced in March 1948. Workshops accumulated points according to various measurements of production and discipline; the easiest way to accumulate points, however, was through participation in factory organizations. If 30 to 40 percent of a shop belonged to one of the artistic circles, or the library, or subscribed to a magazine, or belonged to a sports club, the shop gained five points plus three points for each further 10 percent; participation below 30 percent cost the shop five points. Integration into the factory was therefore as important a result as improved output: it might both reduce turnover and make workers politically reliable. A few months later, a Ministry of Industry inspector recorded an improvement in one of the factory's shops: "The human element [here] is a motley group, raw and undisciplined, exhibiting little diligence. Only rigorous quality control of production, and the introduction of labor competition, have raised work discipline somewhat."[82]

Labor competition gave communist leadership an entry into the work process by making it possible to invest work with ideological content. The party had, of course, been involved in large-scale economic planning from the beginning; now it attempted to shape the way that workers

[80]Kozłowski, *Związek Walki Młodych i Organizacja Młodzieżowa TUR w Łodzi*, 145–48; Rutkowska, "Włókniarze," 77; Studencki, "Młodzieżowy Wyścig Pracy," 85.

[81]WAP Pafawag 173, passim; quotation from 28 November 1948.

[82]WAP KW PPR 1/X/64, k. 5; AAN MPiH 271, k. 118.

performed and understood their jobs. Thus, Polish industry came firmly under the control of the universal state party. But just as the initiatives discussed previously (the Battle over Trade, the reining in of labor organizations, PPR-PPS unification) were products of both party initiative and social pressures or attitudes, labor competition was not merely a repressive instrument imposed on a defenseless population. Workers made use of it in decidedly nonideological ways as if, in spite of socialism, they were reaffirming their own understandings of what it meant to be a worker. But in a state marching toward stalinism whose leaders also adhered to a national vision, traditional views of class were both insufficient and a hindrance. Thus, the state sought to combine mobilization with universal duty to the party; workers could be followers of the vanguard party as well as (in propaganda) individual paragons of socialist achievement.

The state's new conception of labor appeared first in the campaign preceding the party Unification Congress in late 1948. Alongside the internal purges and the acceleration of economic plans, the PPR and the PPS promoted a nationwide labor competition, the Congress Feat, in honor of unification. This competition was a radical break from preceding campaigns. Goals were set in the form of pledges, typically naming a date in December by which the yearly plan would be met. The workers of a factory, or their party or council representatives, also pledged to surpass the yearly plan by a certain percentage, improve discipline by some measurable amount, or complete some repairs or maintenance. Sometimes they also pledged to collect a certain sum for the new party building.

In return, workers did not receive promises of bonuses (except that workers might earn more according to normal piece-rate scales). This was, in other words, a gesture of sacrifice in honor of the party. The Wrocław PPR made this attitude clear in rejecting the proposed pledge of a machine tool factory which had promised that workers would work six hours on each of four Sundays for pay, dedicating the additional production to the Congress Feat. The PPR faulted the proposal for "not educating the workers; this is an idea along the path of least resistance. Lengthening work hours is not a pledge, the more so since . . . workers are presently working twelve hours a day to meet the state plan, which is greatly reduced as it is."[83]

---

[83]WAP KW PPR 1/X/28, kk. 232–35. The PPR took care to discourage any pledges involving overtime, in part to avoid conflict. The few such "excesses" in Łódź, admitted

Before such a pledge was presented to the workers for their formal approval, factory authorities (management, the factory council, and the PPR and the PPS) determined when the yearly plan could conceivably be met or agreed on some other feasible goal; provincial leadership then vetted each proposal. Party leaders were taking no chances; a joint party circular listed conditions that must be met before a pledge could be announced, instructing activists that "a factory Party organization should undertake the initiative of making an appeal [to workers] only with complete certainty that the posited conditions will be met."[84] At the Pabianice cotton mill (which subsequent propaganda showcased as a Congress Feat campaign pioneer) the factory PPR planned to implement the pledge quietly because of worker unrest on other matters. Provincial PPR leadership opposed this plan, and a meeting was called for 29 October. At this meeting, the workers accepted the pledge, although "there wasn't much enthusiasm."[85]

While the PPR still referred to this campaign as a labor competition, the rules had definitely been broken; the workers at Pabianice and some other factories reacted in outrage. A Central Committee inspector checking on the Pabianice pledge's success reported that "hostile elements" in the factory were scrawling graffiti such as "down with communism" and "labor competition is a defeat for the working class" on PPR posters.[86] But protests were not widespread. First, the campaign was hardly intensive; authorities had in most cases simply glorified production that would have been completed anyway, adding a few extra requirements (such as Common Home collections) for good measure. Perhaps workers also hoped this was the last such campaign they would have to endure; the accompanying propaganda did imply that substantial rewards would be forthcoming after unification. And the conclusion of the campaign was accompanied by an impressive amount of ceremony with appropriate sports metaphors about the race to the finish line.[87]

But 1948 was only the first year of last-minute races against the plan

---

the PPR there, caused some workers to protest against the extra work and against the PPR and the government. AAN KC PPR 295/XI/50, k. 129.

[84] AAN CKW PPS 235/XV/2. See also WAP KW PPR 1/V/3, k. 59.

[85] AAN KC PPR 295/IX/31, kk. 370–71. The resolution and other materials on the campaign at Pabianice are in AAN KC PPR 295/XI/47, kk. 35–42.

[86] AAN KC PPR 295/IX/31, k. 403; AAN KC PPR 295/XI/50 kk. 179–80.

[87] See, for example, the article in *Głos Robotniczy,* 2 December 1948: "May 1st pledge accomplished: The tempo doesn't slacken even for a moment at PZPB No. 1. In honor of the Congress, 300 thousand meters above the plan."

and the Congress Feat the first example of a new type of sacrifice. As party unification approached, so, too, did the end of the three-year plan. Through 1948, the goals of that plan were revised upward significantly and the more practical-minded economists of the Central Planning Bureau replaced with Moscow enthusiasts. With the success of the Congress Feat still fresh in planners' minds, meeting and surpassing plan targets became ubiquitous. The Second Congress of Trade Unions, which began on 22 May 1949, was a natural occasion for another campaign. In that campaign, union leaders acted like factory managers; those at a Wrocław textile mill pledged to reach 118 percent of the plan in the precongress period; to eliminate inexcused absences; maintain round-the-clock operation of the factory; and fulfill eight other pledges related to production, culture, and welfare.[88]

On the large scale, the Polish economy began to resemble that of the Soviet Union. On a smaller scale, the meanings that the authorities attached to work also became more like the Soviet model. Such appeals would in the future be issued on every possible occasion, from a trade union congress to Stalin's birthday. As labor competition continued into the early 1950s, it was accompanied by a new idea of work—not for oneself and one's family, or for Poland, but for the party. Labor competitions became a public duty; significant results were now a necessity, not just the by-product of individual contributions to Poland's rebirth and the construction of socialism. As economics gave way to ideology, the reports of hero-workers' accomplishments also began to seem more surreal. Janitor Janina Ryćko, for example, swept floors to the rate of 481 percent of her norm in honor of Stalin's seventieth birthday in December 1949.[89]

To ensure success in pledge campaigns, the PZPR installed permanent agitators in larger factories to exhort workers and sought to convince workers that their standard of living depended on surpassing the plan.[90] A new campaign launched in March 1949 showed clearly that workers would be expected to make sacrifices even without higher wages. In the "savings movement," necessitated in part by the wasteful nature of labor competition, factories made pledges of amounts they would save over a

[88] ARZ KCZZ WO 587, k. 233.

[89] Robert Kupiecki, *"Natchnienie milionów": Kult Józefa Stalina w Polsce, 1944–1956* (Warsaw, 1993), 88–89.

[90] AAN KC PZPR 237/VIII/102, kk. 1–13; AAN KC PZPR 237/VII/93, kk. 34–6, 60–64.

Grinder Ryszard Obrębski (ZMP member), Ursus tractor factory, Warsaw, December 1949. Placard reads: "Citizen Obrębski, 16010, pledges to achieve 300% of his norm for Comrade Stalin's birthday. 19.XII: 250%; 20.XII: 250%; 21.XII: 315%." Archiwum Akt Nowych, Warsaw.

certain period. The obvious message was that the time of extravagance was past and wages would no longer rise so freely.[91] The forced voluntarism of campaigns in 1949–50 occasionally caused workers to rebel. For the 1950 National Loan for the Development of Polish (Armed) Forces, workers were asked to "loan" to the government the equivalent of nine days' basic wage. At the Strzelczyk (formerly John) metal factory in Łódź, the party read over a loudspeaker the names of workers who had given less. The intended intimidation backfired: many workers tried to take back their loans, "saying that this loan is voluntary, and so they will give nothing in this case."[92]

May Day 1949 was an auspicious moment for the new model of obligatory service. It was the first 1 May under the united party and fell three weeks before the Second Trade Union Congress. At Poznański, workers interpreted a proposed one-hour feat *(czyn)* in honor of May Day as a prelude to a nine-hour day. From the comments that the Łódź UB collected, however, it was clear that most workers expected that resistance would be punished and therefore participated in the extra work.[93]

In 1949 and after, workers no longer had the time to protest, even had they not feared the consequences. The pressure to fulfill a variety of plans ranging from yearly goals to campaigns for various occasions consumed the factory. The number of formal requests to the Labor Inspectorate, the Ministry of Industry and Commerce, and the Ministry of Labor and Social Welfare for permission to exceed overtime limits or to employ women in night shifts increased. In most cases, workers accepted more overtime as a way of improving wages; they sometimes opposed it on the grounds of exhaustion or danger resulting from overwork.[94] In 1950, when twelve-hour days were mandated in some factories, workers "literally screamed at production meetings," recalls sociologist Hanna Świda-Ziemba. Older workers in particular "regarded the eight-hour day as a sacred principle. . . . They came to meetings and screamed in fury: 'In a workers' state we have to work twelve hours? So why did we fight with the capitalists? Even the capitalists did not dare to impose this on us! We are not slaves.' " But they came to work; the law on socialist

[91] *Najnowsza historia polityczna Polski: Wybór źródeł,* Part 5: *1949–1956,* ed. Wiesław Kozub-Ciembronowicz and Jacek M. Majchrowski (Kraków, 1993), 19–20. See Tomaszewski, "Zadania 'produkcyjne,' " 32–36; WAP KW PZPR 74/V/3, n.p. (March and April 1949); ŁAP WRZZ 68, n.p. (March 1949); also sources cited in note 90.
[92] ARZ CRZZ WO 636, kk. 17–18.
[93] MSW MBP 17/IX/10 t. 3, k. 126.
[94] AAN KC PZPR 237/XXVIII/1, kk. 100–102; AAN MPiOS 14, kk. 225–27.

labor discipline saw to that.[95] There was a myriad of other control methods: for example, Wrocław factory officials conducted inspections in the apartments of workers who reported sick.[96]

As Świda-Ziemba found, workers did recognize the gap between promises and actual conditions and protested the acceleration of their work, although such protest was rarely recorded in increasingly formulaic documents. Apprehension at the pace of change was voiced by a party member in February 1949:

> I ask you, has someone told us what we will be working for in 1949? . . .
> In 1945, the norm was 40 meters of pavement. . . . In 1947—60 meters, and in 1948—70 meters. Wonderful. We ought to pull ourselves ahead in work, but how? Now I hear that one [worker] is sick, then another. . . . But I ask what will happen in 1950, 1951? Will we [have to] do 100 meters? We'll probably have to fit ourselves with motors. We didn't think that there would be no bonuses for us this year. It won't be 70 meters any more. We will have to think how to take hold of these norms fairly. This is not about quantity, but about quality, and about pay. . . . Where is our raise? Last year, at the basic wage, if the norm of 60 meters was fulfilled, we received about 13,600zł [monthly]—and this year we have only 11,000zł—so where are those 10–20 percent raises? . . . A lot has been done for the union. The union has done nothing for us. Today I stand here without a jacket; next year, I'll be without an overcoat.[97]

For this worker and many others, work was becoming unrecognizable—or rather, thinly clothed in the rhetoric of working-class progress, it was beginning to resemble work in capitalist factories before the war.

Understanding labor competition as a progressive piece-rate system helps to explain more fully workers' anger by putting it into the context of their economic relations with the state as well as their political relations. A crucial part of this story—indeed a significant milestone in postwar economic history—was the pay reform of 1 January 1949. Although it has been little remarked in the historiography, this was a crucial step in the PZPR's effort to set its economic house in order. While econom-

---

[95] Hanna Świda-Ziemba, "Robotnicy 1950," in Hanna Świda–Ziemba, *Mechanizmy zniewalania społeczeństwa—refleksje u schyłku formacji* (Warsaw, 1990), 227–28. On twelve-hour days, see ŁAP WRZZ 19, n.p. (November 1949); ŁAP WRZZ 275, n.p. (December 1949).

[96] WAP WRZZ 23, k. 4.

[97] ŁAP WRZZ 297, n.p. See also June 1949 unrest in the Łódź garment factory, described in Chapter 4.

ically logical and sound, it was also a direct attack on workers or, more specifically, on the labor aristocracy of the early labor competition. Coming just a few weeks after the creation of the PZPR, it symbolized a new era in worker-state relations.

The pay reform, introduced not through collective agreements but by administrative order, introduced a new pay scale that raised the wages of the lowest-paid workers and restricted those of skilled workers and avant-gardists; it also raised norms and eliminated most bonuses, such as the "Western bonus" paid to workers in the Recovered Territories. The idea was to simplify wages, which by late 1948 had accumulated many incentives or additions (bonuses for good attendance or meeting norms, payment-in-kind, ration cards, and so on) that workers had come to regard as permanent. Moreover, workers often had no idea how their pay was calculated or what they were owed. This confusion had been a major point of conflict in previous years, and indeed added to the apprehension workers felt as the reform approached. On average, the basic wage had amounted to only one-fourth of the production worker's take-home pay. Now the basic wage would be at least half the total.[98]

The workers themselves forced the reform through their battles over wages and their reactions to the inequities of labor competition. The pay reform promised to make wage relations fairer; as a slogan at Pafawag expressed it, reform would ensure "to each [person] equal pay for equal work."[99] It struck a complicated balance in favor of three groups: clerical factory workers (who sometimes made as little as one-sixth the pay of a production worker); the unskilled, especially those unable to earn bonuses due to the nature of their work; and, in part, the labor avant-garde. The first two groups in particular had been hurt by the bonus system. Because bonuses were taken for granted (regarded as basic pay, not an incentive) those who could not earn them developed "a psychosis of injustice, as if one worked completely for free."[100]

The bonus system was also incorrect ideologically, for it was unfair to those who ought to profit the most—the avant-garde workers. Because bonuses were calculated as a percentage of base pay, the wages of these workers were also limited under the old system. The authorities wanted to treat enthusiast workers with care lest the movement be

---

[98]See MBP report "Note on the pay reform of 1.1.49," AAN KC PZPR 237/XXXI/197, kk. 1–11; Jankowski, *Przejmowanie i odbudowa*, 236–37.

[99]WAP Pafawag 256, kk. 1–2.

[100]ŁAP WRZZ 297, n.p.

choked off too soon. Even if many achieved fantastic production percentages as a result of artificially low norms or through the favoritism of the foreman or supervisor, they ought to be let down gently, for some stood to lose the most in the pay reform. The PZPR Central Committee proposed a gradually lowering pay supplement, a sort of progressive bonus, whereby after a certain percentage of the norm, pay would equal that of the year before.[101]

Although workers bore the brunt of the reform, the problems it addressed were the fault of management, not the workers. A UB report noted local norms as low as 30 percent of officially set norms and records of even 700 percent achieved by some workers. Factory directors had allowed workers to have overtime work counted as regular work or skilled workers to work less skilled positions at higher rates. These "good uncle directors" were matched by bad directors whose position "has gone to their heads . . . they think that the collective agreement is really a scrap of paper which one can bend and stretch at will."[102] The state's problem was that, even as labor competition politicized the work process, it effectively decentralized control of that process. Each factory manager was able to violate the collective agreement and pay workers more in order to help reduce turnover, raise productivity, and meet the factory's plan.[103] While this practice had not been condoned by the Ministry of Industry or the PPR, they had ignored it while industry got back on its feet. But in order to mobilize society in specific support of larger political and economic goals, it was now imperative that the state gain real control over its economic domains.

Party, union, ministry, and police officials planning and monitoring the reform knew that taking control of wage relations would come at a price. While the reality may have been an overall pay raise for the average worker, in fact whole groups of workers stood to lose money. The cruel irony of the new pay system was that those who had profited under labor competition in the past or had been paid more because management valued their skills would now lose the most. Skilled workers in the metal industry lost 20 to 30 percent of their prereform earnings.[104] Tak-

---

[101] AAN KC PZPR 237/XXXI/25, k. 5.

[102] AAN KC PZPR 237/XXXI/197, kk. 1–2; ARZ KCZZ WO 417, n.p.

[103] See, for example, WUSW WUBP 2/27, k. 9.

[104] See, for example, WUSW KWMO 149/16, n.p. (December 1948); WUSW WUBP 2/27, kk. 29, 36; AAN KC PZPR 237/XXXI/25, k. 5. On metal workers, see AAN KC PZPR 237/XXXI/132, kk. 28–29; and ŁAP WRZZ 77, n.p. (January 1949). For similar information on textile and chemical industries in Łódź province, see ŁAP WRZZ 68, n.p.

ing the threat of worker resistance seriously, the UB prepared for the crucial first payday by placing nearly four hundred factories (employing almost half a million workers) under "special protection"; it conducted "preventative" talks with close to ten thousand nonparty workers in four cities.[105] As usual, the UB regretted that "the lack of a valuable, deep [network of] agents in the hostile circles within and outside the factories turned out to be the most important obstacle to the uncovering and liquidation of inspirers of hostile activity."[106]

Workers were divided over the real results of the reform. Rumors that a new pay system would be introduced right after the Unification Congress had circulated in the factories. Most workers assumed that pay reform meant a raise; as for norms, all thought that their own norms were unfair and would be corrected favorably. Some even believed that new norms would be set according to present productivity; thus, they slowed down to keep future norms low. Some expected raises of 50 percent or more, with a transition to "pure" piece rates and stabilized norms; others feared cuts or perhaps price hikes to match the rise in wages. The concerns of the labor avant-garde, meanwhile, were reflected in rumors that the maximum norm percentage to be rewarded would be 120 percent, above which workers would receive no compensation. With Pafawag's director now claiming that workers reaching 500 percent of norm were actually hurting the factory, such fears were not groundless.[107]

As the reform grew near, workers were less hopeful about benefiting and grew suspicious of the agenda hidden behind promises of equality and simplicity. Remarked a worker at Poznański: "When I get more money, only then will I see that there is a raise—and those papers that they post tell me nothing."[108] In the Lower Silesian textile industry, many new and inexperienced workers had been given lower norms to keep them at work; unified norms raised the likelihood that masses of workers would quit the industry. They, like all workers, feared that "norms would be so high that after working three or four months, a worker [would] be unable to work." In Łódź in particular, there were some signs

[105]MBP MSW 17/IX/38, t. 4, n.p. (January 1949). On party preparations, see AAN KC PPR 295/XI/12, kk. 38–40.
[106]AAN KC PZPR 237/XXXI/197, kk. 10–11.
[107]AAN KC PPR 295/XI/50, k. 180; ŁAP KŁ PPR 1/XI/1, k. 109; AAN KC PZPR 237/XXXI/197, kk. 4; AAN KC PZPR 237/XXXI/187, kk. 1–2; WUSW WUBP 2/27, k. 9.
[108]MSW MBP 17/IX/10, t. 3, k. 1.

of mass discontent as the reform approached, including two brief strikes and some angry factory meetings. These were apparently inspired by widespread rumors of planned price hikes on basic items. It was expected, in other words, that what the state gave with one hand it would surely take with the other.[109]

The ideological goals of the reform were as important as its economic rationale. Coupled with the changes outlined in Chapter 4, the pay reform was a serious challenge to the working-class community and another step in the state's redefinition of work and workers. First, the new pay system, because it de-emphasized bonuses and placed norms under greater control, sharply reduced workers' remaining autonomy and collectivity by taking away their ability to manipulate norms through collusion with management or simple resistance. The authorities hoped that this manipulation of wages might finally provoke genuine norm-beating and real labor competition. Second, the reform was a deskilling of sorts, because the best-paid, best-trained workers came under attack. After the pay reform, workers could not easily act like a community with its own class identity or like individual heroes of labor. Working for a straight wage, they became cogs in the machinery of socialist construction.

Until now, workers had pursued a labor market that they could use to influence pay scales and control their jobs. Early labor competition most certainly fit this idea of the market very well, at least for some workers. The reform ultimately threatened everyone: skilled male workers, who could name their price in any market; the experienced, unskilled workers, who had less mobility but a much greater sense of entitlement to a living and a workplace; the new labor elite, who cultivated a sense of privilege and believed in almost unlimited wage increases; and the masses of unskilled workers, who in some areas could use their mobility to win wages and protection from management. It was time to discover what it would mean to be a worker in People's Poland.

By altering the relations of pay among different groups of workers, the reform intensified wage comparison. Thus, workers who complained about the reform often did so in relation to others. "We make less at our machines than [we would] with a shovel [performing menial roadwork]," complained finishing-room workers at Łódź's Horak mill. Spinners and their assistants in one shift at Eitingon claimed that "other

[109]WUSW KWMO 149/16, n.p. (December 1948); WUSW WUBP 2/27, kk. 30, 38; WAP WRZZ 78, k. 26; AAN KC PZPR 237/XXXI/187, kk. 1–2; MSW MBP 17/IX/10, t. 2, kk. 305–6, 316 and t. 3, k. 4; ŁAP WRZZ 64, n.p. (December 1948).

shifts earned much more." Some workers reacted positively, feeling that the reform had finally recognized their worth. "For this kind of money," remarked a young worker in Łódź, "one could work even three shifts." A spinner's assistant at Eitingon commented, "Though I have more, the spinners have even more—much more—and yet I can manage on the machine." This was the kind of ambition the authorities had hoped to provoke. At other factories, the UB attributed the reform's success (as in labor competition) to the fact that a prominent group of satisfied workers had received significant raises.[110]

The reaction to the reform was muted in the shadow of the newly unified party. Compared even to 1948, a strike was a much riskier enterprise and unlikely to be successful. Sanctions now had more teeth; it was easier for management to fire and blacklist troublemakers and harder for workers to quit and find work elsewhere. Nevertheless, the pay reform did spark a wave of strikes. There were several in the weeks leading up to the reform followed by at least a dozen strikes in January and February.[111] The most common immediate response from workers across Poland was to slow down production, refusing to meet the higher norms even if it meant losing money. This tactic was safer than a strike and well suited to a protest over raising norms. Leaflets imploring workers to "Sabotage! Don't work too much, work slow" were found in downtown Łódź.[112] In a number of large factories, including some of the country's key plants and Silesia's largest mines, workers lowered productivity "to show the unreality of the new norms"; production quality declined, especially in the textile industry. There was significant unrest—"bad moods" (*złe nastroje*), as the UB termed it—in metal, textile, and mining, in Upper Silesia, Łódź, Żyrardów, Częstochowa, Starachowice, Warsaw, and some parts of Lower Silesia, including the Wałbrzych coal mines and the textile mills south of Wrocław. The UB recorded 114 "anti-government protests" of various kinds in January and another 149 in February. It seemed to some people that the future of Poland itself was at stake. The UB ascribed January resistance to the

[110]MSW MBP 17/IX/10, t. 3, kk. 2–4; AAN KC PZPR 237/VII/116, k. 24; AAN KC PZPR 237/XXXI/197, k. 6; ŁAP WRZZ 69, n.p.

[111]MSW MBP 17/IX/77, t. 3, kk. 96–97, 17/IX/38, t. 4, n.p. (January–February 1949); AAN KC PZPR 237/VII/116, k. 52; ŁAP CZPW 447, kk. 17–19. Many official sources had long ceased to use the word *strike* and even euphemisms such as "interruption of work." It is possible that brief strikes lay behind actions described as "lowered productivity" or especially "antipathy to work." See, for example, WAP WRZZ 34 kk. 84–85.

[112]AAN KC PZPR 237/VII/1457, k. 14.

new norms in the Silesian coal mines in part to hostile nationalist activity among Germans, repatriates from France or Romania, migrants from central or eastern Poland, or the native Silesians—enemies of Poland, in the UB's interpretation.[113]

In Wrocław, unrest was greatest at Pafawag, the emblem of progress in the Recovered Territories and a factory whose labor competition movement was considered the strongest in Wrocław; some of its avant-gardists had gained fame across Poland. "Red Pafawag" was also better able than many nearby factories to attract and retain highly skilled workers and technical personnel. Like the rest of Wrocław, it had struck only briefly during the previous three years. But in early January 1949, production suddenly dropped by up to 40 percent. The Wrocław UB reported that workers felt "it isn't worth it to exert oneself, since you can't make any money anyway." The factory PZPR was quick to coun-terattack; by the end of January, Pafawag had achieved 106 percent of its monthly plan.[114]

Protest was most effective when management allowed workers to ma-nipulate norms or labor competition. Some returned to working fewer machines or worked only to their norm. In Lower Silesia, textile workers tried to beat the system by changing their qualifications (presumably with the compliance of the supervisor); their norm was based on work on three sides, for example, but they switched to a norm based on two sides and continued to work on three, thus turning in higher production percentages. Another way to beat the system was to volunteer easy tar-gets—102 percent of one's norm, for example—in labor competition, which benefited the worker more than if higher percentages were met outside competition.[115] Where management had retained workers at high wages, factories made concessions, raising piece rates, awarding supple-ments, or allowing workers to beat the system in other ways. Such con-cessions were particularly common in Łódź. At three garment factories, for example, "excessive abatements from the so-called optimal norm . . . reached 60 to 70 percent. These abatements were to be in effect for a

[113]AAN KC PZPR 237/XXXI/25, k. 5; AAN KC PZPR 237/XXXI/197, kk. 4–7; MSW MBP 17/IX/38, t. 4, n.p. (January–February 1949). On Łódź textiles in particular, see ŁAP WRZZ 77, n.p. (January 1949); and AAN KC PZPR 237/XXXI/135, kk. 1–5, 237/ XXVIII/20, k. 2.

[114]WUSW WUBP 2/37, k. 6; AAN KC PZPR 237/XXXI/187, k. 2; WUSW KWMO 150/ 10 n.p. (January 1949); WAP WRZZ 34, kk. 84–85.

[115]AAN KC PZPR 237/VII/116, kk. 24, 101; WAP WRZZ 34, k. 87; ŁAP WRZZ 69, n.p. (October 1949).

transitional period, [so that workers could] become acquainted with a new assortment. It turned out that the reason for applying the abatements was to reach the level of previous wages, which were often too high. . . . the workers recognized that norms were improper, and expected serious pay cuts in connection with the reform. The high pay turned out to be a surprise for them."[116] In Łódź, the need to retain workers had never been so pressing as in Wrocław; that management offered concessions anyway is a tribute to the power of the labor community.

Unrest continued throughout 1949; there were strikes, threats to przodownicy, incidents of sabotage, and mass absences throughout the summer and fall. Most focused in some way on the loss of workers' control over the speed and the nature of their work, such as management's methods of counting production. Three years after its first attempt, the textile industry in Łódź finally forced a change in paydays from biweekly to semimonthly and faced down at least one strike in the process.[117] The workers had not given up, but their opponent was very different from the one they had defied just a year earlier. Stalinism had finally come to the factory. The Łódź PZPR noted that, while just a few months earlier the slogan in the factories had been "why work intensively, when war will come soon anyway and everything will be lost," the new watchword was even more grim: "Work hard, because otherwise you'll die of hunger."[118]

In one form or another, the basics of labor competition—working to beat plans and norms, with rewards for the most productive factories or workers—remained a staple of the planned economy until its demise. But labor competition in 1949 and throughout high stalinism (until 1953 or so) was vastly different from its first incarnations. The early movement's emphasis on enthusiasm, patriotism, and huge paychecks played a central role in redefining the relationship of the worker to the communist state. The legacy of that relationship was an inordinately high cost of labor because the state feared to rescind too much of what it had given. Despite the reforms of 1949–50, workers' demands continued to limit the stalinist and poststalinist economy; the only thing that really

[116]AAN KC PZPR 237/XXXI/197, kk. 5, 10. In Wrocław, see WAP WRZZ 34, k. 87.
[117]AAN KC PZPR 237/VII/117, k. 402, 237/VII/118, kk. 53, 384, 237/VII/1457, k. 144; MSW MBP 17/IX/38, t. 4, n.p. (May–July 1949).
[118]AAN KC PZPR 237/VII/1457, k. 86.

disappeared in 1949 was the enthusiasm. A truce of sorts had been achieved: although the work was much harder, the pay still insufficient to feed a family, and the supply of goods never reliable, the regime would not for a long time risk raising prices, cutting wages, or punishing workers for their protests. The returns the state received for "competitive" labor declined until eventually the regime went bankrupt, bled to death by (among other things) the wages workers had extracted.[119]

As I noted earlier, one of the goals of the reform of labor competition was to redefine the meaning of *labor* and *worker* in communism. First, the authorities sought to weaken workers' class identity, discouraging conflict with other classes (such as the working intelligentsia or the peasants). Second, they were eager to combine productivity with morality and political consciousness. Fulfilling the plan, even overfulfilling the plan, was insufficient. For example, even though 57 percent of the workers at the Poznański Mill participated in labor competition in December 1949, Łódz union leaders were not satisfied; they complained that workers "do not have a socialist foundation because each competitor tries to get that *złoty*."[120] It would probably be accurate to say that the authorities themselves were divided as to which was more important, socialist morality or production. The division between ideological purity and economic viability has been a part of every state socialist regime. Attempting to remedy this dissonance, the newly dominant party culture sought to create new models of class and morality to integrate the surviving working class into a new society.

[119]Particularly suggestive on the power of labor to derail the economies of late communist Eastern Europe are Charles Sabel and David Stark, "Planning, Politics, and Shop-Floor Power: Hidden Forms of Bargaining in Soviet-Imposed State Socialist Societies," *Politics and Society* 11, no. 4 (1982): 439–75; Burawoy, *Politics of Production*, chap. 4; and Katherine Verdery, "Theorizing Socialism: A Prologue to the 'Transition,'" *American Ethnologist* 18, no. 3 (August 1991): 426–28.

[120]ŁAP WRZZ 2, k. 85.

6 The Battle for Working-Class Identity

The symbolism of change in labor competition or the Battle over Trade was at least as important to stalinist leaders as concrete economic progress. A vital part of this symbolic change, with important ramifications for social peace, was the integration of classes. While there would still be classes in a communist society, the stalinist idea called for them to work in harmony. Stalin himself in 1936 described class relations in developed socialism as consisting of two classes (peasants and workers) and a stratum (intelligentsia); these were simply descriptive categories, not opposing camps.[1] An integrated society was an essential part of the socialist image; progress toward the end of social injustice and class oppression were as central to its ideology as was economic modernization and prosperity. After all, many kinds of states might bring prosperity, but the communist state promised to eliminate conflict between classes arising from that prosperity. To this end, labor conflict—"hurrah-leftist outbursts directed against factory management," in PPR parlance—could no longer be tolerated.[2]

Yet while property relations were, of course, not what they had been before the war, the conflicts of the first postwar years showed that workers still thought in terms of traditional class antagonisms (that is, conflict

---

[1] On stalinist class theory, see Sheila Fitzpatrick, "Ascribing Class: The Construction of Social Identity in Soviet Russia," *Journal of Modern History* 65, no. 4 (December 1993): 745–70.

[2] WAP KW PPR 1/VI/99, k. 67. See also Janusz Gołębiowski, *Walka PPR o nacjonalizację przemysłu* (Warsaw, 1961), 107–9.

rooted primarily in the means of production). They perceived management, whether or not it technically owned the factories, as their opponents for this reason. Workers, then, had to be drawn into amicable cooperation with members of other classes, especially the managerial-bureaucratic class. This was to be accomplished by a number of initiatives, including the education and technical training of workers, promotion of workers into administrative and technical positions, the creation of mass youth organizations as a cross-class means of socialization and acculturation, and the invention of organized leisure time. These programs contributed significantly to the remaking of the working class at the dawn of stalinism. Like labor competition, however, they would both strengthen and undermine the intentions of the stalinist state. As workers accommodated themselves to the evolving system, they also shaped its growth in subtle ways and retained a separate and antagonistic class identity.

The image that the state hoped to use to conquer class conflict was that of the worker as co-owner of the economy. Communist ideologists believed this transformation would take place naturally. As Polish trade union leaders explained to the World Federation of Trade Unions in 1946, "the new economic structure of the state liberates the new working person."[3] Writing primarily about the poststalinist period (1956–89), Zbigniew Kurcz points to the symbolic meanings of various worker self-government schemes (including the factory councils of 1945–47), labor competition (especially the inventor movement), and worker education and advance. All created an image of a worker with a stake in the factory's and the country's future.[4]

Above all, stalinism required that the worker see him or herself as a loyal soldier of the party, and the embodiment of its ideology. In a 1986 study, cultural studies scholar (later Warsaw Solidarity trade union chief) Michał Boni described five dynamic characters frequent in the productivist literature and slogans of early stalinism.[5] First is the "work-

---

[3] Quoted in Salomea Kowalewska, "Wzór osobowy i pożądane postawy pracowników w przemyśle," in *Przemysł i społeczeństwo w Polsce Ludowej,* ed. Jan Szczepański (Wrocław, 1969), 220. See also Jadwiga Kalinowska, *Postawy robotników wobec pracy* (Warsaw, 1978), 32–33.

[4] Zbigniew Kurcz, *Wzór robotnika i jego przemiany w PRL* (Wrocław, 1992), chap. 2. See also Michał Boni, "Stereotyp robotnika w kulturze polskiej na przełomie lat 40/50-tych" (diss., Warsaw University, 1986), 85.

[5] Boni, "Stereotyp robotnika," 268–361.

ing stiff" (*robociarz*), a usually older worker whose work ethic and urge to advance are based on his or her memory of past poverty and injustice and who searches for recognition and peace; this worker is politically conscious but not active, a follower of the labor heroes. Pafawag's Jan Kaniewski, whose folksy, apolitical autobiography will be considered later in this chapter, might be an example. Second is the labor avant-gardist (*przodownik*), the new hero politically active in the class struggle. He or she (see, for example, Wanda Gościmińska's story later in this chapter) has a family and a good home life but is devoted to work. The third model is that of the young enthusiast, a member of the ZMP. This type emerged as early as 1945, but stalinist-era publications such as Halina Lipińska's autobiography (published in 1950) established this character's salient features: loyalty to the collective and the organization, vigilance in the class struggle, and enthusiasm for culture. Fourth is the "advancing worker," who could be any worker advancing from country to city or to higher levels of education and civilization; women workers in general also fell into this category. The universality made this type easier to emulate than a true avant-gardist; many of the people interviewed for this book, such as Stefania K. and Stanisława J. of Wrocław, fit this category. Finally, there was the activist, a model meant not so much for emulation (except by would-be party functionaries) as to illustrate the meaning of the party. This type might appear in the biography of an historical figure or a political leader.

In a communist country, these were still *class* images, but they were stripped of their conflictual heart. The PZPR, as it assumed leadership of the whole nation, became a kind of society in which class as a dynamic phenomenon (that is, based on relations with other classes) ought to disappear.[6] The stalinist party's attack on class went still deeper toward the elimination of the collective identities linking individuals. Hanna Świda-Ziemba has pointed out that the same processes that built the new worker model—industrialization (specifically the influx of villagers to the city), social advance, and the new role of youth—also contributed to the isolation of the worker from colleagues in the factory

---

[6]Marian Surmaczyński, "Klasowe i narodowe aspekty działania Polskiej Partii Robotniczej na ziemiach zachodnich," in *Polska, naród, państwo: Z badań nad myślą polityczną Polskiej Partii Robotniczej, 1942–1948*, ed. Marian Orzechowski (Wrocław, 1972), 138–71.

and the community, tearing workers out of familiar elements and permitting them to ignore or ridicule the labor collectivities of the past.[7]

These processes sound very much like those observed earlier in Wrocław; in the stalinist period, this atomization spread across Poland. But just as in Wrocław, the elimination of class did not proceed so neatly. First, the models just described were also manipulated by their putative subjects to reinvigorate class identity. Older workers accepted the robociarz model in order to regain some authority in the factory. The labor avant-gardists came to see themselves as the new labor aristocracy, the greatest beneficiary of the state's "big deal" (to cite Vera Dunham's phrase) with a new middle class, and positioned itself as an inheritor of working-class tradition and national values.[8] The youth enthusiasts also came to rely on the material aspects of their bargain with the state. Moreover, the new workers who came to the factories from the villages were unreliable in terms of both productivity and ideology. Like the avant-gardists and enthusiasts, the advancing workers demanded more than the state was willing to give. Only the party activist was reliable, but he or she became increasingly isolated and was considered alien by the workers.

Second, the elimination of class in the public sphere allowed it to resurface in the private sphere within social relations outside of work. True, a private identity of class was not nearly so effective a weapon against the state; however, in a state with pretensions to total control *and* social transformation, such a weapon was still dangerous and, indeed, contributed ultimately to the system's collapse. In church, on the streets, and sometimes in the factories, workers showed that class remained a category of identity. This was the Polish communists' greatest failure.

Education and Mobility: Integrating the Worker into Society

The communists staked their political success on urban youth and the great wave of peasants from the countryside. Having filled Wrocław immediately after the war, peasant migrants began to appear everywhere as industrialization gathered speed in 1949–50. By 1950, newcomers

[7]Hanna Świda-Ziemba, "Stalinizm i społeczeństwo polskie," in *Stalinizm*, ed. Jacek Kurczewski (Warsaw, 1989), 31–35.

[8]Vera Dunham, *In Stalin's Time: Middleclass Values in Soviet Fiction* (New York, 1976).

made up more than half of Poland's adult urban population. In cities such as Wrocław in the west, nearly 30 percent of the population was between the ages of nineteen and twenty-nine; Łódź, which fell more toward the median among larger cities, had just over 20 percent in this age group.[9] As Alexander Janta pointed out (see Chapter 5), the state hoped that such workers, along with young workers of any background who came to the factory three or four years after the war, would overwhelm the old labor community and its contentious habits.

These workers could expect to take advantage of promised opportunities for career, social, and cultural advancement; indeed, workers' advance gave some credence to the propaganda about their importance. Although many workers continued to protest material differences, the explosion in wages beginning in 1948 did much to narrow the gap in living standards between blue- and white-collar workers. The Central Planning Bureau estimated in 1948 that workers' food consumption had risen by almost one-quarter from 1938, while that of office employees had declined by even more.[10]

This advance, however, did not come free of conditions; individual success was achieved within the party-structured collective. The ticket to wealth (within limits, after the pay reform of January 1949) and status was assimilation into the new world of the mass organizations (the PZPR and the trade unions), labor competition, and mass culture. Two groups contributed the additional force essential to industrial expansion and became stalinism's key supporters. As Świda-Ziemba explained: "It was not the 'working class' and the 'peasant class' . . . who supported stalinism, but the people who advanced out of these groups."[11]

The image of the new worker was central to the propaganda of the time. In reality, of course, the boundaries among generations or backgrounds was fuzzy; in large measure, the party's emphasis on these distinctions made the generation/culture gap real. Data from two factories

[9]Kazimierz Piesiewicz, "Social and Demographic Consequences of World War II and the German Occupation in Poland," *Oeconomica Polona*, no. 1 (1983): 82; Bogusław Wełpa, *Zagadnienia struktury wieku ludności Polski Ludowej w roku 1950* (Warsaw, 1955), 95, 107; Michał Pohoski, *Migracje ze wsi do miast: Studium wychodźstwa w latach 1945–1957 oparte na wynikach ankiety Instytutu Ekonomiki Rolnej* (Warsaw, 1963).

[10]Helena Gnatowska, *Rola Polskiej Partii Robotniczej w kształtowaniu i realizacji polityki socjalnej Polski Ludowej, 1942–1948* (Białystok, 1986), 255. Still, the median wage for a manual worker in state industry in August 1949 was just over 16,000 zł monthly; for engineers and other technicians, the median was around 27,000 zł. *RS 1949*, 135–37.

[11]Świda-Ziemba, "Stalinizm i społeczeństwo polskie," 25.

in Łódź suggest that the new worker of 1949 was different from his or her predecessors. Workers who were hired at these factories in 1949 were more likely to be from outside the city (and from farther away), younger, and less experienced than their counterparts hired in 1945 or before. Although Wrocław had seen such workers from the beginning, the migrants of 1949 were even more likely to be from a village; they were also less likely to have had experience with migration (during the war, for example) before moving to Wrocław. They were also much younger; in 1948–50, almost three-fifths of workers arriving in Wrocław who came to work at Pafawag were fifteen to twenty-four years old, while in 1945–46 only about half as many were in that group.[12]

Cultural conflict was inevitable. Through 1947 at least, the older generation held the upper hand. As the factories filled up and competition within the factory became more intense, resentment of the newcomers increased. Some in Łódź saw that newly arrived workers did not work by the same code of conduct as did urban workers; others felt that village residents took jobs away from natives and thus should be denied the right to settle in the city and work in factories.[13] Such complaints, of course, simply refocused the anger previously directed (and encouraged by the authorities) at "speculators." These new workers would change the character of urban society, reversing the cultural conflict in their favor as they moved with growing confidence into the factory. By 1948–49, there were two cultures to which one could adapt in Łódź, two urban life-styles, as there already were in Wrocław.[14]

Before the war, a peasant migrant to Łódź felt compelled to become a part of the powerful, well-defined culture that he or she found there; such workers studied the ways and forms of that culture and tried to

[12]The samples are too small (particularly at the John factory) to permit much certainty, but the numbers are suggestive. For example, at Poznański, 72 percent of those working in the factory in 1945 (N = 88) were from Łódź or its immediate environs; for those who entered the factory in 1949 (N = 172), the figure was only 59 percent. Factory samples; Wrocław data: Jędrzej Chumiński, "Motywy migracji ludności polskiej do Wrocławia w latach 1945–1949," *Słupskie Studia Historyczne*, no. 3 (1993): 122–24; Zofia Szapajtis, "Załoga Państwowej Fabryki Wagonów we Wrocławiu," *Rocznik Wrocławski*, nos. 3–4 (1959/1960): 272.

[13]For examples, see ŁAP WRZZ 66, n.p. (August 1948); ŁAP WRZZ 65, n.p. (August 1948).

[14]On the idea of two working classes, see Tadeusz Łepkowski, "Myśli o historii Polski i Polaków," *Zeszyty Historyczne* 68 (1984): 101–2.

dress, act, and talk like their city-born colleagues.[15] After the war, as such workers began to arrive in greater numbers, they experienced the same cultural differences yet felt less need to adapt. Urban-born workers, or those who had acquired (or thought they had acquired) urban culture, resented new arrivals from the countryside for the security they enjoyed (peasant workers often had a little more food or extra income from the farm they had left) and for their eagerness to work hard and impress their superiors; urban workers ridiculed the newcomers' rural habits and speech. An urban-born metal worker remembered them as disciplined and eager to please: "They got along well with the supervisors. They brought eggs, chickens, and ducks, and got easier work, or a better machine, supplements, or prizes. City workers frowned at them, because [we] couldn't afford presents." The newcomers kept to themselves, asserted another Łódź native, "and didn't speak up, because they were ashamed of their speech." This was particularly true at the very beginning when few had yet made the journey to Łódź. New arrivals usually stayed with friends or relatives, who helped them assimilate.[16]

PZPR and industry officials encouraged rural- or urban-born new workers, whether or not they were in fact more disciplined and harder working and despite the barriers that the old labor community might hope to erect, to feel superior to their experienced colleagues. Noting that layoffs most often affected older workers first, Hanna Świda-Ziemba comments: "[The authorities'] wager on the so-called generational conflict was a clever move. The young had a chance at high self-esteem which was unconnected to any effort, yet at the same time was beyond question. By the very fact of one's age, one could entertain the conviction that one belonged to a better race. . . . One could attack without punishment—indeed, with blessing—those who until now had instructed, constrained, dominated: one's parents, teachers, and experienced workers."[17] While young urban workers were encouraged to abandon their traditional class boundaries because of both the war and the propaganda of reconstruction, their older colleagues were more resistant

---

[15]Irena Lechowa, "Relacje wieś—miasto w tradycji robotniczej Łodzi," *Łódzkie Studia Etnograficzne,* 15 (1973): 67–77.

[16]Liliana Podkocka, "Adaptacja ludności wiejskiej do warunków miejskich (w okresie międzywojennym i po zakończeniu II wojny światowej)" (master's thesis, Katedra Etnografii, Uniwersytet Łódzki, 1980), 66–67, 76; texts of informants AZE.B.2250, 2252, and others, Katedra Etnografii, Uniwersytet Łódzki. See also interview with Czesław J. and Eugeniusz S., formerly workers at Poznański, Łódź, 13 March 1990.

[17]Świda-Ziemba, "Stalinizm i społeczeństwo polskie," 33.

to the idea of social advance. Before the war, workers did not place much value in schooling as a means of advance.[18] These ideas remained in the immediate postwar period. For example, foremen at PZPB no. 1 considered the constant reschooling and specialization in 1949 to be "shameful."[19] Unlike urban-born workers, those who came to the city after the war were already advancing; their momentum, as it were, increased their zeal.

What the party was promoting, however, was not advance but the *idea* of advance. Because this process was first evident in Wrocław, it is not surprising that the propaganda of advance caught on especially strongly there. The contemporary autobiography of village-born Jan Kaniewski, an avant-gardist at Pafawag, illustrates this sense of hope; the narrator contrasts present horizons with the past by introducing his children to an imaginary interlocutor: "I would ask him to come to my home in Wrocław on Kotlarska Street. At home, I would find my daughter. I would say: 'look, Halina is thirteen, and is in the fifth grade. Ask her what she wants to do.' And Halina would say, of course, that she will go to conservatory. You understand? 'will go' She doesn't say that she wants to go, but simply that she will. Because she knows that it doesn't depend on how much her parents make, or on their background, but only on her progress in school. So also would my second child, eight-year-old Romek, be very surprised if someone told him that he won't become an engineer. 'How so?' he would say, 'when I have straight A's in arithmetic.' It doesn't even cross his mind that his further study could depend on something other than his interests and abilities." The same, he concluded, was true for young workers, such as two young village-born friends: "When they came to Wrocław, they couldn't do much. But they wanted to work in a factory. That was enough for them to be accepted in Pafawag. And not only accepted: they were sent to the industrial school. What they will become in the future depends on their own desire. Of course, you'll tell me that this is how it is because this is how it should be. Fine, brother. But things have not been how they should be for very long."[20]

[18] Grażyna Ewa Karpińska, Bronisława Kopczyńska-Jaworska, and Anna Woźniak, *Pracować żeby żyć, żyć żeby pracować. Łódzkie Studia Etnograficzne*, 31 (1992): 15.

[19] LAP KŁ PZPR 34/VIII/115, n.p.; Edward Pietraszek, "Etos polskiej klasy robotniczej (kilka wybranych zagadnień)," *Styl życia, obyczaje, etos w Polsce lat siedemdziesiątych z perspektywy roku 1981*, ed. Andrzej Siciński (Warsaw, 1983), 88; Hanna Świda-Ziemba, "Robotnicy 1950," in *Mechanizmy zniewalania społeczeństwa—refleksje u schyłku formacji* (Warsaw, 1990), 231–32.

[20] Jan Kaniewski, *Było to na Pa-Fa-Wagu*, BPP 15 (Warsaw, 1949), 6-7. See Irena Tur-

Kaniewski envisions a meritocratic system of advance, which in the PPR years was more often than not the case. Given the dearth of qualified candidates for any position, politics could take a back seat to ability. In promoting workers beyond the working class, authorities faced a dilemma familiar to Soviet leaders decades earlier—that of choosing between politically active but unprepared workers and neutral but skilled workers; among ability, enthusiasm, and political consciousness. Like their Soviet mentors, the Poles hoped to solve the problem by educating large numbers of sympathetic workers quickly.[21] The exit of members of the working class into the places vacated by the politically unreliable prewar industrial inteligencja could also weaken the cohesion of the working class. But workers were at an advantage as long as ideology took precedence over industrial policy, and the authorities were left vulnerable to the consequences of hasty promotions. As the PPR admitted in a 1947 internal document, "the mere fact of membership in our Party cannot be the decisive motive for advancing workers."[22] A gap opened in the social hierarchy that would not always be filled on the authorities' terms; workers could advance simply because they were workers, not because of their political consciousness. Even in 1949, Stanisław S., not a PZPR member, was chosen to go to a technical school because of his abilities at work. Party membership, he recalled, was not an advantage unless one were an active member.[23] Managers instructed to find appropriate candidates did whatever they could to fill the order, even co-opting unwilling workers; 21 percent of the graduates in the first class produced by the Workers' Textile Technicum in Łódź in 1949 had entered three years earlier without expressing any great desire to study.[24]

In reality, relatively few workers advanced off the shop floor. By March 1948, more than ten thousand workers had been promoted to

---

nau, "Tworzenie się wielkiego miasta z różnorodnej ludności napływowej (Wrocław—miasto przemian społecznych" (diss., Wrocław University, 1950), 224–26. On advance in communist Poland, see also Jacek Leoński, *Drogi życiowe i świadomość: społeczna robotników polskich* (Warsaw, 1987).

[21]On Soviet education and the problems of promoting from the proletariat, see Sheila Fitzpatrick, *Education and Social Mobility in the Soviet Union, 1921–1934* (Cambridge, U.K., 1979), esp. chaps. 3 and 6.

[22]AAN KC PPR 295/V/6, kk. 70–71.

[23]Interview, 9 May 1990.

[24]Salomea Kowalewska and Zdzisław Kowalewski, "Losy absolwentów Technikum Włókienniczego dla Robotników," in *Z badań klasy robotniczej i inteligencji* (Łódź, 1959), 80.

Participants in a course for labor avant-gardists in Łódź, 1949. Note the wide range in ages. Banner reads: "Work Better, Learn to Work." Photographer unknown. Muzeum Tradycji Niepodległościowych, Łódź.

foremen, supervisors, or higher-level managers; more than 60 percent of these advancements were only to the rank of foreman, and another one-quarter became heads of production sections and departments. Barely one-tenth advanced higher, and their numbers declined during the 1950s. In the Łódź textile industry at the same time, 84 percent of 1,212 promoted workers became foremen. The typical candidate had at least twenty years of work experience and was over forty years old, had at most completed elementary school, and was born in the city. Such a background did not fit the profile of the ideologically committed worker.[25]

For the thousands who wished to advance in one way or another, new propaganda models were a valuable guide. Upward mobility was inherent in the biographies of labor avant-gardists, who generally recounted their advance to become an expert, respected worker or a member of the technical cadre. Enthusiasm, duty, and knowledge were the keys to success in the life stories presented to workers in propaganda. Halina Lipińska was nineteen and fresh from a Youth Labor Competition victory when the ZMP asked her in 1948 to take the entrance exams for the Workers' Textile Technicum. She expressed the political bravado expected of her generation in a conversation with her mother:

> "And you will be a technician?" asked my mother, ever unbelieving.
> "I will."
> "And you will work in our factory?"
> "I don't know. I will work where the working class needs me. Where my organization, the ZMP, and my Party, the PZPR, places me!"[26]

The education of workers was both an economic investment and a political necessity. Technical and administrative personnel were in short supply as industry expanded, in part because of losses suffered in the war. The modernization of Poland's more backward industries required higher technical skill at all levels. The PPR and PPS both believed in education as a prerequisite to political activation: education was the

---

[25]ARZ KCZZ WO 333, kk. 31–32; L. Zajczykowa, "Kilka cyfr o awansie społecznym w łódzkim przemyśle włókienniczym," *Przegląd Związkowy* 9 (1950): 412–16; Kowalewska and Kowalewski, "Losy absolwentów," 87.

[26]Halina Lipińska, *Mój awans* (Warsaw, 1950), 26. See also the memoirs of Maria Gałczyńska (Lipińska), "Jak znalazłam się w szeregach uczestników Młodzieżowego Wyścigu Pracy," *Łódzkie Zeszyty Historyczne (Ruch młodzieżowy — tradycje i współczesność)* 1, no. 5 (1985): 133.

mark of the politically conscious, and propaganda would be most effective with the literate. For these reasons, the PPS had established before the war the Workers' University Society (TUR), which continued to run schools and courses throughout Poland until 1948. Similarly, union periodicals strove to bring high culture to their readers. All parties, meanwhile, supported programs that opened universities to workers and children of workers. Preference for such candidates rose steadily until 1949–50.[27] Even if these initiatives reached only a handful of workers, the net result (to modify Świda-Ziemba's comments on youth quoted previously) was that workers could now feel that being a worker was a virtue in and of itself.

The authorities' educational goals were hindered by the fact that many workers had almost no formal education because of the war. As a result, the end of the war brought a mass return of workers and others to school. In 1945–46, some 190,000 adults were enrolled in elementary school, another 34,500 in high school, and thousands more in various technical or professional schools or in courses run by industries, unions, and ministries; their numbers increased throughout the 1940s.[28] Programs at a large factory might include (according to the example of Pafawag) a three-year industrial school, a two-year mechanical lyceum, a three-year vocational school (all of them mostly for younger workers and teenagers), courses for the journeyman, foreman exams, short courses on skills such as welding, and literacy classes for older workers.[29]

In the case of younger students, the inadequacies and poverty of the

---

[27] Alina Woźnicka, "Przyczynek do dziejów aktywizacji zawodowej i społecznej kobiet we Wrocławiu w latach 1945–1948," in *Klasa robotnicza na Śląsku*, vol. 1 (Opole, 1975), 381–401. On the TUR, see Bronisław Syzdek, *Polska Partia Socjalistyczna w latach 1944–1948* (Warsaw, 1974), 297–300, and Stanisław Pajączkowski, "Działalność Towarzystwa Uniwersytetu Robotniczego na Dolnym Śląsku w latach 1945–1948," *Rocznik Dolnośląski* 8 (1983): 95–109. On unions, see Kowalewska, "Wzór osobowy," 219. On universities, see Jan Lewandowski, *Rodowód społeczny powojennej inteligencji polskiej (1944–1949)*, Uniwersytet Szczeciński, Rozprawy i Studia No. 92 (Szczecin, 1991). At Wrocław University, 60 to 70 percent of the new students in the fall of 1948 were workers' or peasants' children: WAP KW PPR 1/V/3, k. 46; also Irena Turnau, *Studia nad strukturą ludnościową polskiego Wrocławia* (Poznań, 1960), 196–98.

[28] *RS 1948*, 204, 206, 208–10; *RS 1949*, 208–10, 212–13.

[29] Julian Cierpisz, "Na 'Dzikim Zachodzie,' " in *Mój zakład pracy: Wspomnienia*, ed. Wiesław Szyndler-Głowacki (Warsaw, 1965), 209. Compare Wiesław Puś and Stefan Pytlas, *Dzieje Łódzkich Zakładów Przemysłu Bawełnianego im. Obrońców Pokoju "Uniontex" (d. Zjednoczonych Zakładów K. Scheiblera i L. Grohmana) w latach 1827–1977* (Warsaw, 1979), 403–18. On industrial education in general, see Anna Magierska, *Przywrócić Polsce: Przemysł na Ziemiach Odzyskanych, 1945–1946* (Warsaw, 1986), 371–93.

national school system made it natural for factories and organizations to pick up the slack. Before the war, employers had to arrange for the education of school-age workers. In 1945, the state took over this task but required employers to pay these workers for eighteen hours of schooling weekly. Nevertheless, many employers disregarded the law, while young workers often preferred to work full time and earn more money. As wages stabilized and schools were rebuilt, the situation improved, but still some 4.5 million adults were illiterate or semiliterate in 1947. Many were workers or would soon leave their villages to become workers. They presented to the state a challenge but also an opportunity to bring them deeper into postwar structures; as in Wrocław, the party could meet these workers first. The widespread belief in the right to education and opportunity may be People's Poland's greatest success; by the end of the 1940s, people began to expect and demand access to education for themselves and their children.[30]

Another purpose of education was to bring the worker into contact with management. A plan at Pafawag in late 1949 encouraged "cooperation between worker inteligencja and their colleague workers" by setting up small study groups run by technicians or foremen on various technical or production topics. The lessons were to be conducted at the home of one of the worker participants or the teacher. In this way, the barriers between the two groups could shrink, and they might recognize their common commitment to improved production. Similarly, when worker autobiographies (such as Łykowski's quoted in Chapter 5) stressed the antagonism between workers and the technical inteligencja, they did so to highlight the anachronism of such relations; other memoirs showed the two in close, progressive cooperation.[31]

According to the images contained in propaganda literature, women were one of the groups that had the greatest opportunity to advance. One of the signal accomplishments of People's Poland was to raise the presence of women in the factory and society, promoting them to new positions of power and economic security. Women did gain access to the same honors and benefits as did men. They could enter vocational

---

[30]AAN MPiH 947 kk. 1–2; Eugeniusz Gudziński, "Działalność związków zawodowych na rzecz awansu społecznego robotników," *KHRZ*, nos. 1–2 (1982): 58–59; Krystyna Bursche and Grażyna Pomian, "Awans zawodowy robotników przemysłowych," in *Przemysł i społeczeństwo w Polsce Ludowej*, ed. Jan Szczepański (Wrocław, 1969), 190–91.

[31]WAP Pafawag 78, kk. 39–41. Worker autobiographies: see, for example, Włodzimierz Gmitrzykowski, *Za przykładem Matrosowa*, BPP 6 (Warsaw, 1949), 18–19.

training and become famous avant-gardists, factory council members, party activists, and politicians. This is the message Janina Strauchold, a union delegate and PZPR activist at Pafawag (where she was a drill operator), conveyed to her Wrocław colleagues upon her return from a national conference: "Like every woman, I had little experience and little faith, and I felt unsure of myself because I was poorly dressed. But it turned out that I was honored in the same way as other dignitaries, and my words did not disappear without a trace."[32] Many women were inspired by the promise of escape from their home lives. The women's magazine *Przyjaciółka* received four hundred to six hundred letters daily; 60 or 70 of these were from women (especially rural women) asking for advice in finding work.[33] The party could boast some successes: the number of women holding union positions increased from less than 2,000 nationwide in December 1947 to more than 22,000 two years later. Female union membership increased from 21 percent of all union members to 31 percent during the same period.[34]

The official advocate for the advance of women was the PZPR-allied League of Women. This organization was in fact only partially aimed at workers, who made up less than half its membership.[35] Only in late 1948 did the league become a mass organization; thereafter, it became another mobilization tool, allowing ambitious women to advance with the party's help. Like the early union leaders before them, league activists saw themselves as primarily concerned with social issues such as day care and housing, yet tried to be both a party mouthpiece and a voice for women as workers and mothers.[36] Women's views of their careers as workers conflicted with activists' visions, as a League of Women representative found when she agitated for the league at a Łódź printing plant in 1949. To stormy applause, a worker named Mikulska retorted that women earn too little and spent too much time in line for purchases

---

[32]ARZ CRZZ WO 766, kk. 83–85. On women's interpretations of work under socialism, see Martha Lampland, "Unthinkable Subjects: Women and Labor in Socialist Hungary," *East European Quarterly* 23, no. 4 (1989): 389–98.

[33]AAN KC PZPR 237/VII/96, kk. 45–46; see monthly reports throughout 1949, same folder.

[34]AAN KC PZPR 237/V/72, k. 33. Total union membership increased from 2,936,100 to 3,705,165, or by 26 percent.

[35]In Łódź, three-quarters of league members were workers. AAN KC PZPR 237/V/72, k. 34, also kk. 7–19; AAN KC PZPR 237/VII/96, kk. 2–3.

[36]An example of this ambiguous role appears in AAN KC PZPR 237/VII/1457, kk. 22–25.

and that men should earn enough to keep their wives at home so that children wouldn't have to go to nurseries. The idea of such a women's organization in the face of these problems, she implied, was absurd.[37]

Indeed, opportunities for advance were often imaginary. In March 1949 there were only 107 forewomen, most of them in the textile industry; only 13 percent of the first 240 graduates of the Workers' Textile Technicum were women.[38] Male skilled workers enjoyed more upward mobility in the party and other organizations and in industry than did women. Women unionists argued that women workers were overworked, unskilled, underpaid, uncelebrated.[39] Their plight reflected a basic conflict between political ideals and national values. A speech by Pafawag drill operator Janina Strauchold showed how politics, national tradition, and gender conflicted. While she celebrated liberation, remarking that "We women, who could not get such training before the war because our husbands didn't want to do politics with us, are . . . training ourselves [in politics]," she suggested a retreat from the heroworker model which she herself represented, drawing attention to family needs: " 'I would . . . ask that women, young mothers of twenty, of whom we have many in this country now, could work in warehouses or in distribution, where work is easier. We see how these young go to the nursery in the morning with one child, while they are expecting another soon. Those women work as welders, or lifting [equipment], while young men sit in the tool room. Can't this be changed? After all, population growth is needed.' (applause)"[40] The intensification of the economy in 1949, like the multimachine campaign of 1947, fell particularly hard on women because their jobs proved the most vulnerable to the pressures of the plan. Nightshifts, overtime, child-care problems, and the difficulties of running a household made study and promotion options for only a few women.[41] Thus, education and promotion, along

[37]Of 183 women in the plant, only 13 volunteered to join. ŁAP WRZZ 68, n.p.

[38]There were just five female factory directors. AAN KC PZPR 237/V/72, k. 34. Kowalewska and Kowalewski, "Losy absolwentów," 80. When a list of thirty-five candidates for party training was drawn up at a Łódź garment factory, the PPR leader reduced the list to twenty-three, explaining that "women are burdened with work, and one cannot burden them with political work." AAN KC PPR 295/XIII/42, k. 112.

[39]See ŁAP WRZZ 19, n.p. (June 1949).

[40]ARZ CRZZ WO 766, kk. 83–85.

[41]A 1949 PZPR report on overtime work found that in one factory only 10 percent of the women considered night work convenient and "the rest work in tears"; the report warned of the likely effect on production. AAN KC PZPR 237/XXVIII/1, kk. 101–2. In

with the premium placed on activism, encouraged not the liberation of women workers but their resubjugation. Working women could not take full advantage of available opportunities as long as advance in the factory remained the domain of skilled men; meanwhile, as the traditional labor community lost control of the factory, even modest gains were vulnerable. Progress for women would have to wait as their patriotic duties as mothers and wives came to obscure their right to a share in the fruits of socialism.

The picture of young women that Strauchold offered was rather different from that which Lipińska's autobiography promised. The promotion or education of a few split the working class between those who were upwardly mobile and those who were not. This split destroyed workers' control over the boundaries and definitions of their class. As the barriers between classes (which had always been important in cities like Łódź) were removed, the meaning of class boundaries and of the working class itself in Polish society changed profoundly. In a way, by promoting workers into administration, the party gave a shadow of workers' control back, but on its own terms. Workers might indeed control industry but only as former workers, bureaucrats in the party hierarchy. Even labor heroism could only carry the worker so far.

The Avant-Gardist: A New Worker in a New Community

What was the hero worker supposed to be like? As I noted in Chapter 5, the avant-gardist might be the young enthusiast familiar from propaganda posters, an experienced worker, or both. The 1949 autobiography of Wanda Gościmińska, one of the first adult avant-gardists in the Łódź textile mills and a prominent figure in propaganda during the three-year plan, exemplifies this mixture. Born to a poor laborer's family in Łódź in 1914, Gościmińska was a typical representative of the old labor community. At the same time, she was not just a concerned, conscious Pole but a true labor avant-gardist and a party exemplar as well. Her participation in the multimachine movement in 1947 helped to spark the Poznański strike. She is the alter ego of the Poznański strikers and recast in her autobiography their collective spirit in the party's mold.

Wrocław, women with children were sometimes fired. WAP Związek Zawodowy Budowlanych WO 16, k. 5.

Wanda Gościmińska, labor avant-gardist and spinning instructor at PZPB Ruda
Pabianicka, c. 1950, Archiwum Akt Nowych, Warsaw.

Gościmińska's story begins with an account of work in the Horak
(PZPB Ruda Pabianicka) mill before the war. After the war (she mod-
estly dismisses her heroism as a saboteur and her years in a Gestapo jail)
she returned to "our factory." The fall of 1947 found her lamenting to
her workmate over the problems of her industry and Poland:

> "You know, Lutka, it makes my heart ache. Look—people need things
> so badly, we have enough machinery, but we produce too little. . . ."
> "There are no people [to work]. You can't do anything about it. . . ."
> "Are you sure that nothing can be done?"
> "Unfortunately, yes."
> I bit my lip. No, that's impossible! We can't wait for someday, maybe
> many years from now, when the new crop trained in the textile schools
> comes to work. A solution must be found *immediately*.

Gościmińska showed where the responsible citizen should turn: to the
party (PPR). Her conversation with the party secretary illustrated the

proper relationship: the party supplied the idea, while the worker avant-
gardist supplied the enthusiasm and natural wisdom:

> The Secretary smiled cordially:
> "But comrade, there is a way! And we were just planning to present it
> to our work force."
> I waited impatiently for what he would say. The Secretary rubbed his
> eyes, red from lack of sleep (there was work up to one's ears in those
> days) and said, "Comrade Gościmińska, have you heard of the Stakha-
> novites?"
> "But of course! Stakhanov was a miner."
> "Well, yes. But Stakhanovites are by no means just miners. . . . Stakha-
> novites work differently. Working two sides of the machine isn't enough
> for them. . . . Do you understand now?"
> It flashed in my mind like a floodlight: switch to multi-machine work!
> I cried: "Comrade Secretary, I'm switching to three sides. And right away,
> next week!"
> The Secretary nodded his head in friendship. He said, in a strangely
> warm voice, "We expected this of you." Then he added, however, "But
> don't think, comrade, that it will be easy. . . ."
> "Oh, but I'm not a child! What do you think, that I decided just like
> that, overcome by emotion? I know how much one can do, and no mir-
> acles are necessary!"[42]

Gościmińska describes how the early antipathy was dispelled by news
of her doubled paycheck and continued high-quality production, the best
on her floor. Then came labor competition, which she encouraged others
to join: "The party warmed me to action, and I tried to influence others." In 1949, Gościmińska was summoned from her machine to become
a roving instructor, teaching younger workers how to improve quality
and quantity. Her story celebrates experience; under the party's tutelage,
her instruction replaced the traditional apprentice-master relationship
(whose cruelty before the war she describes).

Wanda Gościmińska is a model in another way. In a relentless litany
toward the end of her story, she describes her civic duties: she was a
member of the executive of the PZPR factory circle and of the party's
neighborhood committee. She was chair of the factory council: "Someone had to do it, and indeed I know all the factory's problems from the
oldest times." She was then chosen to the Łódź PZPR City Committee

---

[42]Wanda Gościmińska, *Mój wielki dzień*, BPP 16 (Warsaw, 1949), 16–17. See the similar
role played by a party-member foreman in Lipińska, *Mój awans*, 19–20.

and the Textile Workers' Trade Union's Chief Labor Competition Committee. Then she was chosen to the city council: "I hesitated whether to accept still one more responsibility. I calculated that if I left the house one more half hour earlier daily, then I would be up to this task as well! And I was." Next, she was chosen to a position in the League of Women. Finally, she was selected secretary of the Parents' Committee at her oldest daughter's school. Each of these eight tasks Gościmińska portrays as a duty that, however she might value her free time, she had to accept.[43]

In the official pageant of party-society relations, the avant-garde worker was a first among equals, the chosen representative of the working class in the party. The privileged treatment of these heroes was a kind of surrogate for the general privileges supposed to be accorded workers as a class in the socialist state. In their own opinion, these workers were the new labor aristocracy. While workers as a group received some benefits, the avant-garde workers received, and expected to receive, benefits like those of a new nobility. They saw themselves at the forefront of the class struggle, under attack from those who did not understand. Wanda Gościmińska herself had complained to a conference of union activists that although she and her colleagues had been much applauded in the 1947 May Day parade and feted at conferences, "there were very many limousines at the multi-machinists conference, but after the conference they all drove away, and the avant-gardists had to go on foot."[44] Avant-gardists from Pabianice—"We, the representatives of a 12,000-strong army of leading [*przodujących*] men and women workers"—sounded similar themes two years later after an excursion to Kraków. Although they regarded their mistreatment as an affront to all workers, they were particularly offended and discomfited as avant-gardists: "Orbis [the national travel agency] is more interested in well-situated people who have accommodations in a hotel confirmed in advance. . . . One could sleep like that during the occupation, like slaves, but that it would happen today, and to labor avant-gardists at that, is really a scandal. . . . Avant-gardists who have contributed to our factory's winning first-place laurels were treated like non-citizens."[45] As other

---

[43] Gościmińska, *Mój wielki dzień*, 30–31.

[44] AAN KC PPR 295/XIII/7, kk. 99–100. See also a Wrocław railway worker: "At the great rally in the People's Hall on the occasion of the visit of the intellectuals [the 1948 Conference for Peace], railroad worker avant-gardists were not admitted into the hall and had to stand outside." WAP WRZZ 24, k. 21.

[45] ŁAP WRZZ 345, n.p. (June 1949).

avenues of protest were closed, the words of the honored worker remained legitimate; he or she was permitted or encouraged to transmit
real or symbolic worker concerns to the authorities.[46]

But party members who nearly rioted in defense of religious pictures
in Wrocław in 1948 (see Chapter 4) or rowdy youth activists in Łódź
had other ideas about the value of a party card.[47] Their faith in their
position was based in part on older ideas of the valued worker as moral
force. In a way, it was not so far from the idea expressed in a leaflet
found in a Silesian woolen mill in January 1949: "Every citizen-
gentleman-worker battles with communism."[48] Even if the Polish working class was no longer powerful in collective action, the survival of
labor traditions alternative to communism (even within the party) posed
a powerful threat to the building of a stalinist society.

In order to redefine the worker, it was first necessary to redefine the
nature of work itself. Organized factory culture in the stalinist era placed
celebration of the labor process at the center of the work life. Labor
competitions after 1948 honored work in a formal way with pledges
evocative of military or religious oaths. In contrast to Pstrowski's 1947
"defiant sporting challenge," workers participated in the pageant of history as a numberless yet heroic mass.[49] The factory changed rapidly,
becoming a formal, ordered place where everything reminded one of
production goals. Workers had little books by their machine with information about their results so far; successful workers might have little
flags identifying their workplace. "When we walk through the shop,"
exulted an avant-gardist from one textile mill, "we see red pennants
which show us that this is a team of victors. Those pennants speak to
us; we want them to knock at the hearts of all working people."[50] The
"consciously" productive worker, meanwhile, claimed to allow for no
distractions from the business of work. "I lost no time on nonessential

---

[46]Other examples include comments of garment worker Stefan Ślęzak at a December
1949 union conference, CRZZ WO 743, kk. 37–38; comments by Cecylja Sierakowska
in Chapter 4; a letter from avant-gardist worker Władysław Popielski to the Łódź PZPR,
ŁAP KZ PZPR "Wifama" 43 XIV/3–1, n.p.

[47]See complaints of an old PPR member at Poznański in September 1947: "The ZWM
is spoiled; they have brawls in their clubroom; they bring in urchins from Bałuty; they sit
locked up in there at night. Several times the Industrial Guard has had to drive them out
at night, both girls and boys." AAN KC PPR 295/IX/33, k. 14.

[48]Leaflet found at PZPW Myszków, MSW MBP 41/234, k. 19.

[49]Boni, "Stereotyp robotnika," 104–9.

[50]ŁAP WRZZ 19, n.p. (June 1949).

Perhaps the most famous example of Polish socialist realism: "Pass Me a Brick" (*Podaj cegłę*), by Andrzej Kobzdej, 1950. Muzeum Narodowe, Wrocław.

conversation," explained labor hero Lipińska to her readers. "I didn't leave the looms without an absolute necessity. Was this tiring? Not at all! Work absorbed me completely, and time passed more quickly than when I had tried to find ways to entertain myself."[51]

The combination of discipline, productivism, and modernization left many behind. Even a relatively experienced worker could feel lost. Łódź-born Zdzisława G., then eighteen years old but with five years' experience, recalled with regret the difference she noticed when she left the Łódź thread factory [ŁFN], an old, unmodernized factory near her home, for PZPB No. 1 (Scheibler and Grohman), which, as one of the largest factories in the country, was at the forefront of labor competition and modernization.[52]

[51] Lipińska, *Mój awans*, 16.
[52] The factory began modernizing equipment in 1949. Puś and Pytlas, *Dzieje Łódzkich Zakładów*, 326–27.

[Workers at Scheibler] didn't have time, you know. Here [at ŁFN] they went out more often for a cigarette, and talked a bit, or sat down, and there—a spinner had to eat on the run. She set down her thread bag, [took out] a bottle and bread in paper, and was working, tinkering, eating, and walking.

[At ŁFN] the machines were better taken care of, there were more cleaning girls . . . And [at Scheibler] there weren't, the spinner had to do everything herself. On Saturday there was always a half hour when the machines stopped and you had to clean up, and that was it for the whole week. . . . A person talked less. More often, one could quickly talk in the cloakroom when you finished work, or if you came a little early to begin work. Of course people talked with one another. But such chitchats [like at ŁFN] didn't happen any more. Everyone looked after her work.[53]

Although she herself had won medals in labor competition, she felt overwhelmed by the new factory regime. Labor in socialism, it turned out, could be as alienating as under capitalism.[54] While labor competition attracted many workers to the new labor relations, it left many workers behind. Even at Pafawag, where so many workers participated in competitions, only a few truly profited while many others "took only a piece of dry bread for lunch, being unable to allow themselves something better, though . . . there are no idlers in our factory."[55]

Relations among workers, these examples suggest, also changed. The old labor community was shaken by individual competition; the decline of independent labor competition once again placed the collective ahead of individual success. Gościmińska described her six-woman team as close friends who shared meals. "Now one works completely differently," one of the women remarked. "Not to make more, though in fact one finds more change in one's pocket. But—you know—more pleasantly. Like a family. Before, there were always squabbles: who gets no. 24 [thread] to work, and who gets another sort, and now one works in harmony, and happily."[56] This collective was superficially not unlike

---

[53]Interview, Łódź, 10 May 1990.

[54]This alienation was also manifested in propaganda descriptions of work. For example, on the occasion of Stalin's seventieth birthday (20 December 1949) President Bierut spoke of Poland's industrial production (in a special competition in Stalin's honor) as nearly detached from the worker: "The feelings of our nation are forged in thousands of tons of coal and iron, in millions of meters of thread and cloth, in countless forms of workers' labor, hard as steel." Robert Kupiecki, *"Natchnienie milionów": Kult Józefa Stalina w Polsce, 1944–1956* (Warsaw, 1993), 107.

[55]WAP Pafawag 244, kk. 40–41.

[56]Gościmińska, *Mój wielki dzień*, 23.

traditional relations in the Łódź cotton mill, but in fact it was radically new, having been created from above (harnessed to the economy and to the party) and not from below.

On the other hand, to place work again at the center of the factory experience yielded the shop floor to the older experienced or skilled workers again, even as they had been ridiculed by labor competition's rhetoric and left to suffer financially. Indeed, the authorities found it vital to bring those workers back. "The Labor Avant-gardist's Library," a pamphlet series of life stories of successful workers, included a number of experienced workers among its subjects in 1949. These portraits, like Gościmińska's, endeavored to show that labor competition was not contrary to the traditions of the factory community and that older workers, even those set in their ways, could also find their place in the new system. To do so, however, an experienced worker such as Jan Kaniewski of Wrocław's Pafawag, honored for his ideas to simplify and speed up machining, would have to undergo a kind of epiphany, recognizing and welcoming the new world: "So, listen. I was born in 1907, so according to my birth certificate I am 42 years old. But if someone were to ask, 'Say, Jasiu, when were you born?' I would fire back without hesitation: 'you have my date of birth on the birth certificate. But in truth, my life began a second time from the beginning in the fall of 1946, on the day I came to Pafawag.' "[57]

As the party sought to remake the experienced worker, the latter had some success resisting the destruction of old class and community forms by labor competition. This resistance, as much as the shortcomings of youthful labor competition, must be credited for a new labor competition in the cotton industry, the "quality campaign" of 1949. The presentation of this campaign, as captured in a 1950 account by Kazimierz Koźniewski, borrowed from working-class tradition and appealed directly to the experienced worker. Koźniewski's story is a kind of morality play illustrating the isolation and frustration felt by the dedicated older worker, the tension between labor generations, and the party's embrace of experience.[58] Such propaganda was an admission of the vitality and power of working-class traditions. But these traditions were remodeled to fit stalinism: the PZPR assumed the guise of the experi-

[57]Kaniewski, *Było to na Pa-Fa-Wagu*, 6.
[58]Kazimierz Koźniewski, "Extry i primy," in Kazimierz Koźniewski, *Most: Wybór reportaży* (Warsaw, 1951 [originally published in the BPP series, 1950]), 127–53.

enced, knowledgeable senior worker and showed by example what traits ought to be a part of that persona.

Apolonia Bańkowska, the heroine of the story, is a PZPR-member weaver of twenty-five years' experience in PZPB no. 6 (Gampe and Albrecht) in Łódź. Koźniewski shows her torn between two responsibilities, as an activist and as a good worker. "Old trade habits told her to weave the fabric carefully; the ambition of the old worker ached to see how 'number six' sent poor-quality material to the warehouse." Her work on the factory council meant that at any moment she might be called to a meeting,

> and the loom stands idle, the meters of material don't rise, and when the semimonthly calculations come and [others], even that youngster Zielińska, have much more material produced, they get higher bonuses; and when the next round of labor competition is completed, some names are on the list of avant-gardists, others are in the newspapers, are honored and credited—only not the name of old Bańkowska, a weaver who . . . trained 68 students so that many of them are already instructors or foremen. . . .
>
> "And I," she thought to herself, "will return to [just] my machine; I'll show what I know how to do, and finally they will begin to recognize Comrade Bańkowska not only when someone needs to run around and get things done which others couldn't, but also when she stands at her machine."[59]

Bańkowska asserts the value of her work above that of the bureaucrats, explicitly rejecting that avenue of promotion and success as inferior to honest work. "I've had enough of all this bureaucratizing," she shouts at a factory PZPR meeting. "Mine is the factory, the weaving room, the loom, and all Poland, and yours is the office where you officiate, and where I was in over my head." In response, a party official reminds her of the need for teamwork. Bańkowska's place on the sidelines helps others to produce; her "ideological, organizational, social work is no less important in our system than work in a trade."[60]

Bańkowska's dilemma—whether it is wrong to want to return to fulltime work and perhaps win some prizes—was partly material but was presented as a moral one. It is reflective, in Koźniewski's tale, of a similar conflict faced by the party and state as a whole. Until now, labor com-

[59]Ibid., 129–30.
[60]Ibid., 131–32.

petition had resembled a sport; the PZPR official who rebuked Bań-kowska turned this metaphor on its head, reminding her that sport is not just individual accomplishment but teamwork and sacrifice. In this light, ambition was a bad trait; yet as a speaker at a party hearing of Bankowska's case remarked, "one cannot suspect every labor avant-gardist only of personal ambitions, since we would reduce it to absurdity. Labor competition is not a sign of ambition, but is comprehension of the fundamental sense of labor in the new system."[61]

Koźniewski depicts meetings across Poland in mid-1949 in which older workers expressed their frustration at being too good for labor competition. They echo, meanwhile, the sense of civic duty expressed by Gościmińska: "Comrade chair [pleads one such worker in Bielawa, Lower Silesia], it shouldn't go on like this. It's not only that we old weavers . . . are slighted, but that in buying poor material we lose as citizens of this nation. The nation itself loses. Young workers race and race, only thinking of pounding out more meters on the loom, not looking out for breaks or tangles. . . . Believe me, my heart aches, and my conscience doesn't allow me to let it go: I stop the loom, and start untangling. My loom stands still. Others, meanwhile, let a rip go and pound on without a stop. Then I am slighted, through my own honesty. I could let the mistake go and it would be all right: everyone bought [such stuff] until now. After the war, one needed to be clothed all over again. But now all that is over." So, too, Koźniewski is saying, the individualist numbers game of early labor competition was over. In a way, this passage heralded a return to certain aspects of the capitalist labor market. Before the war, one could be fired for too many mistakes; now, lamented another, "anyone who wants to work is accepted to the weaving shop. And that's very good. At last one's bread is certain; but why is bad work rewarded? Why are we, the good workers, losing time in catching mistakes, wronged in the general calculations [of production]? Why, comrade chair?"[62]

As in Gościmińska's story, the party had a solution: a labor competition judged on quality before quantity.[63] This was a symbol of Poland's emergence from the reconstruction era (when people would buy any-

---

[61]Ibid., 134.
[62]Ibid, 139–40; also 146, a similar speech by a worker at Poznański.
[63]The decree of 22 August 1949 announcing the competition appears in AAN KC PZPR 237/XXXI/5, kk. 20–21. Poor quality could be penalized by a deduction of up to 25 percent of one's base pay. Koźniewski, "Extry i primy," 144–45.

thing) into a time of plenty, guided by the nation's reserves of expertise, the keepers of working-class tradition. As Koźniewski tells this story, the young, careless enthusiasts who did not know or care about traditions of honest work lost to the experienced workers who felt "an over-powering antipathy toward the young [workers] who took their work lightly; they had surely deplored the fact that the values of [their] effort were not properly appreciated." Koźniewski's account represented a new future for the old Łódź textile workers within the structures of state-designed production campaigns.[64]

But the party had not forgotten its young enthusiasts. A young non-party worker from Łódź, Maria Terpilakowa, presented the plan for "best quality brigades" at the Second Trade Union Congress in June 1949. "The socialist content of labor competition has done its work," Koźniewski explained, noting the start of a similar campaign in the USSR three months previously. The new workers were not only energetic but politically aware; they "understood not only that one must increase the amount of cloth produced, but that poorly produced cloth is a serious waste for the people's state."[65]

In the new factory envisioned by the party, youth was no longer a virtue of itself but an apprenticeship in a new system of values mentored by workers like Gościmińska and Bańkowska. Those values differed from those of the recent heroic past and those of the workers of Gości-mińska's generation who struck in 1945–47. Just as one could no longer easily become a labor hero, membership in the party also required apprenticeship—or so it was portrayed. In the following scene from Włodzimierz Gmitrzykowski's 1949 autobiography, the leather worker (not yet a labor avant-gardist) considers joining the PPR:

> For several days after the meeting I weighed my decision. Finally I approached Śmietanka, an old Party member.
> "I want to join the party."
> He looked at me, as was his habit, over his glasses which had slipped to the tip of his nose. "Join the party?" he repeated. "But have you shown real activity in the life of the factory? Do you know theory? Brother, you finished school, and you're not a bad craftsman, but you don't know much about the workers' movement. And you do too little in that movement today. Wait a little. Work some with us, learn some more, think it over—then we'll see. Because it's not enough, brother, to join! We don't need

[64]Koźniewski, "Extry i primy," 148–49.
[65]Ibid., 143.

any paper comrades. The party brings one obligations. One must be an activist in everything—a leader![66]

Bańkowska, Śmietanka, and the others are ideal types, as are the young enthusiasts they tutor; nevertheless, these were people over whom the party had at least some control. Having lost its trust in the foremen of the prewar generation as mentors, the party sought to create new models of both teacher and apprentice.

Much more likely than this ideal, surely, were relations like that noted in Łódź metal factories, where older workers were favored at the expense of younger ones: "a tool which could not be found in the tool room for a young worker is found a few minutes later for an old hand. . . . Young craftsmen must search for tools, losing time unnecessarily."[67] Behind the heroic stories of Gościmińska and others, the generation of September 1947 still fought for its dignity. There were even a few strikes in Łódź (including at Poznański) that greeted the quality competition, forcing its delay by one week.[68] Yet the prominence of the other characters in the propaganda literature indicates a hierarchy of values along which workers should progress in the factory.

When party leaders like Władysław Gomułka or Julian Kole charged that party activists were out of touch with ordinary workers in 1945–46, the explanation was incompetence and inexperience. In 1949, this distance was expressed in class terms. Many activists, claimed Łódź unionist Zofia Patorowa, "having [gained] a position, would like to rest and create [for themselves] better conditions than the workers have." She lamented that "though it is not true, [the workers] paint us as better off."[69] Writing twenty years later, Feliks Tomaszewski, an eager party member and a delegate to the Second Congress of Trade Unions in 1949 from the food industry workers' union, still smoldered over the slight he experienced when congress officials refused to allow him to read a poem to the assembled delegates: "the relations of a union comrade to another such comrade—where in this can we see even a touch of a friendly and tutorial gesture toward a weaker comrade-member? . . . There was no place at the Congress for a modest,

[66] Gmitrzykowski, *Za przykładem Matrosowa*, 14.
[67] ŁAP WRZZ 19 n.p. (July 1949).
[68] MSW MBP 17/IX/38, t. 4, n.p. (August–September 1949); AAN KC PZPR 237/VII/118, kk. 350–51, 398–400.
[69] ŁAP WRZZ 19, n.p. (June 1949). See also WUSW KWMO 150/10, n.p. (December 1949).

self-taught average worker, who in his simple language, without fancy style, expressed his position and that of the entire Polish proletariat and society."[70]

Few workers, of course, wanted any part of the podium at such an event. But they had hoped that the revolution would yield a place for the worker at the table. Instead, opportunities for most workers, which had seemed limitless in 1945, looked dim by 1949. Only a few could make fantastic sums in competition or advance to powerful new positions in the factory and society. The rest saw that competition's riches came at too high a price or were eaten away by the demands of ideology, while promises of advance evaporated before the needs of the national economy. To the majority of workers who did not advance, the party offered other incentives for acquiescence. Most important was the opportunity for cultural and social integration.

Mass Culture and the Blurring of Class Lines

In addition to mobility, the communist authorities sought other ways to familiarize and accustom workers to the practices of other classes. Chief among these "alien" practices was the pursuit of higher culture. The new worker-citizen of democratic Poland was to be an enthusiast—if not a patron—of culture. When Pafawag's Jan Kaniewski showed off his musician daughter and engineer son, he expressed a new sense of familiarity with these hitherto alien social groups—the cultural and technical inteligencja. The world into which the party wanted to invite the new workers combined physical labor and mental improvement. The regime did not view workers as simply laborers; they were also potential citizens of a "People's Republic."

Culture for the masses was a key, authorities believed, to the creation of a new political consciousness among workers that was supportive of the state. Many party and nonparty intellectuals hoped that high culture and higher education would at last be accessible to everyone in the new Poland and would reflect the whole society.[71] Before the war, the labor parties and unions had sponsored reading rooms and cultural activities

[70]Feliks Tomaszewski, CRZZ Library memoir 33, 31–32.
[71]Tomasz Szarota, "Upowszechnianie kultury," in *Polska Ludowa, 1944–1950*, ed. Franciszek Ryszka (Wrocław, 1974), 408–70.

for workers; now they endeavored to establish a space for cultural activities, a *świetlica,* in every workplace. While świetlicas were generally supervised by the Ministry of Information and Propaganda (dissolved in 1947), each was actually run by whomever could be found to administer it. A świetlica might begin as a factory council program, its director appointed by management, the trade union, or a party; parties or other organizations often ran competing świetlicas. The PPR was generally most successful in securing control of factory świetlicas and using them as vehicles for propaganda.[72] Much depended on the director, who chose activities and arranged the location; it was not easy to get workers to participate in anything after work. The ambitious świetlica director often faced management indifference to cultural activities; more often, management and even the local PPR allowed świetlicas to fall into neglect. "After holding a few events and having exhausted all their power and hospitality," lamented the Łódź PPR Committee in May 1947, "*świetlicas* fell, one might say, into a state of indolence."[73]

The greatest problem for political leaders was neither money nor direction but matching the cultural form to the audience. First, workers simply had other needs after the war; a reporter visiting a cigarette factory in August 1945 noticed that "baths with hot water . . . are more popular than the *świetlica.*"[74] Moreover, prewar staged culture had been associated in workers' minds with the upper class; right after the war, the same associations were sometimes made with the new upper class, the "speculators." The solution was to distribute free tickets and bring theater and movies into the factory. Workers came readily to concerts, dances, and films, all of which were novelties in the factory. In April 1946, the workers at one textile mill even went on strike to protest the planned closing of the świetlica. Such events, however, accomplished nothing ideologically and might even harm production: when films were shown during work hours at the Widzew manufactory, as its świetlica

[72]On mass culture and the Ministry of Information and Propaganda, see Andrzej Krawczyk, *Pierwsza próba indoktrynacji: Działalność Ministerstwa Informacji i Propagandy w latach 1944–1947,* Dokumenty do dziejów PRL, zeszyt 7 (Warsaw, 1994), chap. 2, esp. 32–34; and Stanisław Kuśmierski, *Propaganda polityczna PPR w latach 1944–48* (Warsaw, 1976), 207–21.

[73]AAN KC PPR 295/XIII/18, k. 105, 295/XI/10, kk. 35–36; AAN MIiP 82, k. 5, and 299, k. 22.

[74]"Tam gdzie powstaje papieros," *Robotnik,* 31 August 1945. See also ŁAP WUIiP 29, n.p., and AAN MIiP 299, kk. 22–23.

director complained, workers left their machines running in their haste to attend.[75]

The best that authorities could hope for was to smuggle in a serious lecture along with the entertainment. The preference of social activists contrasted with the desires of the audience. Amateur groups usually presented vintage light comedies, for until 1947–48 the politically minded theater director could find little appealing material. The more ambitious groups staged selections from Polish classics. Best was a balance between the two, as at a performance by the theater group at the Scheibler and Grohman mill in 1946. Fragments from a patriotic drama by Stanisław Wyspiański, "which was not understood by most of the audience due to a lack of appropriate preparation," were followed by "a light vaudeville which, while effective and profitable, does not possess any social-educational value."[76]

In fact, the regime never entirely succeeded in developing appealing ideological culture; the stalinist years continued the previous tradition of light fare and classics, although activists chose materials more carefully. Even one of the great worker-culture successes of the 1940s, the Workers' Opera in Wrocław in 1948, failed to meet the expectations of proletarian culture. The premiere of its first and only production, Stanisław Moniuszko's *Flis* (Boatman), was attended by PPR and government dignitaries from Warsaw, who were no doubt startled when the first scene opened with a group prayer. At the end of the performance, the actors proved unable to sing the "Internationale" with the audience.[77]

In 1948, the party began to demand a more educational role, with better lectures on topics such as labor discipline. Uncertain about what exactly the party wanted, especially from its older followers, one Łódź tram worker made a plea for reliable models: "We dedicate so little to

---

[75] AAN MIiP 82, k. 10; ŁAP WK PPS 22/XII/7, n.p.; *Głos Widzewa*, 20 January 1946, ŁAP WUIiP 140.

[76] AAN MPiH 947, k. 114. On theater in the factories, see Władysław Misiak, *Działalność kulturalna na Dolnym Śląsku w latach 1945–1949* (Wrocław, 1973), 106–9. See also AAN KC PPR 295/VII/5, kk. 256–62; WAP Pafawag 252, k. 3; and WAP WRZZ 1, k. 12; WAP WRZZ 18, k. 2.

[77] WAP WRZZ 2, k. 208. Ironically, Soviet culture showed the way toward lighter fare. While the first Soviet films shown after the war were "primitive" propaganda vehicles, by late 1946 comedies and dramas such as *Crazy Airport* and *Boy from Our Town* were favorably impressing their audiences, drawing comments like "So they are capable of something after all." AAN MIiP 552, kk. 91, 106.

the modern man. The [Cultural-Educational] Committee [of the tram-workers' union] should create something like standard educational-political-social pictures [films]. Before such a picture, a higher-class lecturer or tutor should give us something human—a speech, or a discussion for the modern man. This should be captured in a social-educational film, because we are far behind other nations of the world. . . . Schools teach children, but we elders would like to catch up to youth."[78] Although still unfamiliar with the vocabulary of a new era, this speaker understood the importance of propaganda and education in shaping a new society. As did formal education, mass culture played two roles: it was a means to establish common denominators between workers and those of other backgrounds but was also a vehicle for establishing models for the stalinist worker.

The autobiographies of 1949–50 suggest an explicitly politicized and ambitious pursuit of organized culture. A successful worker such as Halina Lipińska was thus also cultured. Her autobiography endeavored to show that one could be successful in the factory as well as in a world previously closed to the worker.

If anyone . . . would still think that . . . I achieved my results in competition thanks to some superhuman effort, after which I return home unconscious from exhaustion and fall like a log to bed, I would invite that person to our ZMP *świetlica.*
"Where is your record-holder?" he would surely ask.
"Here she is," would be the answer.
"Here?" the guest would respond with surprise. "I see a party going on. But I am asking about that poor Lipińska, who . . ."
". . . who is dancing the *krakowiak* right now, in the first pair. That tall one on the left."

Lipińska makes clear that her experience is part of the education of a socialist worker. "How many times," she continues, "have I thought with sympathy about my parents, whose youth passed by in gray labor brightened by nothing. . . . Not work itself but the conditions of work and the consciousness of its social meaning determine a worker's personal outlook." Recounting her national successes with her factory's theater, ballet, and choir, she concludes: "Socialism is technical progress and material comfort. But socialism is also culture!"[79]

---

[78]ŁAP WRZZ 297, n.p. (February 1949).
[79]Lipińska, *Mój awans,* 21–22. The *krakowiak* is a lively Polish folk dance.

There was also room in this socialism for the experienced worker of Lipińska's parents' generation. Indefatigable activist Wanda Gościmińska chided her readers:

> To dispel any doubts about "overworking" or "exhaustion," and to amaze unbelievers utterly, I must tell about one more thing. I am a frequent visitor to our factory lending library [attested to by a picture of her there], and have lots of books at home. If someone visits my little apartment . . . they will find books from the Good Book Club and the Rebirth [*Odrodzenie*] Literary Club . . . , and my pride: ten volumes recently bought from the KUK (The Committee for the Popularization of Books). At the moment you read this pamphlet, you should know that I am caught up in Victor Hugo's *Les Misérables*. I set aside 200 to 300 złotys from every paycheck, while it's hot, for the purchase of books.
> . . . I really want to educate myself further. I am 35 years old, but am full of enthusiasm for study. My husband is now finishing the Textile Technical School. When he gets a position after graduation, then I will give a try.[80]

Through culture and political enthusiasm, the road was open for even the senior worker to become more "civilized" than her family before the war.

In the stalinist system, labor was one institution tying the individual to the state. By producing for the state or joining its labor organizations, workers would be socialized into a system that extended beyond the factory. Labor competitions held for noneconomic reasons (in honor of holidays such as May Day, for example, or in connection with national elections) blurred the boundaries between work and leisure. The resulting ceremonies brought mass culture, in the form of ritualized meetings and awards ceremonies, into the factory. As Michał Boni points out, this represented a new chapter in the history of mass culture; now that culture was staged not in one's free time but at work, the workplace was represented as a place where important and politically charged life events were acted out. The factory was a controlled environment with a specific audience; the sense of participation was thus enhanced. The mass meeting (*masówka*) had a special, almost religious connotation, very different from the often unscheduled mass meetings of 1945–47 that had conveyed workers' demands to management or the union during a strike. From the party unification campaign onward, they were pure ritual,

[80]Gościmińska, *Mój wielki dzień*, 32.

marked by symbols (national colors, pictures of leaders, slogans on banners) and gestures such as clapping or standing at appropriate moments. They were "cleansing, revealing Truth, or . . . the solemn celebration of some event"; denouncing class enemies or enjoining self-criticism, they reinforced certain moral lessons.[81]

The most important masówki, of course, were on holidays and special events: May Day, the anniversary of the founding of the PKWN (22 July), the Unification Congress, the Second Trade Union Congress, Stalin's birthday, and so on. While these holidays remained secular shadows of Christmas, Easter, and All Souls' Day, they still afforded an occasion to dress up and gather with one's workmates and march in a parade. To the degree that they were not onerous events—that the speeches were not too long, the beer plentiful, and the weather fair—they were agreeably observed. As a community gathering, the parade was an ideal place for the dissemination of mass culture.[82]

Not until 1949–50 did May Day cease to be cast as a celebration of popular or working-class victory and become instead a vehicle for a controlled ideological message. In Łódź, the PZPR reported 2,891 competition pledges before May Day 1949; workers were chagrined to discover the party's close monitoring of the accomplishment of those pledges. Much more than in the past, authorities carefully planned the look of the parades and rallies. Workers resisted the new formalism, especially because 1 May in 1949 fell on a Sunday, thus eliminating the week's one day of rest. In Wrocław, reported the UB, workers were apathetic and slow to express enthusiasm, while those in Łódź were positively antagonistic toward having to show up at the factory. At eight cotton mills there was talk of shunning the parade; at Scheibler, for example, some eighty workers demanded that the gates be opened to let them go home.[83]

[81]Boni, "Stereotyp robotnika," 101–3, 110–11. On ritual in communist society, see Christel Lane, *The Rites of Rulers: Ritual in Industrial Society—the Soviet Case* (Cambridge, U.K., 1979), esp. chap. 7.

[82]On holidays, see Ewa Pazik, "Obyczajowość rodzinna robotników zamieszkałych osiedle Księży Młyn w Łodzi" (Master's thesis, Katedra Etnografii, Uniwersytet Łódzki, 1980), 84–85. On holidays before 1949, see, for example, AAN KC PPR 295/V/3, n.p. (May–June 1947). On 3 May 1948, the Wrocław police reported absentee rates of 6 to 25 percent at some factories. WUSW KWMO 149/16, n.p. For a list of occasions celebrated in 1946, see Kuśmierski, *Propaganda polityczna*, 254.

[83]AAN KC PZPR 237/VII/95, kk. 68–69, 237/XXXI/133, kk. 25–27; WAP WRZZ 2, kk. 63–65, 70; WAP KW PZPR 74/V/3, n.p. (May 1949); MSW MBP 17/IX/10 t. 3, k. 126.

"Service to Poland" brigade marching on Piotrkowska Street, Łódź, May Day, 1949. Photographer unknown. Muzeum Tradycji Niepodległościowych, Łódź.

Work events outside the factory also helped to eradicate the distinctions between public and private. Two famous programs were the Universal "Service to Poland" Organization and the "Contact with the Village" campaign. "Service to Poland" (*Służba Polsce*), begun in 1948, was a sort of militarized public works/youth employment project. But it did not directly touch most workers' lives; 86 percent of the million-plus participants in February 1949 were rural youth or schoolchildren, and fewer than 9 percent took part as factory workers. Moreover, most work was conducted in villages; in cities, participants worked separately from other workers. Nevertheless, Służba Polsce was a well-publicized example of labor given without compensation to the state.[84]

[84]Jan Hellwig, *Powszechna Organizacja "Służba Polsce"* (Warsaw, 1977), 43. See Jadwiga Michnowska, "Powstanie i działalność Powszechnej Organizacji 'Służba Polsce' na Dolnym Śląsku w latach 1948–1955," *Rozprawy Naukowe AWF we Wrocławiu* 16

The "Contact with the Village" campaign, in which factories provided organized assistance to particular villages, became an important symbol of the stalinist factory. Small groups of workers, usually party members, traveled on a Sunday to a nearby village to help with the harvest or planting, machine repair, building a cultural center or school, and party organizational work. Like most such programs, it was a small "enthusiast" campaign until 1948; by June 1949, more than 1,400 factories throughout Poland (ninety factories in Łódź; 250 in Wrocław province) had sent teams.[85] These teams not only tended to the needs of the peasants (which the state was hard pressed to meet on its own) but served as vehicles of political consciousness and class brotherhood to unenlightened peasants. Workers should not just repair machines while peasants stand and watch, explained party ideologist Roman Zambrowski, but help peasants resolve political problems such as the fight with reactionaries.[86] Participant workers carried a class message: as possessors of political consciousness by virtue of their proletarian identity, they would lift the peasants up, passing on knowledge in the way the inteligencja usually did to workers.

In reality, however, participants were contemptuous of the peasantry and maintained their distance. The PZPR was hesitant to send any but the most trusted workers for just this reason. Even a worker new to the factory and the city selfishly guarded his or her class identity. Łódź workers, proud of their urban culture, particularly despised the village. In Wrocław, most workers came from villages but not from the villages to which they might be sent. In fact, most villages around Wrocław were filled with migrants from eastern Poland, who seemed to workers from central Poland the least cultured of their countrypeople. Reports from 1948–49 describe peasant hostility, brawls, and drunken riots; workers usually returned home drunk. Even worse from a political point of view, workers sometimes received payment for their work from richer peasants. Finally, work on a Sunday, while peasants were in church, only helped to accentuate class differences. As a result, this experiment in erasing class boundaries was short-lived, but the almost ritual clashes between worker and peasant became a motif of stalinist folklore.[87]

(1981): 51–154; Józef Śmiałowski, "Początki łódzkie Powszechnej Organizacji 'Służba Polsce,' " *Rocznik Łódzki* 30 (1981), 17–46; and AAN KC PZPR 295/V/6, kk. 124–35.

[85] WAP KW PPR 1/V/3, kk. 59–60; AAN KC PZPR 237/VII/117, k. 423. On early campaigns, see *Związek Walki Młodzieży: Materiały i dokumenty* (Warsaw, 1953), 317–21.

[86] AAN KC PZPR 295/V/34, kk. 1–3, AAN KC PZPR 237/VII/9, kk. 28–30.

[87] AAN KC PZPR 295/V/34, kk. 10–13; WAP KW PZPR 74/VI/33, passim; materials in

As factory labor became a public duty, new models of working-class leisure also reshaped the meaning of class. Indeed, the time a worker spent outside the factory was the logical place to re-create class as a nonconflictual—indeed, non-economic—identity grounded in propaganda rather than reality. One example of this process was the state-sponsored paid (and organized) vacation, or *wczasy,* for factory employees. The Employees' Vacation Fund, a council made up of representatives from the trade unions and the Ministry of Labor and Social Welfare, allotted partially subsidized spaces at state-owned vacation homes to factories and industries; workers and white-collar employees then applied for them.[88] Wczasy were one of the most significant benefits for the postwar working class; they were not the only example of attempts at interclass contact in this period, but were symbolically the most important.[89] This institution was taken for granted by the 1980s; its beginnings tell us much about the way in which the meanings of class began to change as Poland entered the stalinist era.

Before World War II, fewer than 60 percent of those workers who had the right to take time off (about 50 percent of the total) did so (as opposed to 90 percent of white-collar workers). Very few workers, however, traveled during their vacations, preferring to spend them at home. In 1939, no more than 1 or 2 percent of the blue-collar work force went on wczasy.[90] Workers were not opposed to time off, of course; in fact, vacations were a common demand in conflicts in Łódź in the summer of 1945.[91] Yet to the consternation of the authorities, workers generally did not take advantage of wczasy, even refusing to do so. While hundreds of thousands of factory employees took part (177,000 in 1946; 372,000 in 1948), workers in Wrocław made up only 30 percent of

---

AAN KC PZPR 237/VII/2630, 2631, 2638. See also Stanisław Baranowski, *Pamiętnik robotnika* (Łódź, 1974), 148, and Świda-Ziemba, "Robotnicy 1950," 231–32.

[88] Aleksandra Jacher-Tyszkowa, "Wczasy pracownicze w Polsce Ludowej w latach 1945–1950: Ich podstawy prawne i organizacyjne," in *Robotnicy na wczasach w pierwszych latach Polski Ludowej: Studia i materiały* (PAN, Oddział w Krakówie, *Prace Komisji Socjologicznej,* 1), ed. Danuta Dobrowolska (Wrocław, 1963), 73–81.

[89] A different kind of cultural initiative, garden plots (*działki*) for city residents, may have worked in a complementary way to dissolve contacts between workers. A former Pafawag worker recalled that workers had little contact with one another after work because "you went to your plot, you didn't see your friends, and you won't say anything." Interview, Pafawag, 8 February 1990.

[90] Edward Pietraszek, "Urlop wypoczynkowy robotnika w Polsce w okresie międzywojennym," in *Robotnicy na wczasach,* 50–52, 60–69.

[91] AAN MPiH 41, kk. 422–23; ŁAP KW PPR 1/XI/2, n.p.; ARZ KCZZ WO 41, k. 164.

those in health resorts (one form of wczasy) in 1946; in 1949, they were only 25 percent; of some 1,400 Łódź employees sent on wczasy in one month in 1948, only seventy-two were workers. Nationally, workers were 68 percent of all union members (a criterion for wczasy eligibility) but only 32 percent of vacationers in 1948 and 37 percent in 1950.[92] In 1949–50, a group of Kraków sociologists conducted surveys of vacationers in two resorts in the Tatra mountains in an effort to understand what role wczasy played in workers' perceptions of themselves and of others. Their study, among the last before sociology was banned during stalinism, is an invaluable window on a crucial moment in the transformation of social identities in Poland.

Adam Podgórecki, one of the sociologists involved in the study, suggested a number of reasons explaining why workers might not participate in wczasy. One was a difference in class resources: the technical inteligencja was quick to appreciate and take advantage of wczasy, had twice as much or more vacation time than did manual workers, and might be favored by those bureaucrats who allotted places. Workers, meanwhile, lacked experience with such institutions and travel; those whom Podgórecki considered insufficiently conscious politically could not yet value what they had won. They found it hard to believe that there would not be hidden costs or that there would be enough to eat; rumors of food shortages in vacation homes spread quickly. Many workers were less able to take advantage of wczasy because they were unable to afford transportation or the minimal costs of a vacation.[93] On the other hand, organizers claimed that even when wczasy were free, it was impossible to get blue-collar workers to sign up.[94] The reasons for lack of worker participation, Podgórecki realized, went much deeper—to the roots of class identity and working-class culture. These included the leisure habits of the working-class family, reluctance toward contact with

---

[92] WAP WRZZ 34, k. 125; Jacher-Tyszkowa, "Wczasy pracownicze," 81; AAN KC PPR 295/XI/50, k. 47; Helena Gnatowska, *Rola Polskiej Partii Robotniczej*, 286. On authorities' concern with the success of wczasy, see AAN MPiH 947, k. 95.

[93] Adam Podgórecki, "Pierwszy pobyt na wczasach," in *Robotnicy na wczasach*, 92–97. Those who went on *wczasy* often followed the lead of white-collar workers; as one metal worker remarked, "Look how the mental workers fight over *wczasy!* They know what is good" (94).

[94] ŁAP WRZZ 297, n.p. (February 1949); see also meeting at the Łódź power plant in January 1949 (ibid.) at which a *wczasy* organizer reported that "all last year I went to the boiler room and the machine shop, even threatened [workers], anything so that the working stiff [*robociarz*] would go."

strangers, and perceptions of class differences and hierarchy. Besides deterring workers, these factors influenced the way that workers who did participate interacted with other vacationers and how relations at vacation homes developed.

Unlike white-collar employees (the term used here is *pracownik umysłowy*, "mental worker," as opposed to *pracownik fizyczny*, "physical worker"), blue-collar workers preferred—and needed—to scatter their vacation time throughout the year, a few days at a time. This allowed them to recover from the aches and pains of physical labor and do work around the house. Some tended to their gardens or visited relatives in their home villages. As an older worker from Upper Silesia explained, "Last year I took myself to the village to drink a little vodka and a little clotted milk in good company, because it is never so good in the city as it is in the village. This year I wanted to go to see the family again, but the personalny said, 'We want to do good for you and you don't want to take advantage. Go to the mountains and that's it.' So I came."[95]

For women in particular, a two-week vacation was a luxury: one's time off was for general housecleaning, not for journeys to the mountains. Finally, time in the vacation homes initially did not include families. Especially for workers who put in a great deal of overtime, the vacation was the only time they could spend at home with their families. The two-week vacation was thus a burden on the working-class family.

Subjective class differences played the greatest role. Podgórecki calls them "resistance stemming from an inferiority complex, fear of a new environment, of new, uncertain situations." He quotes a young metal worker from Sosnowiec: "My father never went on vacation, nor sent the family, because he couldn't afford it. There was a bit of field around the house, so he had something to do. . . . After the war, he also didn't want to go, because he was ashamed; he wasn't used to such fancy trips [*pańskie rozjazdy*]."[96] People of another class were strangers; they could go on vacations before the war and knew what to do; they could in every sense afford to go. A young sales worker explained "My father, a foundry worker, never goes because he doesn't know how to eat with others. He doesn't have that breeding. Maybe he could go with my mother. *Wczasy* are good, but for the young people. Our miners and foundry workers go only to Szczyrk, Ustroń, or Wisła [towns in the

⁹⁵Podgórecki, "Pierwszy pobyt na wczasach," 94; see also 99–100.
⁹⁶Ibid., 94.

foothills of the Tatra mountains], no farther. They say that in Krynica [a well-known mountain resort] there is nothing but aristocracy. Everything there is expensive. [Workers] can't dance. They don't have the right clothes. Pyjamas cost money; one must have a suitcase."[97] Workers were being asked to participate in what seemed a distinctly bourgeois form of leisure and felt they would have to measure up to that standard. Older workers treated wczasy as a formal holiday for which one's best clothes were necessary. They were unfamiliar with vacation clothing such as shorts and often stayed at home for lack of a proper suit or dress. Many, particularly older workers, thought it would be best if wczasy for blue-collar workers were separate so that they would not be "inhibited by the presence of the inteligencja and get tongue-tied."[98]

Sharing their first impressions, many workers returned to the problem of cultural class differences. "I'm shy because I'm unlettered," admitted a Lower Silesian forty-five-year-old road worker: "I know, I have no talents. My parents didn't have money, they didn't send me to school. I'm the poorest one here, so poorly dressed. Sometimes it happens that I start talking to someone and they don't want to talk with me and get up and leave. There should be separate homes for blue-collar workers. Sometimes we're walking in a group talking about something, and I throw in a word and no one answers me. . . . That's why three of us stick together, and have gotten to like each other. . . . We are all workers and understand each other."[99]

A forty-four-year-old metal worker saw distinct differences in everyday behavior. Among more experienced white-collar employees, he said, "a worker sometimes doesn't know how to find himself. . . . He doesn't know how to use a fork or a knife, and here is a collection of different people. There might be an engineer, or a bureaucrat, and a person takes an example from these people. Why do they say that a worker doesn't have culture? Because he hasn't spent time with people who have something to give. Now I'm here, I see that this is a great gain for the worker. . . . We mustn't fall down, but lift ourselves up, millimeter by millimeter. A worker doesn't know how to sit on an easy chair. He just sits on the edge, while another, who's used to sitting in one, knows how to do it."[100]

Culture, these workers realized, was a key to class differences in com-

[97]Ibid., 95.
[98]Ibid., 97.
[99]Ibid., 97.
[100]Ibid., 103–4.

munist Poland: one class possessed culture, while others did not. As a
result, such workers seemed uncomfortable with the ideals of social mobility. These are not the voices of prewar worker activists familiar with
workers' clubs, or those of the workers who derided the people who sat
in palaces during the Battle over Trade and earlier (or those of high
stalinism when, presumably, the ability to sit correctly in an easy chair
would be evidence of a suspect background). They seem to have been
unable to accept the model promoted by the state in wczasy (and by the
sociologists) that, in a time of rising living standards, different social
groups should put aside class differences and learn to deal with one
another as individuals. They stayed in the company of other workers,
feeling rejected by other vacationers; for example, researchers noted that
unlike the inteligencja, workers preferred to share a room. They identified with the basic differences that they perceived between worker and
intellectual, thinking of a worker as fundamentally different from the
intellectual.

This does not mean they did not value their own worth. On the contrary, they accepted that, while in one set of values the gentleman might
be "better," their own way of life was just fine. An older miner is quoted
as complaining: "I don't like this elevation of the mental workers above
the physical workers. A physical worker is also an honest person, and
the fact that he has thick hands and doesn't know how to behave gen-
teelly and isn't dressed like a gentleman isn't always his fault."[101] But
these workers reorganized and accepted the concepts of class and of
classes in competition with one another. In virtually the same breath,
this miner affirmed the image of class equality that the wczasy and other
educational-cultural forms promoted and reasserted himself as a worker
in opposition to the "mental workers" despite his supposed inferiority.

The sociologists who interviewed these workers were looking for
something different. In an essentially functionalist view of society, they
saw conflict between classes disappearing as a result of modernization
and progress. As Kazimierz Dobrowolski, an eminent prewar sociologist,
wrote in his introduction to the study, "the strong differentiation of the
working class . . . , so characteristic of the interwar period, has at the
present moment undergone . . . basic transformations which proceed in
the direction of gradual equalization of contrasts." For these researchers,
"transformations" referred to technological and educational advances

---

[101]Barbara Bazińska and Danuta Dobrowolska, "Kształtowanie się społeczności wczasowej," in *Robotnicy na wczasach*, 117.

and the growth of "social organizations," all of which "reach the most hidden corners of the country."[102] Discussing the traditions and attitudes of older workers, the researchers referred to them as "class prejudices" characteristic not of the working class but of the past—words very much like those used by the PPR or state figures when critiquing strikes (see Chapter 1).[103] The sociologists saw older workers such as those quoted above as "isolated," unwilling and unable to bridge the gap between themselves and their fellow vacationers from the inteligencja.

Like labor competition, wczasy were a bet on the younger workers who, organizers hoped, might recognize and welcome the opportunity to experience the fruits of social advance. An eighteen-year-old iron roller remarked: "I feel different in relation to mental workers. Not so high as them. I would like to be their equal, and be like them."[104] This difference between the attitudes of older and younger generations was used to express ideas about progress, a generation of workers trapped by their capitalist upbringing and now-useless traditions of class conflict, and a new generation open to cooperation and advancement. Young workers, as the sociologists wrote, "represented a higher level of education, were more accomplished, comfortable in company, accustomed to contact with the inteligencja. On wczasy they felt sure of themselves; they didn't consider wczasy some charity, but an institution which workers deserved."[105] Older workers could also be convinced through contact with progressive white-collar workers (like the sociologists, who evidently hoped that they themselves could serve as models of approachable intellectuals) who would treat them as equals.[106]

Nevertheless, while barriers might be broken down and exceptions made in a vacation home of some one hundred tourists, both workers and inteligencja retained a sense of fundamental separation, and usually conflict, between classes. Away from the workplace, this conflict was reflected not so much in economic as in cultural relations.[107] "Here we

[102]Kazimierz Dobrowolski, "Uwagi o badaniach nad współczesną rzeczywistością społeczną," in *Robotnicy na wczasach*, 17, 10.

[103]Bazińska and Dobrowolska, "Kształtowanie się społeczności wczasowej," 114. This issue is treated at length by Maria Władyka, "Społeczne funkcje wczasów," in *Robotnicy na wczasach*, 174–80.

[104]Bazińska and Dobrowolska, "Kształtowanie się społeczności wczasowej," 114.

[105]Ibid., 122.

[106]See ibid., 119, where workers praise the sociologists for being different from others of their class; see also Władyka, "Społeczne funkcje wczasów," 166.

[107]Economic relations might also make their mark, as a PZPR member remarked at a

are [considered] inferior," complained a miner. "Supposedly we eat together at dinner, but we talk little with others. . . . What can one talk about with them? They play bridge, and we play *zechcyk* or *szkot* [Scotsman]. 'Bridge' is in English, and *zechcyk* and *szkot* in German, . . . and are the same in Polish. We are people just the same, just at different work, and taught differently."[108] Though the researchers noted frequent examples of workers and office employees who were getting to know one another, an overheard conversation between a miner and a woman office employee illustrated the gulf that prevented communication between them:

> Miner: Will you ladies be coming to our party?
> Woman mental worker: Of course not, there's no one to dance with!
> Miner: How so, since men are in the majority?
> Woman mental worker: That's not for us, we don't have company [*towarzystwo*] here.
> Miner: Oh, you ladies are princesses, and won't deign [to dance with] workers.[109]

"Despite everything," concluded a young machinist from Stalowa Wola, "I learned here the difference [between workers and inteligencja]. . . . I am alien to them. . . . I am from very deep Poland, so they preferred to stand off. . . . Sometimes it's a shame, but this is how it must be. Much water must flow before an educated physical worker will find common ground with an educated mental worker."[110]

That class boundaries were important to these workers is clear in the way they treated those whom they perceived to be between classes and not in their "rightful places." The researchers admitted: "We often encountered among workers the conviction that a truly educated person, 'a true *inteligent*,' is cultured and polite to all. Those who behave coarsely, who slight workers, who emphasize their superiority at every step, are [in workers' opinion] people with a low level of education, often mental workers since only recently, for whom contact with *intel-*

Zgierz union meeting in April 1949: "The comrade . . . said that oppression and exploitation exists in capitalist countries. What do we have here? Oppression and exploitation. . . . [I was] on *wczasy* in Zakopane, and there too *wczasy* employees were very much mistreated and exploited by the director." LAP WRZZ 69, n.p.

[108] Bazińska and Dobrowolska, "Kształtowanie się społeczności wczasowej," 116.
[109] Ibid.
[110] Ibid., 116–17.

igenty 'went to their heads.' . . . They were called 'half-inteligencja' 'shiny inteligencja,' or 'hungry inteligencja.' "[111]

How does this picture of society fit with that held by the PZPR and the state? Although wczasy were not truly a school for stalinism, they did promote what might be called the forced interaction of stalinism. If wczasy were part of a conscious attempt to break down class barriers, then what does workers' rejection of that attempt tell us about their perception of stalinist Poland? As a modern Poland in microcosm, wczasy also reflected the way in which workers, while asserting their equal worth as individuals, defended the importance of division by class. Their recognition of the unequal relationship between classes sometimes signified interest in upward mobility but also indicated their belief in the value of class conflict and separation. The generational distinction made by the sociologists does have some value; younger workers were certainly less inclined to worry about whether or not they could dance with young white-collar employees. But class as understood by workers, upwardly mobile or not, was not something from the past but continued to have real meaning, even in the Tatra mountains far from production.

As I have argued throughout this study, workers manifested class in their communities, their personal relationships, and their recreation. Thus, as the party attempted to remove class conflict from the public sphere, workers simply reenacted it in the private sphere or along the boundary between the two. This internalization of class has been interpreted by many scholars of communist societies as "atomization"; it would be more accurate to understand it as the beginnings of the interior resistance championed decades later by Eastern European intellectuals such as Adam Michnik.[112] Private assertion of class membership, meanwhile, simply resisted the evident disintegration of class boundaries from above and below in stalinist society, for the relative ease with which one could move upward out of the working class or into it from below destroyed the heart of class identity.

One effect of the disappearance of class from the public sphere was the renewed power of national identity. National symbols such as the Catholic church grew in importance.[113] As it became more concerned

[111]Ibid., 120. A cleaning woman at one vacation home made similar comments: workers and "real" *inteligencja* were always polite to the staff and kept their rooms clean, while "poor bureaucrats" acted above their station and treated staff rudely. Ibid., 129.

[112]See Gale Stokes, *The Walls Came Tumbling Down: The Collapse of Communism in Eastern Europe* (New York, 1993), 22.

[113]The events of late 1949, such as the increased presence of Soviet leaders in Polish

with private life and beliefs (particularly among party members, most of whom retained their religious beliefs throughout the communist era), the party perceived the church as becoming more aggressive. One hardly had to look farther than Pope Pius XII's 1949 encyclical on communism, which promised excommunication for those who joined the party, to see that the church had entered into battle with the party on the terrain of private life. Many Poles were faced for the first time with a choice between the two organizations, and some turned in their party cards.[114] Certainly, manifestations of religious belief increased in the worker community. Such manifestations did not express any social class or group identity; they remained instead at the purely individual level, leaving the organizing of society to the PZPR. "A person should begin work with God," explained a weaver, a PZPR and League of Women member from Łódź's PZPB no. 1 who wrote to *Przyjaciółka* in late 1949. She complained that workers were often being forced to work on Sundays and deplored the party's attacks on the church. "I also go to church . . . I have been in many churches and I've never heard that priests were against our government and democratic Poland."[115] Indeed, the church did not take an active social stance; it was both unwilling and unable to lend a public definition to social conflict and limited its political activity to official statements. Not until the 1970s did the church discover its social voice and reach out to workers as workers; even then, its growing role was rather a symptom of the disintegration of class. The church was a place for the individual and the nation but not for the worker as a member of a class.[116]

But even such private manifestations could seem threatening to the

---

political life, Stalin's seventieth birthday, the show trials taking place in other Eastern European countries, and the fall from power of the so-called nationalist wing of the party led by Gomułka, sparked outbursts of national sentiments. See, for example, AAN KC PZPR 237/VII/119, kk. 95, 318, and MSW MBP 17/IX/38, t. 4, n.p. (December 1949).

[114] Jerzy Poksiński, "Przeciw Kościołowi," *Karta* 9 (1992): 137–41. AAN KC PZPR 237/VII/1457, k. 138, 237/XV/1, kk. 39, 42–43; WAP KW PZPR 74/VII/72, n.p. Some Catholics felt that the church should keep to religion and not interfere with politics, according to the PPR Central Committee after investigating reaction in Łódź to a 1948 episcopal letter to youth: AAN KC PPR 295/IX/229, kk. 56–59. See similar observations on other episcopal letters in MSW MBP 17/IX/10, t. 3, kk. 88–89, 193, 230–32.

[115] AAN KC PZPR 237/VII/96, k. 174. On religious belief in Łódź, see also Świda-Ziemba, "Robotnicy 1950," 235.

[116] Some priests in Łódź sought permission even in 1949 to hold masses or erect altars in factories, but it is unclear whether they also sought to address worker concerns. See AAN KC PZPR 237/VII/89, k. 8.

state, as the PPR had shown in its reaction to the demonstration in the Wrocław garment factory (see Chapter 4). In June 1949, some twenty thousand people took part in the Corpus Christi procession around St. Joseph's Church across from Poznański.[117] Factory workers (some of them PZPR members) in Łódź and Wrocław collected money for workplace altars and pictures of the Virgin Mary, spoke out against official antichurch policies, sang religious songs during work, and even used factory equipment to manufacture devotional materials. Such practices may have been common for years, but now the PZPR watched them closely.[118] The climactic event was the "Lublin Miracle" of July 1949, in which an icon of the Virgin Mary in a Lublin church was seen to shed tears. Hundreds of thousands of people from all over Poland flocked to Lublin until sales of bus and train tickets to that city were forbidden. Never recognized by church authorities, the miracle became a folk symbol of opposition to the state's attack on beliefs, traditions, the nation, and the individual.[119]

The concepts of a working class and its culture nevertheless remained as central to state ideology as they did (privately) to worker identity. In 1949, the Ministry of Culture and Art commissioned a study by the Łódź ZMP of proletarian culture. The idea was to document the creation of a socialist proletariat and the effect of świetlicas and party culture on new workers. The ZMP selected a nineteen-year-old nonparty sociology student from Łódź University, Hanna Świda (later the prominent sociologist whose writings on stalinism have been cited previously), to interview workers and organize courses in three textile factories. What she found was not exactly what the ZMP expected. Forty years later, she recalled that period as one of transition: as the old working class retreated, new forms of class emerged to take its place. Świda saw not two but three groups in the Łódź factory: the old workers, who expressed the attitude that, while the government was not theirs, the nation

---

[117]The 1949 Corpus Christi processions—incidentally, the first without participation by state officials—were the largest in years. MSW MBP 17/IX/10, k. 193; AAN KC PZPR 237/VII/117, k. 382.

[118]MSW MBP 17/IX/10, k. 89; AAN KC PZPR 237/VII/116, k. 322; 117, k. 21; 118, kk. 352, 393–94. For other examples of official fears about the church's role in society, see MSW MBP 17/IX/38, t. 4, n.p. (April–August 1949), WUSW WUBP 2/37, kk. 3–4, WUSW KWMO 150/10, n.p. (January 1949), WAP WRZZ 3, k. 191, and AAN KC PZPR 237/XXVIII/20, k. 31.

[119]Grzegorz Sołtysiak, "Cud w Lublinie," *Karta* 9 (1992): 121–36. MSW MBP 17/IX/10, kk. 228–30; WAP KW PZPR 74/VII/72, n.p. (July 1949).

was, and thus one had to work honestly; and two groups of young workers to whom "everything was alien." The older workers took classes that Świda offered on mathematics (so as to understand their paychecks), technology, and literature; the older women "were very moved that [realist writers] wrote about them."[120]

Young workers did not come to such courses. Youth was divided by origin, but all seemed to Świda to be experiencing a crisis of isolation and identity. Those newly arrived in the factory from the village had ambitions of advancing. They lived in workers' hostels far from their families. Isolated from the surrounding society, they were also isolated from one another; because their main allegiance remained to the villages from whence they came, they formed no new community. These workers dominated in Wrocław and other cities (even Warsaw, for example, which, although an old labor community, became dominated by the peasant workers who arrived to rebuild the city in the 1950s). In Łódź, the clash of cultures was different. As before the war, the new workers were absorbed into the Łódź community. This time, however, that culture would not include open resistance to employers, and the physical power of neighborhoods would soon be diluted by the building of huge apartment blocks on the city's periphery. But stalinist society was never successfully rooted in Łódź.

The greatest difference between Łódź in 1949 and Łódź before the war could be seen in the new postwar generation of native Łódź workers. They were indifferent (*olewający*); with both their parents often working twelve-hour days, they, too, were isolated from their families. With work increasingly disciplined, their lives beyond work among friends became more important. Yet they retained a sense of pride, the pride of a native *Łodzianin*. They drank less than newly arrived workers did and sought to retain some semblance of urban style. In 1949–50, these groups of friends and colleagues began to form gangs. This was the origin of the bane of stalinism, hooliganism. There were city gangs and new-city gangs; in the coming years, their rivalry would grow increasingly violent.[121]

---

[120]Interview with Hanna Świda-Ziemba, Warsaw, 23 July 1990; also Świda-Ziemba and Katarzyna Madoń-Mitzner, "Notatki z życia systemu," (journal excerpts and interview), *Karta* 3 (1991): 37–39; and Świda-Ziemba, "Robotnicy 1950," 226–36.

[121]Świda-Ziemba interview; see also Władyka, "Społeczne funkcje wczasów," 153. Jacek Kuroń discusses the origins of hooliganism in his autobiography, *Wiara i wina* (London/Warsaw, 1989), 42–50. For examples of attacks on *przodownicy*, see MSW MBP 17/IX/38, t. 4, n.p. (November 1949); and MSW MBP 17/IX/18, t. 1, n.p. (May 1948).

One of their earliest targets were avant-gardist workers or conformists—but these were not indiscriminate attacks, for workers generally distinguished among the motives of avant-gardists. A worker who sought only to make money and thus caused a rise in norms and lowered pay for everyone else "became an object of aggression, boycott, and sometimes violent revenge (*dintojry*)." For example, "a worker who, for advance or a better position, stayed silent on the matter of raising required work hours—or even worse, who spoke in favor of it—when others protested became 'damaged goods' (*trefny*). One stopped talking with him, he was held in contempt, and could not count on vital help or support from his colleagues if he needed it. At the same time, the same behavior from a worker who for some reason was more threatened with repression than others was treated with understanding: after all, he 'had to.' "[122] As they had done right after the war with accusations of Nazi collaboration, some workers used the system against itself, attempting to convince authorities that spies and saboteurs like those being tried in other Eastern European countries were recruited from among avant-gardists and advancing workers.[123]

Entering the 1950s, stalinism had by no means won the factory. The working class had been driven into private identities yet still defended its community and its class identity. The increasing gap between old and young workers that observers such as Świda noted was, after all, precisely the opposite of what was intended. The class values of the older generation were of no use to the new workers; the class/urban pride retained by native workers was not based on work but on their lives outside the factories, where older workers had no influence at all. On the other hand, the interviews with wczasy participants revealed (and no doubt prompted) a thorough self-examination: workers tried to decide just what class meant, confronting their understanding of class with the definition in official use. We can also glimpse the changing shape of a moral community; as old values were discarded and new ones emerged, there were signs that this community would be as resistant to the regime as the old one was. The problem for the communists as they entered the

---

[122]Świda-Ziemba, "Stalinizm i społeczeństwo polskie," 58–59. Fear of reprisals kept victims from reporting to the police; for most, the need to earn money, whether for ambition, one's family, or just for vodka, remained stronger than fear of attacks. Świda-Ziemba interview.

[123]AAN KC PZPR 237/VII/119, k. 34.

age of high stalinism (1950–55) was that even a pervasive party culture and promise of advancement were not enough to discipline the Polish workers. The outlines of a new society were clear and the pieces in place by 1950; the content, however, would be created by both the stalinist regime and the workers themselves.

CONCLUSION

State, Society, and the
Stalinist Revolution

Postwar Polish history began with the creation of a Moscow-sponsored government. By late 1947, the communists had turned their attention to the control of society and by late 1949 were using language almost indistinguishable from the Soviet variety to denounce enemies of all kinds. The transition to stalinism was apparently complete. One might ask whether anything in Poland had really changed during those five years, apart from the fact that the regime was more repressive. Although the political system itself has remained in the background of this book, it should be clear that the Polish states of 1945 and 1950 were quite different, primarily in the sources of their legitimacy. The state that emerged from the war was a government of renewal and reconstruction, of national rebirth and new social empowerment. The state in the stalinist age, on the other hand, harbored great ambitions to recast society and worked to mobilize that society toward grand economic and political goals. The goal of my study of two working-class communities has been to point the way toward a rethinking of the communist experience in Eastern Europe by showing that this transformation—as well as its consequences—can not be understood apart from the social relations that the communist state inherited and those it created.

The term *revolution*, as used to describe the events of 1945 and 1948–50 in Poland requires some clarification. Usually the term denotes a revolution from above or from abroad. Such interpretations have given society itself far too little credit. To say that workers shaped the revolutions of 1945 and 1948–50 does not in some way blame stalinism on society, but it does restore their agency. Workers were not helpless victims of an omnipotent state and a diabolical ideology but resourceful shapers of their own destiny, able to turn a system to their own advantage and lessen its cruelest aspects.

What does it mean to call a state "stalinist"? The classic definition of communist regimes (now generally out of favor) is totalitarian, defined forty years ago by Carl Friedrich and Zbigniew Brzezinski.[1] It does not, however, illuminate the communist experience very well. Whether or not the state's leaders wished to control every aspect of society, including the means of social organization and identity, is important. But whether or not the state actually tried to penetrate society on its *own* terms or in relation to social pressures and how its efforts were received by society seem to be more essential issues. The course of worker-state relations in Poland between 1945 and 1950 raises doubts about the state's ability to dictate the terms of that relationship and thus questions the usefulness of the totalitarian model. To the extent that the state was corporatist, workers were able to play off the parts of the body (party, union, management, etc.) against one another.

The totalitarian model reduces ideology to a form of control, ignoring the ways in which party rhetoric aimed to mobilize society by using nationalist slogans or promises of material benefits to win supporters. It also implies a well-defined goal toward which society is controlled. It thus cannot be used to describe a regime in which goals (and the means to achieve them) changed frequently under pressure from society itself. For example, Polish communist intentions toward industrial workers were obviously different in 1945, 1947, and 1949. In the first period, workers were imagined as revolutionary allies who were rebuilding industry and conquering the frontier. Two years later, they seemed a recalcitrant, hostile group to be tamed by communist mobilization. By 1949, they were once again a resource of tradition to be harnessed this time for the stabilization and expansion of industry.

My discussion of a somewhat outdated concept is necessary because most of its parameters are also part of standard definitions of stalinism, used here to describe the system that took shape in Poland toward the end of the 1940s. The term *stalinism* is more historically specific than *state socialism* and more descriptive than *authoritarian* or *communist*.[2]

---

[1] For a review of this concept, see Adam Westoby, "Conceptions of Communist States," in *States and Societies*, ed. David Held et al. (New York, 1983), 227–30.

[2] Essential formulations of the stalinist model are presented in *Stalinism: Essays in Historical Interpretation*, ed. Robert Tucker (New York, 1977).

It can, however, imply foregone conclusions and the existence of a master plan in the mind of its namesake. Regardless of the existence of the latter, this interpretation obscures any social agency in Poland, indeed renders study of society a bit superfluous to mere explication of Stalin's master plan. Stalinism was more than just a nasty dictatorship, as the reductive use of the term often seems to imply; it must be redefined so that it becomes a truly useful analytical category. Stalinism was, in fact, an authoritarian system whose practitioners aimed to bring about an economic and political revolution through the transformation of society and the creation of new social forms.

The Polish communists were constructing a system with twin goals, economic and social-ideological. The first—creation of a modern industrial nation—required, in the stalinist view, attention to the second, a mobilized and integrated society. This vision of a participatory yet conflict-free society, not the personality of the dictator or the severity of the repression, qualifies a state as stalinist and differentiates it from the preceding and following periods in the history of that communist state. The regime of discipline and repression that the communists used to achieve their ends was, of course, an essential component of stalinism but not its *most* central. Still, this last component rendered stalinism complete. Although rapid economic progress was implicit in Polish political discourse even before the end of the war, and social transformation began in mid-1947 with the first large competitions, repression did not emerge as a society-wide phenomenon—in the factory and private life—until 1949.

The concept of the "new man" is a useful way to characterize how those governments sought to mobilize society toward certain ideological and economic goals, to interpret the expansion of culture and education, and to explain the millenarianism that some supporters and opponents have seen to be inherent in communism. Poland did not lack the imagery of remade humanity. The posters of shining, bold youth, the mass calisthenics, the socialist realism—all could as easily be found in Poland as elsewhere, even if they are somewhat less omnipresent. Yet stalinism had only five or six years in Poland, much less than it had in its mother country.

The mobilization and integration of society should be understood as not only efforts to remake society according to a particular ideological plan but a means to secure a kind of legitimacy. The state's leaders were after all politicians as well and needed (or at least desired) a semblance of support from their constituents in order to govern. Communist states seek to base their legitimacy on popularity (rather than on legality, for example); their putative revolutionary origins and transformative ideology require their leaders to invoke or elicit real or staged popular support for the development of a political and economic system. Although such support may not have actually come from various groups in society, its genuineness was not necessary. Legitimacy's requirements are minimal: some kind of acceptance of the system and the benefits it offers, and resignation from conflict as a means to political change. This search for legitimacy is crucial to understanding the communist era in Poland.[3] Because the efficacy of terror was limited in the Polish case, a rapprochement with the working class was especially essential. Short of mass labor camps (which were only marginal in Poland), repression alone could not raise productivity, at least not to the levels required for the ambitious industrialization and modernization that were part of the stalinist project. Prosperity, class integration, and (later) appeals to tradition were the tools of communist power in the early stalinist era.

If this is what stalinism is about, then comparison not only with other putatively totalitarian states but also with noncommunist states should help to illuminate the experience of communism in Poland. What, for example, might comparison with the populist dictatorships of mid-twentieth-century Latin America tell us? Like early postwar Poland, these countries were relatively undeveloped economically and mostly agricultural. Approaching such a comparison through political history exposes us to the danger of equating states with very different ideologies; if we recall that stalinism is also a social system, some valuable questions suggest themselves. Like the Polish communists, for example, regimes such as Vargas's Brazil or Peron's Argentina appealed to workers as a source of support for radical transformation. How did the language of those appeals differ, and does that difference tell us anything about each state's dependence upon workers' (apparent) support? In all these cases (Allende's Chile also comes to mind) workers became dissatisfied with the gap between promise and reality. How did the scope and methods of protest vary, and what were workers' limitations and strengths? Each state (in the case of Chile, after the Pinochet coup) eventually attempted to repress worker unrest and achieve rapid economic growth on workers'

[3]Seweryn Bialer, "The Question of Legitimacy," in *States and Societies*, 418–30; Paul Lewis, "Legitimacy and the Polish Communist State," ibid., 431–56.

backs. Were the intentions of the leaders the same (as a crude political comparison would suggest), or did different ideologies produce different responses to social conflict?[4]

In the European context, the efforts of the Polish communists and the obstacles they encountered seem remarkably familiar. The Nazi regime also found that industrial workers' traditions and communities posed a significant impediment to the attempt to remake society. The failure of the dictatorship in Franco's Spain has also been traced in part to its failure to control workers, and thus to the power of working-class communities. Closer to home, the Soviet Union depended upon the mobilization of a new generation of workers to eclipse the old; at the same time, the economics of the planned economy and labor competition gave workers unexpected autonomy. These comparisons suggest that workers may have unexpected power (perhaps unavailable to them in democracies) in ostensibly progressive authoritarian regimes.[5] Placing the Eastern European example in a wider context makes it possible to think more broadly about worker-state relations.

Where does this leave the Polish working class? That the working class occupied a special place in communism is, of course, beyond question; indeed, that honored position fostered a stronger class consciousness among workers. As in the other cases just cited, what is remarkable is the extent to which that special relationship was a product not only of ideology but workers' actions. The first part of this book established the ability and willingness of the Polish workers to resist the state's encroachment in a variety of ways. To end the story there would have been to portray this resistance as the valiant last gasps of a citizenry suffocated by a monolithic state. By reexamining their response to the state's efforts to impose its system, however, we can see these moments as part of a very different chain of events crucial to the success and the

---

[4]See Charles Bergquist, *Labor in Latin America: Comparative Essays on Chile, Argentina, Venezuela, and Colombia* (Stanford, 1986); Youssef Cohen, *The Manipulation of Consent: The State and Working-Class Consciousness in Brazil* (Pittsburgh, 1989); Daniel James, *Resistance and Integration: Peronism and the Argentine Working Class, 1946–1976* (Cambridge, U.K., 1988); Peter Winn, *Weavers of Revolution: The Yarur Workers and Chile's Road to Socialism* (Oxford, 1986).

[5]Tim Mason, "The Workers' Opposition in Nazi Germany," *History Workshop Journal* 11 (1981): 120–37; Geoff Eley, "History with the Politics Left Out—Again?" *Russian Review* 45, no. 4 (1986): 385–94; Sebastian Balfour, *Dictatorship, Workers, and the City: Labour in Greater Barcelona since 1939* (Oxford, 1989). On the Soviet Union, see the works cited in the introduction, note 11.

ultimate downfall of communism in Poland; they place the working class at the center of the story.

In her essay on stalinist society quoted in Chapter 6, Hanna Świda-Ziemba notes a paradox that helps to explain workers' behavior and that of the state in early stalinism:

> I was struck by [workers'] freedom of expression, their aggressive attitudes toward their superiors and the system of the time—revealed sometimes very forcefully at public meetings. . . . This was not a question of personal bravery in that community, but the result of the ruling ideology and . . . the social policy of the stalinist system.
>
> In accordance with the ideology's canons, the opinions of workers, who were pure class-wise, could not constitute a threat to the system. Everything which they said was treated as an indicator of a "lack of consciousness." . . .
>
> In accordance with this policy, the function of the working class was quite different from that of the *inteligencja*. To the latter belonged the construction and realization of a verbal reality, through slogans and postulates. The system of force, control, and repression was therefore directed toward that sphere of behavior. The duty of the workers, on the other hand, was essentially work. . . . They were to be *exclusively* a "work force." Therefore, force and repression toward workers encompassed *just that sphere of activity,* and not their speech. Views and opinions could be expressed without punishment, while the slightest evidence of real refusal to work could be dealt with under all sorts of regulations.[6]

This thesis can be expanded in several ways. First, the labor conflicts that continue through at least 1948, and the inability of the Ministry of Public Security to deal with them, suggest that workers were also not held responsible—were "forgiven"—for strikes. Workers have always occupied an ambiguous role in state communist ideology. A 1953 review of the judicial system, noting with satisfaction that the courts had "grad-

---

[6]Hanna Świda-Ziemba, "Stalinizm i społeczeństwo polskie," in *Stalinizm*, ed. Jacek Kurczewski (Warsaw, 1989), 49–50. In "Robotnicy 1950," (*Mechanizmy zniewalania społeczeństwa—refleksje u schyłku formacji* [Warsaw, 1990], 232), Świda-Ziemba observes that even worker-communists were different from people of other classes in the party; their pronouncements lacked the "fire in the eyes" that the others had at the time. She concludes that, while the party sought out worker members, it did not demand of them enthusiastic ideological declarations. It may also have been the case that the authorities treated workers' speech more leniently than that of peasants. The Łódź UB commented that rumors were generally less active, and less dangerous, in the city compared to the countryside. MSW MBP 17/IX/10, t. 2, k. 150.

ually realized . . . that the reason for [conflicts with management] was not the antagonistic opposition of the two sides' interests," captured the ideological gymnastics the state performed to reconcile its proletarian and productive natures.[7] A cursory glance at the strikes of the later communist period suggests that labor conflict remained unofficially a necessary component of state-society relations. Strikes were the only way for workers to make their demands known, and were tacitly acknowledged by the regime as being so.[8]

Second, immunity was a legacy of the workers' ability to express their version of the revolution in the workers' control movement and in the strikes that followed its demise. The old system of class relations and traditions did not disappear into the past without a fight. Workers had learned to keep quiet and restrict the defense of their idea of class boundaries and content to the private, individual level; but, as Świda-Ziemba's comments illustrate, they also succeeded in expanding that private space to include the shop floor. Workers' power to resist and accommodate was profoundly important in shaping the system of compromise and tactical repression in postwar Poland.

Świda-Ziemba's thesis can be modified in one other way—to point out the disastrous consequences for the regime of making such distinctions between workers and the inteligencja. To lessen the impact of worker resistance and recognize the special role that workers played, the state deployed the weapons of labor competition and social advance to win workers to its side. Materialist appeals to workers continued throughout the stalinist era (1949–56).[9] But these tactics could only wound the authorities in the long run; if the workers' relationship to the state was based on sizable rewards, any attempt to lessen those rewards jeopardized the relationship. The potential for corruption and the institutionalization of worker benefits in labor competition contributed to the unrest and revolution of the 1970s and 1980s; in the shorter term,

[7] AAN MS 1510, k. 48.

[8] This does not mean that the regime did not respond violently to strikes, as it certainly did, but that its leaders seemed to recognize that strikes were an inevitable part of the negotiation process. On state-worker relations in the 1970s, see Roman Laba, *The Roots of Solidarity: A Political Sociology of Poland's Working-Class Democratization* (Princeton, 1991); and Michael Bernhard, *The Origins of Democratization in Poland: Workers, Intellectuals, and Oppositional Politics, 1976–1980* (New York, 1993).

[9] Salomea Kowalewska, "Wzór osobowy i pożądane postawy pracowników w przemyśle," in *Przemysł i społeczeństwo w Polsce Ludowej*, ed. Jan Szczepański (Wrocław, 1969), 223–24.

they may have dampened the effectiveness of stalinist repression.[10] Perhaps, too, the state could have retreated to a less working-class–based description of itself—for example, toward identification with the technical inteligencja—had not workers so vigorously asserted their community and its traditions.

Worker resistance of 1945–50 did not only profoundly affect the communist state; it also influenced future dissent in Poland. The strikes of 1946–47 were still relatively fresh when the uprising of June 1956 began in the Cegielski factory in Poznań; the leaders of that strike were mostly of the same generation as the women of Łódź. The struggles of the 1970s and 1980s were of a later generation, but they bore the marks of their predecessors. Like the earlier protests, they evoked a moral economy, opposing the state through shared ideas of justice and class identity. Workers' control remained a key issue in 1956, 1980-81, and 1989.[11] They continued to use nationalistic rhetoric, both to express solidarity and to label their opponents. Not surprisingly, Łódź continued to play an important role in labor unrest. A strike in February 1971, begun once again in the Poznański mill (renamed Marchlewski), forced the government to rescind price hikes even after it had refused to back down in the face of violent outbursts by workers on the Baltic coast. Some of the leaders of that strike showed knowledge of protest methods and strike tactics. Ten years later a dramatic hunger march through the streets of Łódź in July 1981 intensified the conflict between Solidarity and the government, eventually forcing the latter to make promises of economic improvement it could not hope to fulfill.[12] Wrocław, too, became an important center of conflict, especially in 1980–81. The sons and daughters of the first migrants had nowhere else to go and were as likely to strike as workers in other cities. It does seem, however, that Solidarity was more radical in Wrocław than in cities of longer labor traditions; young, yet perhaps inheriting something of the pioneer spirit,

[10]This relationship has been explored in the East German case by Jeffrey Kopstein, "Ulbricht Embattled: The Quest for Socialist Modernity in the Light of New Sources," *Europe-Asia Studies* 46, no. 4 (1994): 597–615. See Chapter 5, note 119.

[11]See Andrzej Tymowski, "The Unwanted Revolution: From Moral Economy to Liberal Society in Poland" (diss., Yale University, 1995).

[12]Stefania Dzięcielska-Machnikowska and Grzegorz Matuszak, "Łódź między grudniem 1970 roku a lutym 1971 roku," *Rocznik Łódzki* 33 (1985), 227–262; Stefania Dzięcielska-Machnikowska and Grzegorz Matuszak, *Czternaście łódzkich miesięcy: Studia socjologiczne, sierpień 1980–wrzesień 1981* (Łódź, 1984). Memoirs of the strike of 1971 are on microfilm in uncatalogued materials, Slavic Department, Harvard University Library.

these workers often tested the limits of that revolution. During the Solidarity era, Wrocław had the reputation of being the last to strike but the most ferocious: the key to nationwide success.[13]

Thus were the seeds of communism's downfall sown in the years 1945–50. Even stalinism's successes were not all of its own making. One must question to what extent the "new man," stalinist or otherwise, was truly the product of the communist state. The Polish communists did not invent the masses of young peasants who flocked to the cities or the young workers who entered the universities, each with his or her own values (or antivalues) in addition to what the party hoped to instill. Chapter 3 referred to the workers of Wrocław as a blank slate; as subsequent chapters showed, that characterization was too simple: the PPR was unable to inscribe what it liked on that slate. Peasant workers proved dangerous material on which to build a revolution. Although perhaps inclined toward radicalism in a more malleable way than were the militant established factory workers, they could as easily destroy the system they helped to build. The course of Polish history since 1956, in which the same workers, peasants and intellectuals who once participated in various stalinist forms as the representatives of the new society came to oppose that system (or rather its even less oppressive successors), should be sufficient proof of the power unleashed by mass urbanization.

The era's social hallmarks—labor competition, social advancement, mass education, organized leisure—enhanced many lives; they were the backbone of the "little stabilization" under Gomułka in the early 1960s. Meanwhile, the intended social effects of these programs (to weaken the collective of the working class and create a society of cooperative, fluid classes in which class prejudices and conflictual class identity were a thing of the past and workers would subscribe to a new collective order created by the PZPR) were at best inconclusive. Workers, whether they retreated into private identities or repudiated everything connected with the system, resisted the intrusion of the state into their lives.

The state's apparent victory was thus subtly altered by the ways in which workers resisted or accommodated to change. Working-class mobilization and integration were clearly double-edged weapons. Even as workers were drawn into participation in organizations and campaigns

---

[13]The leader of Wrocław's Solidarity, Władysław Frasyniuk, was a twenty-six-year-old bus driver in 1980. See Włodzimierz Suleja (Stanisław Stefański), *Solidarność na Dolnym Śląsku* (Warsaw, 1986). Thanks also to Krystyna Ziółkowska.

and into contact with other classes, they did so on their own terms, turning these same mass institutions—organizations such as the party or the unions or events such as May Day parades—into battlegrounds themselves. The workers would eventually develop a mass organization of their own (Solidarity), and the church became an important mobilizing force. Meanwhile, the incentives for mobilization, such as increased prosperity, gave the workers aspirations and resources unavailable to them before. As for integration, contact with the technical inteligencja would bear fruit in a powerful alliance in 1980–81.[14]

The years 1949–50 were the beginning of the stalinist transformation of Poland. The old world was still passing, the new not yet established. Indeed, it would never be established; only six years later, workers' control was temporarily reestablished, private trade revived slightly, and the shackles taken off the private peasant and the intellectual. A search for a fully fledged, Soviet-type, stalinist society in Poland must be in vain. The intent of this book has been, however, to look over the divide that separates prestalinist Poland from that new era and to examine the foundations of the coming system.

The period 1945–49 was one of negotiation: social resistance, pressure, and accommodation versus the state's search for legitimacy and control. The workers' control movement of 1945; the battles over aprowizacja and wages; the multimachine movement and the great control strikes; lack of discipline, theft, and labor turnover; the Battle over Trade; the war scares and the growing indifference to organizations and politics; labor competition; education and advancement; the construction of social models; initiatives such as working-class leisure—all can be understood as events around which such negotiation took place and part of the process of negotiation itself. Each action by the state addressed social needs or pressures in some way; each action by the workers either affected the way the state carried out its plans or contributed to the state's search for expression of popular legitimacy. What I have described here are the foundations of a sociopolitical system far more complex than a more limited view of Eastern European communism can show. Stalinism in Poland was not a system popularly acclaimed but was nevertheless a product of both ideology and society, profoundly affected by the very forces it would control. The same society that sta-

---

[14]See Michael Kennedy, *Professionals, Power, and Solidarity in Poland: A Critical Sociology of a Soviet-Type Society* (Cambridge, U.K., 1991).

linism enlisted on its behalf during Poland's industrialization would rebel when it was once again possible and necessary in 1956 and after, and workers would reassert their solidarity and identity as a class and as a community.

Sources

The archives of communist-era Poland began to open in 1989, when research for this book began. While such archives have been used for years to produce some important works on economic and political history (many of which have been cited in this book), they also contain a wealth of material for the social historian. The Archiwum Akt Nowych in Warsaw includes the files of state ministries and other bureaucracies and (since 1990) the archives of the communist and socialist parties as well. The provincial state archives also contain the files of regional trade union offices, which at the national level are housed in a separate archive, the Archiwum Ruchu Zawodowego. Important documents in these archives range from minutes of local party or union meetings, to letters to the editor of the women's magazine *Przyjaciółka*, to regular reports by factory management and party officials, to confidential reports on strikes or assessments of workers' moods. In all these archives, the materials are well organized and remarkably comprehensive. Some documents were still just coming to light in 1993, and more are undoubtedly still to come.

The archives of the Ministry of Internal Affairs presented special difficulties: in the spring of 1990, a rather hostile interrogation was still the norm for the applicant researcher, and access was very limited. No access at all was permitted in Łódź, and promising documents in Wrocław had a way of disappearing from day to day. In Warsaw at least, the situation improved greatly in 1993. Nevertheless, many materials are still unavailable, including files on cases pursued by the security police; in the state archives, "cadre files" containing the records of individual party members are still off-limits.

Personnel files from four factories supplied valuable data used in the figures in Chapter 3. The exhaustive data in Wrocław were collected by Jędrzej Chumiński; the brief time available to me in Łódź made it possible to collect a representative sample only. Interviews conducted in each city with workers from the period were another source. These interviews were not intended to be representative in any way; moreover, interview subjects did not (and were not expected to) provide any insight on the politics of the postwar era. Instead, they offered a look at the lived experience of the time in ways not recorded in any archive. Finally, a number of published and unpublished memoirs supplemented these perspectives.

Because of the lack of social history of communist Poland, I used most secondary sources only obliquely. The following bibliography thus contains primary sources only, including several key secondary works that contained large amounts of valuable primary data.

Archives

(Abbreviations used in the notes are given after each archive. Other abbreviations: k./kk. [kartka/kartki]: leaf/leaves [in archive folder]; t./tt. [tom/ tomy]: volume/volumes.)

Archiwum Akt Nowych, Warsaw (AAN)—New Documents Archive
  Ministerstwo Przemysłu i Handlu (MPiH)—Ministry of Industry and Commerce
  Ministerstwo Pracy i Opieki Społecznej (MPiOS)—Ministry of Labor and Social Welfare
  Ministerstwo Informacji i Propagandy (MIiP)—Ministry of Information and Propaganda
  Ministerstwo Sprawiedliwości (MS)—Ministry of Justice
  Komisja Specjalna (KS)—Special Commission for the Struggle against Abuses and Economic Sabotage
  Komitet Centralny Polskiej Partii Robotniczej (KC PPR)—Central Committee of the Polish Workers' Party
  Centralny Komitet Wykonawczy Polskiej Partii Socjalistycznej (CKW PPS)—Central Executive Committee of the Polish Socialist Party
  Komitet Centralny Polskiej Zjednoczonej Partii Robotniczej (KC PZPR)—Central Committee of the Polish United Workers' Party
  Miscellaneous other materials
Wojewódzkie Archiwum Państwowe, Wrocław (WAP)—State Provincial Archive in Wrocław

Wojewódzka Rada Zwiazków Zawodowych (WRZZ)—Provincial Trade
Union Council
Miscellaneous trade union archives
Pafawag
Komitet Dzielnicowy/Komitet Miejski/Komitet Wojewódzki PPR/PZPR (KD/
KM/KW)—District Committee/City Committee/Provincial Committee of
the PPR/PZPR
Dzielnicowy Komitet/Wojewódzki Komitet PPS (DK/WK)—District Commit-
tee/Provincial Committee of the PPS
Miscellaneous other materials
Wojewódzkie Archiwum Państwowe, Łódź (ŁAP)—State Provincial Archive in
Łódź
WRZZ
Wojewódzki Urzad Informacji i Propagandy (WUIiP)—Provincial Bureau of
Information and Propaganda
Centralny Zarzad Przemysłu Włókienniczego (CZPW)—Textile Industry Cen-
tral Administration
Dyrekcja Przemysłu Bawełnianego (DPB)—Cotton Industry Administration
Local bodies of PPR (there were two province-level PPR organizations: Ko-
mitet Łódzki [KŁ]—Łódź Committee, and the KW), PPS, PZPR
Miscellaneous other materials
Archiwum Ruchu Zawodowego, Warsaw (ARZ)—Archive of the Trade Union
Movement
Komisja Centralna Zwiazków Zawodowych (KCZZ)—Central Trade Union
Commission; and Centralna Rada Zwiazków Zawodowych (CRZZ)—
Central Trade Union Council
Wydział Ekonomiczny (WE)—Economic Section
Wydział Organizacyjny (WO)—Organizational Section
Biblioteka Historii Ruchu Zawodowego, Warsaw (CRZZ)
Memoir collection
Trade union newspapers: *Trybuna związkowca, Drogowiec, Życie
włókiennicze*
Factory Personnel Archives
Poltex Conglomerated Textile Works (formerly Poznański), Łódź: data on 608
workers (estimated 5 percent of total employed in 1945–49)
Strzelczyk Machine Tool Factory (formerly John), Łódź: 201 workers (esti-
mated 5 percent of total)
Garment Complex, Wrocław: 1,354 workers (estimated 50 percent of total)
State Hydrometer Factory, Wrocław: 2,139 workers (estimated 80 percent of
total)
Centralne Archiwum Ministerstwa Spraw Wewnętrznych (MSW), Warsaw—
Central Archive of the Ministry of Internal Affairs
Ministerstwo Bezpieczeństwa Publicznego (MBP)—Ministry of Public Security
Opposition materials: Polish Peasants' Party (PSL), Labor Party (SP), miscel-
laneous underground organizations

Archiwum, Wojewódzki Urząd Spraw Wewnętrznych (WUSW), Wrocław—Provincial Bureau of Internal Affairs
    Wojewódzki Urząd Bezpieczeństwa Publicznego (WUBP)—Provincial Bureau of Public Security
    Komenda Wojewódzka Milicji Obywatelskiej (KWMO)—Provincial Citizens' Militia Command
    Katedra Etnografii, Uniwersytet Łódzki—Faculty of Ethnography, Łódź University
    Interview transcripts
    Master's theses

Interviews

Łódź

Group interview, five men, Strzelczyk (John) metal factory, 18 January 1990.
Group interview, three women, Harman (Biederman / PZPB no. 8) mill, 27 February 1990.
Wacław A., worker at Poznański mill, born 1931, interviewed 8 May 1990.
Stanisław and Filomena S., knitwear workers (Schweikert hosiery factory), 9 May 1990.
Zdzisława G., thread/cotton worker, born 1932, interviewed 10 May 1990.

Wrocław

Group interview, four men, Pafawag factory, interviewed 8–9 February, 1990.
Stefania K., worker at Pafawag, born 1918, interviewed 4 June 1990.
Tadeusz S., worker at Pafawag, born c. 1925, interviewed 15 July 1990.
Stanisława J., garment worker, born 1928, interviewed 18 July 1990.

Selected Published Primary Sources

Archiwum Ruchu Robotniczego [ARR]. Vols. 7, 9, 10, 11. Warsaw, 1982, 1984, 1986, 1988.
Baranowski, Stanisław. *Pamiętnik robotnika.* Łódź, 1974.
Biuletyny Informacyjne Ministerstwa Bezpieczeństwa Publicznego, 1947. Vol. 1. *Źródła do historii Polski XX wieku—ze zbiorów Centralnego Archiwum Ministerstwa Spraw Wewnętrznych.* Series C. Warsaw, 1993.
Chumiński, Jędrzej. "Kształtowanie się środowiska robotników przemysłowych Wrocławia w latach 1945–1949." Diss., Akademia Ekonomiczna we Wrocławiu, 1992.

Dobrowolska, Danuta, ed. *Robotnicy na wczasach w pierwszych latach Polski Ludowej: Studia i materiały.* PAN, Oddział w Krakowie, *Prace Komisji Socjologicznej,* 1. Wrocław, 1963.

"Dokumenty PPR i PPS dotyczace działalności zwiazków zawodowych." *Kwartalnik historii ruchu zawodowego [KHRZ]* nos. 2/3 (1964): 191–212.

Głos Widzewa. 1946–48.

Gmitrzykowski, Włodzimierz. *Za przykładem Matrosowa.* Biblioteczka przodownika pracy (BPP) 6. Warsaw, 1949.

Gościmińska, Wanda. *Mój wielki dzień.* BPP 16. Warsaw, 1949.

Gudziński, Eugeniusz, ed. "Zwiazki zawodowe wobec problemu aktywizacji produkcyjnej załóg robotniczych (1945–1948)." *KHRZ,* no. 4 (1981).

Janta, Aleksander. *Wracam z Polski.* Paris, 1948.

Jarosz, Dariusz, and Tadeusz Wolsza. *Komisja Specjalna do Walki z Nadużyciami i Szkodnictwem Gospodarczym (1945–1954). Wybór dokumentów.* Warsaw, 1995.

Jędruszczak, Hanna, ed. *Upaństwowienie i odbudowa przemysłu w Polsce (1944–1948): Materiały źródłowe.* 2 vols. Warsaw, 1967–69.

Kalinowski, Stefan. "Z działalności Komisji Specjalnej do Walki z Nadużyciami i Szkodnictwem Gospodarczym (1946–1947)." *KHRZ,* no. 2 (1976): 47-57.

Kania, W. "Pamiętnik z lat 1945–1948." *Sobótka* 7 (1952).

Kaniewski, Jan. *Było to na Pa-Fa-Wagu.* BPP 15. Warsaw, 1949.

Koźniewski, Kazimierz. *Most: Wybór reportaży.* Warsaw, 1951.

———. *Żywioły: Rzecz o ziemiach zachodnich Rzeczypospolitej.* Poznań, 1948.

Kozub-Ciembronowicz, Wiesław, and Jacek M. Majchrowski, eds. *Najnowsza historia polityczna Polski: Wybór źródeł. Część 5: 1949–1956.* Kraków, 1993.

Krawczyk, Andrzej. *Pierwsza próba indoktrynacji: Działalność Ministerstwa Informacji i Propagandy w latach 1944–1947.* Instytut Studiów Politycznych Polskiej Akademii Nauk. *Dokumenty do dziejów PRL.* Zeszyt 7. Warsaw, 1994.

Krupa, Julian, ed. "Udział Związków Zawodowych w walce ze spekulacją i procesie normowania sytuacji rynkowej w latach 1944–1948." *KHRZ,* no. 2 (1977): 40–56.

Kształtowanie się podstaw programowych Polskiej Partii Robotniczej w latach 1942–1945 (wybór materiałów i dokumentów). Warsaw, 1958.

Lipińska, Halina. *Mój awans.* Warsaw, 1950.

Łykowski, Mieczysław. *Ja tylko usprawniałem.* BPP 5. Warsaw, 1949.

"Materiały na 40-lecie Młodzieżowego Wyścigu Pracy." *Łódzkie Zeszyty Historyczne (Ruch młodzieżowy—tradycje i współczesność)* 1, no. 5 (1985).

Mroczkowski, Władysław, and Tadeusz Sierocki, eds. "Protokóły posiedzeń Rady Gospodarczej PPS (1945–1946)." *Z Pola Walki,* nos. 1/2 (1982): 227–62.

Nieuważny, Andrzej, ed. "Pierwsze dokumenty normujace podstawy prawne tworzenia i działalności zwiazków zawodowych w początkach Polski Ludowej." *KHRZ,* no. 4 (1986).

Paczkowski, Andrzej, ed. *Aparat bezpieczeństwa w latach 1944–1956: Taktyka, strategia, metody. Część 1: Lata 1945–1947.* Instytut Studiów Politycznych Polskiej Akademii Nauk. *Dokumenty do dziejów PRL.* Zeszyt 5. Warsaw, 1994.

Pafawag. 1946–47.

Pamiętniki robotników z czasów okupacji. Vol. 1. Warsaw, 1949.

Partia w cyfrach 1944–1948. Warsaw, 1948.

Polonsky, Antony, and Boleslaw Drukier, eds. *The Beginnings of Communist Rule in Poland.* London, 1980.

Rocznik statystyczny (RS). Warsaw, 1947–49.

Rocznik statystyczny miasta Łodzi, 1945–1947. Łódź, 1949.

Świda-Ziemba, Hanna. "Robotnicy 1950." In *Mechanizmy zniewalania społeczeństwa—refleksje u schyłku formacji.* Warsaw, 1990.

Świda-Ziemba, Hanna, and Katarzyna Madoń-Mitzner. "Notatki z życia systemu." *Karta* 3 (1991).

Szyndler-Głowacki, Wiesław, ed. *Mój zakład pracy: Wspomnienia.* Warsaw, 1965.

Tranzytem przez Łódź. Łódź, 1964.

Trudne dni: Wrocław 1945r. we wspomnieniach pionierów. 3 vols. Wrocław, 1960–63.

Turnau, Irena. *Studia nad strukturą ludnościową polskiego Wrocławia.* Poznań, 1960.

Wojtanowicz, Janina, ed. *17 opowieści prawdziwych: Wspomnienia dolnoślązaków.* Wrocław, 1968.

Wspomnienia działaczy związkowych. 2 vols.: *1909–1949* and *1944–1972.* Warsaw, 1971, 1974.

Wyka, Kazimierz. *Życie na niby: Pamiętnik po klęsce.* Kraków, 1984.

Zaremba, Józef. *Atlas Ziem Odzyskanych.* Warsaw, 1947.

Związek Walki Młodzieży: Materiały i dokumenty. Warsaw, 1953.

Index